KU-337-012

Lord Liverpool

The Life and Political Career of
Robert Banks Jenkinson
Second Earl of Liverpool
1770–1828

NORMAN GASH

FABER & FABER

This edition first published in 2016
by Faber & Faber Ltd
Bloomsbury House, 74–77 Great Russell Street
London WC1B 3DA

Printed and bound by CPI Group (UK) Ltd, Croydon, CR0 4YY

All rights reserved
© Norman Gash, 1984

The right of Norman Gash to be identified
as author of this work has been asserted in accordance
with Section 77 of the Copyright, Designs and Patents Act 1988

This book is sold subject to the condition that it shall not, by way of
trade or otherwise, be lent, resold, hired out or otherwise circulated
without the publisher's prior consent in any form of binding or cover other than
that in which it is published and without a similar condition including this
condition being imposed on the subsequent purchaser

A CIP record for this book is available from the British Library

ISBN 978-0-571-29637-8

Glasgow Life Glasgow Libraries	
BM	
C 006165890	
Askews & Holts	13-Apr-2016
941.073092 /H	£20.00

'He was a very honest, upright man
& deserves a higher character as a statesman
than I dare say History will grant to him.'

Mrs Arbuthnot

TO
HARRIET AND SARAH
carissimis

Contents

Notes are grouped at the end of each chapter

Illustrations

Acknowledgements

I am grateful to the Earl and Countess of Liverpool, to Mrs Colthurst of Pitchford Hall, to Mr George White of Hawkesbury, to Captain C.S. Rawlins and Mr Brian Davidson of Chipping Sodbury, and to Mr Geoffrey Moorhouse for their generosity in allowing me to see pictures, busts and papers, or otherwise helping to elucidate the family history of the Jenkinsons. The staff of the National Portrait Gallery, especially Sarah Wimbush, and Mr John Kennedy Browne kindly gave me information about paintings and statuary relating to the second earl and his wife; the school secretary of Charterhouse and Mr Fernandez-Arnesto the school archivist details of his school career. I am glad to have this opportunity of thanking also the Deputy Clerk of Records in the House of Lords, the National Trust officials at Ickworth, Suffolk, and the staff of the Gloucester and Bristol Libraries, for their help in obtaining other information.

Among historian friends who good-naturedly responded to my enquiries I would like to thank in particular Charles Stuart and John Mason of Christ Church, and A.F. Thompson of Wadham College, Oxford, for obtaining details of Lord Liverpool's university career; Ian Christie of University College, London, and John Ehrman, for advice on several points in the history of the period. To two old friends I am even more deeply indebted. Dr John Taylor, MB, ch.B., FRCPE, of St Salvator's College, St Andrews, patiently and at length discussed with me Lord Liverpool's multiple and often obscure medical symptoms. Dr Arnold Taylor, FSA, as on past occasions, not only allowed me to draw on his unfailing knowledge of the sources for genealogical, topographical and architectural history, but often extracted for me what I at a distance needed to know.

Finally I acknowledge with gratitude the support of St Andrews University and the British Academy in meeting some of the costs of travel and typing.

LANGPORT, SOMERSET   *Norman Gash*
OCTOBER 1983

List of Abbreviations used in the Notes

Unspecified five-figure numerals refer to the British Library Additional Manuscripts (Liverpool Papers, Private Correspondence of the first and second Earls of Liverpool).

AR: *The Annual Register.*
ARC: *The Correspondence of Charles Arbuthnot*, ed. A. Aspinall, Camden Society Third Series, Vol. LXV (1941).
ARJ: *The Journal of Mrs Arbuthnot*, ed. F. Bamford and the Duke of Wellington, two vols (1950).
Auckland: *Journal and Correspondence of Lord Auckland*, by the Bishop of Bath and Wells, four vols (1861–2).
Bagot, Josceline: *George Canning and His Friends* (1909).
Bathurst: *Hist. Man. Comm. Report on the Manuscripts of Earl Bathurst* (1923).
BCG: Duke of Buckingham, *Memoirs of the Court of George IV*, two vols (1871).
BCR: Duke of Buckingham, *Memoirs of the Court of the Regency*, two vols (1856).
CMC: *Memoirs and Correspondence of Viscount Castlereagh*, ed. Marquess of Londonderry, twelve vols (1848–53).
Colchester: *Diary and Correspondence of Charles Abbot, Lord Colchester*, ed. Lord Colchester, three vols (1861).
Cookson, J.E.: *Lord Liverpool's Administration 1815–22* (1975).
Creevey: *The Creevey Papers*, ed. Sir Herbert Maxwell (1923).
Croker: *The Croker Papers*, ed. L.J. Jennings, three vols (1884).
Dixon, Peter: *Canning* (1976).
FD: *The Farington Diary*, ed. J. Grieg, eight vols (1922–8).
Fortescue: *Hist. Man. Comm. Report on the Manuscripts of J.B. Fortescue at Dropmore*, nine vols (1892–1927).
Foster: *The Two Duchesses*, ed. Vere Foster (1898).

GCFM: *The Formation of Canning's Ministry*, ed. A. Aspinall, Camden Society Third Series, Vol. LIX (1937).

GCHT: *George Canning and His Times*, by A.G. Stapleton (1859).

GCOC: *Some Official Correspondence of George Canning*, ed. T.J. Stapleton, two vols (1887).

GD: *The Diaries of Sylvester Douglas, Lord Glenbervie*, ed. F. Bickley, two vols (1928).

George 3: *The Later Correspondence of George III*, ed. A. Aspinall, five vols (1962-70).

George 4: *Letters of King George IV, 1812-1830*, ed. A. Aspinall, three vols (1938).

GM: *The Gentleman's Magazine.*

Gray, D.: *Spencer Perceval* (1963).

Greville: *The Greville Memoirs*, ed. L. Strachey and R. Fulford, seven vols (1938).

Herries, E: *Memoir of J.C. Herries*, two vols (1880).

Hilton, Boyd: *Corn, Cash, Commerce: The Economic Policies of the Tory Governments 1815-1830* (1977).

Hinde, Wendy: *George Canning* (1973).

Hobhouse: *Diary of Henry Hobhouse*, ed. A. Aspinall (1947).

Huskisson: *The Huskisson Papers*, ed. Lewis Melville (1931).

Knight, G.D.: *Lord Liverpool and the Peninsular War 1809-1812*. (Florida State University) XEROX University Microfilms, Ann Arbor, Michigan (1976).

LGC: *Lord Granville Leveson Gower, Private Correspondence 1781-1821*, ed. Countess Granville, two vols (1916).

LM: *The Private Letters of Princess Lieven to Prince Metternich 1820-26*, ed. P. Quennell (1937).

LWF: *The First Lady Wharncliffe and Her Family*, ed. C. Grosvenor and Lord Stuart of Wortley, two vols (1927).

Marshall, Dorothy: *The Rise of George Canning* (1938).

Oman, Carola: *The Gascoyne Heiress* (1968).

P. of W.: *The Correspondence of George Prince of Wales 1770-1812*, ed. A. Aspinall, eight vols (1963-71).

Parker C.S.: *Sir Robert Peel from his private papers*, three vols (1891).

Pellew, G.: *Life and Correspondence of Viscount Sidmouth*, three vols (1847).

Pemberton, S. Childe-: *The Earl Bishop, The Life of Frederick Hervey, Bishop of Derry, Earl of Bristol*, two vols (1924).

Rede, L.T.: *Memoir of George Canning* (1827).

Rose: *Diaries and Correspondence of the Rt. Hon. George Rose*, ed. Rev. Leveson Vernon Harcourt, two vols (1860).

Stanhope, Earl: *The Life of the Rt. Hon. William Pitt*, four vols (1861-2).

Stuart, Dorothy M.: *Dearest Bess, Life and Times of Lady Elizabeth Foster* (1955).

Twiss, H.: *Life of Lord Chancellor Eldon*, three vols (1844).

Walpole, Spencer: *Life of the Rt. Hon. Spencer Perceval*, two vols (1874).

Ward: *Memoirs of R. Plumer Ward*, ed. E. Phipps, two vols (1850).

Webster, C.K.: *The Foreign Policy of Castlereagh*, 1812-15 (1931).

Wellesley: *The Wellesley Papers*, ed. Lewis Melville (1914).

Windham: *Diary of the Rt. Hon. William Windham*, 1784-1810, ed. Mrs Henry Baring (1866).

WND: *Despatches, Correspondence and Memoranda of the Duke of Wellington 1819-32*, ed. Duke of Wellington, eight vols (1867-80), new series.

WSD: *Supplementary Despatches, Correspondence and Memoranda of the Duke of Wellington*, ed. Duke of Wellington, fifteen vols (1858-72).

Yonge, C.D.: *The Life and Administration of the Second Earl of Liverpool*, three vols (1868).

The Jenkinson Family

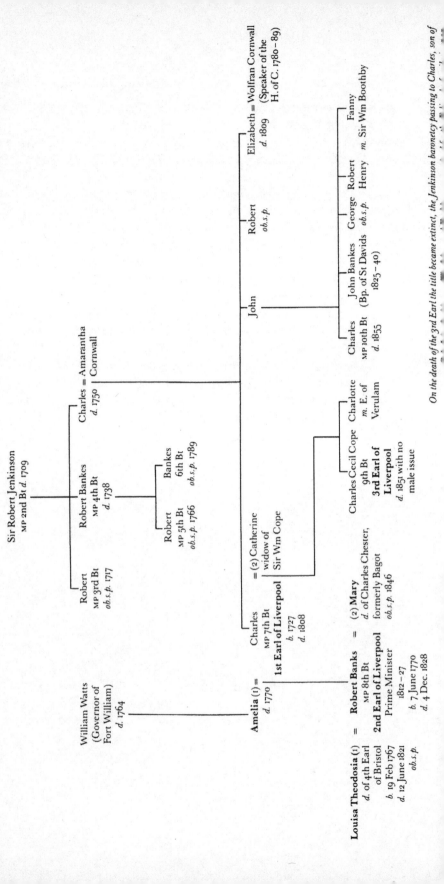

Sir Robert Jenkinson
MP 2nd Bt *d.* 1709

Robert
MP 3rd Bt
ob.s.p. 1717

Charles = Amarantha
d. 1750   Cornwall

Robert Bankes
MP 4th Bt
d. 1738

Robert
MP 5th Bt
ob.s.p. 1766

Bankes
6th Bt
ob.s.p. 1789

William Watts
(Governor of
Fort William)
d. 1764

Charles
MP 7th Bt
1st Earl of Liverpool
b. 1727
d. 1808

= (2) Catherine
widow of
Sir Wm Cope

John

Robert
ob.s.p.

Elizabeth = Wolfran Cornwall
d. 1809   (Speaker of the
H. of C. 1780–89)

Charles
MP 10th Bt
d. 1855

John Bankes
(Bp. of St Davids
1825–40)

George
ob.s.p.

Robert
Henry

Fanny
m. Sir Wm Boothby

Amelia (1) =
d. 1770

Robert Banks
MP 8th Bt
2nd Earl of Liverpool
Prime Minister
1812–27
b. 7 June 1770
d. 4 Dec. 1828

= (2) **Mary**
d. of Charles Chester,
formerly Bagot
ob.s.p. 1846

Charles Cecil Cope
9th Bt
3rd Earl of Liverpool
d. 1851 with no
male issue

Charlotte
m. E. of
Verulam

Louisa Theodosia (1) =
d. of 4th Earl
of Bristol
b. 19 Feb 1767
d. 12 June 1821
ob.s.p.

On the death of the 3rd Earl the title became extinct, the Jenkinson baronetcy passing to Charles, son of

Introduction

Only a few British prime ministers have had the distinction of leading their country to victory at the close of a long and desperate war. More have presided over successful domestic policies. Some, less fortunate, have had to grapple with prolonged periods of economic depression and social unrest. Only of Lord Liverpool can it be said that in the course of fifteen years at the head of government he experienced all these things. Having been called to power for the last three testing years of the struggle against Napoleon, he next had to deal with the disorders and discontents of the age of the Luddites, Peterloo and the Six Acts; and finally brought the country through to the prosperity and liberal reforms of the 1820s. His government, the last of the great eighteenth-century administrations in its structure and duration, was the first of the great nineteenth-century administrations in its problems and achievements.

Liverpool's long rule as prime minister will not easily be matched, if only because the changes in the electoral system since his death have made it difficult for any ministry to remain in power for that length of time. The voice of the people as it comes through the modern ballot box has many sounds, but a sustained note of trust is not commonly one of them. Part of the explanation then for Liverpool's unique place in British political history is the sheer accident that he lived in the unreformed parliamentary era when the choice of prime minister was decided by a very small number of people in a relatively small political society. The characteristic pattern of eighteenth-century government was an alternation of some long and many short administrations. Between the accession of George I in 1714 and the death of George IV in 1830 five prime ministers out of a total of twenty-one had ten or more years continuously in office. The first four were Walpole, Henry Pelham, Lord North and the younger Pitt; the fifth was Lord Liverpool. For ministries to last so long, a number of conditions had to be present. The first essential was the confidence of the monarch. With it all things were possible; without it, very little. There was more than this, however, to the secret of political longevity. Royal favour was usually necessary to gain power; it was insufficient to sustain in office men who were either clearly inadequate or peculiarly unlucky.

To meet the needs and face the accidents of political life a chief minister (to use the old-fashioned phrase still common in Liverpool's day) had to possess further qualities. The attributes which commanded success in the unreformed era were not the same – or, more accurately perhaps, did not have the same weighting – as today; but a variety of talents was still required. It was desirable, and sometimes indispensable, for a prime minister to have skill in the management of men and assemblies, a measure of administrative ability, good fortune in keeping the country either honourably at peace or successful in war, and dexterity in avoiding private scandal and personal unpopularity. Given the unpredictable hazards of politics, the longer a ministry lasted, the greater the probability that all these different qualities would be called upon at some time. It was a measure of Liverpool's political stature that after fifteen years his administration was more popular in the country, more firmly entrenched in the good opinion of Parliament and the Crown, than at any previous time. It came to an end not because it had lost the favour of the King or of the legislature but because the Prime Minister's health made it impossible for him to serve any longer.

To achieve such success was not easy; the history of the administration reads sometimes like a chronicle of endless difficulties. Some of these difficulties were personal and accidental; others inherent in the political constitution of the time. It was Liverpool's misfortune to serve a king who lacked the steadfastness and sense of duty of his father, and was not always conscious of what he owed to himself. These defects of character were compounded by a broken marriage and an attempted divorce. It followed that there were at times bitter disagreements between George IV and his cabinet. What saved the government on more than one occasion was merely the King's physical indolence and political timidity. A change of ministry involved the Crown in trouble and responsibility. An administration with a record of efficiency over a number of years acquired an authority of its own. It could not easily be dismissed; it could not easily be replaced. Unlike his immediate predecessor or successor, George IV never actually dismissed any of his ministries, unless the confused end of the demoralised Goderich administration in 1828 comes under that heading. The ministry which served him longest was the one he inherited from his father and had simply confirmed in office. Though he lacked political initiative and courage, however, his substitute tactics of obstruction, petulance and delay imposed a heavy burden on his ministers.

Next in importance was the problem of retaining the confidence of Parliament. It was true that up to 1830 general elections were not among the more pressing of ministerial preoccupations. They commanded a degree of attention from the Treasury secretaries when the time came, since the executive had electoral interests of its own to safeguard; candidates of its own to be returned. But elections did not decide the fate of governments; as a rule they merely confirmed in power those who already possessed it. Parliament did not think it had a duty to prescribe a set of ministers for the monarch; it was content to have the right to criticise and obstruct those he had appointed: a traditional task for which it was historically well equipped. General elections were still primarily a mechanism for finding men to fill the benches of the House of Commons. Such ideas and opinions as they took up to Westminster were for the most part a reflection of the views and interests of their patrons and constituents. Few had any coherent plans of securing office for a particular group of men. The task of governing the country was regarded as the duty of the executive; and the choice of the executive was the responsibility of the Crown.

Nevertheless, government required the assent of the legislature for much ordinary and all important business. The House of Lords, though not unimportant as a forum of debate, was under strong Court and ministerial influence and could be relied on in normal circumstances to support the government of the day. The House of Commons was a different kind of animal. Though the imperfections of the electoral system were coming under increasing criticism, it was still the representative branch of the constitution and proudly conscious of its character. It was not only an influential body which had to be treated with tact and understanding; it was also a barometer of public opinion. The members for the more popular constituencies - the English counties and the larger towns - were of particular importance. They could not easily be controlled; frequently criticised; often voted in opposition; but had to be listened to with attention. The fact that government was rarely defeated in the House of Commons was beside the point. Any ministry that did not on all vital issues secure the substantial backing of the House was at once suspect; small arithmetical majorities were not enough.

As ballast to what would otherwise have been an unstable, almost unmanageable assembly, the government - any government - had a party of its own. It consisted of office-holders and aspirants to office, followers of individual ministers, nominees of friendly peers, and MPs, especially the Scottish and Irish, with indifferent political views but small, patronage-hungry constituencies. These provided a nucleus of strength round which more transient majorities could be collected on specific topics. For that larger support the ministers had to rely on the merits of their proposals, skill in presenting their case, the commonsense and patriotism of uncommitted members, and in the last resort the reluctance of MPs and their patrons to risk the expense and hazards of frequent general elections. Even so, the House of Commons was a difficult body and in Liverpool's time was getting more difficult. A steady process of 'economical reform', starting as far back as 1782, had gradually been eliminating most of the less defensible but highly useful means of attracting neutrals and rewarding friends which had been enjoyed by previous prime ministers. Outside Parliament the growth of an articulate and critical public opinion (to which 'economical reform' itself was a concession) constituted a new element in political life. It was one which neither MPs nor ministers could afford to ignore. The rise of an independent newspaper press, relying on circulation and advertisement revenue rather than government subsidies, was a sign of this rival power in the state. Once the war ended in 1815 it was soon evident that the relationship between the executive, the legislature and the public had changed considerably since 1793.

The Liverpool administration also faced a comparatively recent innovation in public life, the presence of an organised parliamentary opposition. There was no proper party system and party affiliations were for most MPs either fluid or non-existent. Yet there were times when the opposition whigs behaved like a party in the modern sense: a body of politicians with a common outlook, aiming at office, and ready to oppose on principle everything proposed by the ministers they sought to replace. Throughout Liverpool's fifteen years as prime minister, however, the official opposition were never in a position to unseat him by their own efforts. Unable to gain the confidence of the Crown, unable to 'win' a general election in the modern style (since 'winning' implies a fixity of organisation which did not then exist), they acted as a kind of Greek chorus, lamenting and warning, but never able to usurp the central roles in the drama. Their danger lay in the fact that as against the governmental 'party' they too formed a hard nucleus which in association with other temporarily discontented elements in the House might be able to defeat or damage the ministry on particular issues.

In itself the word 'party', as used by Liverpool's contemporaries, was a vague expression applied to many different forms of political connection. In one sense all professional politicians were whig or of whig background, since this was the inescapable legacy of the Hanoverian succession. From the end of the American war the Foxite whigs had made themselves conspicuous by personal opposition to George III, just as Pitt had become conspicuous as leader of the monarchical whigs who rallied to the King's defence in 1783-4. The French Revolution and the Catholic Emancipation issue later created other cross-divisions; and the influx of a hundred Irish members in 1801 helped to dilute party spirit and party distinctions still further. Politicians in office tended to regard themselves primarily as servants of the Crown and did not feel a dependence on 'party' to keep them in office; they had little interest therefore in party labels. In the course of Liverpool's career the adjective 'whig' became by default almost a monopoly of the old Foxite opposition.

For Liverpool, undoubtedly of good whig background, 'party' (when he thought in such terms) usually meant something more personal and more ephemeral - Mr Pitt's party (to which he belonged) or Mr Addington's or Lord Grenville's (to which he did not). That his strong sense of loyalty to the Crown and his devotion to the Church of England were shared by others who could be described as 'tory', was of no special significance. There was no 'tory party' in the Commons; though doubtless many of the 'country gentlemen' (to use the conventional contemporary expression), who sometimes voted with the government and sometimes against, would have been called tories in the age of Sir Robert Walpole. A vague Anglican and monarchical sentiment among the landed gentry helped to perpetuate the tradition of dutiful support for the king's government; but no ministry after Waterloo could exist on such a tenuous basis. The task of securing the votes of the floating, independent members of the House of Commons was a more practical, undoctrinal, earthy matter. Appeals to the traditional loyalty of the backbenchers were of little value in the presence of felt grievances. The House, in other words, had to be managed.

It was a disadvantage to Liverpool in these circumstances that he himself was in the House of Lords. The history of his administration would have been very different had he sat as Prime Minister in the Commons. Not only would it have meant that his government always possessed a spokesman of authority (and incidentally of marked debating skill) in the lower house; but his presence there would have prevented that historic rivalry between Castlereagh and Canning for the leadership of the house which coloured so much of the internal history of the administration. As it was, the problem of ministerial weakness in the Commons was one that continually plagued the Prime Minister. It explains much of what his critics regarded as his obsession with the need to retain Canning's services. In fact Liverpool was never able to find a satisfactory team of ministers in the House of Commons until the last five years of his administration. Until then this internal weakness was a constant source of anxiety and his attempts to solve it a recurrent and wearisome part of his work.

It says something for Liverpool's ability as prime minister that he was able to overcome all these handicaps. With only fitful support from the monarchy, without the means to ensure steady support from the legislature, he and his colleagues depended to an unprecedented extent on their own political skill and personal authority. As time passed they also began to reap certain accrued benefits. Continuity in office nourished a sense of both independence and solidarity; and the fifteen years of Liverpool's premiership marked an important stage in the development of the modern cabinet. He was always a strong constitutionalist and his difficult parliamentary position between 1815 and 1822 was in itself an incentive for upholding the rights and powers of ministers of the Crown even against the Crown itself. The decline in the prestige of the monarchy which came with the Prince of Wales's accession to the regency in 1811 made it possible for Liverpool to press his views on his royal master more firmly than he would have been disposed to do in the previous reign. Though ready to allow a certain latitude to the Crown in matters of patronage and ministerial appointments, he limited it more tightly than his colleagues always thought prudent. On issues of any importance he tended to take the rigorous constitutional view that the sovereign, having chosen his chief minister, should accept his advice and recommendations as long as he kept him in office. The king's remedy, if he disliked that advice, was to change his minister. It was impeccable constitutional doctrine but (as most Hanoverian monarchs discovered) though legally unchallengeable it was not always politically practicable. Exceptions to this rule, however justified, were in Liverpool's view politically objectionable even when constitutionally admissible. The most crucial issue of all was the prime minister's right to select the senior members of his administration. On this Liverpool recognised that circumstances might occur which would warrant a crown veto in particular cases, such as uncongenial political views, disloyalty, or moral depravity. Nevertheless, he once wrote, the king 'should be most cautious in acting on such a principle, for the effect of it will generally be to exalt the individual and to lower the King'.[1]

As prime minister Liverpool fought consistently to maintain the authority of his own office and the unity of his administration. He had to face both the wilfulness of George iv and his intermittent attempts to deal behind Liverpool's back with individual ministers. Though not always agreeing with their leader's high notions of ministerial authority, his colleagues stood by him in every serious crisis. A feature of Liverpool's administration is in fact the remarkable degree of discipline it exhibited both in Parliament and against the Crown. This had not always been a characteristic of British cabinets in the years preceding 1812; and Liverpool's long rule helped to consolidate this more modern but as yet far from established convention. For the time being, however, the executive remained in a curiously isolated position. In a literal sense, this was an age of cabinet government. Liverpool's role in some respects resembled that of a United States president rather than that of later British prime ministers. His authority was of a different origin from that of the legislature with which he had to deal. There was still a confrontation between two essentially different branches of the constitution. Though the prime minister had means at his disposal of influencing the legislature, they were not unlimited. In turn, though Parliament could in practice force a ministry to resign, it was normally reluctant to encroach so drastically on the legal rights of the Crown. What it could do was to obstruct and nullify the government's policy and reduce it to a cypher. The primary task therefore of Liverpool's executive was to secure, by influence, persuasion or threats, the cooperation of the legislature. This absorbed a great deal of the ministerial time, and involved a constant calculation of what would, and what would not, be acceptable to Parliament.

The proof of Liverpool's political ability was that though he made mistakes and was more than once frustrated in his purpose, he never made a disastrous error and was always able to retrieve a damaged position. The reproach that his administration might have done more constructive work than it did, must be balanced by a consideration of the narrow limits within which it exercised effective authority. In the uneasy equilibrium which existed after the decline in the personal power of the Crown and before the rise of party rule, Liverpool's government had to supply from its own resources what it could not obtain from institutional strength.

One day, perhaps, the life of Lord Liverpool will be written as it deserves to be, on the basis of the massive archival material now available and on a scale that will require more than a single volume. The purpose of this book is simply to uncover more about Liverpool as a person and as a politician. He gave his name to the longest, and one of the most important, British administrations of the nineteenth century. Yet the man himself has remained a shadowy figure. The three-volume *Life and Administration* by C.D. Yonge, published in 1868, is full of essential information drawn from the Liverpool Papers now in the British Library. Like many Victorian official biographies, however, its effect was to bury rather than to resurrect its subject. Much fresh and important work has been done in recent years on the Liverpool administration; but the only modern biography has been Sir Charles Petrie's *Lord Liverpool and His Times* which appeared thirty years ago. Even that, as the title half-betrays, is too much concerned with the times to deal adequately with the man. For nearly a century and a half Lord Liverpool has remained one of the least known and most underrated of British prime ministers.

NOTE

1 Bathurst, p. 490 (27 June 1821).

CHAPTER I

Old Jenkinson and
Young Jenkinson

In July 1786 at the end of the parliamentary session the Prime Minister William Pitt found time to write to his mother. He included among other items of political gossip (the only kind of gossip he knew) the news that Mr Jenkinson was to become President of the reorganised Committee of Trade and receive a peerage. 'This, I think, will sound a little strange at a distance, and with reference to former ideas; but he has really fairly earned it and attained it at my hands.'[1]

The defensive note was understandable. Charles Jenkinson was a professional politician and administrator who had worked his way up from a modest start as unpaid private secretary to Lord Holderness twenty years earlier to become Secretary at War in 1778. A trusted servant and adviser of George III, credited with more influence among the 'King's Friends' than he actually possessed, he might have attained even more responsible office had it not been for the engrained caution and secretiveness of his character. Narrow, dogged, loyal only to his master the King, he lost his post when the discredited North ministry fell in 1782 but remained in contact with George III during the difficult twenty months which followed. When Pitt formed his first administration at the end of 1783 he failed, perhaps deliberately, to give office to Jenkinson, as though demonstrating his political independence from the older set of 'King's Friends'. Nevertheless, there was no open breach and when appointed unpaid member of Pitt's new Committee of Trade in 1784 Jenkinson applied himself diligently to his new duties. The subsequent energy and initiative displayed by the Board of Trade (as it became known) under his presidency vindicated Pitt's judgement even though collectively the Board remained noticeably unsympathetic towards Pitt's liberal, free-trade views.

The new Lord Hawkesbury was a bureaucrat rather than a politician; though the distinction was not one to which the eighteenth century paid much attention. The closets and corridors of office were clearly more congenial to him than the floor of the House of Commons. As an MP he spoke frequently and knowledgeably but he had no eloquence and lacked charm. Though avoiding excessive public responsibilities, he had not neglected his private interests. In addition to the salary from a string of minor offices, including a not unprofitable sinecure as Master of the Mint, he had become auditor of accounts to the Queen Dowager, purchased the lucrative Irish office of Clerk of the Pells in 1775, and on the death in 1789 of his relative Sir Bankes Jenkinson, secured his sinecure post of Collector of Customs Inward. Wealth and rising social station, however, sat awkwardly on him. His brother-in-law, Nathaniel Dance, the royal portrait painter, described him in 1796, unkindly though not without truth, as 'a common kind of man whom luck and perseverance have made'.[2] The pompous formal manner he affected in society created amusement in the royal family despite their appreciation of his loyalty and usefulness. His attempt to assume the air of a man of fashion, his mispronunciation of the occasional French phrase with which he garnished his conversation brought him ridicule in smart London circles. Yet with much of the pedant about him, he had some of the pedantic virtues: industriousness, an appetite for knowledge and a zest for writing. Youthful verses on the death of the Prince of Wales in 1751 were followed by a *Dissertation on the Establishment of a National and Constitutional Force* in 1756 and a *Discourse on the Conduct of the Government with respect to Neutral Nations* in 1758. Even office and promotion did not extinguish his scholarly zeal. A three-volume *Collection of all Treaties of Peace ... between Great Britain and other Powers 1748–1783* appeared in 1785 and in 1805 came his *magnum opus, A Treatise on the Coins of England,* which remained the standard authority for the rest of the century and was reprinted by the Bank of England as late as 1880. These learned labours, which in another century might have earned him an honorary degree from his old university, did little to enhance his reputation in the aristocratic world of Pitt and Fox.

For all his affectations and snobbery, however, Lord Hawkesbury belonged to a class which had governed England for a century or more. Like many other rising gentry of the Tudor and Stuart periods the Jenkinsons first made their way in trade and then consolidated their social position by the purchase of land. The founder of the family fortunes was Anthony Jenkinson of Bristol, merchant, sea-captain and traveller, who became agent for the Muscovy Company, served as diplomatic representative of Queen Elizabeth to the Tsar of Russia and the Shah of Persia, and was granted that certificate of gentility, armorial bearings, in 1568–9. The family acquired land at Walcot in Oxfordshire and later bought the Gloucestershire manor of Hawkesbury from the Crews. One of Anthony's descendants, Robert, was knighted by James I; and his son, a good royalist, was created a baronet by Charles II. In the eighteenth century the Oxfordshire Jenkinsons produced a succession of county MPs and a few army officers, and in the early nineteenth century one undistinguished bishop. Charles Jenkinson's father, a younger son of the second baronet, fought at Fontenoy and Dettingen, reached the rank of colonel, and married the daughter of a naval captain. The Jenkinsons were not, however, even allowing for the generous standards of the age, a very prolific family. The third, fifth and sixth baronets all died childless and in 1789 the baronetcy and the family estates passed to Lord Hawkesbury as the nearest male descendant of the second baronet. The inheritance included the manor of Hawkesbury from which he took his new title.

With the old manor house, which then stood opposite the present parish church in the remote little hamlet of Hawkesbury, he already had a tragic personal association. In 1769 he had married Amelia Watts, the daughter of a former governor of Fort William in Bengal. It was doubtless a marriage of prudence rather than passion. Jenkinson at the age of forty-one was more than twice the age of Miss Watts. She on the other hand probably brought more than the qualities of youth to the altar. Her father, William Watts, was one of Clive's not over-scrupulous young men in India who had been of considerable assistance to his chief in handling the arrangements with Mir Jaffa, the puppet ruler in Bengal set up after the battle of Plassey. His own share of the lucrative proceeds of the settlement was said to amount to £117,000, equivalent to a small fortune in the reign of George III. At any rate he shook the pagoda tree vigorously enough during his brief Indian career to enable him on his return to England to purchase land in Berkshire and a town house in Hanover Square. In the eighteenth century, before the arrival of respectable white women in any number, mixed marriages were not uncommon among officials of the East India Company. William Watts married a well-known Eurasian woman, already twice widowed, who is best remembered in Calcutta history as the 'Begum' Johnson after the name of her fourth husband, the Residency chaplain. As Mrs Watts she became the mother of two children, Amelia and a younger brother Edward. In 1764, on the death of their father at the early age of forty-two, Edward while still a minor inherited the bulk of his fortune. His trustees subsequently bought an estate for him at Hanslope in Buckinghamshire. It is unlikely, however, that no provision was made for his sister on her marriage. There was certainly a marriage settlement; and it would have been out of character for Charles Jenkinson to have taken a bride, however young and pretty, who lacked a dowry.[3]

The future prime minister had therefore a tincture of Indian blood through his mother's side of the family: a genetic oddity which does not seem to have attracted any comment in England from his contemporaries and is not mentioned in standard genealogical reference books. He was born on 7 June 1770 when his mother was still only nineteen. For Amelia's convalescence after the birth, her husband's cousin Bankes Jenkinson, the sixth baronet, offered the use of the quiet old house at Hawkesbury. His own family had not lived in it for over a century, ever since (according to local tradition) a sister of the first baronet had fallen to her death from an upper window after her father had forbidden her to marry a son of the neighbouring Roman Catholic family of Paston. A second pitiful tragedy now followed. The young Mrs Jenkinson died on her way down from London to Hawkesbury and it was her lifeless body which arrived at the manor. After her burial in the parish church across the road, the ill-fated house was abandoned and soon fell into a ruinous state.

Twelve years later Charles Jenkinson married again. His second wife was Catherine, the widow of Sir Charles Cope, who besides bringing with her a town house at 26 Hertford St, Mayfair, later presented him with two children, Charles Cecil born in 1784 and a sister Charlotte.[4]

The infant Robert, left motherless when he was only a month old, grew up therefore in his early years as an only child in the house of his widowed father. He did not, however, altogether lack gentler influences and a certain amount of feminine spoiling. The orphan son of a minister of state is calculated to arouse warm interest in the female breast and for many years his father's private correspondence regularly included tender enquiries from women friends and relations about the health and progress of his little boy. There was a Sophia Watts on his mother's side of the family, and an even closer connection with the Cornwalls. Charles Jenkinson's mother Amarantha was a Cornwall and his sister Elizabeth had married Charles Wolfran Cornwall MP, who became speaker of the House of Commons and was generally regarded as a political protégé of Lord Hawkesbury. He had an estate at Barton Priors near Winchester and as a child Robert frequently spent Christmas and part of the summer with his grandmother Cornwall at Winchester and even for a time attended school there. His regular education, however, started at Albion House, a private school for boys at Parsons Green, Fulham, where his curriculum was varied if not alleviated by dancing lessons under the supervision of M. du Rosel of Chelsea. During these juvenile years he seemed a high-spirited and generally healthy little boy, though in the summer of 1781 he was reported very thin, principally and not surprisingly because he 'has worms which devour him'. The attentive M. du Rosel hastened to acquaint his father with a safe and infallible cure which had been effective with a young gentleman much of Master Jenkinson's age, namely five glisters and five grains of aloes.[5]

On 23 September 1783, when he was thirteen, Robert Jenkinson entered Charterhouse where his father had been a foundation scholar or gownsboy forty years earlier. He was placed as a boarder in the house of Dr Berdmore, the Schoolmaster, as the headmaster was officially designated. The school still stood on its original site in the heart of London close to those places of grim memory, Smithfield, Newgate and the Old Bailey. Here among its dingy grass lawns and soot-encrusted plane trees, with the smoke and clatter of the City all about, he spent the greater part of the next four years. Built over a medieval plague-pit, dusty in summer and foggy in winter, it could scarcely be said to have had the most salubrious of situations. Charterhouse was also an asylum for aged men; but though the Old Codds, as the ancient pensioners of the foundation were nicknamed, died off regularly each winter, the boys kept healthy enough.[6] All these things signified less to Robert's ambitious father than the quality of the education his son was receiving. Writing to 'my dear Bob' at the start of his second year at Charterhouse, he expressed the opinion that he was already sufficiently advanced in Latin and Greek to ensure that by the time he left school, he would be master of both languages. He was, however, to pay great attention to his exercises 'in which you are not very forward'. Every leisure moment was to be applied to the study of algebra and geometry in order to acquire 'a habit of reasoning closely and correctly on every subject'. Any hours not so employed should be given to works of history and criticism of which his knowledge of French would furnish him with excellent examples. For the time being, Lord Hawkesbury added repressively, he wished Robert not to read any novels, since they would only waste time which (he observed a trifle unnecessarily) he would not find 'more than sufficient for the pursuit of more useful and important studies'.

Yet book-knowledge alone, he continued implacably, was not enough. He was to pay proper attention to his person. Every failing in this respect would expose him to disgust or ridicule and detract from any advantage of talents or learning he might otherwise possess. It was particularly important for Robert to attend to this since he was 'just at an age when improper manners and tastes are acquired, which will become habitual if they are not now corrected'. Was it his own experience or natural boyish untidiness in his son which made him dwell on this point? Dwell on it he certainly did. 'You will recollect the advice I have of late repeatedly given you on this subject, and I am sure you will attend to it.' He ended this Polonius-like discourse by reminding Robert how he and the rest of the family 'look forward with anxiety to the figure you will hereafter make in the world'. For himself, he concluded resignedly, the chief happiness he expected to enjoy in his declining years would be derived from his son's 'prosperity and eminence'.[7] It was an oppressive homily for a boy of fourteen to receive, but eighteenth-century society regarded childhood as something to grow out of as quickly as possible; not as a state of innocent happiness to be artificially prolonged.

Robert responded dutifully and without resentment to his father's admonitions. By the time he left school he was for a boy of his years unusually well-read, not only in the traditional classics and the additional university requirement of mathematics, but in the more unconventional subjects of French, history, European politics, and political economy, prescribed by the new president of the Board of Trade. Long afterwards it was stated with some authority that 'a catalogue of the best writers on the different branches of the public economy was put into his hands, and a selection from their purest and most perfect works was prepared for him, to blend with his college exercises. Commerce and finance were especially attended to, and while the more abstract departments of knowledge were not neglected, chief attention was paid, by both father and son, to the more practical and popular.'[8]

It was at first uncertain which Oxford college he should enter. His father had been at University College where he took his BA in 1749; but since 1783, under the stimulus of its energetic Dean, Cyril Jackson, Christ Church had taken a decisive lead, politically and academically, in the university. It was this probably that decided his father's choice rather than his friendship with Dr Jubb, Regius Professor of Hebrew and Canon of Christ Church. All such

relationships had their uses, however; Dr Jubb was of assistance in getting
suitable rooms for Robert in college, and his wife, declaring that she had 'ever
felt a Mother's affection for Him', offered her services in any way that might
be useful.[9]

The transition from school to university was remarkably sudden. On 20
April 1787 Robert Jenkinson left Charterhouse; exactly a week later he matri-
culated at Oxford University. Though not yet seventeen, his life as a boarder
at Charterhouse, his father's sedulous training, and youthful familiarity with
some of the great political figures of the day – Pitt, Burke and Thurlow – whom
he met at his father's house, had already given him a precocious air of sophis-
tication. To Anne Jubb, meeting him after a lapse of time in the summer of
1786, he seemed 'grown up into Man' and, writing to his father, she professed
herself lost in admiration at his 'extraordinary abilities'. Other women, with
less need to flatter a fond father, were not so rapturous. Staying at Addiscombe,
Lord Hawkesbury's country house near Croydon, in May 1787 the shrewd and
intelligent Lady Stafford reported:

> Mr Jenkinson was at Home, from Oxford – he is well educated, well informed, and
> sensible ... [But, she continued more critically] if he had been my Son, I should have
> wished him to be more inclined to listen to what the Chancellor and Mr Pitt said,
> than to express his own ideas on Politicks, Government, and Commerce ... but he
> spoke well, and his Language was good, and it was obvious that he had really a great
> Deal of Knowledge. I have a Notion that at Oxford, if they are good Scholars, they
> contract High Ideas of themselves, which wear off when they come to live with the
> rest of the world.[10]

Among his contemporaries at Christ Church, possibly because they too had
high ideas of themselves, this intellectual cocksureness passed with less comment. J.F. Newton, who entered the college the same year, later described
Jenkinson's eminence as an undergraduate in terms so lavish as to prompt the
reflection that he was writing forty years later at an age when men's memories
are apt to paint the past in kindly colours. He was, recorded Newton, a first-
rate classical scholar, with a greater share of general knowledge than any of his
contemporaries and an excellent historian, who as a result of his father's tuition
was already well informed on the relationships of the great European states.
With such a dangerously inflated reputation, it is comforting that Newton also
remarked on his conciliatory temper and benign manner in ordinary society:
an impression confirmed more shortly and convincingly by another Christ
Church undergraduate, George Canning, who told his uncle that Jenkinson
was 'very clever and very remarkably good natured'.[11]

These were young men's opinions. For Lord Hawkesbury, nearing his six-
tieth birthday, there was still much to be done before his son's education could
be regarded as complete; and he was as sedulous as ever in requiring a strict
account of his studies. Herbert Croft, the writer and barrister who at that time
was carrying on some research at Oxford, lent Robert books of his own

including a volume by that unsettling modern sceptic David Hume, which 'your Lordship did not, I trust, dissapprove'. From Robert himself came a dutiful flow of letters keeping his father informed of his progress and reading. In December 1787, for instance, he was able to report that he had acquitted himself satisfactorily in his college examinations on Herodotus, had begun Mitford's *History of Greece* and Plutarch's *Lives*, and revised 'in the most accurate manner the Books of Euclid, attending very minutely to every Part of the Demonstrations'. The following term he was to embark on a programme of 'Thucydides, Logick and a continuation of the Mathematics'. As his reading progressed he favoured his father with his youthful views on the successive classical authors he encountered. Plato he admired for his language and philosophy; Demosthenes earned a respectful tribute; Livy, rather condescendingly, was read for relaxation. Yet he was modest enough both to accept and acknowledge criticism. In his second year his tutor warned him that he was too prone to general ideas and did not weigh up a book critically enough. This, he assured his father, was a fault he was trying to correct.

Robert Jenkinson was clearly an industrious and sober undergraduate. In his first year at Christ Church he even failed to spend his whole annual allowance of £200: a remarkable act of restraint in a university student at any period. For his first Christmas vacation, as a result of his college friendship with Lord Henry Spencer, he was invited to Blenheim by the Duke and Duchess of Marlborough to take part in amateur theatricals. This was hardly Robert's line, but 'as I perceive them willing to pay me every Civility,' he informed his father seriously, 'I have accepted the invitation. I have pleaded inability as an excuse for not acting, which I trust will be sufficient.' He also promised to gratify Lord Hawkesbury's insatiable desire for backstairs information. 'I will certainly let you know when I am at Blenheim their manner of living and everything that goes forward.'[12] His one verifiable diversion, and that hardly frivolous, came in his first few terms when he took an active part in a small and exclusive Christ Church debating club. Its half-dozen members, while affecting much secrecy as to their proceedings, provoked college curiosity by ostentatiously appearing in hall clad in brown coats of an uncommon hue, with velvet cuffs and collar, and adorned with buttons bearing the initials of Demosthenes, Cicero, Pitt and Fox. Two of his early friends at Christ Church – Canning and Lord Henry Spencer – were members of the club as was also J.F. Newton who later published an account of its activities. They met each Thursday evening in the rooms of one of their members and debated contemporary political issues, often with Canning championing the whig and Jenkinson the tory side.

It was not an age when authorities at public schools and universities looked with favour on the participation of the young in current controversies. Canning, lacking both private fortune and aristocratic connection, was destined for the Bar rather than the House of Commons and received a warning from the formidable Dean not to put his professional prospects at risk by too open an identification with one political party. In consequence, much to the ire of its members, he abruptly withdrew from the club. It is possible that in his second year a gentler hint was also conveyed to Jenkinson. He confessed to his father that in his first two or three terms he had contracted a bad habit of 'disputing in company' but was now convinced of its ill effects and was avoiding mixed society, contenting himself with the companionship of only one or two people. His closest friends during the rest of his stay at Oxford were Canning and Leveson Gower, son of the Marquess of Stafford, both of whom he praised warmly in letters to his father. For Canning, who came up to Christ Church seven months after Jenkinson, he conceived an instant admiration. Like other young men, then and later, he was immensely impressed by Canning's command of language, his quicksilver mind and acuteness of argument, his humour and constant high spirits. His only fault, in the eyes of his more solemn friend, was his incurable habit of turning serious matters into a jest and exercising his wit at other people's expense.

It was an uneven friendship. Part at least of Canning's motives for joining the Christ Church debating club was to measure his ability against Jenkinson's established reputation. As he admitted a year later to Newton, 'Connected with men of avowed enmity in the political world, professing opposite principles and looking forward to some distant period when we might be ranged against each other on a larger field, we were perhaps neither of us without the vanity of wishing to obtain an early ascendancy over the other.'[13] The words 'we' and 'perhaps' are disingenuous. There is no evidence that Jenkinson ever thought in terms of gaining ascendancy over Canning; it was rather the opposite. In Canning's attitude towards Jenkinson, by contrast, there was always an undercurrent of condescension. Theirs was an attraction of opposites; but to Canning, with his hard, crystalline mind and temperamental inability to appreciate the effects of his actions on others, Jenkinson's moral seriousness and emotional sensitivity made him a natural subject for teasing. It was one way of expressing an ascendancy; not perhaps the most convincing. Whether Canning's levity infected his more sober companion is uncertain. Josceline Bagot in George Canning and His Friends refers to wine parties at which Jenkinson was accustomed to sing satirical verses composed by Canning and aimed at one of their friends who 'usually threw a glass of wine in his face when he had finished'. As an isolated example of undergraduate boisterousness, this may pass. As a regular occurrence, even with such a mild-tempered person as Jenkinson, it hardly rings true; the laundry-bill alone would be a material consideration. He himself in later life had apparently forgotten such incidents (if indeed they ever took place) and simply recorded that when at Oxford 'I had the good fortune of living in a very quiet and orderly set.'[14]

Such as it was, his effective undergraduate career at Oxford lasted only twenty-six months. The next stage in his formal education was the Grand Tour of the continent. In May 1789 Lord Hawkesbury was negotiating with a M. Boutin of Paris, to whom he had previously been of service on a visit to England, for the hiring of a room and engagement of a French servant for his

son. Leaving Christ Church at the end of June Robert crossed almost immediately to France, reaching Paris on 7 July. In retrospect it was not perhaps
the most favourable time for the arrival of an earnest young Englishman
anxious to see something of the great European capital and perfect his French.
In May had come the meeting of the Estates General for the first time in nearly
two centuries; on 17 June the Third Estate had constituted itself the National
Assembly and subsequently forced the King to agree to the formulation of a
new constitution. Yet though the unprecedented political events at Versailles
were alarming enough to make the more timid French upper-class families
desert the capital, there seemed no real danger. While appreciably thinning
the number of polite salons in which M. Boutin had hoped to present his young
Englishman, the increasingly unpleasant tone of politics did not unduly restrict
Robert's activities. He visited the Tuileries; M. Boutin was indefatigable
in procuring invitations to dine with French families of his acquaintance;
he was taken out for carriage drives, and made sight-seeing visits to places
of interest. He received lessons in fencing and horsemanship, French language and literature; learned something about the fine arts (a taste for which
was to grow with the years); and practised his conversation with increasing
fluency on the thirty or forty good-natured French people to whom M. Boutin
was able to introduce him. Occasionally too he seems to have slipped away
from his mentor's vigilant eye to go about Paris on his own; for on 14 July he
was in the great crowd of Parisians who watched the storming of the Bastille
and saw the rioters, including numbers of women, at their horrid work of
destruction and slaughter. It was a spectacle which gave him a distaste for
revolutions.

Despite the regrettable events taking place around him, however, he was
able to write regularly to his father with reassuring reports of himself and his
mode of life in Paris. Lord Hawkesbury also received from his French host
glowing accounts of his son's progress and deportment, together with assess-
ments of his character which were not without penetration. He was, said M.
Boutin, well-conducted, good-natured, easy to get on with, receptive to advice
and criticism, and though lacking a degree of social polish, of good appearance.
He had more sense and wisdom than was ordinarily to be found in a man of his
years, and it was easy to see (observed the courteous Frenchman) that his
education had been carefully attended to. His qualities of integrity, mildness of
temperament and reasonableness of mind were certain to make him popular,
despite a certain shyness and reserve which, the good M. Boutin hastened to
add, at his age were not unattractive. In short, he had all that was necessary to
make him a likeable as well as a dependable man. From another French
observer came a similar verdict, perhaps more to be credited since he was not
writing to Lord Hawkesbury and was by his profession trained to scrutinise
human nature. 'His modesty and simplicity of manner,' wrote the Abbé Barthelemy to his nephew at the end of October, 'form an interesting contrast to the
firmness of his character. He has an excellent heart and his conduct has been

perfect.'[15] Even allowing for the reservations, these were not altogether unsat-isfactory judgements.

Robert Jenkinson was not quite twenty when he left Paris at the end of October; and his education had still to receive some finishing touches. The barrister John Reeves, whose great five-volume *History of the English Law* had already started to appear, was engaged to instruct him in the mysteries of that subject and by way of preparation asked him to look at the laws of Justinian as described by Mr Gibbon in his recently completed *History of the Roman Empire* (which Lord Hawkesbury prudently proposed to read with him), together with a shorter (but perhaps less entertaining) history of the laws of Rome by the learned Schomberg.[16] It was possibly at this time also, following his Paris experiences, that he took lessons with Henry Angelo, the celebrated swordsman who kept a fashionable fencing school in Soho. After passing the winter at his father's house in Hertford Street, he returned to Christ Church for thirteen weeks in the spring and early summer of 1790 where he found Canning in all the dignity of an official studentship and a minute termly stipend. Under the liberal statutes of the university, and the even more liberal interpretation placed on them in the eighteenth century, sons of peers were absolved from the perfunctory examination required for the degree of BA and allowed to proceed at once to their MA by decree three years from matriculation. Having finally completed his nine terms of residence, Jenkinson was duly created Master of Arts in May 1790.

The same summer saw him acquire with equal ease an even more desirable pair of letters after his name. Having run its full course, Pitt's loyal parliament of 1784 was dissolved in June 1790 and in the ensuing general election the twenty-year-old Mr Jenkinson was elected (by a superabundance of caution on Lord Hawkesbury's part) for both Lord Lonsdale's pocket borough of Appleby and the Treasury borough of Rye. He chose to sit for Rye for reasons not difficult to guess. His father had sat for Cockermouth and Appleby in two successive parliaments but having had differences with the Lowthers found a safer seat in the government borough of Harwich. Nevertheless, with charac-teristic Jenkinson prudence, it was decided that his son should not attempt to enter the House of Commons while still under age. Instead he spent the following winter in a second and more extended instalment of European travel.

Taking with him a small but chaste travelling library, which included Virgil, Horace and Blackstone's four-volume *Commentaries on the Laws of England*, he proceeded by way of Holland to Italy, reaching Rome on 17 January 1791. While waiting there for a pass to enter the Kingdom of Naples he made a punctilious round of all the conventional sights of the Eternal City. On the very first day after his arrival he visited St Peter's and immediately wrote off to his father in his thin slanting scrawl a dutiful letter replete with the aesthetic reflections proper to a serious tourist. As compared with St Paul's in London, he informed Lord Hawkesbury, St Peter's was less smoke-blackened and much larger, possessed a better approach and boasted a more ornate interior. On the other hand, he observed patriotically, the west front of St Paul's exhibited a purer and more correct taste than St Peter's, which seemed a temple rather than a church.

With usual Italian dilatoriness it took several weeks for the Neapolitan permit to materialise and the daily round of Roman sight-seeing began perceptibly to pall. He had seen almost all the places of interest, he wrote somewhat perfunctorily at the end of February, and hoped to complete his inspection by the following week. He had been extremely delighted with everything. It was impossible, however, to give in a letter an adequate idea of his impressions but he looked forward to many conversations with his father on the subject when he returned to England. What took his fancy was a story circulating in Rome about the Cardinal of York, the last of the exiled Stuarts. Having heard that Mr Burke's recent pamphlet on the French Revolution contained a stout defence of Church establishments, he sent for a copy to be read aloud to him. When, however, his secretary came to the passage in which the Revolution of 1688 was defended, the cardinal stopped the reading abruptly, left the room and had not looked at the pamphlet since. To Jenkinson, loyal Hanoverian and good Protestant, this was too good an anecdote to wait until he arrived back, and he promptly related it in a letter to his father.

When he finally gained entry to the Kingdom of Naples it did not find much favour in his eyes. The landscape was certainly more picturesque than the 'unhealthy and disgusting' flat countryside round Rome; but the people were given to criminal habits, the legal system was corrupt, the upper classes uncivilised; and the women, added the young moralist disapprovingly, though 'gallant' were for the most part neither 'amiable or pleasing'. However, he saw an eruption of Vesuvius, which was not a spectacle readily available elsewhere, and on the return journey he was able to visit Florence before travelling on to England where his father was impatiently waiting for him to take his seat in the House of Commons.[17] Though the session which was nearly over had witnessed a dramatic quarrel between Fox and Burke over the significance of what was happening in France, the attention of the Commons had been mainly fixed on other matters: the financial arrangements proposed in the budget, affairs in India, Pitt's Canada Act, and the growing tension with Russia because of its aggressive actions against Turkey. With only three days intervening between his twenty-first birthday and the end of the session on 10 June, the opportunity for Jenkinson to make his entry on the stage of the House of Commons was brief enough. The surviving parliamentary records do not particularise the new members who took the oaths on any given day and it is in fact not clear when he took his seat, though the probability is that it was not until early in 1792.

Certainly his maiden speech was deferred until that year. In the meantime, with the maturity and assurance created by election to Parliament and foreign travel, he visited his old friends in Christ Church. Leveson Gower for one was conscious of the change and resented it. He wrote somewhat sourly to his mother in December,

> Jenkinson has been here for a few days. We were not upon such intimate terms as formerly; there were some traits in his character I heard from different people (Strathaven among others) which inclined me not to look so favourably with regard to him as before, and his excessive importance (unless one is prejudiced in his favour) becomes very disgusting. I do not think his abilities are of the highest class, but a wonderful fluency of words and no share of *mauvaise honte* may cause his making some figure in the House of Commons.[18]

Three years younger and still an undergraduate, it was not surprising that Leveson Gower felt a twinge of jealousy, though a little odd that he could be swayed so easily by other people's judgements about an old friend. No doubt, if he was disposed to be captious, there were faults to be found. Clever, over-educated, the self-conscious centre of his father's unremitting hopes and ambitions, and still at heart perhaps lacking a natural self-confidence, Jenkinson might well have put on airs in front of an old acquaintance still in *statu pupillari* at college. It would be equally natural for his rapid rise to evoke some disgruntlement among contemporaries whom he had momentarily outstripped. To a jealous onlooker his path so far had been singularly easy. Unlike Canning with his disorganised family background and uncertain choice of career, Jenkinson had not only had his course mapped out from birth but had enjoyed every material advantage that money and influence could secure in pursuing it. It would have taken more objectivity than is usually present in a young man of twenty-one to appreciate how much he owed to his father and how little to himself. If the Abbé Barthelemy was to be trusted, however, he had firmness of character and an excellent heart; and these were good correctives to youthful vanity and conceit.

NOTES

1 Stanhope, I, 306.
2 FD, I, 162.
3 Geoffrey Moorhouse, *India Britannica* (1983), pp. 48, 50, 184; and *Calcutta* (1971), pp. 27, 34. See also the Watts of Hanslope in Burke's *Landed Gentry* (1894), Vol. II.
4 For the history of the Jenkinson family see Rev. H.L.L. Denny, *The Manor of Hawkesbury and its Owners* (privately printed, Gloucester, 1920); *Gloucestershire Notes and Queries*, ed. W.P.W. Phillimore, Vol. V (1891–3), 91–2, 252, 267–8.
5 38470 fos 138, 156, 166, 204, 236; 38471 fo. 17.
6 W. Haig Brown, *Charterhouse Past and Present* (1879); E.P. Eardley Wilmot and F.G. Streatfeild, *Charterhouse Old and New* (1895).
7 Yonge, I, 6–8.
8 GM (1829), Pt I, p. 81.
9 38471 fos 1, 98, 137.
10 LGC, I, 8.
11 J.F. Newton, *Early Days of the Rt. Hon. George Canning* (1828); Dixon, p. 8.
12 38471 fos 176, 183, 189; Yonge, I, 9–12.

13 Newton, *op. cit.*, pp. 20-21.

14 38475 fo. 146 (in 1824).

15 'Sa Modestie et la Simplicité de ses Manières font un Contraste très intéressant avec la fermeté de son Caractère. Son Coeur est excellent, sa Conduite a été parfaite.' 38471 fo. 262. See also fos 225-55.

16 Ibid, fos 276 ff. (Reeves to Hawkesbury, Nov.-Dec. 1789).

17 38472 fos 2, 8, 19; Yonge, I, 13.

18 LGC, I, 35.

CHAPTER II
Politics and Love

In the parliamentary session of 1791 the ministry had experienced an uncomfortable defeat over its foreign policy. For some years the aggressive activity of Russia and Austria in south-east Europe had been causing anxiety to other states. In 1791 the British and Prussian governments had sent ultimatums demanding the evacuation of Oczakov, a Turkish fortress on the Black Sea occupied by Russian troops in 1788. Though the containment of Russian expansion was to become in the nineteenth century a classic British interest, at the time Pitt's policy received little comprehension or support. To the public Oczakov seemed an obscure place in a distant country. The cabinet was divided; and there were suspicions that the Prime Minister was being unduly influenced by his Prussian allies. To the opposition, smarting over their defeat on the Regency issue in 1788, it provided an admirable platform from which to launch a fresh attack on the administration. Pitt was obliged to abandon his armament plans and withdraw his ultimatum. It was the most humiliating defeat he had yet experienced and the opposition were not disposed to let it be forgotten. The matter was brought up on three occasions during the first four weeks of the following session and on the last of these (29 February 1792) Whitbread moved what was in effect a retrospective vote of censure.

He was answered by Jenkinson in a maiden speech which, reported the *Annual Register*, excited 'uncommon attention and admiration'. With a clear delivery and no sign of nerves, he ranged for more than an hour over such high matters as the European balance of power, the value of the Prussian alliance, and the eclipse of France as a military state as a result of internal weakness. There was, however, he warned the House, a power that had succeeded France 'no less deserving of attention from its restless politics and ambitious views: this was Russia.... Were she suffered to accomplish these, the balance of Europe would be totally destroyed.' It was a prophetic utterance; less so his closing passage when, in seeking credit for mediation, he observed that the present time was not calculated for invasion and conquest. Nevertheless, it was a good speech and probably seemed all the better because of the mediocrity of other speakers on the government side. Congratulations flowed in to old Lord Hawkesbury. Pitt made a complimentary reference both publicly when closing the debate and in private when writing to the King.

No doubt Jenkinson had been well primed with advice and information by Pitt and his father; and the occasion was well chosen. Though much publicised, the issue was recriminatory rather than real, and Whitbread's motion was soundly defeated by a majority of more than two to one. Yet it must have been satisfactory to the Prime Minister to feel that he had added a young man of obvious talents to his slender team of House of Commons debaters. With Fox, Sheridan, and Grey on the opposition benches, good speakers in debate were almost as important to the government as good numbers in the division. However strong the ministerial case, it had to be seen to be strong by the independent members of the House. The youthful orator himself was wisely content for the next few months to rest silently on his laurels. In the debate on Wilberforce's motion for abolishing the slave trade, along with Colonel Tarleton, MP for Liverpool, he urged a variety of ingenious reasons for continuing that suspect traffic. Otherwise his parliamentary activities for the remainder of a not particularly eventful session were unmemorable. Even his intervention in the slavery debate owed more to filial loyalty than political conviction. In the upper house Lord Hawkesbury was one of the leaders of the majority which ultimately frustrated the efforts of the emancipationists to bring the slave traffic to a halt before the end of the century.

The session ended in June and the following month Jenkinson departed once more to the continent. This, however, was no mere sight-seeing trip. Since the previous year, even since his speech of February, the political landscape of Europe had darkened. Though it was true that the military power of France had been eclipsed, the rapid and unpredictable slide of French politics towards anarchy and republicanism was watched with horrified fascination by the European public. From the summer of 1791 the royal family were virtually prisoners; in April 1792 the hapless French King had been forced by his Girondin ministers to declare war on the Emperor. In June the first coalition against revolutionary France signalled to an unprescient Europe the start of what was to prove one of the longest conflicts in its history. Before Jenkinson left London the dusty columns of Austrian and Prussian troops were already creeping west towards the French frontier. In the circumstances it was hardly surprising that his journey aroused some speculation. The *Leyden Gazette* took note of it and by professing ignorance of its object contrived to give it an air of importance and mystery. It was not long before the belief was being expressed in French circles that he had been sent by Pitt to make contact with the Allies.

Travelling by way of Holland Jenkinson ran into Leveson Gower who went with him as far as Mainz. Though outwardly friendly his old Christ Church companion was as hypercritical as ever in his private comments. His impression was that though Jenkinson denied being an emissary of the Prime Minister, he was not displeased by the interest he was exciting. He was certainly indefatigable in picking up information, visiting both the headquarters of the two armies at Coblence and the French *émigré* force of several thousand which was to cooperate with them. The tuition he had received under M. Boutin was clearly being put to good use. 'His eloquence in the French language,' Leveson Gower reported sarcastically to his mother, 'is nearly equal to that for which he is so famous in the House of Commons.' His eloquence, however, failed to persuade Gower to accompany him any further and they parted at Mainz: Gower to continue his journey to Dresden, Jenkinson to hurry after the Austrian army as it moved up to the French frontier. To his father he sent the results of his observations and for good measure a copy of the Duke of Brunswick's famous proclamation, announcing the intention of the two monarchs to restore the French King to his former authority. A year's experience of politics had sharpened Jenkinson's faculties. His Rhineland despatches of 1792 show a noticeable advance in shrewdness and objectivity compared with the tourist letters of his previous travels. Though he was only twenty-two, they could have been the products of a much older man. He was impressed by the machine-like discipline of the Prussian troops and quoted a remark made to him by the Duke of Brunswick, the allied commander-in-chief. 'They are great blockheads but, all the same, they know their job.' He reflected, nevertheless, that if any disaster happened to the Prussian army, it would be difficult to replace it. The Austrians, on the other hand, while decidedly less efficient, had the more indestructible reserves of manpower in their large dominions. He noted also the German contempt for the French and the Austrian dislike of the Prussians.[1] If his views on the two Germanic allies ever came under Pitt's eye, they could only have fortified the Prime Minister's reluctance to intervene on the continent.

Events in France, however, moved at a speed which completely outpaced the calculations of neutral politicians. In August came the massacre of the Swiss Guards and the setting-up of a national convention; in September the first wave of guillotinings and the inconclusive cannonade of Valmy which brought a premature halt to the cautious allied advance; in November the proclamation of assistance to revolutionary movements in other countries. Before the new parliamentary session began in London, Louis xvi in Paris was on trial for his life. An early date had been fixed for the meeting of Parliament because of the government's decision to call up part of the militia. The response of the opposition to this precautionary act was to table a motion requiring the immediate despatch of a mission to Paris to negotiate a settlement of all differences between the two countries that might lead to war. The resolution was moved by Fox, seconded by Grey, and answered among others by Jenkinson. Fresh from his continental experiences, he treated the House to a speech of considerable length and surprisingly bellicose spirit. Britain, he argued, was financially in a better position to wage war than revolutionary France; and radical movements at home would be dampened rather than encouraged by actual hostilities. The threat of opening the Scheldt was a direct challenge to British commercial interests and treaty rights, and to send an ambassador to 'bow his neck to a band of sanguinary ruffians' at the very moment when the French King was about to be sentenced – was perhaps already executed – would be infamous.[2]

His oratory went ahead of events. It was to be another five weeks before Louis XVI ascended the scaffold; but his fate had long been certain and the emotional tone of Jenkinson's speech reflected the passions that the French Revolution was beginning to arouse in British society. His attitude of revulsion was shared by most of the House of Commons. Fox's motion was negatived without a division and the eloquent young speaker received the congratulations of both Pitt and Burke. He was evidently emerging as a young war-hawk on the government side. After the French had started hostilities against Britain and Holland in February 1793 Jenkinson was again prominent in defence of ministerial policy. The same month Fox moved a set of resolutions condemning the outbreak of war and Jenkinson was given the task of moving the previous question that put a triumphant end to the debate. He did so, wrote the Prime Minister to his monarch, 'in a speech of uncommon ability and effect'.[3] This, from such a quarter and in a debate graced by Fox, Burke, Grey and Sheridan, was praise indeed.

He was again conspicuous, though less happily, in a debate of April 1794 when the government spokesmen had to address themselves to the task – one which was to become depressingly familiar over the next fifteen years – of explaining British military failures on the continent. It occurred on an opposition motion for an enquiry into recent operations at Dunkirk and Toulon. In the course of his speech (one of several he made this session vindicating the ministry's conduct of the war) Jenkinson expressed the opinion that the soundest military policy would be to strike at the heart of the enemy and march on Paris itself.[4] It was one of those innocent remarks – one of the well-known pitfalls of a parliamentary career – which inexplicably appeals to the public's sense of the ludicrous and is never forgotten. To a generation brought up on the deliberate strategy of mid-eighteenth-century warfare and made cynical by the continued ill-success of allied arms, the idea seemed amateurish nonsense. A then unknown French captain of artillery, who had been largely responsible for the British defeat at Toulon, was later to demonstrate the political as well as military value of a direct strike at the enemy's capital. In Britain, however, the intelligent but unpopular Windham was one of the few politicians with pretensions to military knowledge who ever admitted that in principle what Jenkinson suggested was the correct strategy. At the time, and for many years to come, 'Lord Hawkesbury's March on Paris' was a stock jest. Though Canning in the same debate referred to Jenkinson's 'very admirable speech', he himself was not above using the old jibe in a satirical poem he wrote against the Addington administration seven years later.

It was not only in foreign and military affairs that Jenkinson was making his mark as a parliamentary speaker. A year earlier, in May 1793, he had demonstrated both his versatility in debate and his conservatism in politics, by opposing Grey's motion on parliamentary reform. Though employing arguments made familiar by Burke's speeches and pamphlets, it was his most elaborate oration so far and was followed by promotion to office. Under a bill which passed through the House of Commons the same month, the Board of Control set up by Pitt's India Act of 1784 was reconstructed to permit the appointment of men who were not privy councillors. When the new board was gazetted, Robert Banks (he dropped the 'e') Jenkinson's name appeared as the most junior of a list which included such leading politicians as Pitt, Dundas, Lord Grenville and Lord Mornington, the future Marquess Wellesley. In Hickel's painting of the House of Commons in 1793, exhibited in the Haymarket in 1795, Jenkinson appears sitting next to Mornington on the government front bench: a tall, youthful figure in wide-skirted coat, cream waistcoat, fawn breeches, elegant cravat, and fashionable tight boots. He was there again on 31 January 1794 when Canning made his maiden speech.

Since Canning had come down from Oxford in the summer of 1791, the friendship between the two young men had continued as warmly as when they were undergraduates: perhaps even more so, since it was no longer marked by any difference of opinion over political matters. Within twelve months Canning had been equally disillusioned by the study of law as a professional career and by the Francophil democratic enthusiasms of Fox and Grey as a guide for his political attitudes. Once these distractions had been cleared from his path, the way ahead was clear. There is no reason to doubt the firm contemporary belief that it was through Jenkinson that he gained access to Pitt. One account is that the first meeting of any importance between Pitt and Canning took place when both were invited to dine at Addiscombe, Lord Hawkesbury's home. When Canning had his first private interview with Pitt in August 1792 there was certainly much mention of Jenkinson in their conversation. In less than a year Canning was furnished with a parliamentary seat and at the start of the following session he made his first speech. Before that momentous occasion Jenkinson, from his two years' experience of the House, gave practical advice on how to avoid that familiar 'sensation of sinking and emptiness' which habitually afflicts the novice speaker; and when safely delivered of his oration, it was Jenkinson and a couple of other friends with whom he went off to dine.[5]

While not a great admirer of Canning's speeches, which struck him as florid and generalised compared with his own closely argued debating efforts (his Oxford tutor's criticisms had clearly not gone unheeded), Jenkinson was as devoted as ever to his old college friend. When in November 1793 he established himself in a house of his own in Conduit Street, Canning frequently ate there before going on to the House of Commons or dined there alone with Jenkinson afterwards. 'The inseparables', as they had been nicknamed at Oxford, seemed inseparable still. In the famous cartoon published by the satirist Gillray in 1796, 'Promised Horrors of the French Revolution', one of the more striking details in its lively scene was the bodies of Jenkinson and Canning, lashed together and dangling from a street-lamp outside White's Club, with a placard affixed entitled 'New March to Paris'. Though they were identified with each other in the public mind, however, Canning's feelings towards Jenkinson still had an element of contempt of a kind not uncommon in a clever, witty young man towards a duller, loyal companion. It was an example followed by many of Canning's friends and admirers. The habitual use in Canning's circle of such derisive variations on Jenkinson's name as Jinks, Jenky, and later Hawky, Hawsbury, Jinksbury and Jawkes, spoke for itself. His moral seriousness, his slightly odd physical appearance, made him something of a butt among the bright, amusing, slightly malicious young men who gathered round Canning.

In these early years Jenkinson had a frequently melancholy expression; though tall, he was not robust, and his long neck helped to give him a lanky, shambling appearance. James Hare, professional wit and friend of Charles James Fox, who described Jenkinson as always looking 'as if he had been on the rack three times, and saw the wheel preparing for a fourth', declared that he had the longest neck in England.[6] While much must be allowed to the dinner-table humorist, there was obviously enough truth in this caricature to amuse his listeners. To the young Canningites it was vexing that such an unmodish figure should be ahead of them in the parliamentary race.

In the patriotic defence movement that was launched at the start of the war, Jenkinson characteristically was among the first of the junior ministers to volunteer for service. In the winter of 1792-3 he was busy getting a commission in the militia, undeterred by Canning's unkind assertion that his knowledge of music better qualified him to be a trumpeter. Most official men clearly thought it was their duty to set an example to the country. Pitt as Lord Warden organised a force from the Cinque Ports; Addington raised a troop of Woodley Cavalry in Berkshire; Rose several units in Hampshire; while the City of London Light Horse positively bristled with MPs and future ministers of the Crown, including Perceval, Vansittart, C.W. Wynn, Charles Abbot, and Manners Sutton. In the course of 1794 Jenkinson became colonel of Pitt's Cinque Ports Regiment of Fencible Cavalry and was conscientiously practising his parade-ground horsemanship. The absence of most of the regular forces threw additional burdens on the militia and his new duties frequently kept him away from London. For several sessions, in fact, he only attended the House of Commons when his vote or his voice was particularly needed by the government. In 1796 his regiment was up in Scotland, he himself being quartered at Dumfries. Among other tasks he had to furnish a guard at the funeral of Robert Burns, a poet of whom he disapproved on political grounds. In the eyes of Colonel Jenkinson he was a revolutionary whose acquaintance he had previously declined to make. In general he was only a degree less censorious of Scotland than he had been of Naples five years earlier. His regiment was hospitably received by the good people of Dumfriesshire; but he commented critically on the difficulty of getting servants, the dirtiness of those who were obtainable, the quantities of meat put on the table, and the excessive circulation of the bottle afterwards.

Canning, who easily evaded Jenkinson's efforts to make him take a commission as captain in his regiment, had from the start viewed these military activities with a sardonic eye. When Jenkinson proudly showed him one of his recruiting sergeant's posters, he could not resist the temptation to dash off a wicked parody in the form of a burlesque appeal for

> Tight lads, who would wish for a fair opportunity,
> Of defying the Frenchmen, with perfect impunity....
> 'Tis the bold Colonel Jenkinson calls you to arm,
> And solemnly swears you shall come to no harm.

And so on for another fifty lines. It was all unfair and highly amusing. It was standard practice in recruiting placards to assure potential militiamen that they would not be sent for service abroad; which was the point of Canning's joke. The verses, printed in the form of a poster with the picture of a militia sergeant, were used for an elaborate practical joke at a dinner-party given by Charles Ellis MP, one of Canning's friends. After the guests had assembled a packet of these posters arrived addressed to Jenkinson with an accompanying note as though from a printer, acknowledging a non-existent order, and implying that copies had already been put up in the streets. The company, all of whom were in the plot except the victim, insisted on having the poster read aloud by one of their number. The joke misfired; poor Jenkinson was so mortified that he began to cry; Ellis and Lady Malmesbury (at whose house the verses had been written) tried to compose him but without success. Eventually Lady Malmesbury took him away to another room and sat with him on a sofa for two hours until he had recovered sufficiently to go off to dine elsewhere. He was not angry with anyone, he told her miserably, but he felt that coming from Canning it was so unkind.

When informed by Ellis of what had happened, Canning was distressed to the point of tears himself and went off to find Jenkinson. Going home together in Jenkinson's carriage he explained that it was all a misunderstanding and he had never meant to show unkindness or cause pain. When Jenkinson failed to respond to this limited expression of regret, Canning stopped the carriage in a huff, and went away home on foot. For a few weeks there was a complete breach between the two old friends. Finally, when Canning was about to leave town for the summer vacation, he wrote to Jenkinson offering to call on him. They met, and after some meaningless conversation Canning picked up his hat to depart, observing that Jenkinson had behaved badly but he would forgive him and think no more about it. At this characteristic piece of egotism Jenkinson did not know whether to be amazed or amused. When able to speak he observed good-humouredly, 'well, after all, this is the oddest and most unreasonable thing, that I am to be made out in the wrong and to have need of forgiveness'. Canning airily explained that he considered he had already made sufficient apology and that it was therefore Jenkinson who was responsible for the continuing coolness between them. On that they shook hands, laughed over the whole episode, and spent the rest of the morning together before going down to the House of Commons. It was a revealing incident, Jenkinson's emotional vulnerability, good-nature and lack of vindictiveness contrasting with Canning's insouciance and genuine though superficial kindliness. When Cyril Jackson, the Dean of Christ Church, was told about it, he remarked trenchantly that it was as foolish a business as he had ever heard and just like their behaviour in college, when they were perpetually quarrelling and making it up again.[7]

It was, admittedly, for all three men concerned – Ellis, Canning and Jenkinson – conduct hardly befitting the dignity of an MP and legislator for the Empire. At this particular period, however, Jenkinson was emotionally in a disturbed state: which explains to some extent his tearful exhibition at Ellis's party. He had fallen in love for the first time and Canning the practical joker had been his sole confidant. The woman who had aroused his ardour was Lady Louisa Hervey, youngest daughter of the Earl of Bristol. It was in certain respects an unconventional alliance for the young Jenkinson to set his heart on; but in his mid-twenties, freed from his father's immediate supervision, he was in an ardent mood. The portrait painted by Lawrence (himself only a year older than his sitter) about 1796 in his early romantic style, shows a sensitive and intense young man with long hair, worn naturally in a kind of studied disorder, and a curiously intent look beneath the dark level eyebrows. Nevertheless, even by the lax standards of the eighteenth century, the Herveys were an exceptionally odd family and none odder than Louisa's father, the eccentric fourth earl. As Bishop of Derry he had fortuitously inherited the secular title as a result of the deaths without heirs of his two elder brothers. An admirer of Rousseau and Voltaire, liberal, optimistic and humanitarian, amateur scientist, patron of the arts, and insatiable traveller, he was an engaging specimen of the spirit of the enlightenment which dominated European thought before the French Revolution arrived to cast doubts on the complete goodness and perfectibility of human nature.

To those indifferent to his personal charm, and they unfortunately included his wife, he seemed restless, impetuous, vain and self-indulgent. He struck others more tolerantly as a man with an innocent zest for life, an indefatigable eagerness for fresh scenes and experiences, whom no misfortune or disappointment could long depress. In 1782, after thirty uneasy years of marriage, he separated from his patient and sorely-tried wife. They never saw each other again, though he continued to correspond in the friendliest manner with his three daughters. Two of these, Mary and Elizabeth, had themselves made disastrous marriages and were living apart from their husbands. The elder, Lady Erne, for many years spent an unsettled existence first on the continent and later alternately in London and Hampshire. Her sister, the fascinating Elizabeth Foster, joined the household of the Duke of Devonshire as friend and companion to the Duchess, governess to the Duke's natural daughter, and in little over a year as mistress to the Duke in a much-chronicled *ménage à trois* at Devonshire House.

The third daughter Louisa could have had as a child very little of her sisters' companionship. There was a considerable gap of age between them and, before she was ten, both had married. For a few brief years she was the spoiled child of her oddly assorted parents, accompanying them with her governess on their protracted tour of Europe in 1777. Most of the time they spent in Italy where Louisa took music and drawing lessons, was petted by the artistic circle which gathered round the eccentric earl-bishop, and nearly died of malarial fever. Because of the long convalescence she required they did not get home until September 1779. Three months later her father succeeded to the earldom and at the age of twelve Lou (as Lord Bristol always called her) became Lady Louisa Hervey. Ironically her father's elevation to the peerage marked the end of the first and happiest part of her childhood. With her parents' separation a few years later her life took on a more restricted pattern. Hard pressed for money, Lady Bristol was forced to let their London house and live permanently with her daughter at their country home at Ickworth, near Bury St Edmunds in Suffolk. The old Tudor manor house had already been demolished and the great new house with the magnificent rotunda seen today was no more than a grandiose idea in the fertile mind of the fourth earl and a few preliminary sketches on an architect's drawing-board. In the interval the family lived at Ickworth Lodge, a converted farmhouse fitted up by the first earl in the middle of the great park in leafy but somewhat solitary rural seclusion. There, as an emotional compensation for her husband's desertion, Lady Bristol devoted herself in a grimly evangelical spirit to the formation of Louisa's morals and disposition. 'I now am only intent,' she wrote to her second daughter soon after the separation, 'on drawing all the good possible out of this evil in favour of Louisa ... and to acquire in solid advantages to her mind and character what she loses in accomplishments.'

To be the sole object of a pious mother's unremitting attention is a doubtful advantage for a small child. The regime Lady Bristol instituted at Ickworth was to outward appearance both dull and oppressive. Reading aloud to her mother; playing picquet with her mother; exercising on the piano while her mother drank tea – 'which saves her a temptation and gives me a pleasure'; being read to by her mother – 'one book of *Iliad*, – a little talk on the notes on it after it is over', until her French governess came to take her to bed – this made up a typical day. She had no companions of her own age; the books she was allowed were carefully censored. When they read together Richardson's improving novel *Clarissa Harlowe*, Lady Bristol (fearing that Louisa was becoming enamoured of the scapegrace hero Lovelace) tore out one of the letters as 'a little too *descriptive* of the night he got into her room'. Louisa dutifully made clothes for a poor girl she was supposed to be maintaining at school; and there were visits in the summer from dancing and music masters. Apart from these rare apparitions from the great world beyond the park gates and occasional descents on Ickworth by her sisters and her uncle General Hervey, her life was cloistered and uneventful. Though she greatly missed her father's society, she was a willing and affectionate child and tried as much as was possible for a girl of fifteen not to give way to what her mother unsympathetically characterised as 'a selfish and pining discontent'. Lady Bristol was satisfied, perhaps too complacently, that she had convinced Louisa of her ability not only to bear with their altered mode of living but to profit from it.

The consequences were foreseeable. The 'little snip of a musician' who returned home from Italy, the child who got up early on May Day 1780 to pick flowers and sing under her mother's window 'as wild as the winds, her face like Aurora', in five years became a nervous, irritable adolescent, pining away in what must have seemed to her the desolation of the vast park and the flat, windswept Suffolk landscape outside. In 1785 her mother took her to London for medical advice. There the celebrated Court physician Dr Farquhar pronounced her free from any physical disorder and, with a commonsense unusual in the medical faculty of his day, prescribed an eminently sensible regimen of mineral waters, moderate exercise, and cheerful amusements. For the next few years mother and daughter lived quietly but more happily at Bristol House. While avoiding fashionable festivities and late nights, in St James's Square they had congenial families around them and for Louisa company of her own age and sex. Nevertheless, she was slow to shake off the effects of the oppressive years at Ickworth; in some respects she never did. Though in 1792 her mother took her off for a long holiday by the sea at Ramsgate, during the next two years she was still suffering from nervous depression. Her father, writing to Lady Erne (his favourite daughter) in August 1794, opined that the troubles of 'dearest Lou' derived entirely from the effects on her nervous system of her Italian illness. As confident in his medical as in his aesthetic judgements, he prescribed a glass of fresh spring water each night when she went to bed. This at least was harmless; but another and probably more efficacious remedy was close at hand.[8]

Robert Jenkinson made the acquaintance of the Hervey ladies in 1793 or even earlier. Certainly by May of that year he was on friendly terms with Lady Erne since he was writing to her with all the authority of an officer in the Cinque Ports Cavalry that it would be safe for her and her daughter to take a holiday on the south coast. 'You must admit unless you mean to affront me,' he wrote, 'that the objection on the Ground of Danger is entirely removed, and that all Persons that are wise enough to establish themselves on the Coast of Kent will be certain of Protection.' The following winter he was seeing much of Louisa and her mother, despite the fact that to save expense they had moved from Bristol House to Wimbledon.[9] Almost before he realised it, he was deeply in love. It was the attraction of similar rather than of opposite temperaments. Both were serious young people, both strictly brought up, both somewhat shy and reserved, both essentially kind and warm-hearted. Physically Louisa had her full share of the traditional Hervey good looks. A portrait of her painted about this time by Romney shows a slender young woman, leaning on a harp, dressed in the simple, high-waisted fashion of the period, her delicate face framed by dark hair and a large mob-cap, with full, expressive eyes and a wistful expression. There was a clear family likeness to her two sisters in the regular features and heart-shaped face; but where Lady Erne in her portraits appears grave and maternal, Elizabeth Foster calm and assured, the younger Louisa seems fragile and uncertain. In temperament too there was a difference. They were all sense; she sensibility. In her impulsiveness and generosity she was like her father; in her piousness she had something of her mother's evangelicalism. She was genuinely concerned to help the poor and afflicted; but she sometimes showed a morbid tendency to moralise over the accidents and mortalities of human existence (especially when manifested among the rich and powerful), as being the salutary chastening of Providence.

She took longer than Robert to make up her mind: but by the summer of 1794, though she had not positively given her consent, Canning (the only other person in the secret) felt confident that she would do so. By November everything was settled between them; it was the first decision of importance affecting his own life that Jenkinson had made. The next step was to obtain the consent of the two fathers. Since the Earl of Bristol was as usual on the continent, and his probable reaction, from all experience, unpredictable, the two young people decided to obtain his approval before applying to Lord Hawkesbury. It proved an unfortunate error of judgement. The disciple of Rousseau replied not only promptly but in a spirit of benevolence that surpassed their hopes. Meanwhile Lord Hawkesbury had heard rumours of his son's attachment but refused to credit them. When finally told, he was highly offended at being kept in the dark so long. Approached by his son, first by letter and then face to face, he expressed a decided opposition to the match. This was not altogether surprising. Even if he were prepared to overlook the marital peculiarities of Louisa's family (three broken Hervey marriages were no recommendation for a fourth), she was three years older than his son and possessed little or nothing in the way of a dowry. In any case he thought it folly for Robert to marry at the age of twenty-four at the very outset of his career – unless of course it was to an heiress to a fortune, which would materially alter the case. He himself had prudently postponed matrimony until he was over forty and saw no reason why his son should not wait at least until he was thirty. In short, marriage was improvident and the prospective bride not particularly eligible. Having roundly stated his objections he was at first prepared to let Robert consider them at leisure and then make up his own mind. The interval for reflection merely hardened his own heart; when again approached, he angrily ordered his son to put all thought of the match out of his head.

His usually docile son, however, showed an unexpected determination of his own and for a time there was deadlock. Accustomed all his life to please and defer to his father, of whom he was genuinely fond, Robert was in deep distress. Others were brought in to give advice: Louisa's younger brother Frederick Hervey, and her close friend Jane Dundas, the recently-married wife of the cabinet minister. In turn Dundas talked with Pitt. These two wily politicians agreed with Canning that only strong measures would overcome Lord Hawkesbury's resistance and that it would be useless to wait (as his son thought of doing) for persuasion and affection to operate on his tough old heart. It was settled therefore that Jenkinson should tell Lord Hawkesbury that his low spirits made him incapable of any parliamentary exertion and that he proposed to absent himself permanently from the House of Commons. Pitt and Dundas concurred with these tactics since, according to Canning, they thought with worldly shrewdness that in Hawkesbury's mind 'the pride which he feels in his son's consequence is a passion much more powerful, and to which it is much more prudent to appeal, than his affection'. In the end the ruse proved successful, though not before the King himself took up the cause of the young lovers and pressed Lord Hawkesbury to yield. The involvement of Court and cabinet in smoothing the course of true love lent the episode a comic air which was probably lost on the two persons most concerned. It said much for the strong-mindedness of old Lord Hawkesbury, however, that it needed the monarch and the Prime Minister to unite against him before he gave way on a matter affecting his son's future.

The wedding took place at Wimbledon on 25 March 1795 with Lord Hawkesbury's kinsman Folliott Cornwall, then Dean of Canterbury, officiating. The bridegroom on the previous day was reported as being in such a state of nerves that it was uncomfortable for anyone even to sit near him. When, after a brief honeymoon, they returned to town, Canning went to dine with them. He described Lady Louisa as delightful, the house handsomely furnished, the dinner pleasant, and his host benevolently disposed to all his old friends.[10] Nevertheless, between Louisa Hervey and George Canning there could have been little temperamental affinity. Even if she did not feel any of the natural jealousy of a young bride towards an old, intimate and somewhat cynical friend of her husband, she probably thought Canning too frivolous and he perhaps found her too strait-laced. Lady Holland spoke a few years later of her 'extreme prudery' and added waspishly that 'prudery comes with an odd and questionable aspect from a Hervey'.[11]

Jenkinson had certainly acquired a peculiar set of relations, though he seemed on the best of terms with both his sisters-in-law. Indeed, despite their whiggishness, he seemed rather proud of his Devonshire House connections. Many years afterwards Mrs Arbuthnot ascribed the award of the blue ribbon of the Garter to the sixth duke entirely to Jenkinson's family partiality, though he said it was the wish of the King. What had provoked Lady Holland's outburst, however, was a report that Louisa had been shocked at hearing of an acquaintanceship between Lady Holland and her own niece, Elizabeth Hervey. It must be said, however, that Lady Holland herself was one of the more scandalous ladies of her generation, enjoying a notoriety similar to that of Caroline of Brunswick a generation later; and with equal cause. Louisa was not the only one to regard any connection with her as compromising. Nevertheless, her marriage inevitably meant the end of Canning's easy, patronising relationship with her husband. There was no sudden break. As late as April 1799 when Windham dined with Jenkinson, he found the familiar trio of

Canning, Leveson Gower and Ellis among his fellow-guests. The change was one of circumstance rather than of intention. After 1795, however, the old bachelor intimacy that they had carried on from their Oxford days slowly waned.

Matrimony, however, did not diminish Jenkinson's zeal for amateur soldiering. Fortunately it was a patriotic activity that could be pursued without undue separation from Louisa; since it is evident that he continued to spend all his summers, once the parliamentary session was over, with his militia unit. It was a call of duty he took seriously. To a distant relative he wrote in February 1798 that 'my Military duties make it difficult for me to obtain leave of absence from my Regiment during the Summer'. This devotion to the demands of the service was all the more admirable on this occasion as he was writing about a meeting to discuss the possibility of his inheriting an estate in Shropshire. Catherine Jenkinson, the sister and heiress of Sir Bankes Jenkinson, sixth baronet, had married Mr Thomas Ottley of Pitchford Hall. By 1798 he had reached the age of eighty-two and his only son Adam was unmarried and in poor health. The two Ottleys were agreed that the estate, with a rent-roll of over £2,000 per annum, which had been in the possession of their family for thirteen generations, should pass to their relations on the mother's side, the two younger Jenkinsons. The difficulty was to choose between Robert, the heir to the title, and Cecil, the impecunious younger brother. Adam Ottley favoured Robert; his father and uncle preferred Cecil, as being more likely to reside on the estate. These matters Adam Ottley put candidly before his kinsman in January 1798, asking him to discuss them fully with Lord Liverpool, as Hawkesbury had become meanwhile.

Robert, while duly passing his letter on to his father, not surprisingly showed a warm interest in his chances of becoming the Ottley heir. He assured Adam Ottley that he had no settled home of his own and that if Pitchford Hall came into his possession, 'I should certainly make it the established residence of my family'. However, much was to happen that would change his mode of life before the Pitchford estate passed from the Ottleys to the Jenkinsons. Adam Ottley and his aged father lived on for another nine years and family discussions on the disposal of the estate continued. Louisa and her husband were clearly anxious to obtain the property but it is probable that this happy opportunity of providing for the younger son had certain attractions for Lord Liverpool. It is to be presumed also that his second wife, Cecil's mother, favoured her son's claims.[12]

Apart from these delightful but tantalisingly vague prospects, Robert's more immediate attention was fixed on the great events passing on the continent; in these he took an intense, almost emotional, interest. To his friend Lord Mornington he expressed later in 1798 his fervent hope that the European war would recommence and that the great powers would come to see that their only chance of survival lay in a great combined effort against what he called 'the common enemy of the human race', though whether by that resounding expression he meant General Bonaparte or the French republic generally was not clear. This was the year of Bonaparte's expedition to Syria and Egypt, of the battle of the Nile, and of the ferocious Irish rebellion. Taking Louisa with him he had gone down to Walmer to join his regiment and from there in September he sent apologies to Mornington for the long gap in their correspondence. 'The constant state of anxiety in which I own my mind is kept by the events that are daily occurring is apt to make me put off many duties in a way which may appear unpardonable to those who do not feel as strongly as myself on the present state of the world.'[13] It was clear that as a youthful student of European affairs he still took his duties seriously.

NOTES

1 Yonge, I, 24; LGC, I, 49.
2 15 Dec. 1798.
3 George 3, II, 8.
4 10 April 1794.
5 Marshall, pp. 53-5.
6 LGC, I, 329.
7 For the whole incident see Marshall, pp. 125 ff.
8 For Louisa's childhood see Pemberton, I, esp. 159-263; B. Fothergill, *The Mitred Earl* (1974), esp. pp. 59-114; Foster, pp. 28-118.
9 LWF, I, 32-6.
10 For the courtship see Marshall, pp. 135 ff.
11 Pemberton, I, 583.
12 Ottley Papers (transcripts at Pitchford, originals in Nat. Library of Wales).
13 Wellesley, I, 79-81.

CHAPTER III

War and Diplomacy

In the half-dozen years after Robert's marriage the political fortunes of what Lord Bathurst once ironically called the 'House of Hawkesbury' continued to thrive. In May 1796 Lord Hawkesbury was created Earl of Liverpool and his elder son was thereafter known by the courtesy title of Lord Hawkesbury. The corporation of Liverpool, sensible of the compliment and mindful perhaps of the new earl's constant championship of British mercantile interests (not to speak of his defence of the slave trade) requested him to quarter the arms of the city with his own. The King sanctioned the change and accordingly that unusual heraldic bird the cormorant *argent* of the town of Liverpool was added to the *fesse, cross-patée* and *estoiles or* of the Jenkinsons to form the coat of arms of his new dignity. Since the cormorant is an emblem of voracity his critics may have thought it a peculiarly appropriate addition. A more decorous and, for father and son equally appropriate, sentiment was expressed in the armorial motto *'palma non sine pulvere'*. Even this blameless device, however, did not escape the merciless wit of political opponents who announced that the correct translation of the Latin was 'this is the reward of my dirty work'. Wraxall, who not without relish records the anecdote, admitted nevertheless that a man who did not begin his public career until his mid-thirties, became a trusted servant of George III, a baron before he was sixty and an earl before he was seventy, must have possessed great, as well as rare, endowments of mind.[1] While the first Lord Liverpool was not widely liked, at least he exacted a grudging respect from the politicians of his day.

Three years later his son was promoted to the Mastership of the Mint. Previously something of a sinecure, it was now intended to have a fixed salary and a certain amount of work. If Bathurst was right, the main object of the change was to create a vacancy for Canning on the India Board; but Lord Liverpool improved on the occasion by persuading his son to stipulate for a salary of £3,000 rather than the £2,500 originally proposed. Hawkesbury himself was less interested in the remuneration than in the privy councillorship annexed to the post which opened the way for more important administrative appointments.[2] On 13 March 1799 he was presented to the King at a levee and afterwards sworn in as a member of the Privy Council. So, quietly and inconspicuously, he mounted another rung in the ladder of politics. Work of a somewhat miscellaneous description certainly came his way. In 1800 he served on a committee on the new London Bridge and another on the state of public records. He was also one of the small parliamentary delegation which presented the articles of the Irish Union to the King and heard George III make the significant remark that one good result of the measure was that it removed any pretext for the admission of Catholics.[3] These activities, however, hardly constituted the stuff from which political reputations are made. He was without doubt a rising politician, though contemporary observers were puzzled to know why. He was recognised as a useful debater on a variety of topics. He had simplicity and good nature, though his manners were sometimes awkward. He stood well with Pitt; through his father he had the favour of the Court; and his reputation in the Commons was good. These were solid rather than showy claims to distinction. On the whole, it was simpler to conclude, like that elderly and disappointed ex-minister Lord Glenbervie, that he stood out more because of the dearth of talents on the government benches than from any outstanding qualities of his own.[4]

Meanwhile, overshadowing all the trivialities of domestic politics and the careers of individual politicians, the incessant drum-roll of French victories on the continent – Fleurus, Lodi, Arcola, Rivoli, Marengo and Hohenlinden – threatened not merely to deprive Britain of any European ally but to expose her own coasts to attack. Howe in the Channel, Duncan off the Texel, and Nelson at the Nile maintained British naval supremacy; but the mutiny at the Nore in 1797, and the Irish rebellion in 1798, revealed a certain defensive vulnerability and for a time there was actual fear of invasion. These were the years when in the libraries of sedate politicians helmets and sabres lay among the daily newspapers, and manuals of military tactics alongside the parliamentary orders of the day. The cabinet had hoped for quick victory and a short war. When their hopes failed to materialise, Pitt, under pressure from the Wilberforce peace party and the Foxite opposition, turned his thoughts to negotiation. Hawkesbury, with an optimism and resolution from which he never wavered throughout the war, was not entirely in agreement with his leader. 'I am still for war,' he confided to Addington, the Speaker of the House of Commons, in August 1796. 'I never will doubt of our ultimate success.' Though he did not underestimate the influence of the Wilberforce group, he hoped it would not be given too much weight. Any discouragement to the war effort at home, he thought, would delay rather than hasten a satisfactory end to hostilities; and while he was not opposed to peace, he was emphatic that it should not be peace at any price.[5] When, in the second coalition war, a renewed British military expedition to the continent under the Duke of York expended itself fruitlessly in the mud and malaria of the Dutch coast, his confidence remained unshaken. He was critical of the cabinet's strategy. He considered Holland entirely unsuitable terrain for war and blamed the government for the disaster rather than the unlucky Duke. His chief concern, however, was that the right lessons should be extracted from the defeat. 'Let us be persevering,' he wrote to Addington with unusual feeling in October 1799, 'let us be bold, let us be intrepid, but in God's name let us feel what we have lost, and that the greatest part of what we have lost, we have lost for nothing.' He took the trouble to discuss the whole campaign with officers returning from Holland and concluded that while neither Abercromby, nor Dundas, nor Moore had unduly harmed their reputations, the Duke of York was at best neither fortunate nor popular. Hawkesbury doubted indeed whether the Duke would ever be employed in an active command again.[6] As junior member of the government he could only express such views in private; but that he had firm views was obvious. Windham, the Secretary at War, had a number of conversations with him at Bath in the spring of 1797 and thought that he was right in everything he said about the faults in the cabinet's management of the war.[7]

By 1800 the government was in serious difficulties. Military failures, bad harvests, popular discontent, food-riots, inflation and high taxation pointed to peace as the only sensible policy. Yet, as Pitt's earlier negotiations had demonstrated, peace seemed unobtainable on terms that would be acceptable either to British public opinion or to the more militant party within the administration headed by Lord Grenville and the King. Meanwhile Pitt's control of his cabinet had broken down over the Catholic question. His solution to the Irish danger – a parliamentary union on the lines of the Scottish Union a century earlier – had been accepted by both parliaments between 1799 and 1800; but his implicit pledge to Irish Roman Catholics that Union would be followed by full political equality failed to win the wholehearted backing of his colleagues. This setback was compounded by errors of judgement sufficiently startling to raise doubts whether his mental powers, which had shown such astonishing maturity when he was young, were not beginning to pay the price of that abnormal precocity. Sixteen years at the head of affairs, growing political strain, and increasing dependence on alcohol to sustain his nerves, had left their mark on the Prime Minister. He omitted to prepare the King for the new measure, despite his notorious opposition to it; and when the secret was betrayed to George by the strong anti-Catholic minority in the cabinet, a crisis occurred which ended in Pitt's resignation.

The retirement of the head of the government, after a longer period of unbroken power than any of his predecessors and at the height of a great European conflict, was an event sufficiently staggering to provoke more than one interpretation. Few men seemed able to credit the publicly-stated and probably correct explanation. It was widely believed – by the King, by Addington, and by countless others – that Catholic Emancipation was only a pretext; that in reality Pitt resigned because he could no longer carry on a disastrous war and was unable to make a satisfactory peace. To this, Lord Liverpool (never a friend of Pitt) added the rider that the Prime Minister also wanted to rid himself of Lord Grenville, his obstinate Foreign Secretary, with whom his disagreements over policy were causing increasing difficulties.[8] On any of these interpretations the implication was that the Addington administration was only formed to make a settlement with France and when that was accomplished, Pitt would return to office. Hawkesbury may not have shared his father's cynicism, but he certainly disagreed with Pitt's decision. As early as 1798 he had been permitted to see an outline of Pitt's plan of Irish Union and thoroughly approved of it as a remedy for the separatist republicanism which he detected in the Irish rebellion of that year. As he then understood it, the Prime Minister's intention was to merge the two parliaments, establish free trade between the two countries, and find a substitute for the tithe on the Irish peasants' potato crop, which Hawkesbury thought the greatest practical grievance of all. On religion he mentioned briefly and somewhat obscurely the proposal 'to give the Catholics (if possible) the little that remains to be given them'. What that implied is not clear, but since he said he agreed with Pitt in 'every part' of the plan, he presumably saw no reason for Anglican alarm. On what was to become known as Catholic Emancipation his views perhaps at that date were only half-formed. Castlereagh, the Irish Secretary, with whom he had become very friendly, later tried to persuade him of the justice of the measure; but Hawkesbury, while admitting that, in certain respects and with certain safeguards, it might be the right course, refused to commit himself.[9]

The immediate issue was Pitt's resignation. On 4 February 1801 the Prime Minister told Hawkesbury privately of his determination and asked him to stay on with Pitt's other friends to support Addington. Shocked by the news, Hawkesbury urged him to remain in office and make some compromise arrangement which would keep the ministry together. When this plea proved useless, his first instinct was to resign along with his chief. Two days later he had another interview when Pitt, distressed to the point of tears, made it clear that his administration was at an end. Only then did Hawkesbury, together with others whom he had consulted, agree to serve under the man whom Pitt himself promised to support. The mixture of agitation, anxiety and regret in the Hawkesbury household came out clearly in a letter Louisa wrote to her sister Mary.

> The crisis is an awful one, the event wholly unexpected, but we must not be dismayed. Let it reassure you to know that the door is still shut against opposition and jacobinism. ... The first inclination of all was to go out with Mr Pitt, but on considering the matter with him, and with themselves, they finally agreed it was their duty to stand firm and brave the storm, and not to forsake the King at such a crisis and drive him into the Hands of Opposition.[10]

A fortnight later her husband was sworn in as secretary of state for the foreign department.

On giving him the seals, Lord Liverpool proudly related, the King observed that he had often given them away but in no instance with so much pleasure. It may be doubted whether Hawkesbury enjoyed the same unalloyed feelings. From Master of the Mint to Foreign Secretary and the cabinet was a steep and unexpected promotion justified only by the desperate needs of the new prime minister. To carry on a Pittite administration not only without Pitt but without the formidable group of colleagues who resigned with him – Grenville, Dundas, Spencer and Windham from the cabinet, others including Castlereagh, Canning, and Leveson Gower from subordinate posts – could only be accomplished by bold improvisation. The rest of Addington's cabinet had to be made up of peers like Westmorland, Portland and Chatham, who appeared and re-appeared in almost every administration, adding little beyond their name and electoral influence to the strength of the government. For the inexperienced Prime Minister, left solitary in the House of Commons, it was essential to have at least one cabinet minister alongside him, and Hawkesbury, with his solid debating ability, was an obvious choice. The appointment was one of the first to be made; in fact Hawkesbury, and the Earl St Vincent at the Admiralty, were the only ministers to complete the formalities of taking office before the King's illness suspended all further proceedings. Addington himself did not take his seat as First Lord of the Treasury until 23 March.

Pitt, who may have suggested Hawkesbury as one of the principal figures in the new government, undoubtedly approved his appointment and paid him a public and generous compliment. 'He knew of no one,' he told the Commons at the end of March, 'superior to his noble friend in capacity for business' and none on the opposition benches his equal except Fox. At first these tributes seemed to be justified. Hawkesbury made a good impression on Otto, the French diplomatic agent in London, and on Rufus King, the American minister. He was good-natured, and pleased people by his readiness to grant interviews – a welcome change from his cold and forbidding predecessor of whom it was said (perhaps with exaggeration) that he scarcely saw anybody, and when he did, never spoke to them.[11] Yet there was much prejudice to overcome. The older members of the diplomatic service, who had served Grenville for a decade, were not pleased at having a young and untried man put over them. Their contemptuous surprise was matched by the comments of some of the young Pittite followers at home. Canning himself, huffed at Addington's failure to make any offer to him, and morbidly conscious of Pitt's disapproval of his resignation from his newly-acquired post of Paymaster-General, was from the start a critic of the new administration. The tendency of the Canning circle to idolise Pitt had a less pleasant side in their ostentatious contempt for his successor. When Leveson Gower's parents warned him not to be involved in any general attack on the government, he answered crossly that Canning undoubtedly had a low opinion of Addington as prime minister and for his own part 'we that have known Hawsbury well at Oxford cannot certainly look up to him with any admiration, and it would be ridiculous for all of us (I mean Morpeth, Boringdon, Ellis, Sturges) to be observing a cautious silence to each other respecting our opinions on these chief Pillars of the New Administration'.[12]

The hostility of the Canningites was embittered by a conviction that Hawkesbury, his family, and friends, had spread lies about Canning to damn him in the eyes of the public in general and Pitt in particular. For this there seems no evidence; Canning's jealous mind was always prone to leap to unwarranted conclusions. There was evidently much disapproving gossip about Canning in the political world; but this he had largely brought on himself. 'I find the town is full of abuse on Canning,' wrote Glenbervie at the beginning of April. 'His hot-bed promotions, his saucy manners and his satirical songs and indiscreet epigrams and buffoonery have already indisposed almost all Pitt's friends. Not only Addington but Lord Hawkesbury, and I believe Dundas, Ryder etc. had been the frequent subjects of his ridicule.' [13] Political society in London was already sharply divided over the wisdom of Pitt's resignation; but the Canning-ite group excelled all others in the bitterness of their vituperation. In the heat of the moment it was natural for them both to regard Hawkesbury as a renegade and to decry his abilities.

These personal unpleasantnesses were small, however, compared with the magnitude of the task confronting him in his new office. It was clear that whoever took the foreign secretaryship would be occupying the most vulnerable seat in the new government. The Addington administration was committed by the circumstances of its creation to two principles: postponement of the Catholic issue and an early peace with France. Not only could its Foreign Secretary have little freedom of action but he would be, inevitably so in the situation he inherited, under the close supervision of the Prime Minister and the cabinet. That was not all. With Addington's ministry admittedly a cast of understudies, it also seemed reasonable in the circumstances to expect the former principals to prompt their successors from the wings. The Prime Minister had regarded Pitt's support as virtually a condition of taking office and it was assumed that both Pitt and Grenville would be available as technical advisers and parliamentary allies in the difficult diplomatic negotiations which lay ahead. Finally there was Lord Liverpool: a member of the cabinet, though his rheumatism made him a virtual absentee from its meetings, whom habit and duty made it natural for his son to regard as an additional personal counsellor. Though to a new and perhaps diffident foreign secretary, still only thirty years old, this galaxy of support might offer some reassurance, it also promised considerable awkwardness if his elderly advisers disagreed among themselves.

With Pitt, fortunately, Hawkesbury continued to be on the best of terms. After he took office they dined almost fortnightly with each other. In October 1801 Hawkesbury visited Pitt at Walmer and Pitt stayed with Hawkesbury for a few days the following December. Throughout the protracted negotiations with the French government Pitt was kept constantly informed of their progress. Since his cabinet memorandum of 1800 had been transmitted to Addington and made the basis of the new administration's policy, the eventual peace treaty bore as near the hallmark of a Pittite product as was possible. So close indeed was the relationship between the ex-prime minister and his successors that it added force to the common belief that everything since January had been a juggle on Pitt's part to obtain a peace settlement without incurring direct responsibility for it. From Grenville, on the other hand, came in the end little assistance and even less encouragement. In the beginning all promised well. When Hawkesbury wrote to him early in February, he received a reply thanking him for his 'very obliging message' and promising to assist at any time not only as an ex-minister but as 'a sincere friend and cordial well-wisher'. As an earnest of his desire for cooperation Hawkesbury promptly sent the draft of a note to the Danish minister asking Grenville to 'criticise it without mercy' and make any alteration he thought proper. He also asked for advice over diplomatic appointments; and all through the summer the Foreign Office, on Hawkesbury's instructions, continued to send foreign news to their late chief. It is obvious that Addington and Hawkesbury spared no effort to retain Grenville's goodwill. They offered embassies to his brother and brother-in-law, and gave diplomatic posts to Wickham and his other protégés. Even when they disagreed with Grenville, they always treated his views with deferential respect.[14]

Their conciliatory attitude was to prove of no avail. By midsummer Grenville's early assurances of friendship had given way to criticism and distrust. When in July the terms of the convention with Russia, together with the relevant despatches from St Petersburg, were submitted to him, he sent them back with a long covering letter expressing 'great uneasiness' and proposing endless alterations – some, according to Lord Liverpool, solid but others 'frivolous or captious or literal'. The former were accepted, the latter, on Pitt's advice, ignored since it was thought useless to attempt to persuade Grenville to change his mind. If Lord Liverpool is to be believed, Pitt also advised Hawkesbury not to communicate the terms of the peace preliminaries with France to Grenville until they were agreed.[15] When they were finally signed in October, Hawkesbury wrote to Grenville the same day giving him the substance of the agreement and promising to send him the full text within the next few days. He hoped, he said with an apparent confidence which perhaps he did not feel, that Grenville would regard it as an honourable peace; at all events, though difficulties still confronted them, a continuance of the war was not justified and would not have secured better terms. All he got back was a frigid letter which, according to his father, hurt him very much. With Pitt, who had sent his old colleague a friendly but firm letter expressing full support and approval for Hawkesbury's peace terms, Grenville was more outspoken. All his trust in the government, he wrote, was completely and irrevocably destroyed. He had evidently made up his mind to attack the administration over both the preliminaries with France and the convention with Russia.[16] From the narrow and bitter attitude he displayed, many people (including Hawkesbury) concluded that no terms which could possibly have been negotiated would have earned his approval.

The formal decision of the cabinet to open peace negotiations with France had been made on 19 March and within two days Hawkesbury had sent off his first note to Paris. Otto, the commissioner for prisoners of war in Britain, was appointed by the French government as their diplomatic representative and a brisk correspondence was carried on all through the summer. Two military successes in the first half of the year helped to strengthen the negotiating position of the new Foreign Secretary. Nelson at Copenhagen in April destroyed the rickety 'Armed Neutrality' of the Baltic powers and made possible the despatch of a British envoy to St Petersburg and the signing of a highly satisfactory neutrality convention in June. Abercromby's victory at Alexandria, news of which reached London in May, ended French hopes of a permanent occupation of Egypt. With Otto, a Protestant Alsatian and professional diplomat, Hawkesbury's relations were good, but behind Otto stood Talleyrand and Bonaparte. It would be difficult to imagine a more daunting pair of opponents for a young and inexperienced Foreign Secretary at the outset of his term of office. The two wily and unscrupulous Frenchmen in Paris indulged in a variety of manoeuvres to intimidate the British government and draw out the proceedings until a bargaining position more favourable to themselves had been reached. Among their tactics were complaints of assassination plots hatched in England, ostentatious preparations for invasion, and pressure on the Spanish government to attack Portugal. In the negotiations proper there were bewildering changes in demands and shifts of argument. In September Hawkesbury was driven to a threat of breaking off negotiations if any fresh requirements were put forward by the French government.

The peace preliminaries were finally signed in Hawkesbury's office in Downing Street on the evening of Thursday 1 October and it was agreed to send plenipotentiaries to Amiens to conclude the definitive treaty. In broad terms Britain was to return to France, Spain and Holland all its colonial conquests except Trinidad and Ceylon. The Cape was to revert to the Dutch, subject to freedom of commercial access; Malta was to be returned to the Knights of St John; France was to evacuate Egypt, Naples, and the Papal States and guarantee the integrity of Portugal. The negotiations with Otto had been carried on in admirable secrecy and both the signing and the terms of the peace preliminaries came as a surprise. For the British public, however, after eight years of war, it was not the detail but the event which mattered. Bells were rung and towns were illuminated in scenes of rejoicing unparalleled, according to the *Annual Register*, since the restoration of Charles II. When the French envoy carrying his government's ratification of the articles arrived in London on 12 October, his carriage had its horses removed and was dragged by enthusiastic volunteers from Oxford Street to Downing Street and back past cheering crowds. While the generality of people welcomed the peace, not all those behind the scenes felt confidence in its duration. The King, in approving the terms, expressed a strong hope that the country would be kept in a proper state of defence, since, he wrote shrewdly to Hawkesbury, he could 'never think any Treaty with France can be depended upon till it has a settled and regular form of Government'.[17]

When Parliament met in October the anticipated Grenville attack was easily beaten off. In the Commons, where the Foxite liberals and the Wilberforce peace party joined with Pitt and Castlereagh in approving the peace - and even Canning forbore to oppose - the debate ended tamely without a division. Hawkesbury, in the main speech on the government side on 3 November, made what was by common consent an able and convincing defence. Unlike the principal opposition speaker Windham, who on the following day expatiated on the immorality of the French Revolution and the continued danger of Jacobinism, Hawkesbury argued from the facts of the situation. His tone was realistic and the expectations he held out limited. There was no advantage, he said frankly, to be secured from a continuation of the war. Neither Britain nor France could strike an effective blow against the other. The terms, tone and temper of the peace were right. It had been negotiated from strength; it could be accepted with honour. The retention of Trinidad and Ceylon provided a tangible recompense for past efforts. He began his speech by saying he gave no pledge for the stability of the peace and he ended with an assurance that if war was renewed 'in seven, eight or ten years', Britain would face it on more advantageous terms than in 1793. Ten days later he was on his feet again defending the Russian convention in a speech which most observers thought even better than that on the preliminaries. 'His character in the House of Commons,' wrote one MP, 'rises daily and justly.'[18]

Peace was not finally assured until the signing of the definitive Treaty of Amiens in March 1802 and much wearisome negotiation had still to be endured before that event. At one stage the submission of a French counter-project containing six points, which were either entirely new or had already been rejected, raised doubts of ever concluding a settlement. It was only on Hawkesbury's insistence, in fact, that Spain and Holland, the allies of France, were brought into the negotiations to ensure that it became 'one general treaty of peace'. Signed in the end it was, however, and the gift from Napoleon to the Foreign Secretary of a dinner-service of Sèvres china and a snuff-box of blue and white enamel with an N on the lid in diamonds, marked the resumption of normal diplomatic relations. When the treaty was debated in May, Hawkesbury was even more prominent than in the previous November, his speech being (according to one reporter) 'by much the ablest defence of the treaty which was made in either house of parliament'.[19] There was even some talk of printing it, in view of the importance which the government attached to the arguments in favour of the treaty. Tom Grenville reported to his brother Lord Grenville on 19 May that Hawkesbury was giving all his time to arranging the material, though in the event the idea of publication was abandoned.[20]

The concern of the ministers was understandable. Once the extravagant rejoicing over the return of peace had subsided, a reaction soon set in. In the twelve months which followed the conclusion of the peace preliminaries the aggressive activities of Bonaparte and the unresolved problem of Malta steadily undermined public confidence in the permanence of the settlement. By the autumn of 1802 Hawkesbury's 'seven, eight or ten years' had shrunk in most people's minds to one, two or three. If, in reality, the peace was to be no more than a truce, it was easy to believe that it was one that should never have been made. What was forgotten was that the terms of the settlement were probably as good as Pitt or anyone else could have obtained; that the country at the time wanted peace and was unconvinced of the need for prolonging hostilities; that the rest of Europe might have regarded Britain as an aggressive power, bent only on the acquisition of other countries' colonies, had it not shown a willingness to treat; and finally that Bonaparte's unquenchable ambition still had to reveal itself to Europe.

For the Addington administration the end of the 1802 session marked the summit of its power and popularity. With peace concluded and financial measures agreed, the general election of 1802 passed off quietly and, for the government, satisfactorily. In July Castlereagh joined the ministry as President of the Board of Control and a growing understanding with some of the Foxites resulted in a notably friendly attitude by Sheridan, friend and spokesman of the Prince of Wales, when Parliament met in November. Hawkesbury thought the new House of Commons, larger now by a hundred Irish members, was more likely to support the ministry and less likely to split into party factions than its predecessor. The country gentry were no orators; but they continued to look with favour on Addington and to approve a pacific policy abroad. Hawkesbury had no reason to be dissatisfied with his own prospects either; as secretary of state he enjoyed close relations with the King who in his punctilious way complimented him at an early stage on his 'tallents, assiduity and good temper'. By the summer of 1801 George III seemed to have recovered from the malady which had clouded the start of the Addington ministry. In August Hawkesbury reported from Weymouth that the King looked wonderfully well and better in all respects than when he had left London. The sea air agreed with him and he appeared to get considerable benefit from sailing on the royal yacht several times a week. This was an activity which he refused to give up, despite the alarm caused to the Admiralty, which had to provide protection against any lurking French privateers, and the occasional discomfort inflicted on the ministers he took with him on board. According to the rueful Eldon the King made a deliberate practice of this in the hope that a little dose of sea-sickness would discourage them from bothering him with business when he was on holiday. Hawkesbury on one occasion sailed with him from six in the morning to six at night: fortunately with no recorded symptoms of unease. Either he was a better sailor than Eldon or it was a calm day.[21]

At Addiscombe his elderly parent was living a more restricted life than his sovereign. Though Lord Liverpool retained his post as President of the Board of Trade until the end of the Addington administration, his physical deterioration virtually confined him to his own house. He was losing the use of his legs and arms; sometimes was unable even to write a letter. He still carried on his official duties but his memory and concentration were going. Lord Bristol, with his usual unreflecting kindness, urged him in the summer of 1802 to take advantage of the peace to come to the south of France – Marseilles, Hyères or Toulon – to convalesce. With old age, the ill-feeling over his son's marriage had long dissipated and he took a close and affectionate interest in everything that affected their welfare. At Christmas 1801 he sent the young couple a Dickensian present of a sparerib, hogs pudding and sausages. At the 1802 election, when the corporation of Rye contrived to transfer sundry debts of its own to Hawkesbury's election bill, his father philosophically agreed to meet the full amount rather than risk making difficulties in the borough. The cost of the previous election had been about £1,300 for the two members and the inflated figure for 1802 of £2,596 was something Hawkesbury had not anticipated or could afford to pay. As his own world slowly closed round him, old Lord Liverpool, as he had promised, lived on vicariously in his son's career.

> The only pleasure I have [he wrote from Addiscombe in January 1804] is in hearing what is read to me, and in the enjoyment of what I hear of your Publick Conduct. I can have less Communication with you than formerly and I have no Messenger to employ. I send today by Cecil's servant a fine Pine Apple for you but I am afraid you will not get it till tomorrow. I beg my love to Lady Hawkesbury and I remain with sincere regards, Dear Hawkesbury, Your affectionate Father, Liverpool.[22]

He was seventy-six at the date of that letter and had another five years to live. To the last he maintained his constant and jealous oversight of his son's political fortunes.

Hawkesbury's difficulties over the Rye election may have been a temporary embarrassment since he had just bought a country house to the south-west of London in a district which was becoming increasingly fashionable in aristocratic circles. The Hawkesburys had already sampled the Surrey air in 1801, when they rented a house at Roehampton; and they had been looking for something more permanent. Their new purchase, Coombe House or Coombe Wood, as it was indifferently called, was located at the end of Richmond Park on the south side of the Putney road, about one and a half miles from Kingston on Thames. The grounds seem to have been fairly extensive. When the property was sold after the middle of the century it comprised, according to a note in the family records, 670 acres. It is possible that the third earl added to the original purchase, though since he was already a considerable landowner and possessed four houses, there seems no reason for him to have done so. Certainly even in Liverpool's times the house struck visitors as extremely secluded and difficult to find in its surrounding woodlands. When that formidable bluestocking Mme de Staël was in England between June 1813 and May 1814, she included Coombe in a number of other residences of well-known public figures which she visited. Her companion, the whig lawyer Mackintosh, proved a singularly inept guide. In his ignorance he first took her to Addiscombe, the house of the first earl who had been dead for over four years. When after several more mistakes they eventually arrived at Coombe, darkness had fallen and it was not easy to see the way. In the end they had to get out of their carriage and walk along a miry road through a wood to reach the house. They arrived at Liverpool's door, tired, bedraggled, and two hours late for dinner. 'Coombe par ci,' exclaimed the voluble and possibly exasperated Frenchwoman, 'Coombe par là: nous avons été par tous les Coombes d'Angleterre.'[23]

When the Hawkesburys acquired Coombe, probably in 1801 or soon after, it was a relatively small house on a frontage of under 100 feet, built on a simple symmetrical plan with drawing room and dining room at opposite ends and two central bay windows at the back. Evidently many repairs and alterations had to be done which John Soane, the fashionable architect, was employed to supervise. It was some years, however, before the house was totally comfortable. As late as 1808 Louisa was complaining sharply to Soane about the continuous delays which threatened to deprive her of a laundry for the whole summer.[24] Nevertheless, by August 1802 the Hawkesburys had moved into the house which was to be their home for the rest of their lives. Louisa's mother Lady Bristol had died in 1800 at Ickworth Lodge. Her errant husband the Earl Bishop followed her two and a half years later, characteristically dying on the road between Albano and Rome, to the consternation of an Italian cottager who was unprepared for the arrival of a heretic bishop *in extremis* and banished him to an outhouse. The fascinating Elizabeth Foster (now the mother of two illegitimate children by the Duke of Devonshire) was a distant and elusive figure. She did not even come down from Chatsworth for her mother's funeral. Early in 1803, however, Louisa's elder sister Lady Erne was installed nearby in Hampton Court where Hawkesbury had been instrumental in obtaining for her a grace and favour apartment which Louisa helped to furnish.

For the Hawkesburys Coombe Wood had much to recommend it. Secluded and rural, it was near enough to town to be reached in less than two hours, far enough away to discourage casual callers. With its sheltered garden and verandah (Louisa reported in December 1806 that mignonette and china roses were still in bloom), its poultry, pigs, dogs, lawns and lake, it was an oasis of peace after the dirt, smell and noise of London and the continual bustle of boxes, messengers and official visitors. In the spring of 1803 Louisa described to her sister how on one occasion Hawkesbury at her suggestion came away early from the House of Commons. After dinner they left between seven and eight in the evening, taking with them in their chaise some cold meat for supper. 'By nine we were out of the clatter of this Town and with a feel of comfort not to be express'd, and this morning we had above an Hour's walk and potter in the midst of workmen, pigs and Turkeys' before returning to the round of interviews and engagements in London that were a minister's lot.[25] With her husband's promotion to the cabinet and a secretaryship of state, Louisa's social activities had greatly increased in size and splendour. Her role as hostess reached its height in June 1805 when, following a review of troops on Wimbledon Common, the King dined at Coombe Wood and his servants were regaled with venison on the lawn.[26] Though she complained to her sister of constant tiredness and the strain on her nerves of all her engagements, it is clear also that she enjoyed the excitement and sense of being behind the scenes in great events. She sent scraps of war news and diplomatic gossip to her relatives, and used to call in at her husband's office for the latest titbits of information. To her irreverent Hervey relations this bland assumption of importance created some amusement; they nicknamed her circle of friends 'the cabinet'. Though gossip had it that she interfered with her husband's business, this seems unlikely. He occasionally employed her for copying confidential documents but she had neither the knowledge nor the capacity to form opinions of her own. Her chatter to friends and relatives about public affairs simply reflected her quick, emotional response to everything around her. Politics, the latest fashion in dress, moral reflections, the state of her health (always an engrossing subject), and family news, came pouring out in her letters in one artless stream.

The year 1803 gave no respite either to her or to her husband. The signatures at Amiens the previous summer had procured a treaty but not made a peace. Both sides were distrustful; both had grievances. While Britain delayed the evacuation of Malta, Egypt and the Cape, Napoleon, now consul for life, seized Piedmont, Parma, Piacenza and Elba, and forcibly reconstructed the Batavian Republic and the Swiss Confederation as satellite French states. With offers from Bonaparte's family to allow Malta to remain in British possession in return for a substantial bribe from the British government (Whitworth the ambassador in Paris suggested one or two millions, Hawkesbury more economically thought £100,000 adequate), it was difficult to believe in London that the island itself would ever be a *casus belli*. The cabinet was ready in fact to acknowledge the new Italian states set up under French patronage in return for Malta or its equivalent. What was depressingly evident was the disinclination of the great continental states to lend their efforts to limiting French expansion. Russia was displeased by the Malta settlement but unwilling to risk French hostility. Following the French military intervention in Switzerland Hawkesbury sent a special envoy to Vienna to ascertain whether the Austrian government would cooperate in encouraging the Swiss to resist. Neither this nor a vigorous protest to Paris nor the despatch of a further envoy to the Swiss themselves produced any result. By the end of 1802 Hawkesbury had moved from his guarded optimism after Amiens to a noticeably harder attitude.

When in November the new ambassador Whitworth went to Paris, he took with him instructions which reflected both a profound suspicion of French intentions and the determination of the cabinet not to remain passive in the face of French expansionist designs. At the start of the session the government had announced a restoration of some of the cuts made in the army at the end of hostilities. Hawkesbury still advised, however, the 'experiment of continuing the Peace' and by February 1803 was able to point to the fact that Britain had fulfilled all its treaty obligations except in relation to Malta where the failure to secure a guarantee from Russia and Prussia, and the obvious unsuitability of the Knights of St John as a governing body, made delay advisable until some additional security had been obtained. This in effect was a tacit invitation to the French to negotiate and was followed in April by specific British proposals for a compromise settlement. Nevertheless, the drift to war continued with hardening diplomatic attitudes and growing military preparations on both sides. The British ambassador, tardily acting on his instruction, finally left France on 17 May. The next day the British government declared war. It was a legitimate criticism of their handling of foreign policy that, having been too conciliatory in 1801-2, they were too inflexible in 1802-3. Tactically perhaps it was an error to make Malta a central issue when the heart of the matter was Napoleon's aggressive actions on the mainland. Yet this was a criticism of methods rather than of objective. Of the rightness of their decision to oppose Napoleon's expanding military ambitions there could be little doubt. For the rest ministers could plead that Pitt had dinned into them the importance of Malta; that they had sought peace honestly; and that they had forborne from hostilities as long as possible in order to let the world see the insatiability of French aggrandisement in Europe.

For all that, when the Addington administration renewed the war in 1803, it was without a single ally on the continent and with a widespread impression at home of weakness and indecision. One final episode contributed to confirm the general sense of mismanagement. A last-minute offer by the Tsar to mediate over Malta, taken in Paris as a sign of support for France, in London was ignored. When in May Fox raised the matter in the Commons, Hawkesbury defended himself on the grounds that the proposal had been too vague to justify a suspension of the government's preparations and in view of previous French intransigence unlikely to have any useful outcome. The Tsar, not unnaturally, took offence at this forthright language. When, under pressure from Fox and Pitt, the Foreign Secretary later sent a note inviting Russian mediation not only on Malta but on the affairs of Europe generally, he was duly snubbed. The eventual Russian propositions, put forward after the French occupation of Hanover, were in fact so unrealistic as to ensure rejection by both belligerents. Hawkesbury suspected that the Russians had designs of their own on Malta and saw no immediate prospect of finding any reliable ally on the continent. As he observed caustically to his father, 'the Court of Vienna appeared to be very feeble, that of Petersburg very flat, and that of Berlin very false'.[27] Nevertheless the opposition made capital out of the Russian mediation fiasco and, even worse, Pitt for the first time showed signs of associating himself with Foxite criticisms of the government.

A cabinet whose two major decisions are first to make peace and then to declare war labours under a certain embarrassment in vindicating its policy. In the fourth week in May came a full-scale debate in both houses on the resumption of hostilities. Hawkesbury opened for the government with a long, elaborate speech which won the praise even of opposition whigs like Creevey ('fair and reasonable representation of his case and justification of the war') and Sheridan ('judicious, imposing and statesmanlike'). For posterity, however, it went largely unrecorded. The public interest in the debate was so intense that the parliamentary reporters were crowded out of their usual places in the gallery and Hawkesbury himself was so tired that his voice failed and his peroration ending with the quotation 'if England to itself do rest but true', was almost inaudible.[28] The honours of the debate were carried off by Pitt with what was generally regarded as among the finest of his war speeches. The government secured its expected majority but, as speakers on all sides made clear, support for the war did not necessarily imply support for the ministers' handling of negotiations. There was a growing feeling that despite his parliamentary skill, Hawkesbury had not proved a successful foreign secretary.

It is a criticism which has been repeated by historians without a great deal of factual evidence other than the complicated and controversial argument over the course of Anglo-French relations from the Treaty of Amiens to the resumption of the war in 1803. The one published study of his work as foreign secretary is concerned with the secondary field of Anglo-American diplomacy and the charge here is not so much one of inefficiency as of slowness in coming to a decision. For this there was obviously some excuse. What necessarily engaged most of his attention during his term of office were the European issues – the convention with Russia, the peace preliminaries with France, the definitive Treaty of Amiens, the growing deterioration of Anglo-French relations, and the renewal of the war. Against these the problems with America, mainly legacies of the War of Independence, must have seemed of minor importance; the more so since Hawkesbury's knowledge of foreign affairs was almost exclusively European. For the technical background to the American disputes he had to rely largely on his under-secretary Hammond. Even so, despite Rufus King's occasional and justifiable impatience, his relations with Hawkesbury were friendly and the two conventions signed during these years – one settling on generous terms the protracted Philadelphia debt controversy, the other regulating the disputed Maine boundary – left Anglo-American relations on a more cordial footing than they had been at any time since the colonies had won their independence. Nor was Hawkesbury invariably tardy. When war broke out between the United States and Tripoli he offered the use of British naval bases in the Mediterranean for American warships even before an official request from Secretary Madison arrived on his desk. In his official actions and public utterances Hawkesbury showed not only great conciliatoriness towards the United States but a confidence rare among Englishmen at the time that there was no inherent barrier to friendship between the two countries.[29]

What undoubtedly contributed to the contemporary impression of his inadequacy as foreign secretary was the sustained hostility of the Russian ambassador in London, Count Woronzov. A passionate Anglophil, an equally passionate opponent of Napoleon, and a close friend of Lord Grenville, Woronzov had viewed the change of government in 1801 with profound regret. An early clash with Hawkesbury over the latter's refusal to deal with the Russian consul except through an accredited representative of the Russian government, provided the excuse or the reason for an unconcealed dislike of the new foreign secretary himself. In addition Woronzov was as savage a critic as Grenville of the whole policy of peace with France. By April 1802 he was treating Grenville to resentful denunciations of Hawkesbury as being governed by his brother-in-law Lord Hervey (then under-secretary at the Foreign Office) who in turn was accused of being dominated by the French diplomat Otto. He held even more extravagant language to other and perhaps less discreet men. When Pitt's old Treasury Secretary Rose was visited by Woronzov in August 1803 he was solemnly told by the Russian that Lord Hawkesbury was 'absolutely incapable of transacting common business' and that there was 'an actual imbecility in his Lordship, as a man of business, which no man can have a comprehension of who has heard him speak in Parliament'. Given the natural prejudices against Hawkesbury of many senior British diplomats and the more malicious attitudes of the Canningites, this kind of talk going round London society probably did more damage to Hawkesbury's reputation than he ever realised.[30]

The real weakness of his position in 1802-3 was his identification with a peace which had foundered and a ministry that was floundering. The 'new opposition' led by Grenville and Windham was more hostile than the old; Canning was showing signs of joining them; and Pitt, once benevolently neutral, was now simply neutral. In November 1802, when sent a packet of papers on the French negotiations, he returned them to Hawkesbury with a note excusing himself from offering any opinions. He made similar excuses when Hawkesbury wrote the same month pressing him to make an appearance at the meeting of Parliament. In the spring of 1803 he absented himself for long periods from the House of Commons. Increasingly the only way to ensure his support seemed to be through his return to office and when he made it clear to Addington that he would only return as prime minister, serious negotiations were opened up at Easter 1803. At the crucial conference at Long's house at Bromley on 10 April Pitt stipulated not only for the entry into the cabinet of Lord Melville (as Dundas had become), Grenville, Spencer and Windham, but also for a general reconstruction of the administration. He also indicated that it would be necessary to remove Hawkesbury and St Vincent from their existing posts.[31]

Whether Addington informed his cabinet or Hawkesbury personally of this last proviso, does not appear. In any case it was hardly necessary. If Grenville came back, it was almost certain that he would insist on having the Foreign Office. The question was whether he should come back at all. Pitt had been warned by Long before his meeting with Addington that while Hawkesbury and Castlereagh were anxious to have Pitt in the government, there was a general feeling that the return of the bellicose Grenville would endanger the fragile peace and, if war came, would be regarded as one of its proximate causes. When the two men met, Addington asked Pitt specifically not to insist on office for Grenville, Spencer and Windham. Failure to agree on this point was the official, and undoubtedly part of the real, reason for the failure of the negotiations. When the cabinet discussed Pitt's terms, Hawkesbury was the most prominent of those who argued that it was not in the public interest at that juncture to bring Grenville and Windham back into office. Behind this objection lay perhaps a deeper feeling that what Pitt demanded was not so much a coalition as wholesale surrender. The changes he had in mind would demonstrably amount to a remodelling of the entire administration.

Pitt's insistence to Addington that Hawkesbury and St Vincent would have to give up their posts was a decision which had probably been arrived at the previous year. While he conscientiously felt that Hawkesbury and Castlereagh, whom he had urged to remain with Addington, must be offered posts in any ministry he formed, he knew that others, on whom he might have to depend, felt differently. Grenville had told him as early as the spring of 1802 that he would object to the retention of Hawkesbury and Addington in any posts of importance. When he learned the following year that Hawkesbury had been the leader of those who opposed his return to the cabinet as not being in the national interest, his stiff Grenville pride was touched to the quick. He made up his mind then that Hawkesbury would never be a member of any future administration in which he himself held office. His 'apparently irreconcilable bitterness towards Hawkesbury', as Pitt described it to Canning, was one of the many difficulties confronting the ex-premier when contemplating a return to power in the summer of 1803.[32] That he was now contemplating it, however, was clear to all. A proof of the chillier relationship with the government came in a debate in June on the conduct of the war. Pitt ostentatiously declined either to approve or condemn the administration; instead he resorted to the evasive expedient of moving to the orders of the day. Hawkesbury on behalf of the government refused to compromise, demanded a clear expression of opinion from the House, and pointedly expressed his regret that Pitt had not made up his mind to vote for or against the ministers. The courage of the government in refusing to take refuge in what Sheridan called 'the shabby shelter of the previous question' was rewarded. With Fox and his friends voting for the ministry against Pitt's amendment and abstaining on the main motion, the government secured massive majorities in both divisions. Pitt in fact left the House after his amendment had been lost, though Canning stayed on to vote for the censure resolution. Writing to his father afterwards, Hawkesbury characterised Pitt's conduct as 'most extraordinary and most unaccountable'.[33]

The session ended with the government in a far weaker position than the voting in June suggested. An overture after Easter to the 'old opposition' had petered out in the face of exorbitant demands which reflected only too clearly the contemptuous attitude of Fox and his friends towards the Prime Minister. All that Addington secured, and it was only a modest catch, was the recruitment at the beginning of June of the dissatisfied Foxite Tierney. Since Tierney was on notoriously bad terms with Pitt this appointment, like the pamphlet war that broke out during the autumn, suggested that all hope of conciliating

Pitt had been given up. It was the more surprising, therefore, that Addington at this point asked Hawkesbury to move to the House of Lords and take over the leadership of that House on behalf of the government. Certainly he now had both Castlereagh and Tierney to assist him in the Commons, where he himself was a lamentable performer even in his chosen field of finance. He seems to have thought also – or been prepared to argue – that Castlereagh, though no orator, was a readier speaker than Hawkesbury in miscellaneous and extempore debating. His prime reasons, however, were the need to strengthen the weak team of ministerial spokesmen in the upper house against Lord Grenville and the likelihood, in view of Lord Liverpool's failing health, that he was only anticipating an imminent event.

Hawkesbury, who with some justification regarded himself as the most effective front-bench speaker in the Commons, was reluctant to make the move. His father, oblivious of his own mortality, was even more opposed to it. The death he was expecting was not his own but that of Pitt. He did not think that the late prime minister, even if he returned to power, would last very long; and on his death his son would be admirably placed to reunite the Pittites, if not the Grenvillites, together with some of the Foxite opposition. For this it would be an obvious advantage to be, at any rate at the outset, in the House of Commons. While not disagreeing with this flattering sketch of possible developments, Hawkesbury characteristically felt it his duty to defer to Addington's view of parliamentary necessities. Accordingly in the middle of November he was formally called to the House of Lords as Baron Hawkesbury. His colleagues in the upper house welcomed his presence. 'Lord Hawkesbury has a readiness and confidence about him that will be useful in the House of Lords,' wrote Hobart, the Secretary for War, in December 1803, 'and which will put the business there upon a footing that will be extremely advantageous.'[34] The gain in one house, however, was balanced by the loss to the other. In the session following Hawkesbury's departure there was a growing lack of control in the House of Commons which marked an important stage in the decline and fall of the Addington administration.

Meanwhile, from the summer of 1803 to that of 1805, Britain was faced with a more imminent threat of invasion than at any time during the war. A large French army was concentrated round Boulogne with fleets of flat-bottomed vessels in the adjacent harbours; the navies of France, Holland and ultimately of Spain were being mobilised to cover the crossing; a diversionary expedition to Ireland seemed likely; and virtually the entire remaining military force at Napoleon's disposal, in all nearly half a million men, was strategically disposed along the western European seaboard in a menacing arc from the Texel to the Pyrenees. In England preparations proportionately as great were being made to resist attack and one of Hawkesbury's first tasks as Leader of the House of Lords was to introduce a new volunteer bill for the organisation of some 400,000 men additional to the total regular and militia force of 184,000. Though among the British people at large there was a sturdy confidence in the outcome, the government prudently made contingent plans against the possibility that a French force might successfully be landed on British soil. The Queen and the treasure from the Bank of England were to be evacuated to Worcester; Cornwallis, the most experienced of all the British generals, was to take command of the main reserve army, including the volunteers; and the King, with his unflinching Hanoverian sense of duty, taking with him Addington and Yorke, the Home Secretary, was to go to an advanced headquarters – Chelmsford if the landing took place in East Anglia, Dartford if it was in the south-east of England. A small Privy Council, including Hawkesbury, Eldon the Lord Chancellor, and St Vincent, was to act in London as the operational centre of government to issue all necessary acts and orders.[35]

The sustained warlike excitement, however, only strengthened the public conviction that Pitt should be recalled to power; and the ministry was further weakened by the serious illness of the King from February to May 1804. The similarity with earlier attacks of George III's mysterious illness (now diagnosed as porphyria), especially with that which brought on the Regency crisis of 1788, was too marked to be ignored. 'It reminds one of the *first* great illness,' Louisa wrote emotionally to her sister Mary on 16 February, 'it makes one's heart sick.'[36] With the prospect of a renewed dispute on the question of a regency, some of the royal family thought that Addington would not be able to stand up against the Prince of Wales's party and lent their influence to persuade the King on his recovery to bring back Pitt. Among old parliamentarians the rats began to scent the emanations of a sinking ship and made their own individual preparations for flight. In the unreformed House of Commons anything less than a three-figure majority for the government in an important division was a sign of weakness. When Parliament met in February after several weeks' adjournment, Pitt signalled his decision to oppose with a hostile motion on naval defence. Supported by Fox he was able to beat the government down to a majority of 71 in a thin house.

That was only the beginning. In March and April 1804 Addington's administration saw its margin of strength shrink to a mere 52 (in contemporary terms a moral defeat) on a Foxite censure motion on defence; and finally on 25 April to an impossible 37. Long before that point was reached most of the cabinet had made up their minds that the administration could not go on. A secret overture from Eldon had already resulted in an interview with Pitt in March. By the second week in April Pitt was confident that Eldon, Portland, Chatham, Yorke, Castlereagh and Hobart were convinced of the inadequacy of their own government and the need for his return. 'I believe too by Lord Hawkesbury,' he added, when reporting all this to Lord Melville, 'but of him I have not heard it so pointedly.'[37] Addington, however, was determined not to retire until he was compelled and his colleagues, whatever their private misgivings, were too loyal to desert him as long as he remained in office. It was the voting in the Commons that clinched the matter, especially the disastrous division of 25 April. The following day Addington broached the question of his resignation to a disturbed and reluctant King and on 29 April informed his colleagues of his decision to retire. The cabinet meeting which heard the news was made additionally unpleasant by his resentful attack on Eldon for being the bearer of a letter from Pitt to the King conveying expressions reflecting on the conduct of the administration. On 7 May Pitt saw the King for the first time since his resignation in 1801 and three days later received his seals of office. The Addington administration which was his creation had finally perished at his hands.

For the outgoing Prime Minister it was a species of betrayal which he never forgave. In justice to Pitt, however, he was only acting as a tardy public executioner on behalf of a country which had lost all confidence in its own government. The real criticism of Pitt is not that he destroyed the Addington administration in 1804 but that he made its creation necessary in 1801. No member of that ill-starred ministry left it with enhanced reputation. Yet, with the curious obliquity of human affairs, for many of them it had been a not unimportant stepping-stone in their personal careers. For Hobart, for Eldon, for Castlereagh, and not least for Hawkesbury, all of whom had entered the cabinet for the first time under Addington, the events of 1801–4 gave them a status which they had not possessed before. Even Addington himself, refusing the earldom pressed on him by a grateful monarch, was a force to be reckoned with in future. His administration had disappeared, unloved and unlamented; but in its own ambiguous way it left an indelible mark on British politics.

NOTES

1 Sir N. Wraxall, *Posthumous Memoirs of His Own Times*, 2nd edn, three vols (1836), II, 166–9.
2 Wellesley, I, 90; George 3, III, 196.
3 GD, I, 151–2, 389.
4 Ibid, 221–2.
5 J. Pollock, *Wilberforce* (1977); Yonge, I, 35.
6 George 3, III, 283; Yonge, I, 41.
7 Windham, p. 238.
8 Fortescue, VII, 111; GD, I, 277–9, 294–5, 389. Addington lived to change his mind. Cf. his remarks to Croker nearly forty years later when he was eighty-two. Croker, II, 340.
9 Wellesley, I, 80; GD, I, 157–8.
10 LWF, I, 62–3; GD, I, 158.
11 3873 fo. 11 (C. H. Hall, the future Dean of Christ Church to Lord Liverpool).
12 LGC, I, 298–9.
13 GD, I, 209.
14 Fortescue, VI, 443–74. See also Intro. to Vol. VII.
15 GD, I, 295; Fortescue, VII, 29–30.
16 Fortescue, VII, 45–51; GD, I, 269.
17 George 3, III, 613 ff.
18 Colchester, I, 378.
19 AR, 1802, p. 152.
20 Fortescue, VII, 95.
21 George 3, III, 592; Twiss, II, 357.

22 38473 fo. 165. See also fos 117, 119, 121.

23 Croker, I, 326.

24 Plans, accounts and letters relating to Coombe House are in the Soane Museum.

25 LWF, I, 109. The suggested date 1805 is clearly wrong, since Hawkesbury went to the House of Lords at the end of 1803. The only possible date is the spring of 1803.

26 George 3, IV, 333 n.

27 Yonge, I, 129.

28 LWF, I, 88; AR, 1803, p. 150; Creevey, p. 15; W. S. Sichel, *Sheridan* (1909), II, 441.

29 Bradford Perkins, *The First Rapprochement: England and the United States 1795-1805* (University of Pennsylvania Press, Philadelphia, 1955), esp. pp. 89, 133-53.

30 Fortescue, VII, 89-93; GD, I, 408-9; Rose, II, 46-51.

31 Pellew, II, 120 n.; Rose, I, 493 and II, 30 ff.

32 Marshall, pp. 241-3; Stanhope, IV, 28-30; Rose, II, 30-32.

33 Yonge, I, 125; Pellew, II, 136-42.

34 Auckland, IV, 186; Yonge, I, 128; GD, I, 333.

35 Colchester, I, 471.

36 LWF, I, 102.

37 Lord Stanhope, *Secret Correspondence connected with Mr Pitt's Return to Office in 1804* (privately printed, 1852), pp. 28-45.

CHAPTER IV
At the Home Office

The resignation of Addington and the return of Pitt produced a buzz of speculation. For the moment the war was forgotten. Had the French arrived in London, Lord Auckland sardonically observed, they would only have been asked which way they meant to vote. The public had hoped for a ministry that would be visibly stronger than its predecessor; they were disappointed. With four discernible parties in existence – those of Pitt, Grenville, Fox and Addington – not one of them large enough by itself to provide an effective administration, it was a reasonable assumption that the Prime Minister would ask his old colleague and cousin Lord Grenville to join him. Grenville, however, had set his stubborn mind on a broad-based national government and refused to take office unless Fox, with whom he had been brought into closer association by their common detestation of Addington, was also invited. The King refused to agree to this, and Pitt was left to construct a new ministry out of the ruins of the old and a few followers of his own who, except for Melville, lacked any political distinction. Of the new cabinet five came in with Pitt and six were retained from the outgoing cabinet – Hawkesbury, Castlereagh, Eldon, Portland, Westmorland and Chatham. The first two Pitt felt it a debt of honour to keep in office, though not in Hawkesbury's case the office he held under Addington. Apart from any general criticisms of his performance at the Foreign Office, to have left him there would have guaranteed the bitter opposition of the Grenvillites; and Pitt's frail-looking administration was in no position to offer gratuitous hostages to fortune.

To Hawkesbury he explained that he wanted the foreign secretaryship for Moira, the reputed head of the Prince of Wales's party, and asked him to move to the Home Office, while retaining the leadership of the House of Lords. The alliance with Moira would undoubtedly have been a political asset since it would have signalled the favour of the heir to the throne and detached a number of MPs from the general body of Foxite liberals. Hawkesbury was not anxious to move but eventually consented in order to facilitate Pitt's plans. Moira, however, rejected the overture. Pitt then told Hawkesbury he wanted to offer the foreign secretaryship to Harrowby on the grounds that his health was so poor that he could only undertake that particular office. This, as an explanation, was barely plausible. Hawkesbury again demurred but again gave way. His father was more vociferous. He had recognised the advantage of gaining Moira; he saw none in appointing Harrowby whom he thought had neither talents nor business habits nor political influence sufficient to justify displacing his son. To soothe his understandable indignation the King wrote flatteringly to say that he wished to have Hawkesbury, in whom he expressed great confidence, in a position near him; and as a minor gratification Pitt agreed to Hawkesbury's request that Wallace, an old Christ Church friend, should be retained on the India Board despite the opposition of Canning and others. By 14 May it was all settled.[1]

Canning, who out of office had drawn closer to Grenville and joined in urging Pitt to make a change at the Foreign Office, was far from satisfied with the shape of the new administration. He was maliciously pleased that Hawkesbury had been relegated to the Home Office; but it irked him that Hawkesbury and Castlereagh, whom he regarded as deserters to Addington, had been retained in the cabinet while he himself had to be content with junior office as Treasurer of the Navy. His accumulated ill-feeling broke out a couple of months later in a debate on the defence bill. Speaking on 18 June, the third day of the debate, he denied suggestions that Pitt's second administration was little more than a continuation of Addington's. He went on to point out the differences.

> He [i.e. Canning] should content himself with vindicating his own consistency; he had objected to the administration of foreign affairs, and that had been changed, he had objected to the naval administration, and that had been changed; he had objected to the military administration, and that had been changed; he had also objected to the general superintendance of the whole, and that had been changed. In objecting to the inefficiency of the late ministers he had been joined by almost all those who were now in opposition.

The implications of this tirade were glaring. Bragge Bathurst, Addington's brother-in-law, rising immediately afterwards made a home-thrust by recalling that Canning's introduction to public life and ultimately therefore to the office he now held, was mainly due to his early friendship with the same Hawkesbury whom he was now attacking. Though this assertion was not denied, to moralise on the brevity of political gratitude was no answer to a charge of political incompetence. Of the four ministers to whom Canning referred, three – St Vincent, Hobart and Addington – had been discarded when Pitt formed his administration. The fourth, Hawkesbury, had been transferred to another department. The reason for the move given to Hawkesbury by the Prime Minister had nothing to do with any shortcomings in his work as Foreign Secretary. Yet in the face of Canning's wounding remarks, Pitt made no attempt to explain to the House of Commons what that reason had been.[2]

After reflecting on the matter for twenty-four hours and consulting some of his friends, Hawkesbury sent in his resignation. Pitt was now seriously embarrassed. He had long ago made up his mind to move Hawkesbury from the

Foreign Office. The Harrowby explanation was patently a pretext; the real reason had understandably been withheld from Hawkesbury. It was a minor dishonesty of a kind which most prime ministers (and not only prime ministers) have to commit at some time or other. What Canning had said was true as far as it went; but to say it publicly was both offensive and unnecessary. In a couple of arrogant sentences he had irritated his party leader, insulted Hawkesbury and offended half the cabinet. To have allowed Hawkesbury to resign in those circumstances would have shaken the whole administration. Castlereagh in fact declared that if Hawkesbury went, he would go too. Other Addingtonian ministers in the cabinet might well have followed his example. Pitt sent back a placatory letter asking Hawkesbury not to say or do anything until they could talk it over together. When they met the following day he first tried to dissuade Hawkesbury from resignation and then, when he stood firm, offered to dismiss Canning if he insisted on it. Hawkesbury took a day to consider this. In the interval Canning came three times to the Home Office to see him and on the third occasion forced himself into Hawkesbury's room to explain that he had not meant to give offence and that having delivered his sentiments in the Commons, he considered the matter was over and was prepared to go on as cordially as ever. It was precisely the airy attitude he had adopted over the bogus recruiting poster, applied to a more elevated sphere of human action. Hawkesbury, more proof against his old friend's effrontery than ten years earlier, made no direct answer. Instead he wrote to Pitt saying that he did not want anyone to resign or be dismissed on his account. He added, however, with some courage, that he thought the Prime Minister was at fault in not immediately explaining to the House that the reason for Hawkesbury's transfer to the Home Office was simply to facilitate his arrangement of offices; and he asked the Prime Minister to make this explanation at the first suitable opportunity. This Pitt promised to do and the incident was officially closed.

Nevertheless, details had leaked out; varying versions of what had happened were circulated by the partisans of each man; and echoes of the dispute rumbled on in the political press until the following year. Lord Liverpool sent his friends an account of the episode and the prejudice created against his son by the little knot of Canningites, adding aggressively that 'he must destroy their influence, or they must destroy him'. Canning for his part denied that he had apologised to Hawkesbury or asked his pardon for what he had said in his speech, and sent Morpeth to get a written statement to that effect from the Home Secretary. To his friend Sneyd he observed that Hawkesbury was 'a lying snuffling hound' against whom it was essential to have documentary proof. Despite his noisy protestations, however, it is clear that there had been an apology in substance, if not in form; and that was only the least of his resentments. He had the humiliation of knowing that he had only kept his office through the magnanimity of a man whom he regarded as his inferior. Even worse was the mortification of realising that Pitt had been prepared to sacrifice him in order to retain Hawkesbury.[3] His mood was made even more bitter by what happened at the end of the year. Following an accident in his home, Harrowby was obliged to give up for a time his work at the Foreign Office. Canning at once offered to take over the department without pay or promotion until the Foreign Secretary was able to resume. Pitt declined this embarrassing offer; he told Canning there were difficulties, though the only one he specified was 'the feelings of the person who held that situation up to May', namely Hawkesbury. When in December Harrowby finally resigned office, the Prime Minister chose as his successor the blameless though not conspicuously talented Mulgrave. Canning was sore at being passed over; his only consolation was the thought that Hawkesbury would be equally sore at not getting back his old post.

As he admitted to Pitt, in an emotional interview the following autumn, he had suspected that Hawkesbury had used his influence to secure the rejection of his volunteered services for the Foreign Office; and his resentment at Pitt's readiness the previous year to make what he called 'a propitiatory sacrifice' of him to please Hawkesbury was still fermenting in his mind. He spoke in violently abusive terms of his rival, though he added more placatingly that he recognised his value to the government.

> My opinion of him is this. He speaks as much above his talents, as he talks (in common conversation) below them. But he is not either a Ninny - or a great and able man. He has useful powers of mind, great industry and much information.

Pitt replied mildly that this was a pretty fair judgement, though he thought Canning underestimated his talents. 'He *is* useful,' the Prime Minister continued.

> I could not do without him in the House of Lords and though I do not say he is the man to whose decision singly I would commit a great question of policy, yet with his information - that I think you hardly put high enough - and the habits of reflection which he has acquired, he is by no means a contemptible adviser.

He then dexterously turned the conversation to the more soothing topic of a possible early promotion of Canning to the cabinet.[4]

If Hawkesbury had been disappointed at Mulgrave's appointment to the Foreign Office, he did not show it. He sent instead a graceful note to Pitt which was an illuminating contrast to Canning's outbursts.

> I am perfectly aware that there are many circumstances which must influence a decision in a question of this nature of which you alone can be thoroughly apprized, and for Mulgrave individually, I have a very sincere regard and esteem.[5]

Though still sensitive about his period as Foreign Secretary, he was probably already appreciating the advantages of the Home Office. Since the formal separation of the secretaryships in 1782, the home department had always ranked lower in prestige than the foreign. Nevertheless, war had added to its limited peacetime functions of preserving law and order; and the Union with Ireland had brought a large even if indirect additional responsibility for that country. Throughout the summer of 1804 Hawkesbury's correspondence was dominated by the defensive measures being taken against French invasion, the threat of which reached its height in August. On the 14th of that month he wrote to his father that the most recent intelligence reports indicated that an attempt at a landing would soon be made. Six days later he sent out a circular to all lords-lieutenant about local arrangements for maintaining order and preventing panic in the event of invasion.

Even in the midst of war, however, there were mundane matters to which he had to attend. On the question of trade unions, for example, he maintained a cautious neutrality. When the master boot and shoemakers of the metropolis petitioned against alleged illegal activities by their employees (traditionally a radical and argumentative breed of men) he took advice from Perceval, the Attorney-General, and declined to initiate any prosecutions. He devoted much time to the improvement of the police in London, a complicated matter (as Peel was to find twenty years later) which engaged his attention throughout his period of office as Home Secretary. He was also drawn into the tangled relationships within the royal family where he had to intervene to settle differences between the Prince of Wales and his estranged wife. During the winter of 1805–6 he took part, in company with the Lord Chancellor, in the negotiations which led to the assumption of the guardianship of their only child, the Princess Charlotte, by the King himself.[6] His work at the Home Office had this further advantage that it allowed him to consolidate his already good relations with George III. Harassed by scandal within his own family, burdened by the recollections of his own recent mysterious illness, depressed by the death in 1805 of his younger brother William, the King clutched for support at the few sympathetic and congenial persons around him. After Hawkesbury had been down at Weymouth with the King in the summer of 1805 Rose noted how much he had gained in favour by 'constant assiduity and attention, particularly at the time of the Duke of Gloucester's death, when His Majesty's mind was deeply affected'.[7]

Across the water George III's kingdom of Ireland continued to produce its unfailing crop of problems great and small. Among the latter which came to Hawkesbury's attention was a case of seditious libel which was eventually traced to one of the Irish judges. When there were fears of a potato famine he told Sir Arthur Wellesley, then Chief Secretary, in the severe tones of the classical school of economists, that any interference by the legislature would be calculated to 'derange trade and give an impulse to unhealthy speculation'.[8] Overhanging everything else, however, was the strategic weakness presented by a country still only half-pacified after the rebellion of 1798 and the Union of 1800. The activities of the Catholic Committee and the campaign for Emancipation in themselves were real enough; but intelligence reports coming to the central government spoke of plans for invasion by ships of the Dutch fleet and a projected landing near Dublin. While urging Irish Catholics to postpone their demands until more propitious times, Hawkesbury was convinced that the Grenville party were secretly encouraging the Catholic Committee to continue its agitation. It was this, in particular, among other considerations, which made him anxious to bring Addington back into the ministry so that a more solid front could be presented against Grenville and Fox. Since such a reunion was also the King's long-standing desire (and anything which calmed the King's mind was of advantage to his ministers) Hawkesbury soon became the chief royal instrument for bringing together the two estranged statesmen.

In October 1804 he got in touch with Addington and after some friendly overtures the ex-prime minister and his wife dined with the Hawkesburys on 1 December. It was their first social meeting since the change of government. With Addington clearly ready for a reconciliation, Hawkesbury was now given the authority of Pitt, sanctioned by the King and approved by the rest of the cabinet, to open serious negotiations. On 12 December he had a three-hour talk with Addington on the possibility of his rejoining the government, and another two days later. Addington's initial profession of reluctance to take office personally was soon overcome by the argument that unless he did so, the alliance would not be taken seriously by the public. Hawkesbury's own plan was for Addington to take over from the elderly and invalid Portland as President of the Council and combine it with the lead in the House of Lords. He did not think that Addington should stay in the Commons without the prestige of the premiership to support him, since he lacked the debating skill to become an efficient lieutenant to Pitt in the lower house. That to promote Addington as leader of the upper house involved a personal sacrifice for himself was characteristically disregarded. Addington hankered for a secretaryship of state but he saw the awkwardness of remaining in the Commons and was prepared to accept the presidency of the Council provided suitable provision was made for his relatives and friends - Hiley Addington, Bragge, Bond, and Vansittart. He also wanted some compensation for the victims of the Pittite spring purge - St Vincent and above all Hobart (now Lord Buckinghamshire). When broad agreement was reached on these points, Pitt and Addington met at Hawkesbury's house at Coombe Wood on 23 December and talked alone for three hours. Pitt, who had brought Castlereagh with him, stayed the night and Addington returned the following day for further discussions. The meetings went off well and both men seemed pleased. Reporting to the King, Hawkesbury suggested that they should be left for a few days to consider the various matters which had been raised. Louisa, more ardent and optimistic, wrote delightedly to Lady Erne of her pleasure at seeing Pitt and Addington so easy and comfortable together. 'The dear King is most pleased with this Peace and with the peace-maker.'[9]

Further talks in January 1805 between Pitt and Addington proved necessary before the new arrangements were finally announced. Addington became Viscount Sidmouth and succeeded Portland as President of the Council, though in the event Hawkesbury retained the leadership of the House of Lords.

Buckinghamshire became Chancellor of the Duchy of Lancaster and minor political rewards went to Addington's disconcertingly large parliamentary retinue. The new alliance had barely been cemented, however, before the first cracks appeared. In February the naval commission of enquiry appointed by Addington when Prime Minister presented its notorious tenth report containing damaging reflections on the conduct of Lord Melville when, as plain Henry Dundas, he had been Treasurer of the Navy. A further irony was that at the Admiralty Melville had succeeded St Vincent, the Addingtonian minister whom Pittites like Canning blamed for shortcomings in the state of the navy. Pitt's instinct, chivalrous but politically misguided, was to hush the matter up. Addington, strongly supported by Hawkesbury, took the view that Melville should either face an independent enquiry or resign. To this Pitt reluctantly consented but in the House of Commons an opposition vote of censure on Melville, obviously designed as the preliminary to impeachment, was carried against the government in April by the casting vote of the Speaker. After Melville's inevitable resignation Addington put forward various alternatives for his successor, including Hawkesbury, and volunteered in the latter case to take the Home Office himself. Pitt rejected the other candidates suggested but did make an offer of the Admiralty to Hawkesbury only to have it declined. To his father Hawkesbury confessed characteristically that if pressed, he felt he could not in the circumstances persist in his refusal. Lord Liverpool, out of office and always critical of Pitt, was made of sterner stuff. He told his son that no minister within his recollection had ever added to his reputation by going to the Admiralty and that Pitt was merely trying to shore up his shaky administration while taking care that Hawkesbury should never return to the office most suited to his talents and wishes, by which presumably he meant the Foreign Office.[10]

Pitt, however, did not press the matter. Hawkesbury was indispensable to him as Leader of the House of Lords and if, as he suggested, it was impossible for him to combine that with the Admiralty, the Prime Minister had little choice but to leave him in the more accommodating Home Department. For the Admiralty, much to the disapproval of Sidmouth who wanted Buckinghamshire, he selected Sir Charles Middleton, a professional sailor nearly eighty years old but of undoubted competence who was brought into Parliament as Lord Barham. At this Sidmouth promptly and intemperately offered his resignation. To Hawkesbury, who essayed the ungrateful task of mediator, he poured out his particular objections to Middleton and his deep suspicions that he and his friends were simply used by Pitt as a 'political convenience'. Pitt tried to smooth away some of this resentment and eventually Sidmouth agreed to make what he ominously called 'the experiment of continuing in office'.[11]

In May there was a brief respite from the ministry's smouldering internal disputes when Grenville in the upper and Fox in the lower house moved resolutions in favour of removing Catholic disabilities. In the Lords the main speeches against the motion were made by Hawkesbury and Sidmouth and it was defeated by a majority of more than three to one. In the Commons, though the debate was chiefly in the hands of Irish MPs, the majority was almost as large. It was the first time that Hawkesbury had expressed his views at any length on the Catholic question. He went to considerable pains over his speech and obtained the assistance of that learned cleric Dr John Ireland, later Dean of Westminster and founder of the well-known Oxford chair of exegesis, but at that time in the humbler position of vicar of Croydon and chaplain to Lord Liverpool. In the debate Hawkesbury contended that the King, by virtue of the British constitution, was in a special relationship with the Church of England and that as long as Roman Catholics refused to take the oath of supremacy, it was proper that they should be deprived of political power. It was a broad, moderate argument; in private perhaps he felt more strongly against Lord Grenville for raising the issue at all at such a moment. When there was talk of Grenville's candidature for the chancellorship of Oxford University, he wrote sharply to his father at the end of May that the university would disgrace itself if it abandoned the King, who had risked so much to defend the Establishment, and selected a man who was not only a systematic opponent of the government but even worse a supporter of Catholic claims. He was sufficiently pleased with his performance in parliament, however, to get his speech printed as a pamphlet.[12]

In June the disagreements in cabinet over the Melville case came to a head. Sidmouth's followers in the Commons, whose zeal against Melville seemed to go beyond a proper concern for administrative probity, voted with the opposition for a criminal prosecution in the courts: a decision which Pitt, by a piece of parliamentary sharp practice, was able to convert a couple of weeks later into the milder alternative of impeachment. This was the last straw for Sidmouth and in July he and his friends resigned from the government. Pitt, distressed beyond measure at the public disgrace of his old friend Melville, had shown a certain lack of composure in dealing with the recalcitrant Addingtonians. Sidmouth, on the other hand, displayed all the resentful sensitivity of an ex-prime minister sitting in the cabinet of his victorious successor. Hawkesbury himself had by that time come to the end of his sympathy and patience as far as Sidmouth was concerned and in the last two months of the session there had been little contact between the two men. He thought Sidmouth had allowed himself to be swayed too much by others and he was charitable enough to believe, unlike some, that he had not acted dishonestly in either entering or leaving the ministry as he did. His own assessment, given to Plumer Ward four years later, was different though scarcely more flattering.

Lord Sidmouth was not a man of falsehood, though he might be a man of folly; that his ruling passion was vanity; that vanity, and regret at having missed all the popularity which he would have acquired in consequence of the discoveries against Lord Melville (which was his work), and which made him often intimate to Mr Pitt what he had renounced by joining him – all this combined to make him take the part he did.[13]

Sidmouth, by contrast, who could never entirely free himself from his old emotional allegiance to Pitt, by a typical transfer of resentment was now inclined to blame Hawkesbury for the failure of 'the experiment'. He wrote bitterly to Bragge on his retirement that it was through Hawkesbury's 'coldness and neglect' that opportunities had been lost of cementing the union which he had been instrumental in securing and 'counteracting the machinations of those whose object it was to dissolve it', by which he meant Canning and his friends.[14]

Pitt, by now a sick and weary man living on his last reserves of energy, fell back on the old idea of a coalition with Fox and Grenville. In the cabinet Hawkesbury, Eldon, Mulgrave and others argued against such a move. Hawkesbury, in fact, told his father that if Pitt persisted with his scheme for a broad-bottomed administration, he would have nothing to do with it. He and Eldon were down at Weymouth with the King during the summer and probably strengthened his resistance to such a plan. When in September Pitt saw George, he was told that there was no need for any coalition and that neither Grenville nor Fox could be permitted to enter the cabinet. Everything now depended on that other coalition, the alliance between Britain, Russia and Austria which Pitt had secured by August 1805. Early in September Hawkesbury was able to tell his father that the camp at Boulogne had been broken up and that Napoleon had turned east against his continental opponents.[15] Relieved of their invasion anxieties, ministers were now able to direct their thoughts to active military intervention on the European mainland in support of their allies. For that much depended on the course of events in the Danube valley. Out of the fog of the early vague reports came the news of Nelson's victory and death at Trafalgar, known in London on the night of 5/6 November. It was followed almost at once by information of the capitulation of an Austrian army at Ulm. In all the bustle Hawkesbury found time to write a brief note to Sidmouth, who he knew was a close friend of Nelson, conveying the Trafalgar news. As Home Secretary it fell to him to arrange with the King for a day of thanksgiving for the victory, the funeral of Nelson at St Paul's, and the commission of a public monument. Meanwhile public attention was riveted on the Danube where Napoleon faced the combined Austrian and Russian armies. Austerlitz was fought on 2 December but three weeks later there was still no trustworthy intelligence of the outcome of the battle. The government was as much in the dark as the public. When Hawkesbury heard a report that a private gentleman in Putney had received reliable information from Berlin, he and Mulgrave rode down in person to enquire, only to find the rumour groundless.[16]

The authentic news, when it came, of the surrender of Austria and the withdrawal of the Russians, was shattering. Many were inclined to blame Pitt for the precipitancy and ill-preparedness of the coalition. The Prime Minister was by now a dying man. He was seriously ill at Bath when the news of Austerlitz came. The meeting of Parliament, due for 7 January, was postponed for a fortnight. Hearing that Pitt had been advised to leave Bath because of an attack of gout, Hawkesbury wrote on 7 January: 'I wish I could persuade you to come directly to Coombe; you will be there not only in good air, but you will find a particularly warm house.'[17] It was his last letter to the man who had dominated British politics ever since he could remember. With the machine of government virtually at a standstill, the funeral of Nelson took place on 9 January. Lady Hawkesbury, exemplifying in herself the public mood of pathos and pride, had watched the procession arrive by water at Whitehall on the preceding day and then persuaded her husband and brother to go with her to the lying-in-state at the Admiralty. She described the scene to her sister.

> You can easily imagine our feelings as we look'd at that *little* coffin and thought of what it contained. The dead silence too of the room - hung with Black - the funeral Torches - the melancholy chaplain in his mourning cloak at the head of the bier - altogether spoke more directly to the heart than all the pageantry of the morning.[18]

On the day of the funeral she was up by candlelight. Since her husband had to be in his official place in St Paul's, he detailed two Bow Street Runners to look after Louisa as she gazed for six hours at the long, slow procession - general officers, military trumpeters, pipes and drums, horse and foot, a party of Greenwich pensioners, veterans of the Egyptian campaign, a detachment of the crew of the *Victory*, banners, heralds, court officials, princes of the blood, an endless column of mourning coaches, in the centre of which rolled the great funeral car bearing the coffin - as it wound its way from Whitehall along the Strand, through Temple Bar, to St Paul's where the congregation had been waiting for several hours. The dusk of that dull January day had already fallen when the coffin finally arrived and part of the service was carried out by torchlight. It was late in the evening before Hawkesbury was back in his house again.

Two days after the funeral Pitt arrived from Bath at what Louisa called his 'damp and cold' house at Putney Heath. There, on 13 January, he was visited by Hawkesbury and Castlereagh who came to break the news that the British expeditionary force operating with the Russians and Swedes in north Germany would have to be withdrawn. It was the last time they saw Pitt alive. After 15 January the doctors forbade any more visitors; on the 19th the cabinet considered what to do if Pitt died. Hawkesbury, who was now virtually in charge of the government, was firmly opposed to any formal discussion on whether they should resign or stay in office. Informally it was known that he, Castlereagh, Chatham and Camden favoured some arrangement which would enable the existing administration in one form or other to continue. Mulgrave, Montrose, and possibly Harrowby, shared the growing public view that Grenville and Fox should be given their chance. Parliament met on 21 January and

Hawkesbury drew up the speech from the throne in studiously uncontroversial terms. With the Prime Minister on his death-bed and the King, now almost blind from cataract, unable to be present, it seemed that the ministry was already defunct. The following day there was a small family gathering of Pittites at Hawkesbury's house in St James's Square: Castlereagh and his wife, Louisa, her brother Lord Bristol and her sister-in-law Lady Hervey. While they talked dejectedly together, information arrived for Hawkesbury of Pitt's steadily worsening condition. Visitors kept coming in to hear the latest reports and eventually Castlereagh became so agitated that he left. Hawkesbury sat down to write to the King and asked Louisa to send a similar note to Lord Liverpool. Later in the day he rode over to Putney and returned to say that Pitt was in a dying state though still calm and collected. That night the Hawkesburys had little sleep. They were woken by the news that Pitt had died at half-past four that morning.[19]

Hawkesbury saw the King at one o'clock and in the evening held a special cabinet. The King, himself in a state of great distress, had asked for the advice of his ministers on what was to be done. On 24 January the cabinet finally decided that they could not carry on. Next day Hawkesbury had a three-hour interview with the King who had come up to town for the purpose. Deeply disappointed by their decision, George pressed him hard to accept appointment as prime minister; and for a time Hawkesbury may have wavered. He told his sister-in-law Elizabeth Foster the same day, though perhaps with rueful exaggeration, that he had been minister for two hours but had not the courage to go on.[20] Instead he urged the King to abandon his veto on the return of Fox to office and so far succeeded as to return home confident that George would now, at whatever personal sacrifice of feeling, negotiate with the opposition. One last satisfaction the King allowed himself before approaching that distasteful task. As a mark of special favour to his outgoing minister he appointed Hawkesbury to the Wardenship of the Cinque Ports, the lucrative sinecure made vacant by the death of Pitt. Over the next few days negotiations were carried on with Lord Grenville and though at one point, when difficulties arose over the military powers of the Duke of York, there was another summons for Hawkesbury's assistance, the new government was announced in the first week of February. It proved to be that union of politicians which the public in general wished to see: the Grenvillites, the Foxites and the Sidmouth party – in effect all the identifiable parliamentary groups except the members of the late administration. If it hardly deserved its nickname of All the Talents, at least it comprised most of the parties.

There can be little doubt that Hawkesbury was right to refuse the King's offer of the premiership. It was not an unexpected invitation; even in the summer there had been speculation that he might take the responsibility of government off Pitt's shoulders. In the hubbub of talk which followed Pitt's death it was widely forecast that he would succeed as prime minister. Tom Grenville in fact wrote to his brother on 25 January as a positive fact that 'Lord

Hawkesbury is First Minister'. If the old administration was to carry on, he was clearly its natural leader.[21] Yet the task that had broken Pitt would have proved even more difficult for his successor. From the start Pitt's second administration had lacked both prestige and public support. By the beginning of 1806 its authority was exhausted, its war policy in ruins, its members discredited. The attraction for the public of a complete change of ministers was understandable; and politically there was much to be said for letting Grenville and Fox lay aside the heroics of opposition and experience the realities of office. Hawkesbury's refusal was generally approved; what damaged his reputation was the acceptance of the Cinque Ports sinecure. It was assumed that he had angled for it as a final perquisite before he relinquished office. Had it been given to Pitt's brother, the Earl of Chatham, as a reward to the dead statesman's family, it might have earned public approval. Bestowed on the son of Lord Liverpool, who had already extracted so much from the public purse during his long career, it seemed another example of his family's remarkable talent for amassing official emoluments. 'The Jenkinson craving disposition will revolt the whole country,' observed Lord Sheffield sourly.[22]

In this there was a shade of injustice. It would have seriously affronted the King, already agitated by the prospect of Fox and Grenville, to have refused his grateful gesture to a man who had been rising steadily in his esteem over the last few years. Moreover, though Lord Liverpool was affluent, Hawkesbury was so only in his expectations. Financially he was entirely dependent on his official salary and his father's generosity; Louisa had nothing apart from the interest on a legacy of £5,000 left to her by her father. She at least had no qualms about accepting the Lord Wardenship. The Princess Mary had told her how the King had spoken with tears in his eyes of the comfort it had been to him to give the Cinque Ports to Hawkesbury as a testimony of his appreciation. With an increased allowance from Lord Liverpool, loss of office, which in any case reduced their expenses, now seemed unlikely to have serious financial consequences. As Louisa confided to her sister,

> Thanks to the Dear King's Gift and Lord Liverpool's liberality, we shall be perfectly well off in circumstances. Our income will remain precisely the same. The Cinque Ports are £3,000 and Lord Liverpool is to give Lord Hawkesbury £4,000, these two make just the amount of the Secretary of State office and Lord Liverpool's present allowance of £1,000.[23]

A further attraction of the Wardenship was that it carried with it the use as residence of Walmer Castle on the Kent coast which Louisa hoped would be beneficial to her husband's health.

Out of office and in opposition for the first time in his life, Hawkesbury moved with the caution advisable in such unfamiliar territory. He, Castlereagh and Camden agreed to keep a small Pittite party together with regular dinners and consultations on tactics. Until the Melville impeachment was over it was pointless to make any move against the new government. The more prudent course was to support Grenville against Fox and Sidmouth. Nevertheless the King was informed that if he wished for a change of government an alternative was at hand and, further, if he decided to dismiss his existing ministers, it should be before and not after a general election so that new men would have the opportunity to redress the parliamentary balance in their favour. Hawkesbury, Castlereagh, Melville and Canning agreed among themselves, before they left town in the summer, that in the event of their being asked to form a ministry, the Attorney-General Spencer Perceval, who had earned his parliamentary spurs as a defender of the Addington administration in the Commons, should be Chancellor of the Exchequer and Leader of the House. Canning acquiesced in this decision and Hawkesbury went even further by saying that there was no reason, if it seemed expedient, why Perceval should not be prime minister.[24]

Though the King's sense of constitutional proprieties forbade any expression of opinion on his part, it is probable that by the summer of 1806 he was perfectly aware of the situation. At that point, however, a new element was introduced by the rapid deterioration in Fox's health. From mid-June he was absent from Parliament and from mid-July was unable to do any effective business. Grenville made overtures to the opposition through Lord Wellesley and Canning; but after consultation with Hawkesbury, Castlereagh and Perceval, the answer went back that they were not ready to make any arrangements without the general agreement of their friends. This pointed to something more than the recruitment of a few individuals and though Canning carried on his own personal negotiations with Grenville up to the end of the year, it was clear by the autumn that the only way to bring over the main Pittite opposition was by a wholesale reconstruction of the ministry.[25]

Fox died in September; the following month, partly to strengthen his weakened ministry, partly to forestall the opposition, Grenville dissolved Parliament and called a general election. The old parliament still had a couple of years to run and there was some criticism of this unusual though not unprecedented use by ministers of royal prerogative to gain a party advantage. At some point Hawkesbury drafted a formal protest to the King against the dissolution; but the document is undated and there is no proof that it was ever sent. What he did, more constitutionally though with little profit or credit to himself, was to make a protest in Parliament at the start of the next session. Even so, he refrained from moving a hostile amendment. The dilemma for the opposition was that they were unwilling to attack the King's ministers until the King had given them the signal; and the King was unwilling to move against ministers, whom he had after all brought into office, until they had done something to forfeit his confidence. In the 1807 session, however, the requisite conditions arrived. The misunderstanding between King and ministers over the new Catholic relief bill need not have led to their resignation; but Grenville by then was sick of being prime minister and sick of trying to hold together his far from talented cabinet. His peace efforts had broken down; his army reforms were encountering as many objections as those of Addington and Pitt; and Ireland was a perpetual irritant. A poor manager of men, he had annoyed several members of his cabinet by his negotiations with Canning. When on 11 March Sidmouth tendered his resignation, it was as much on this account as on the Catholic issue.

For the opposition the crisis had come too soon; and indirectly they endeavoured to persuade both cabinet and King to patch up their differences. The ministers, however, were probably bent on resignation and the King provided them with a convenient pretext by his demand for a pledge that they would never trouble him again over Catholic Emancipation. Hawkesbury was as much surprised as anyone by the sudden dismissal of the administration. Returning home late at night from visiting his father on 18 March, he found a letter commanding his presence with Lord Eldon at Windsor at ten o'clock the following morning. It is possible that the King would still have liked Hawkesbury as prime minister; but the opposition had already agreed on Lord Portland, the elderly but respected survivor of Pitt's cabinet of 1801, as a figure (more brutally perhaps as a figurehead) under whom all the younger men could agree to serve. This presumably was the advice which Hawkesbury and Eldon tendered to the King. On their return from Windsor the two men went straight to Portland, and discussions with other influential peers and politicians followed next day. On 23 March, the day Portland submitted his ministerial list to the King, Hawkesbury himself wrote to George III to support the appointment of Perceval as Leader of the House of Commons. With the Prime Minister in the upper house, it was in fact a crucial position. Though Hawkesbury had anticipated a sharp attack by the displaced ministers, he was not discouraged by the many difficulties which lay ahead. 'If they had good nerves,' he opined, 'they should get through it.'[26]

In the last week of March came the announcement of the new appointments. Hawkesbury returned to the Home Office; Canning became Foreign Secretary; Castlereagh at the War Department took the third and potentially the most hazardous of the three secretaryships. Mulgrave went to the Admiralty, Eldon resumed as Lord Chancellor and other familiar names – Camden, Westmorland and Chatham – added their quota of family connection or electoral influence to the new administration. Sidmouth was left out; he had worn thin too many people's patience to be welcomed back; but his recent breach with Grenville and his known loyalty to the King guaranteed for the time being his benevolent neutrality. Even so, during April the government was being run too close for comfort in Parliament and as a final safeguard the cabinet decided at the end of the month to use their predecessors' precedent against them and dissolve Parliament. With a new House of Commons and the customary shift of allegiances that normally accompanied a change of ministry, their first trial of strength in June after the general election yielded them a comfortable majority of nearly two hundred.

The Hawkesburys, who had given up their town house and spent most of the previous winter in the seclusion and cheapness of Coombe, faced a return to their old ministerial way of life with mixed feelings. Louisa, who had a taste for the melancholy, viewed it with some misgiving.

> I find our year of Holyday has spoilt me. I hope it has not Lord Hawkesbury. I never can tell you how I shrink from the renewal of hurry, bustle, anxiety and worry . . . we must now have a large house in Town . . . Walmer Castle at Easter is of course out of the question now. Alas I fear even in autumn it will be very different from the tranquil *séjour* of last year. But I must not complain, tho' I cannot rejoice. If Lord Hawkesbury's health and Peace of mind do not suffer by this unexpected and unwish'd for return to Power I am content.[27]

Her husband perhaps saw the future more placidly. Whatever his father said, he had no wish to return to the Foreign Office where he thought there had been a deliberate set made against him during Sidmouth's administration. Canning, moreover, had made it clear to others that he could not bear the idea of Hawkesbury's resumption of that department and would regard it as a renewal of their quarrel of 1804. With Hawkesbury in the double obscurity of the Home Department and the House of Lords that quarrel could be allowed to sink into the past. His jealous instincts were now directed against Castlereagh and Perceval, the only two cabinet ministers who sat with him in the Commons. Free of such rivalries and relieved of direct responsibility for the limping progress of the British war effort, Hawkesbury was content to keep the noiseless tenor of his departmental way, wait upon the old, tired, half-blind king, and manage the daily business of government in the House of Lords. With a prime minister in the upper house who never opened his mouth, Hawkesbury became in many respects the utility man of the administration. From October to December 1807, when Castlereagh was seriously ill, he even took over the considerable additional burden of the War Department.

Castlereagh was not the only government invalid. From the start of 1808 Portland's health grew steadily worse. He was unable to concentrate on matters of business for very long or act as effective head of the administration. To look about for a successor was natural; to find one more difficult. Of the inner group of cabinet ministers Hawkesbury and Canning were thirty-eight; Castlereagh thirty-nine. Perceval, at forty-six the oldest, was the least experienced politician of the four, having only recently abandoned a professional legal career. Their claims were too finely balanced, and Canning at any rate too firmly ambitious, to permit any mutual agreement on the choice of one of them as successor to Portland. A possible candidate from outside the government was Lord Welles-ley, whom Portland had tried to recruit as foreign secretary. Two years older than Perceval, he had won prestige and a marquessate by his vigorous and victorious administration in India, and was known to be interested in a political career at home. Qualities which kept the gorgeous East in fee, however, were not wanted or appreciated in the prosaic atmosphere of Westminster, as his contemporary nicknames of 'the Lama' and 'the Grand Mogul' sufficiently indicated. Hawkesbury, Perceval and Chatham disliked both his old connection with the Grenvilles and his new intimacy with Canning. Sidmouth, on the other hand, growing more peevishly critical of the ministry as the months passed, was even less acceptable as a possible head of the administration. In the end nothing was done, and it seemed nothing could be done, to replace Portland's failing leadership. Increasingly the government degenerated into a bundle of separate departments with no single impetus and no centre of loyalty. The ministry lacked even the bracing stimulus of a powerful parliamentary opposition. With Fox's death, with Howick's succession to his father's earldom, the ineffective Ponsonby installed as leader of the opposition in the Commons, and the emergence of a small controversial group of radical reformers, the old Foxite liberal party had neither present shape nor future purpose.

Abroad, after the Russian defeat at Friedland and Alexander's pact with Napoleon at Tilsit, British war strategy had come to one of its periodic halts. Vigorous and high-handed action saved the Danish and Portuguese fleets from falling into enemy hands; but after the French occupation of Portugal in November 1807, Britain had no point of leverage anywhere on the mainland of Europe. The inability of the two great belligerents to come to grips with each other had led in November 1806 to Napoleon's Berlin decrees declaring Britain to be in a state of blockade. This was answered on the British side by Orders in Council forbidding trade with France or with ports in French hands. In November 1807 Portland's cabinet, influenced largely by Perceval, Hawkesbury and Castlereagh, widened the economic war-front by imposing a system of licensing on all neutral vessels wishing to trade with ports from which British ships were excluded. Napoleon retaliated with the Milan decrees ordering the confiscation of all ships coming from British ports. The neutral powers, among which the United States were first in importance for European trade, were thus placed by the belligerents in an intolerable dilemma.

The opportunity to strike a more orthodox blow at Napoleon's empire came with the Spanish revolt in the summer of 1808. It was the first national uprising against Napoleonic tyranny and British public opinion was not slow to seize its significance. Encouraged by the feeling in both houses of Parliament, the cabinet pledged itself to assist the revolt. The strong language used by Hawkesbury at the end of June reflected not only the government's determination but his own personal conviction that everything possible should be done to support the Spaniards in their efforts to rid themselves of what he called in his characteristically forthright language 'a powerful and sanguinary tyrant'. The resolution of the government was soon tested. Following the meeting of the two emperors at Erfurt in September, a joint peace-offer was made by them. In October emissaries from the two states arrived under a flag of truce at Dover. Hawkesbury, who was at Walmer on his customary autumn visit, ordered the Frenchman to be detained and the Russian to be sent up to London. The British government expressed a willingness to negotiate but only in association with their allies, among whom they included the Spanish people. This was rejected by France and a royal proclamation was therefore issued in December regretting the continuation of hostilities but declaring that it would not be possible to begin peace discussions by abandoning the Spanish.[28] The problem of helping Spain was not one of ends but means. Inconsistency of army policy in previous years and concentration on home defence had left their inevitable mark. When Castlereagh took over the War Department he found that the resources were totally lacking to mount an expeditionary force of more than divisional strength. Organisation and expansion were his first tasks rather than any ambitious overseas strategy. The hasty despatch of 10,000 men under Sir Arthur Wellesley and his victory at Vimeiro were followed by the unnecessary and humiliating convention of Cintra arranged by senior generals. Another failure came in January 1809 when Moore's larger forces operating from north Portugal had to be hastily evacuated from Corunna.

For Hawkesbury it was a grim winter. On 17 December his father died at his home in Hertford Street. 'My beloved father,' he wrote the same day to the King in language that could not for all its formality hide the genuineness of his emotion, 'departed this life at six o'clock this morning after an illness of several days, during which we have the satisfaction of believing that he never suffered a moment's pain.' In his reply the King referred in stately words to his father's 'integrity and fidelity' in the able discharge of his duties over a period of forty years.[29] Two days before Christmas his body was taken out in state to begin the long journey to Hawkesbury where on 30 December it was interred in the family vault. Three weeks later the new Earl of Liverpool stood up in the House of Lords to defend the government's decision to make no peace without Spain. In the aftermath of the Cintra Convention it seemed an expression of faith rather than confidence; and Lord Grenville made much play with the folly of sending a force of 30,000 men into the interior of Spain to meet 200,000 Frenchmen. 'I can compare such a measure,' he observed satirically, 'only to the far-famed march to Paris to which it is equal in its wildness and absurdity.' Unmoved by this sixteen-year-old witticism, Liverpool made a stout defence of the government's strategy. History, he observed coolly, offered many examples of nations struggling for their independence which had eventually succeeded after years of defeat. A better prospect of success was offered in Spain than anywhere else. 'It was the only instance since the first outbreak of the French Revolution in which a whole people had taken up arms in their own defence.' He ended on a characteristically steadfast note. 'We have done our duty. We have not despaired; we have persevered, and will do so to the last, while there is anything left to contend for with the slightest prospect of eventual success.'

It was as well perhaps for his peace of mind that he was denied the aerial vision of Thomas Hardy's *Dynasts* which would have shown him at that moment Moore's tattered, hungry army outside Corunna, shooting their foundered Cavalry horses and blowing up ammunition dumps prior to embarkation and withdrawal. When Sir Arthur Wellesley returned to Portugal in April, it was still unclear whether the peninsula was going to be a main theatre of war or a sideshow. With Austria about to re-enter the war, it seemed to Castlereagh a better use of limited resources to bring pressure to bear on the central, sensitive area of western Europe. The Austrians urged an expedition to northern Germany in order to encourage the Prussians. The cabinet, with unhappy memories of similar expeditions in the past, preferred the nearer and logistically more manageable option of an attack across the narrow seas on the great port and naval base of Antwerp, preceded by a landing on the island of Walcheren. The final decision to go forward with the Walcheren expedition was made towards the end of June. It was taken by a cabinet already riddled by internal divisions and rivalries. Government by departments presupposed a readiness by ministers not to interfere with the work of their colleagues. Canning, by common consent the mainstay of the administration's debating strength in the Commons, had too much energy and too much ambition to observe this self-denying ordinance. In April, restless at the stalemate into which the war seemed once more to have fallen and at the general looseness of the administration, he approached Portland with a demand for a reorganisation of the cabinet and, in particular, for the replacement of Castlereagh by his new political ally the Marquess Wellesley.

Under the threat of Canning's own resignation, the Prime Minister consulted some of his colleagues, notably Bathurst and Camden, and eventually the King himself. No immediate action, however, was taken on Canning's proposal. Portland's health, the awkwardness of moving Castlereagh from the War Department in the middle of planning an overseas military operation, the difficulty of finding suitable cabinet reinforcements, were all arguments for delay. The summer wore on with fitful discussions of plans for a ministerial reshuffle and periodic talk of resignation from the impatient Canning. Meanwhile the unsuspecting Castlereagh continued with the preparations for the Walcheren expedition. In July Liverpool learned for the first time of the move to displace him and on the 11th wrote a stiff letter to the King. He pointedly regretted Portland's failure to inform him of a matter so crucial for the government. If the issue had merely been a public one, he observed, he would have had no difficulty in concluding that it was more important to retain Canning in the administration than Castlereagh; but, in fact, Canning had objected to Castlereagh's continuance as Secretary for War 'on no ground to which Lord Liverpool, as far as he is acquainted with it, could subscribe'. To remove Castlereagh in the middle of his work on the Walcheren expedition would be 'an act of manifest cruelty and injustice'. Having relieved his mind with these blunt expressions, he put forward some constructive proposals. If, as had previously been suggested, Castlereagh took a peerage, he himself was prepared to vacate the Home Office and the leadership of the House of Lords in his favour, on the understanding that Castlereagh would remain in charge of the Walcheren business. For himself, he added finally, he wanted no other post nor even to remain in the cabinet. To Canning, who the same day at last took him into his confidence, he said exactly the same though in more circumspect language.[30]

To this uncommonly generous offer George III made no reply. With a clear eye for the real weakness of the ministry he could see little purpose in getting rid of any of his younger, efficient ministers and leaving the elderly, inefficient one. After Portland had suffered a minor stroke on 11 August, he spoke privately with Liverpool and Camden, to the effect that Portland could not remain as prime minister much longer and the rest of the cabinet ought to be considering the question of a successor. What he hoped was that the personal issue of Castlereagh might be settled without open recrimination under cover of a general reconstruction of the government. Canning himself was against allowing Liverpool to sacrifice himself simply to provide an honourable way out for Castlereagh. Whoever succeeded Portland, it was clear that Liverpool was regarded as the cornerstone of the government in the upper house. Other members of the cabinet – Camden, Bathurst, and probably even Westmorland – were ready to give up their offices to facilitate a new partition of responsibilities. The critical problem was to find a successor to Portland. In August Perceval opened negotiations with Canning; he told him that all their colleagues wanted Castlereagh to stay in the government and suggested that they might agree on a peer – Bathurst, Harrowby, Liverpool or Lord Wellesley – under whom they could both agree to serve. Canning, having consulted his friends, took the line that the new prime minister must be in the Commons; that he could not expect Perceval to acquiesce in Canning's promotion to that office; and finally that, if Perceval took it, Canning would have to resign. What he evidently intended by this uncompromising attitude was to create a situation in which he himself would have to be chosen as the simplest way out of all the difficulties. What he did, in effect, was to force the rest of the cabinet to take sides. He gambled on the assumption of his own indispensability; and overplayed his hand.

If a choice had to be made, Liverpool for one had no doubt what choice he would make. Perceval showed him his correspondence with Canning on 2 September. After taking time for reflection he sent Perceval the following day an explicit letter of support. As Leader of the House of Commons, he wrote, he was already the second man in the government and could not be expected to serve under Canning. On the other hand, Canning would incur no loss of status if Perceval became prime minister; and, he added, irrespective of Perceval's situation, he was convinced that Canning's appointment would meet with 'insurmountable' difficulties – by which he probably meant the refusal of most of their cabinet colleagues to serve under him. Stiffened by this heartening support, in which Bathurst joined, Perceval resolved now to stand firm. The three ministers agreed that Portland should be pressed to retire and that in the circumstances no move should be made to displace Castlereagh. In fact Castlereagh's resignation four days later nearly brought about those of Liverpool, Perceval, Camden and Bathurst as well. Their reasoning was clear. If Castlereagh went, while Portland and Canning stayed on, the administration would be completely under Canning's domination. Liverpool's instinct was to keep the main body of the ministry together, even if it necessitated taking in some new men. Others, like Eldon and to some extent Perceval, were less anxious to recruit new allies and less optimistic about their chances of survival.

Events now happened quickly. Between 6 and 13 September Portland tendered his resignation; Canning ostentatiously absented himself from the cabinet; Castlereagh learned what had been going on and indignantly resigned; and finally the King, having contemptuously ignored Canning's unabashed offer of his services as prime minister, instructed Perceval to consult with his colleagues on a reconstruction of the cabinet. It is possible that the inner group of ministers – Perceval, Liverpool, and Eldon – decided as early as 12 September that without Canning and Castlereagh and those of their friends likely to go out with them, it would not be possible to carry on. With Lord Wellesley on a diplomatic mission to Spain, Lord Melville aggrieved, and Sidmouth unacceptable, the only conceivable alliance was with Grenville and Grey. This at any rate was the substance of the advice presented to the King in a formal cabinet minute of 18 September. While emphasising the weakness of their own position, however, the ministers added drily that if Canning were to undertake the government, his difficulties would be equally great. The overture to Grenville and Grey (the two Gs), reluctantly sanctioned by the King, was undertaken by Eldon and Liverpool. It was wrecked at the outset by Grey who refused even to travel to London to discuss it. On 4 October the King finally accepted the unanimous advice of the cabinet to choose his next prime minister from the House of Commons and appointed Perceval as head of the government.[31] He regarded him as a straightforward and honourable politician; he also knew that if Canning were given the post, most of his colleagues would at once resign. Meanwhile, on 21 September the two ex-secretaries of state, Castlereagh and Canning, fought a duel on Putney Common. Canning received a pistol ball in the thigh; Castlereagh, unscathed except for the loss of a coat-button, returned home to his house in St James's Square where almost immediately Liverpool called on him.[32] Though Castlereagh's anger was directed as much against his late colleagues, especially Portland and Camden (his uncle by marriage), as against Canning, he could have had little resentment against his visitor. Even if Liverpool had been unable to avert his resignation, he had done as much as anyone in the cabinet to ensure that the premiership did not pass to Castlereagh's rival.

NOTES

1 Yonge, I, 147 ff.; Rose, II, 132-6.

2 *Cobbett's Parliamentary Debates*, 1804, II, 722-3; LGC, II, 4.

3 For rival accounts of this episode see Yonge, I, 147 ff.; Marshall, pp. 274 ff.; GD, I. 409-10; Bagot, I, 217-20.

4 Marshall, pp. 288-91; George 3, IV, 274 n., 275 n.

5 George 3, IV, 276-7.

6 AR, 1804, p. 603. For the work at the Home Office see generally Yonge, Ch. v; Auckland, IV, 220-28 has information on the business of Princess Charlotte.

7 Rose, II, 202.

8 Yonge, I, 162.

9 LWF, I, 107; for the reconciliation generally see Yonge, I, Ch. v; Pellew, II, 325-6; George 3, IV, 260-64.

10 38473 fos 207 ff. (draft letter n.d. but clearly April 1805); Yonge, I, 193; Pellew, II, 355-64; Colchester, I, 545-7; Bathurst, p. 45; George 3, IV, 315.

11 Pellew, II, 362-3.

12 38473 fo. 206.

13 Ward, I, 254.

14 Quoted by A.D. Harvey, *Britain in the Early Nineteenth Century* (1978), p. 164, from Sidmouth Papers.

15 38473 fo. 226.

16 LGC, II, 150.

17 Stanhope, IV, 370.

18 LWF, I, 113-15.

19 Ibid, 115-17.

20 LGC, II, 166.

21 For the change of government in 1806 see esp. Fortescue, VII, 279-83, 334-5, 337-9; Rose, II, 226-9; George 3, IV, 382.

22 Auckland, IV, 269; cf. AR, 1806, p. 19.

23 LWF, I, 119.

24 Bathurst, p. 53. See also Rose, II, 246-7, 262-4; Muriel Chamberlain, *Lord Aberdeen* (1983), p. 94; George 3, IV, xxv-xxxvi.

25 Fortescue, VIII, 210-12, 331.

26 Yonge, I, 228. See also for change of ministry Auckland, IV, 308; Twiss, II, 36-8; Bathurst, p. 50; Colchester, II, 30, 104.

27 LWF, I, 136.

28 AR, 1808, pp. 227-8, 364-5.

29 George 3, V, 160.

30 George 3, V, 310-11.

31 The best account of the end of the Portland ministry is in George 3, V, Intro. and pp. 310-62. See also Twiss, II, 78, 88; Walpole, II, 19 n.

32 Rede, p. 192.

CHAPTER V

At the War Office

The administration formed by Perceval in the autumn of 1809 was to be the basis of British government for the next seventeen years. At the time nothing seemed less likely. The old body of Pittites were split into more hostile groups than at any time since 1801. Few of its own members thought that the rump of Portland's ministry could long survive. Even if it lasted out the rest of the year, its intrinsic weakness would be exposed as soon as Parliament met. Perceval took the better part of two months in finding men for all the vacancies he had to fill; even so, after half a dozen refusals, he had to take on the Chancellorship of the Exchequer himself. Little prestige or respect was now attached to government. The scandal early in 1809 over the alleged sale of army appointments by the Duke of York's mistress, coming on the heels of the Melville impeachment, confirmed the public suspicion that almost all politicians were corrupt and politics little more than a sordid scramble of aristocratic factions for place and profit. Abroad the war was doing no better than before. The disastrous failure of the Walcheren expedition, and Sir Arthur Wellesley's enforced retreat into Portugal after his victory at Talavera had both helped to precipitate the cabinet crisis in September. It was not surprising that politicians held aloof from Perceval's stricken administration; and not only politicians.

In October Liverpool's name was being canvassed for election as Chancellor of Oxford University in anticipation of Portland's death which took place at the end of the month. His unwillingness to stand was probably due to a justified doubt of success. In normal circumstances, as a leading minister and backed by the influence of the government, he would have been sure of election. The prudent academic and clerical electors, however, with an earnest sense of the importance of favours to come, were discouraged by the sight of what the Bishop of St Asaph described as 'a tottering ministry'. In the event, strengthened by the widespread conviction of an early change of government, Lord Grenville was put at the head of the poll against the opposition of Eldon and Lord Beaufort.[1] In continuing to shoulder the burden of office, ministers were acting less from any hopeful calculation of their chances than from loyalty to the old, blind King who had begged them not to desert his service and expose him to his enemies. In his perplexity and distress George leaned for support on those of his political servants he trusted most like Liverpool and Eldon, his

Lord Chancellor. To Liverpool he wrote pathetically at the end of the crisis month of September, 'you are my eyes, and I know I can trust you that I shall not be imposed upon'.[2] Liverpool himself took the simple view that the ministry had taken office two years earlier to protect the King and could not now abandon him. If, as was likely, they were defeated when Parliament met (he wrote to Wellington), 'we shall at least have the satisfaction of keeping a respectable party together, which may be able to afford some protection for the King, and, I trust, some security to the country'.[3]

The two largest gaps Perceval had to repair were the secretaryships of state vacated by Canning and Castlereagh. As far as the Foreign Office was concerned, Liverpool was averse to returning to his old department; Harrowby's health disqualified him; Bathurst was reluctant to move. In the end it was decided to offer it to Lord Wellesley, who was still in Spain. One of Canning's last official acts had been to send off a letter recalling him to England; but Liverpool on behalf of the cabinet went to the Foreign Office and instructed Bagot, the under-secretary, to arrange for an immediate despatch conveying the government's view that Wellesley should not leave Spain until he could do so without damage or inconvenience to the public service. To Lord Wellesley himself he sent a private note expressing his personal hope that he would take the Foreign Office. Wellesley in fact vigorously rejected any suggestion that he was politically bound to Canning; and his letter of acceptance arrived in London in November a few days before the 'Grand Mogul' appeared himself.[4]

For the War Department Perceval proposed Liverpool himself. For him this was almost as unwelcome as the Foreign Office, where as the only surviving secretary of state he was already temporarily in charge. He had grown accustomed to the Home Office and its less exacting duties fitted in well with his responsibilities in the House of Lords. The War Department, on the other hand, had been as much a graveyard of political reputations as the Admiralty. Yet Perceval insisted; and with good reason. He needed at least one other cabinet minister with him in the House of Commons and the only possibility seemed Ryder. Yet he was another of those politicians of indifferent courage or stamina who professed himself unequal to the rigours of the War Office and fit only for the less demanding Home Department. In the end, as no doubt Perceval calculated, Liverpool's sense of loyalty made him yield; though the Prime Minister still had to overcome resistance from the King. 'As the Home Department suits Lord Liverpool so well and is so ably filled by him,' he wrote to Perceval at the end of October, 'as it is the first in rank and therefore desirable on that account to be held by him, it would be more consistent with Lord Liverpool's situation and wishes not to remove him from it.' Having made his decision, however, Liverpool came to his chief's assistance and wrote a persuasive letter to George, pointing out the difficulties of the government and the reluctance of other politicians to take office.[5] The War Office had in fact been offered first to Dundas, Lord Melville's son, who had been deterred by his aggrieved father from accepting it, and then to Yorke, who had been dissuaded from taking it by his brother, Lord Hardwicke. It was therefore in some desperation that Perceval had finally turned to Liverpool.

The new War Minister did not, however, allow these circumstances to sit too heavily on him. In communicating all that had passed to the commander-in-chief in Portugal Arthur Wellesley, now Viscount Wellington, he added with modest assurance: 'I feel very strongly the additional weight of anxiety this change will bring upon me; but I could not, under the circumstances, refuse it, and I think I may be, perhaps, of more use to you in your command in Portugal than any other person who could be placed in the same situation.'[6] As an earnest of his good intentions he invited Wellington to let him have the names of the general officers he wanted to be appointed to his command and promised to do his best to see that they were selected. For his own end of the business he took care, even before he formally assumed responsibility for the department, to secure the services of an experienced professional soldier as his military under-secretary. Both King and cabinet were anxious to make the appointment a permanent post dissociated from party politics or patronage. On the advice of the Horse Guards (the army administrative headquarters) the choice fell on Lt-Col. Bunbury, a product of the new military college at High Wycombe and of Moore's training camp at Shorncliffe. He had served in the Duke of York's campaign of 1799 in North Holland and at the battle of Maida (one of the few British victories in the field so far) in Sicily in 1806. It proved an admirable selection and Bunbury (though in party sympathies a whig) remained in his post until after the conclusion of the war, contributing not a little to the steadily increasing efficiency of the department.[7]

On the larger issue of policy Liverpool made up his mind from the start that if the war in the peninsula was to continue, the government should not allow any part of its military effort to be diverted elsewhere. The question, however, in the autumn of 1809 was whether they should persevere with the campaign at all. His own view was that the French would have great difficulty in reconquering Spain and that the right strategy would be to remain in the peninsula as long as it could be done without risking the actual destruction of the British army. On the other hand the Austrian surrender would clearly enable Napoleon to concentrate in massive strength against the little British expeditionary force. He made it his first task, therefore, to elicit from Wellington his own views on the chances of ultimate success. Even while contemplating a possible evacuation of Lisbon, however, Liverpool was looking to a defence of Cadiz and Gibraltar rather than a complete withdrawal from the peninsula. The replies he received from Wellington, though not entirely specific, were sturdily optimistic. If the French attacked Portugal, the British commander was confident that they could be resisted; and even if defeated, he would still be able to re-embark his army safely. This letter Liverpool laid before the cabinet together with a statement of the reinforcements that would be needed. Before the end of the year he was able to promise Wellington that his army would be maintained at an effective strength of 30,000 men. Equally heartening was the cabinet's acceptance of Wellington's proposal that an auxiliary force of Portuguese troops should be raised and paid by the British government. By Christmas 1809 Liverpool had done everything in his power to reassure the British field commander that he had a minister and a government disposed to support him.

The doubt was whether that government could long survive. In the first week of the new parliamentary session ministers were beaten on a motion for an enquiry into the Walcheren expedition and on the appointments to the important Finance Committee. Though they escaped a direct motion of censure, Lord Chatham was forced to resign; before the end of the session there were further defeats on the perennially sensitive issues of pensions and sinecures. It was obvious that this grinding pressure, damaging both to the efficiency and the prestige of the administration, could not be allowed to continue and the cabinet decided at Easter to make simultaneous overtures to Sidmouth, Canning and Castlereagh. Sidmouth, however, refused to serve with Canning; nobody except Lord Wellesley wanted Canning by himself; and Perceval thought it useless in these circumstances to approach Castlereagh. Perceval's hopeful project of a grand reunion of Pittites merely demonstrated in fact their continued disunity.

At the end of the session another effort was made with no better result. Since Sidmouth was still obdurate, the cabinet agreed on a simultaneous invitation to Canning and Castlereagh. Lord Wellesley objected to taking the second without the first; his colleagues would not take the first without the second. The problem in any case was to find them suitable offices, since there was a strong feeling that neither should be allowed to return to his former post. Liverpool once more offered to make a vacancy by giving up his secretaryship for war and taking the presidency of the Council. His colleagues were not, however, anxious to see a change at the War Office even though Wellesley was also prepared to move. The alternative of putting Liverpool in the Foreign Office and making Wellesley President of the Council was probably rejected because it would be unacceptable to Canning. In the end the Admiralty and the Home Office were jointly offered to Castlereagh and Canning, leaving the individual choices to be decided by themselves. This frustrating cabinet game of noughts and crosses ended in September when Castlereagh refused the offer outright, Canning more conditionally. The whole episode probably left some ministers with a feeling that the covert Wellesley–Canning axis represented a new danger to Perceval's fragile administration.

In the autumn of 1810, as the retreating British army faced the French across the triple lines of Torres Vedras, Wellington's equally beleaguered political masters faced a mortal danger at home. On 27 October Liverpool wrote to Bathurst that the protracted illness of the Princess Amelia (she died on 2 November) had produced alarming effects on the King and that it had been decided that the whole cabinet should be informed of the position. By the beginning of November it was plain that George III was no longer in full possession of his faculties. There were moments of lucidity when he realised what was going on and the ministers hoped that as in the past there would be a substantial recovery. Liverpool was particularly anxious to avoid a regency since it could not be kept secret from the King and the knowledge might in itself cause another relapse. It became distressingly evident, however, that the old malady had taken a new and remorseless hold. Parliament met as summoned (since no further prorogation was now possible) at the start of November and after two adjournments even Liverpool had to agree to an enquiry into the King's mental state.

The report of the royal physicians left ministers with no choice but to seek legislation. In a repetition of the constitutional procedure of 1788-9 a regency bill modelled on Pitt's original proposals was carried by narrow majorities through both houses and became law in February 1811. What would happen next nobody knew. Grenville and Grey were hopeful of being called to office but the irresoluteness of the Prince of Wales defied rational calculation. The ministers were as much in the dark as the disjointed opposition. 'We have no share whatever of his confidence,' Liverpool wrote to Wellington on 17 January. All he could say was that if the Prince thought his father might recover, he would hesitate to change his government. Already the Irish members were beginning to drift away; in three weeks' time the fate of the administration would be decided. Meanwhile, he added more cheerfully, Wellington's reinforcements were about to embark and he doubted whether a new government would dare to countermand the order even if the transports were held up by contrary winds.[8] Perceval's stout and dextrous defence of the regency proposals enhanced his reputation in the Commons; but the passage of the bill was itself a suspended death sentence on his administration. Nevertheless, for the first twelve months there would be restrictions on the Regent's powers; there was still a possibility of the King's recovery; and after much speculation the minds of the ministers were set at rest by a message on 4 February from the Prince Regent that he did not propose to remove them. That this was a respite rather than a pardon was made clear by his further observation that his restraint was attributable solely to his desire to do nothing that might interfere with his father's return to health.

For the time being ministers could carry on with their work, and Liverpool devote himself more singlemindedly to the war in the peninsula. That the campaign should be carried on at all was a measure of the government's courage. Had the decision been left to Parliament in the winter and spring of 1809-10, Wellington's forces would probably have been ordered home. Most MPs were unconvinced of the chances of success and resented the increasing cost of the expedition. Only the determination of the ministers upheld the strategy of the peninsular war against the doubts of their supporters and the defeatism of the opposition. That strategy, however, was subject to severe limitations. Given the inferiority of British manpower resources and the absence of conscription, there could be no rational expectation of total victory in the field. Wellington could never hope to drive the French out of Spain even if, after the defence of Torres Vedras in 1810-11, the French could not hope to drive the British out of Portugal. Only with superficial hindsight can the peninsular campaign be depicted in terms of steadily mounting British pressure which in the end took Wellington and his victorious infantry into southern France. In the wider panorama of the Napoleonic Wars it was no more than a large-scale diversionary activity - a running ulcer, in the classic phrase, but not a mortal wound.

From his impregnable position on the western seaboard Wellington's role was to give support and encouragement to the Spanish and Portuguese resistance movements. Three times he advanced into Spain and three times withdrew before a numerically superior enemy. Not until 1813, five years after he first landed, and when Napoleon's Russian campaign had destroyed the flower of the French army, did he start a continous advance towards the French frontiers. In the circumstances it was inevitable that the security of Wellington's expeditionary force was a constant preoccupation of ministers and that contingency plans for evacuation were kept under discussion until the summer of 1811. Wellington's command was not simply a British army; it was, as Liverpool pointed out on more than one occasion, the only army in the field which the country possessed. Within this strategic framework there were other limitations; in particular the rate at which the military organisation at home could produce trained replacements for disease and battle casualties, and the financial ability of the government to meet the mounting cost of Wellington's operations. The Secretary of State for War, as Liverpool soon discovered, was only one authority among others in matters of military administration. The Treasury, headed by the Prime Minister, controlled not only the financing of the war effort but the actual commissariat branch responsible for supply. The Master-General of the Ordnance was responsible for equipment; and the commander-in-chief at the Horse Guards dealt with discipline, promotions and postings. In many matters affecting the war in Spain, Liverpool could be no more than an intermediary between Wellington and other departments and his office no more than a sorting-box for requests and requirements coming in from the peninsula.

The system was one of deliberate decentralisation and divided authority that had existed since the Revolution of 1688 and was to last until the Crimean War nearly half a century later. It was a recipe, perhaps, for constitutional liberty but it hardly made for the efficient conduct of war. With the Treasury, controlled by politicians like himself, Liverpool's relations were close; with the two successive commanders-in-chief, first Sir David Dundas and then, from May 1811, the Duke of York, they were correct; with the Ordnance, distant and sometimes difficult. A measure of the latter department's independent and somewhat hidebound outlook was provided by the inter-departmental argument in 1810 over the use of Congreve's rocket and Major Shrapnel's new type of exploding shell in which Liverpool took a lively personal interest. To his suggestion that they be used in Portugal, the Ordnance returned the remarkable answer that it would be inadvisable to employ these weapons in circumstances where they might fall into the hands of the enemy.[9] Outside the administration there were other distracting influences at work of which Liverpool had to take note even if he did not allow them to control his decisions. Court opinion, in the person of the Regent and most of the other royal dukes, was less than enthusiastic about the Spanish sideshow and would have preferred a more direct intervention in north Germany where something could be done to defend Hanover. Within the peninsular theatre they favoured Spanish Cadiz rather than Portuguese Lisbon as a base. Some at least of Liverpool's queries to Wellington were probably designed to forestall this kind of pressure.[10]

The man with whom above all good relations were essential was the commander in the field. From the start Liverpool tried to make it clear to Wellington that he had the confidence of the ministry and they would be largely guided by his advice. For the first year or two this was not always an easy task. With all his superb qualities Wellington was a confirmed grumbler and under the strain of tiredness and frustration allowed himself on occasions some heated and intemperate language. Moreover he had an initial distrust of the ministry which only slowly dissipated. Moore's ill-fated campaign, the Convention of Cintra and the court of enquiry which followed, were not calculated to instil confidence into future field commanders; Castlereagh, his friend and supporter, the only politician he trusted, had left the government under a cloud. The violent attacks in Parliament, lack of support from the public, the pessimistic views of the military profession in England, gave an added significance in Wellington's mind to the emphasis in Liverpool's early letters on the importance of not risking the destruction of his army and to the continuing discussion of ports suitable for evacuation. The cabinet was undoubtedly gravely concerned for the safety of Wellington's force in the spring of 1810. They were agreed that a large discretion must be given to the commander in the field; but they also knew that another disaster like that suffered by Moore would bring down the government. Wellington himself had warned them of the coming onslaught by the French armies being collected against him. With an effective British force of some 32,000 men facing Massena's 138,000, Liverpool in March wrote what was perhaps his most pessimistic letter of the war, deprecating any 'desperate resistance' and telling Wellington that he would be excused for bringing his army away too soon rather than too late.[11]

Between the assurance that the final decision would rest with him and the reiteration of the broad principles which were to govern his operations, there was an uncertain area which Wellington was quick to resent, and less justifiably, to suspect. His political chief in London, however, remained admirably calm and conciliatory. He assured Wellington of the cabinet's complete trust, passed on in friendly fashion private news of Lady Wellington and his two boys, and forwarded an extract from a flattering letter from the King, praising Wellington's ability and recommending the cabinet to allow him to act according to his own judgement and discretion. The commander's snappish mood continued, however, all through the summer of 1810. His military operations had not been distinguished; he had been severely criticised for failing to relieve Ciudad Rodrigo; promised reinforcements had not arrived; opinion in England, as he knew from his own officers, was pessimistic. All these grievances came out in a petulant letter he wrote to Liverpool in August implying that the ministry had no confidence in his operations and hinting that if he could not have more troops the contest might as well be abandoned. In his long reply Liverpool wrote patiently that he was at a loss to know how Wellington could imagine that the ministry had no trust in the measures he had taken for the defence of Portugal. There was little disagreement in the cabinet on the strategy of the war, as their parliamentary defence of the campaign should have demonstrated; and already the earlier critical opinion in England was beginning to shift. He wrote again in November to the effect that Wellington's decisions should be governed by his own judgement of what was necessary, not by any presumptions about the feeling in England: 'In short you know our objects to be the defence of Portugal and the support of the cause of the Peninsula as long as they are practicable; and I trust you feel that you possess the entire confidence of the Government with respect to the measures which it may be desirable to adopt for those purposes, whether they may be of a cautious or more enterprising character.'[12] Nevertheless, he warned Wellington that if, as seemed probable, the war was to be prolonged, material and financial difficulties would necessarily make it a limited, though steady and continuous operation.

During 1811 Wellington's irascibility and distrust slowly receded, though to the end Liverpool and the rest of the cabinet showed more understanding of his difficulties than he of theirs. Some of Wellington's accusations were in fact wide of their target. The leakage to the press of military information, of which he complained in February of that year, was discovered by Liverpool to have come not from his own office but from letters sent home by peninsular officers. The remedy for this, he suggested, lay in Wellington's own hands. When Wellington wanted his despatches kept confidential, Liverpool replied that having carefully censored them before publication in the *Gazette*, he had on occasion learned that the complete versions appeared in the Portuguese newspapers. It would be better, he suggested in May, to leave out of his official despatches any matters he did not want published and reserve them for private letters to the minister.[13] All the time he laboured to build up Wellington's confidence. In April he assured him that though the government's means were limited, they were determined not to be diverted from the peninsula to any other object. If they could strike a blow, they would strike it there. Next month he told him explicitly that while his main consideration should be the security of Portugal, he should feel at liberty to undertake any operation he thought fit for that purpose. After Massena's retreat there was a new mood in Parliament and the public of which Wellington could not have been unaware. Nor could he have been indifferent to Liverpool's tribute, in a great parliamentary debate on the war in April 1811, to Wellington's 'transcendent merit' as military commander, and his unequivocal defence of the peninsular campaign as 'the cheapest and easiest mode of defending our own country'.

Liverpool was far from being a sleeping partner in the direction of the war but he sensibly assumed that his task was to advise, encourage and warn the man on the spot rather than impose his own authority from a distance. He was not without constructive ideas. On occasion he suggested the use of small diversionary attacks on the coasts of Biscay and Calabria, and the despatch of selected officers to stimulate local Spanish insurgents. In view of the great drain on the French resources in guarding their long lines of communication, these ideas were neither impracticable nor foolish. Wellington, however, like most commanders, preferred to keep his forces under his own hand and Liverpool was always perfectly ready to give up his ideas when the commander in the field expressed strong objections. His method was to put forward suggestions, ask questions and state difficulties as though to elicit Wellington's views rather than press his own. As a technique it had the double merit of making Wellington clarify his own mind and of providing the secretary of state with reasoned arguments for domestic consumption.

Liverpool also shared Wellington's desire to develop the peninsular war on a larger scale, particularly after the retreat of the French from Torres Vedras in March 1811. One obvious limitation was manpower. Sickness and battle casualties needed a constant flow of fresh drafts merely to keep the army up to strength. In August 1810 there was not a single battalion of infantry in the whole United Kingdom available as additional reinforcements except the Duke of Brunswick's corps in Ireland which Liverpool promised to send to Portugal as soon as it could be relieved. The Corunna disaster left a shortage of seasoned cavalry horses which was still being felt eighteen months later. In the summer of 1811 the War Department had to resort to the unpopular device of dismounting the 12th Dragoons and sending their horses to Portugal for use by Wellington's army.[14] Nevertheless, the hard work of the department in 1810 had a measurable effect. In January 1811 the nominal total of the army in the peninsula had been raised to 48,000. It was little enough in comparison to the French but substantially more than the original plan for a force of 30,000 bayonets (in the contemporary phrase) which with officers and supporting arms meant in effect a total of something like 40,000. This did not seem a large number when set against the nominal total for the whole British army of over 200,000 regular troops. Half of these, however, were locked up in overseas colonies; a quarter, including most of the elderly and unfit, were engaged in garrison and training duties in Britain and Ireland. Recruiting was bringing in so few men that the strength of the army by 1810 was actually falling at the rate of 8,000 a year. As Dundas, the commander-in-chief, pointed out in that year, strong legislative action was needed to prevent a further decline. Liverpool's response was to devise a measure allowing up to 10,000 militia annually to volunteer for the regular army and receive a bounty of fifteen guineas (about half a year's agricultural wage) for so doing.

The Duke of York, with whom Liverpool had discussions on the manpower problem in the winter of 1811, took the view that no more men could be spared from existing home units and overseas garrisons; any further reinforcements for Wellington would have to come from an actual expansion of the army.[15] Fortunately the militia bill which Liverpool introduced in April 1811 proved a success. That year 11,500 men joined the regular army from the militia; these, together with other British and foreign recruits, added 27,000 troops to the army strength. After the bloody battle of Albuera in May 1811 Liverpool was able to gather reinforcements of 16,000 infantry and cavalry from various sources which were despatched to Wellington between June and October. In all, during Liverpool's period at the War Office some 25,000 additional men were sent out to reinforce the army in the peninsula. Whether that effort could have been greater is arguable. Wellington's elder brother Lord Wellesley was the politician who argued most forcibly that it could. In a minute of May 1811 he declared that the campaign in the peninsula had been conducted 'on an inadequate and imperfect scale'. Liverpool's comment on this was that there had been no limit on the government's exertions except what arose from 'the means of increasing and supplying our armies' and that nobody had put forward any proposals which would enable more to be done than had been done.[16]

Logistics (failure to comprehend which is the snare of the amateur strategist) involved among other things finance. Between Perceval's justifiable concern at the growing cost of the war and Wellington's insatiable demands for gold and silver coinage (treasury notes were useless as currency in the Iberian peninsula) Liverpool's position was not an easy one. For the Treasury the financing and supply of the overseas campaign was the most complicated of all their problems. The machinery for the purpose was exiguous and it was singularly difficult to obtain either reliable estimates beforehand or accurate accounting afterwards. Wellington's original estimate for the cost of his army proved a gross under-statement. Expenditure jumped in 1810 from £3 to £6 million and in 1811 to nearly £9 million: a figure three times that on which the government had originally based its calculations. Little wonder that Liverpool in February 1811 had to convey the view of Perceval and the Treasury that it would be virtually impossible to undertake financial responsibility indefinitely for both Wellington's force of 50,000 and another 40,000 Portuguese troops. Neverthe-less, while the Treasury extended its desperate search for silver dollars (the preferred currency in Spain) as far afield as Mexico and China, Liverpool continued his efforts to persuade Wellington that bills of exchange drawn on London could equally well be used. In this he was clearly right; £5 million of the total peninsular expenditure of £6 million in 1810, and £8½ million of the £9 million spent in 1811, were raised by bills.[17]

Perceval's government in fact had made and was making prodigious efforts to keep the war going. As time passed Wellington was increasingly ready to recognise the debt he owed to the ministers in London. If they were fortunate in finding in him the successful general who had eluded all previous administrations, the credit was theirs for supporting him morally and materially to the limit of their powers. In the combination of Wellington, Perceval, Liverpool and Bathurst (his successor at the War Department) the country at last secured an efficient and single-minded direction of the war. By the winter of 1811/12 it was becoming clear to the British public, even to the parliamentary opposition, that the war in the peninsula, so far from being a useless diversion likely to end in defeat and disaster, constituted a safe and effective means of bringing unrelenting pressure to bear on Napoleon's European empire. To that extent the political basis of Perceval's government was marginally strengthened.

In the summer of 1811 there was still no assurance on what was going to happen when the restrictions on the Regency expired. At most there was a growing feeling that perhaps after all the Regent might not dismiss his existing ministers. He himself gave no clear indication of his intentions either by words or actions; and his equivocal behaviour, while probably no more than the device of a lazy and uncourageous man to delay an awkward decision, only prolonged the uncertainty. Having dined with the opposition and entertained them in return, for example, he discomfited the pundits of Brooks's Club by dining with Camden, Perceval and Liverpool in succession during the course of July. He seemed to be getting on well with his ministers and they, as duty and interest both dictated, did their best to please. Liverpool, for example, was careful to supply him with copies of Wellington's more important despatches, supplemented when necessary by extracts from his private letters; and sometimes took the trouble to wait on the Prince personally with the more confidential documents. The ministers found the Regent dilatory and unbusinesslike compared with his father; but apart from the ever-present problem of the Prince's debts, there was considerable agreement between them on public issues and the conduct of the war. As he became accustomed to dealing with them his natural indolence ensured that any original thought he may have entertained of changing the government was reduced to a vague inclination to add to its solidity and pay a sentimental debt to his Foxite past by bringing in a few of the more prominent men in opposition. Grey and Grenville, who had unsuccessfully signalled to the Prince in January their readiness to take office, were by the autumn completely disillusioned. Without compelling political ambitions of their own, they were now more concerned with preserving their credit in the eyes of the public than with any serious expectation that they would be called upon to form a ministry.

For Lord Wellesley, on the other hand, the opportunity seemed ripe to make his own bid for power. With the authoritarian outlook instilled by his Indian career and an elevated notion of his own public value, he found membership of Perceval's workaday and equalitarian cabinet somewhat distasteful. His political conceit and literary vanity were piqued by his colleagues' comments on his diplomatic despatches and their occasional insistence on emendations; but his fundamental grievance was that he did not possess the weight in the government which he assumed he would have when he entered the cabinet. He complained loftily that he had imagined he was joining a cabinet of statesmen but found himself among a set of critics.[18] His particular dislike was for Perceval; but Liverpool, a steady supporter of the Prime Minister against his patrician Foreign Secretary, had little patience with Wellesley's unwillingness to accept normal cabinet discipline. He told Wellington that his brother had not attended half the cabinets held since he entered the ministry and mixed very little with his colleagues. 'Government through a cabinet,' he observed characteristically, 'is necessarily a Government *inter pares* in which every man must expect to have his opinions and despatches canvassed.'[19] Official reticence prevented him from adding, as he might have done, that Wellesley's recent behaviour in siding with the Prince Regent against his own colleagues in the acrimonious matter of the arrangements for the Civil List and royal household had exasperated the whole cabinet.

On 17 January 1812 Wellesley sent in his resignation or, more accurately, intimated to Bathurst his intention to resign. Meetings between him, the Prime Minister, the Lord Chancellor and Liverpool at Carlton House failed to resolve the dispute. Wellesley then appealed directly to the Prince Regent to mediate: a disruptive device promptly rejected by the cabinet. Perceval told the Prince that Wellesley's resignation must be accepted and asked permission to approach Sidmouth and Castlereagh. Something approaching deadlock now ensued. The Prince was critical of Perceval's potential recruits, for the moment shelved Wellesley's resignation, and adopted a frigid attitude towards the Prime Minister. Castlereagh when approached was disinclined to come in as a stopgap for Wellesley and doubted whether even an alliance with Sidmouth would bring enough strength to the ministry. It was the old story: most leading politicians were ready to criticise; few ready to assist.

Wellesley and Canning were now confident that they could construct a central coalition which, while displacing Perceval, would relieve the Prince of the need to resort to the Foxite whigs. Their plan envisaged the return of Castlereagh to a cabinet post but with a peerage, thereby conveniently freeing the House of Commons leadership for Canning; and the retention of Liverpool as working manager of the House of Lords under the capricious suzerainty of Wellesley. 'I should wish of all things to have Jink,' Canning observed complacently to his aristocratic ally, 'as I think him an able and honourable man, and think too that he acted with peculiar fairness in all the affair of 1809.' Time and circumstance had apparently obliterated the petulant opinions about his old friend which he had expressed to Pitt in 1805. Their illusions of grandeur were soon shattered. Unpredictable – or as more jaundiced politicians put it – unreliable as ever, the Regent chose this moment to authorise negotiations, through his brother the Duke of York, with the two Gs. When those suspicious and stiff-necked peers contemptuously rejected his overtures, the offended Prince sent for Perceval, told him he was to continue as prime minister and authorised him to make what official arrangements he deemed necessary.

Even so, the crisis was not over yet. On 17 February Lord Wellesley once more saw the Prince, offering this time to serve with Perceval but not under him, and claiming that he alone could bring both Canning and Castlereagh back into the government. When the outraged cabinet heard of this latest manoeuvre they agreed unanimously that Wellesley's resignation must now be positively accepted and that none of them would continue in office if he remained in the government. It was the climax of months of political uncertainty and the Regent bowed to the cabinet's ultimatum. Next day he accepted Wellesley's resignation. The Prime Minister's courage and the cabinet's loyalty had in effect enabled the ministers to impose their will on the Prince at the outset of his full regency. For the future everything depended on Perceval in the Commons and Wellington in Spain. The Prince, relieved at last from any royal responsibilities, indulged himself with fretful criticisms. He grumbled to the Archbishop of York that he would be left with a very weak government. All his old friends had cruelly deserted him; he did not care for Perceval or Sidmouth; Canning, though 'most useful and brilliant in the House of Commons' was 'insincere and intriguing'. In fact, 'he has now only Lord Liverpool'.[20]

In reality Perceval had already taken steps to strengthen the administration. Yorke and Camden had indicated their readiness to retire, and a number of smaller posts were also at his disposal. Sidmouth consented to come back as President of the Council in place of Camden and brought with him Buckinghamshire and Bragge Bathurst; a price reluctantly paid by the cabinet as the only means of securing the Addington party. Castlereagh, the other notable capture, with some hesitation took Wellesley's vacant place at the Foreign Office where Liverpool was temporarily in charge. Plumer Ward saw him there on 22 February, busy interviewing all the foreign ministers still accredited to the British government, namely four: a circumstance which moved Ward to reflect on the grand spectacle of England defying almost the entire continent.[21] Though its duties had lightened, however, Liverpool himself had no desire for a move to the Foreign Office and it is unlikely that the cabinet wanted him to shift. Mulgrave in fact had told Ward only the day before that 'Lord Liverpool was too good a War Secretary to be spared there'. After two and a half years of growing experience, with Wellington at that moment breaking into Spain through the frontier fortresses of Ciudad Rodrigo and Badajoz, he had every reason for staying in a department which at that stage in the war was of more consequence than the other two secretaryships. On 16 February he wrote to Perceval that while he had only reluctantly accepted the post in 1809, the objections to his leaving it were now insuperable, involving as they did 'a great degree of personal awkwardness to myself' and possible prejudice to the military operations in the peninsula. It was a firm letter; though it is conceivable that it was written to strengthen Perceval's hand if Castlereagh needed persuasion to relinquish any claim to his old office.[22]

The reorganisation of the cabinet came none too soon for the parliamentary fortunes of the administration. The early part of the 1812 session brought difficult debates for the government on Catholic claims and the unpopular Orders in Council. The rigid line taken by Perceval on both issues disconcerted some of his friends and fortified many of his enemies. The Catholic question had been alleged as a reason for the difficulties felt by Grey, Grenville, Wellesley and Canning in working with him; and the severe provisions of the Orders in Council had come under sharp attack both from the opposition in Parliament and from many manufacturers in the country. They were, it was argued with some plausibility, responsible for the distress in the industrial areas which had already produced the first wave of Luddite riots, as well as for steadily worsening relations with the United States, Britain's best customer. The debates on these issues between February and April produced only marginally satisfactory majorities for the government. The continued flood of petitions against the Orders in Council, in fact, allowed the young radical barrister Henry Brougham at the end of April to obtain an enquiry by a committee of the whole house. Then the unpredictable, the almost unimaginable, happened. On 11 May, on his way to an examination of witnesses before the committee, Perceval was shot dead in the lobby of the House of Commons. The assassin was a discharged bankrupt who had unsuccessfully sought redress from the Prime Minister for a five-year imprisonment for debt he had endured in a Russian gaol. A single pistol bullet, entering '3 inches above the left pap' (an anatomical detail noted by Nollekens the sculptor who took a plaster cast of the dead statesman's face),[23] once more plunged the political direction of the country into disarray at the height of the struggle against the greatest military opponent in its history.

Perceval's death was a stunning blow, even if, in the minds of the public and most MPs, the seriousness of the loss was enhanced by the brutality of the act. The first instinct of the Regent, in an audience with Liverpool and Eldon the same day, was to express the hope that it was not the intention of the government to abandon him. When the cabinet met to consider their future, however, of its twelve members only the hardbitten Lord Westmorland returned a positive Yes to the question whether they could carry on without either the two Gs, Wellesley, or Canning. Eldon, with less assurance, held that it might be possible. Of the others five thought it either impossible or at best extremely doubtful; five, including Liverpool, Castlereagh and Sidmouth, doubtful but not desperate. They were all unanimous in declining to serve under Wellesley; unanimous again in agreeing to serve under any of their number whom the Regent might select; but divided on the final issue of authorising overtures to Wellesley and Canning. Castlereagh said ominously that while not wishing to be an obstacle, he would have to reserve his freedom of action. It was generally felt, however, that their prospects of retaining public support would be better if they could demonstrate that fair offers had been made to some at least of the four whose names had been under discussion. On 16 May Perceval's body was buried in the Egmont family vault at Charlton in Kent; the pall-bearers were four of his closest political allies – Liverpool, Eldon, Harrowby and Ryder. By the time these ministers took their seats in the mourning coach which carried them back to Downing Street, it had probably been settled by the cabinet that Liverpool was to be head of the government, Castlereagh Leader of the House of Commons, and offers made to Wellesley and Canning.[24]

Most ministers thought, and perhaps some hoped, that on this basis the offers would not be accepted. In that case they were prepared to carry on the government by themselves. If this proved impossible, the alternative for the Regent would have to be Grenville and Grey. With the Regent's approval Liverpool called on Canning and Wellesley the day after Perceval's funeral. Apart from one question about Catholic relief, Canning reserved comment until he could consult his friends. Wellesley, more grandly, catechised Liverpool on a number of points – the Catholic question, the war in the peninsula, the retention of Sidmouth, and the possibility of approaches to other politicians. It made little difference. The following day replies came from both declining to serve; Canning on the sole ground of the government's opposition to further Catholic relief, Wellesley on a wider range of disagreements with the existing ministers.

While the government felt that they had now disposed of the issue, the country and the House of Commons were less happy. The cabinet's gesture to public opinion had seemed too quick and too contrived. When it became known that no ministerial changes were to take place, Walter, the proprietor of *The Times*, hesitated at supporting 'a body of men so critically situated, and so doubtful of national support'.[25] Within twenty-four hours his journalistic sense was vindicated. On 21 May the House of Commons carried by 174 votes to 170 a motion proposed by Stuart Wortley for an address to the Regent asking him to appoint 'a strong and efficient administration'. It was a disconcerting defeat for the government, the worse for being slightly fortuitous. The division had taken place in a small House and some half a dozen government MPs had been momentarily absent. Wortley himself, a backbencher who usually supported the government and had formerly opposed Catholic claims, had put forward his motion mainly because he thought the time had come for concessions to be made on that issue. An infrequent speaker, he had not even troubled to arrange for the motion to be supported. It was seconded, in fact, by an opposition member, his Yorkshire neighbour Lord Milton. What was particularly stinging to the Liverpools was that Wortley was their nephew by marriage, his wife being the only child of Lady Erne. He had informed Liverpool of his intention; but this did little to allay the hurt felt by his relatives. Louisa promptly cancelled a social engagement she had in order to avoid a meeting with her niece; and Lady Erne, according to her sister Elizabeth, now Duchess of Devonshire, 'was so fretted and vexed that she went back to

Hampton Court'.[26] The damage was done, however, and the cabinet had no choice but to tender their resignations to the Regent and request him to take such measures as seemed necessary to meet the sense of the Commons' resolution.

The Prince was in no mood to expose himself once more to the tedium and occasional humiliation of a personal intervention to construct a new administration. Instead he asked Wellesley to discover whether it would be possible to form a government from the existing ministers reinforced by the Grenville-Grey party. Wellesley delegated to Canning the task of approaching the ministers while he negotiated with the two Gs. Accordingly on 23 May Canning wrote to Liverpool and, curiously, also to Melville (perhaps because of his Catholic sympathies and Scottish electoral influence), inviting them to discuss a coalition on the basis already agreed between himself and Wellesley of a final settlement of the Catholic question and a more vigorous prosecution of the war in Spain. As a formula for political union it was something of an oddity. The first stipulation was calculated to alienate half the cabinet; the second both Grenville and Grey. Having listened to Canning's arguments, Liverpool conferred with his colleagues and the same day returned a brief and chilly answer. The cabinet, he wrote, saw no point in discussing principles of policy since they declined to become members of any administration formed by Wellesley. The feeling against their ex-colleague had in fact grown even harder because of the publication in *The Times* of 20 May of a statement by Lord Wellesley not only justifying his resignation but attacking the character of the dead prime minister and the general competence of his colleagues. Though the document was printed without his permission, its authenticity was never challenged and, coming when it did, might well (as the ministers believed) have contributed to the outcome of the Commons' vote next day on the Wortley motion. Liverpool made an unmistakable reference to this fresh cause of offence when, in answer to an appeal by Canning to be more conciliatory, he wrote once more on 24 May to reiterate his unwillingness to serve under Wellesley or discuss policy.

Displeased by this peremptory refusal, the Prince demanded further explanations. On 27 May, therefore, having held a cabinet to discuss the issue, Liverpool sent the Prince a formal minute of their conclusion that no beneficial result could be expected from any attempt at a union with Wellesley and Canning. When requested, with the rest of his colleagues, to put his individual reasons on paper, he wrote the next day that his objections were two: his disagreement with them on the Catholic question and his conviction that the advantages of securing their services would be counterbalanced by loss of support 'in other quarters no less important' by which he meant (as the letters of the other ministers made clear) Castlereagh and probably also Sidmouth. Since the two Gs themselves returned discouraging answers to Wellesley this first design for a 'broad-bottom administration' of the best men in all parties (constantly advocated by the well-meaning and as constantly proved unworkable in practice) collapsed within a week. The Prince then commissioned Lord Wellesley, for whom he had a high if somewhat sentimental regard, to form an administration himself. When he met with yet another rebuff from Grenville and Grey, the Prince transferred the somewhat shop-soiled commission to the even less convincing figure of his old friend and favourite, Lord Moira. Meanwhile the Perceval ministers continued in office simply as caretakers. On 3 June, in response to a question from the Duke of Norfolk in the House of Lords, Liverpool confirmed that he was still in his old post but only until the Regent signified his pleasure as to other arrangements.

Though Moira, for form's sake, conducted a polite but meaningless exchange with the two Gs, the real intention of himself and the Prince was to isolate those two aristocratic politicians and draw the main body of the Foxite whigs into a coalition with some of the available Pittites. All that emerged from his activities, however, was a shadowy sketch of an administration under the nominal leadership of Moira, the professional soldier, with Canning as First Lord of the Treasury and Leader of the House of Commons, and other Pittites like Melville, Leveson Gower, Wellesley Pole (Lord Wellesley's less distinguished younger brother), Huskisson and Arbuthnot making up the rest of the ministerial team. If this was in fact the only alternative to Grey and Grenville, Liverpool was prepared to support it, though not to participate in it; and he took care to convey this assurance to Moira. To evict the existing ministry, however, simply to put into office a kind of reserve team of Pittites seemed a curious response to the House of Commons' request for a stronger and more effective administration. The Prince, who could display on occasion sound Hanoverian commonsense, saw the absurdity of it. When Moira finally threw up his commission, the Prince is said to have observed, on looking at the list of his intended appointments, 'you see, my dear Moira, they are chiefly Pittites, so the best way is to make it up with the present men, and you may settle it all with Eldon and Liverpool'.[27] Eighteen days of uncertainty ended on 8 June when the Prince finally appointed Liverpool Prime Minister and First Lord of the Treasury with authority to complete all necessary ministerial arrangements.[28]

It was exactly four weeks since Perceval's death and the cabinet had been living in a state of crisis virtually the whole time. Liverpool's immediate task was twofold: to reorganise and if possible strengthen his ministry and to steer it away from the twin rocks towards which Perceval's policy had been taking it in the early part of the session. On the day after he took office he called a meeting of government officials and supporters at his house at which he announced the intention of the ministry not to propose or oppose the question of Catholic relief as a government but to leave all their members free to act as individuals whenever the issue came up in Parliament.[29] It was a policy of expediency and improvisation; a policy which was to have its critics and lead to internal difficulties; but a policy which in 1812 was perhaps the only way of establishing cabinet unity, postponing a difficult decision and, more immediately, preventing a renewal of Stuart Wortley's motion. Like many other temporary expedients it was to last longer than any of its authors could have anticipated: for sixteen years, in fact, during which the attitude it enshrined became one of the fixed principles of Liverpool's cabinet. The same month, on 24 June, the Orders in Council were revoked: a pacific gesture which, though the cabinet did not know it, was already too late. Five days earlier, in response to a Congressional motion, the United States President had declared war.

The rest of Liverpool's attention was devoted to men rather than measures. He had been given several weeks in which to consider the problems and it is evident that he had made up his mind on the more important offices. When he met his colleagues on his return from the Prince Regent, his first words were to Sidmouth – 'you must take the Home Department, Lord Sidmouth – it will be everything to me'.[30] It was a flattering compliment to the touchy ex-prime minister who had been so bitterly offended with him seven years earlier; it was also a sound appointment. Sidmouth wanted more active employment and was at his best in an office where diligence, integrity and courage were needed rather than flair or intelligence. From a narrower point of view it installed a stout Protestant in an office which had ultimate responsibility for Ireland and for a wide area of patronage. It was also a senior post at which Sidmouth could not cavil, though with the Prime Minister in the House of Lords, it did not carry with it the leadership of that house. Flanked as it was by the Chancellor-ship of the Exchequer for Vansittart and the Duchy of Lancaster for Bragge, the old Sidmouth connection had no grounds for complaint. For the rest the sound and sensible Lord Bathurst was moved from the Board of Trade to the War Department and Harrowby replaced Sidmouth as Lord President of the Council.

The changes were not dramatic; but they resulted in as good a distribution of offices as was possible with the material Liverpool had at his disposal. Whether it would be good enough to weather the storms ahead remained to be seen. 'You have undertaken a most gigantic task,' Wellington wrote laconically on the eve of his own risky advance into Spain, 'and I don't know how you will get through it. . . . However, there is nothing like trying, and I can assure your Lordship that I shall be happy if I can be of any use to you in any way.'[31] The last great test of the session came at the end of June and the beginning of July when Canning in the Commons and Wellesley in the Lords moved that Parliament should take Catholic claims into consideration early in the follow-ing session. Carried by a decisive majority of 129 in the lower and only defeated in the upper house by one vote, it at least put off for six months another debate on that disruptive issue.

Before the session ended Liverpool was quietly able to dispose of a further religious issue which had promised to become a political and electoral liability. In 1811 Sidmouth, as a private member, made a well-intentioned but unfor-tunate attempt to pass a law defining more precisely the status and qualifica-tions of dissenting ministers. The Methodists, still only separating and not yet separated from the Established Church, were alarmed both by the threat to their ministers and by the prospect of being legally registered as dissenters. Perceval had already been preparing a new law to allay the widespread dismay and opposition in the country among classes who, he was convinced, were politically loyal and socially conservative. Liverpool inherited his task. He had shared Perceval's dislike of Sidmouth's bill, not least because he felt that it might force English dissenters into an alliance with the Roman Catholics. In collaboration with Thomas Allan, the influential London Methodist solicitor, a 'new toleration bill' was drafted which not only quietened Methodist fears but gave the main body of English dissenters relief from various ancient legal restrictions to which they had long objected. In private conversations with the Archbishop of Canterbury and other bishops Liverpool was able to persuade them that the undefined position of the Methodists, who assented to most of the doctrines of the Church of England and some parts of its discipline, was more of an advantage than an injury to the Establishment. On a more mundane level Liverpool's 1812 Act was not without its political benefits. It broke the whig monopoly of posing as the 'friends of Dissent' and it reinforced the feeling of the Methodists that a continuation of their privileges was closely connected with their political loyalty and dissociation from political radicalism. Electorally it was no bad thing for the new prime minister to be hailed by dissenters as the author of the most generous measure of toleration passed in England since the Revolution.[32]

Before the long session of 1812 ended, Liverpool made one more attempt to bring Canning back into the ministerial fold. Of the three cabinet members in the House of Commons, Castlereagh (whatever Sidmouth might have said) was not a good speaker, except on the defensive; Vansittart and Bragge Bathurst even worse. The need for at least one good debater was obvious; and both Castlereagh and Sidmouth were ready for a reconciliation with Canning. Liverpool's negotiations, by letter and private talks, went on for ten days, from 17 to 27 July. Canning was offered the Foreign Office or as possible alternatives the War or Home Departments. The sticking point was always Canning's jealous refusal to accept the degree of superiority implied by Castlereagh's position as Leader of the House of Commons. On that point Liverpool declined to give way. His courteous and patient if perhaps unconvincing explanation that the title simply indicated responsibility for the management of the House of Commons rather than any precedence over other ministers, failed to remove Canning's objections. The more he was offered, the more he seemed to be raising his price. In the end Castlereagh, who had been perfectly willing to hand over the Foreign Office, himself began to grow suspicious. Led on by foolish friends such as Leveson Gower, Canning pushed his pretensions beyond all reason and in so doing revived the old distrust of his character and ambitions that went back as far as 1801. His final refusal came on 27 July and the only consolation for the Prime Minister was that he had made fair offers to Canning and it was not his fault that they had failed. He wrote to Wellington on 19 August:

I have had therefore no resource but to bring forward the most promising of the young men, and the fate of the government in the House of Commons in another session will depend very much on their exertions. I should be most happy if I could see a second Pitt arise amongst them, and would most willingly resign the government into his hands, for I am fully aware of the importance of the minister being, if possible, in the House of Commons.[33]

Young men of Pitt's precocity do not occur in every generation; but among the promising junior politicians promoted or given office for the first time that autumn were two future prime ministers (Peel and Robinson) and a future cabinet minister (Vesey Fitzgerald).

One other resource was left to Liverpool. Since the last general election there had been three prime ministers; for practical purposes two monarchs; and what had been virtually a vote of no confidence. There were ample grounds for seeking to strengthen the new administration's position in Parliament through a fresh appeal to the electorate, and the autumn of 1812 seemed a propitious moment. Ireland was quiet; the harvest was good; in Spain Wellington's victory over Marmont at Salamanca had enabled him to enter Madrid and raise the siege of Cadiz. 'In short, the prospect in the Peninsula was never so brilliant,' Liverpool wrote in September to his late civil under-secretary at the War Office, Robert Peel, now Chief Secretary in Dublin. At the end of the month, to the surprise of the political world, Parliament was dissolved. Despite the limitations on government influence imposed by the recent Curwen's Act against the purchase of seats (which Liverpool had in fact supported), the result of the general election justified the Prime Minister's decision. With many MPs of independent or fluctuating allegiance, exact calculations of strength were impossible; but the most conservative estimate furnished to him by his experts in November suggested that both the extreme radicals and the Foxite opposition had lost ground and that the ministers had improved their position by more than thirty seats in England and one or two in Ireland. It was not, however, the official opposition which posed the greatest threat. As Liverpool expressed it at the start of November,

Our danger is not from Opposition, but evidently from the third parties headed by Lord Wellesley and Canning, who will represent themselves as holding the same opinions as we do on all popular topics, who will say that they have as much right to be considered as the successors of Mr Pitt's party as ourselves, and whose object will consequently be to detach as many of our friends as possible. The practical question in the House of Commons for the next session will be, who are the true Demetriuses? and on the issue of that question the fate of the Administration will in a great measure depend.[34]

If, as some suspected, the dissolution had been intended primarily to weaken the third party, government could also take some comfort on this account. Though Wellesley had gained some seats, Canning had lost even more and Liverpool estimated that the Canningite group in the new House of Commons would not number more than twenty, or at most, twenty-five. In the event, the solid strength of the Canningites in 1813 proved to be never more than twelve.

What was to be of incalculable importance in the new Parliament was the progress of the war in Spain. Already the victory at Salamanca in July, which earned Wellington a marquessate, had enabled the government to carry £2 million of taxes through Parliament with little opposition. 'You have made the army,' Liverpool wrote to him in August, 'as popular as the navy': and the ministers were duly grateful. To support Wellington in his new dignity Liverpool decided to propose a parliamentary grant of £100,000. 'I know,' he wrote to Bathurst the same month, 'that at this time he is rather poor.' This was not his only mark of appreciation. Before his death Perceval had intended to purchase the Manor of Wellington as a complimentary gift to the new marquess but subsequently the estate of Wellington Park came on the market which Liverpool was able to obtain for the reasonable sum of £20,000. Wellington was not insensitive to these attentions. Perceval and Liverpool, he felt, had done the handsome thing in a handsome manner.[35] His early misgivings over the departure of Castlereagh from the War Office had long vanished; and, unmoved by his elder brother's political vagaries, he acknowledged a genuine obligation to the ministers, particularly Liverpool, Bathurst and Castlereagh, who had given him their confidence and supported him so stoutly. Perceval's replacement by Liverpool had meant not only a continuation but an intensification of the war effort and Treasury restraints on expenditure were loosened still further. In the autumn of 1812 the government, overriding the protests of the directors, requisitioned £100,000 of gold coin from the Bank of England and told them that this was only a first instalment. The same year saw the start of secret transactions between Liverpool, Vansittart and Herries (the efficient new Commissary in Chief), and Nathan Rothschild, the British representative of the great international banking family, which resulted in large quantities of gold and silver coin, collected from all over Europe, being conveyed to the British army in Spain, sometimes through France itself. In the last months of 1812 and in 1813 a flood of guineas, Napoleons, dollars and gold bars was pouring into Wellington's coffers.[36]

At a time when Canning was encouraging Wellesley to claim his brother's authority for his attack on the ministers' conduct of the war, Wellington's political loyalty, as well as his military skill, was a priceless asset for the government. It was all the more valuable because the Salamanca campaign of 1812 ended, in a manner distressingly familiar to the British public, in a precipitate and disorderly British retreat to the shelter of Portugal in the face of superior French armies. Lord Wellesley, at the meeting of the new Parliament in November, tried to put the blame for the withdrawal on what he alleged to be the tardy and parsimonious policy of the government. Liverpool's reply was caustic. It was extremely easy, he observed, for the noble lord to sit in his study and think out a desired effort of any given magnitude; but in real life every policy depended on the available resources of the country and the sum of demands made on them. The current operations in the peninsula, he reminded their lordships, were greater than anything that could have been imagined three or four years earlier. In the course of 1812 reinforcements of 20,000 men and 7,000 horses had been sent to Wellington and in June he had under his command a force of 58,000 British troops, exclusive of the Portuguese. A similar attack by Canning in the Commons was repelled by Castlereagh in much the same style; and in neither house did either critic venture to divide.

Liverpool himself, at the end of 1812, was in good spirits. He assured Wellington that the retreat from Burgos and Madrid, despite opposition criticisms, had not weakened the parliamentary position of the government; and he wrote hopefully of plans for the coming campaign. Bathurst had been discussing, in the event of the French being driven from Spain, the possibility of an Italian expedition. Liverpool's strong preference was for an invasion of the south of France; clearly the strategy of the march on Paris still held his allegiance. As always, his chief concern was to elicit Wellington's own opinion. He ended a long letter of 27 October with a modest apology for going into so much detail. 'I have in fact been thinking aloud on them, and I thought there would be no harm in bringing under your consideration those ideas.' What also heartened the government in the autumn of 1812 was Napoleon's invasion of Russia and the prospect that French reinforcements would be going off to eastern Europe which might otherwise have been on their way to Spain. Reporting the hard-fought French victory at Borodino, the Prime Minister observed cheerfully that Napoleon was nearly 800 miles inside Russia with the main Russian army in front of him and formidable Russian forces on either flank. 'What a moment for Austria to strike a blow!' Simultaneously he was telling Cathcart, the British ambassador in Russia, to hold up the example of the Spanish war, the only national conflict in which Bonaparte (it was fashionable among British leaders to use his bourgeois surname) had until then been engaged, and to keep the Russian spirit of resistance alive by the strongest assurances of British interest and support.[37] In December, when the news came of Napoleon's defeat at Smolensk, the guns were ordered to be fired in Hyde Park and the Tower of London to mark the significance of the event for the whole allied cause. For the first time there was a feeling in government circles that the tide had at last turned.

NOTES

1 Fortescue, IX, 332–410.
2 Ibid, 332-3.
3 Yonge, I, 297; WND, VI, 412-13.
4 Wellesley, pp. 258, 277-8.
5 George 3, V, 425-8.
6 WSD, VI, 421.
7 *Memoirs of Sir H.E. Bunbury*, ed. Sir Charles J.F. Bunbury (1868).

8 WSD, VII, 45.

9 Knight, pp. 167-9.

10 Cf. Knight, pp. 76-80.

11 WSD, VI, 493.

12 Ibid, p. 641.

13 WSD, VII, 61, 120.

14 WSD, VI, 567; VII, 119.

15 Knight, pp. 194-8.

16 Ibid, pp. 194, 211; WSD, VII, 167.

17 Knight, pp. 93-4, 119 ff.; see generally Yonge, I, Ch. XI.

18 Ward, I, 429.

19 WSD, VII, 250; Gray, pp. 439-40.

20 Fortescue, X, 220-23. For details of the crisis see P. of W., VIII, 302-16; George 4, I, 2-9; Gray, pp. 444-5; Wellesley, 71-8; Bathurst, pp. 160-61.

21 Ward, I, 428.

22 Gray, p. 448.

23 FD, VII, 84.

24 Walpole, II, 305; Bathurst, p. 173; Twiss, II, 209-12.

25 Croker, I, 38.

26 Foster, p. 369; LWF, I, 184-7.

27 W.S. Sichel, Sheridan (1909), II, 360.

28 For the negotiations see Yonge, I, 79 ff.; George 4, I, 84-109; Wellesley, II, 88 ff.; Memoirs and Correspondence of Marquess Wellesley, ed. R.R. Pearce, three vols (1846), III, 213 ff. A full selection of letters is printed in AR, 1812, 346 ff.

29 Creevey, p. 165.

30 Pellew, III, 78.

31 WSD, VII, 343; Yonge, I, 400.

32 Yonge, I, 433-4; Pellew, III, 62; See also D. Hempton, 'Thomas Allan and Methodist Politics 1800-1840', History, Vol. 67 (1982), pp. 13-31.

33 WSD, VII, 402.

34 Parker, I, 37, 44-5.

35 WSD, VII, 401, 408, 423, 426; Bathurst, p. 195.

36 Herries, I, 76-113; Bathurst, p. 219; Knight, pp. 133-7.

37 Yonge, I, 440-43; WSD, VII, 462 ff.

I have for convenience used the term War Office as well as War Department to indicate what in official contemporary language was the Office of the Secretary of State, Colony and War Department. The 'War-Office' strictly speaking was a small separate office under a junior minister, the secretary-at-war. It seemed pedantic, however, to abstain from a familiar general expression which, like Home Office and Foreign Office (also slightly anachronistic titles), conveys to the non-specialist reader a clearer idea of the status and functions of the department concerned.

CHAPTER VI

Prime Minister and Peace

Few men have come to be prime minister in such a paradoxical way as Lord Liverpool. It is true that for six years he had been one of some half-dozen politicians who were generally considered as possible heads of government. He had been offered the post in 1806; perhaps only his membership of the House of Lords prevented him from succeeding Portland in 1809. He had served in all three secretaryships of state - with debatable success at the Foreign Office; competence at the Home Office; and distinction at the War Office. His gradual ascent to the highest office of all had in retrospect a certain inevitability. Yet the actual circumstances under which he became prime minister in 1812 bore all the marks of accident and improvisation. For over a year the administration had been deprived of real political strength by the widely held conviction that it was only a temporary arrangement. After Perceval's death his post was hawked round among five other independent or opposition politicians. When in the end the Prince Regent turned to Liverpool, it seemed that, far from being a first choice, he was a last resort.

In reality the administration was never so weak as people thought because the Prince was never so interested in making a change as people assumed. He could have cashiered his father's ministers at any time after February 1811; the Regency 'restrictions' were not important enough to have restricted him from doing that. The fact that he did nothing during this first year was significant, though not many observers fully understood its meaning. Only two completely fortuitous and unpredictable events forced the Prince out of his passivity: Perceval's assassination and the Stuart Wortley resolution. Even though he went through the motions of looking for a new ministry, however, there was no urgency in his search; and it was with evident relief that he fell back on the existing ministry when he had done enough to satisfy the House of Commons. Parliament and the public took the hint; and after its momentary disturbance the pattern of politics resumed its customary shape. If the prolonged ministerial crisis of 1811-12 proved anything, as the editor of the *Annual Register* for 1812 sagaciously noted, it was the relative unimportance of political 'parties' and the existence of a 'preponderating mass of power' provided by the influence of the Crown and the authority of the executive government. The old Perceval ministry survived because it was more congenial to the Prince than the possible alternatives; and more efficient than any since 1801.

In turn the strength of Liverpool's position was that he had been the choice of his colleagues and presented by them to the Prince Regent as their preferred leader. The reasons for their choice are not difficult to guess. Divided as the Pittites had become, there was always a central core of men who felt a loyalty to the King and to each other, and were ready to carry on the government of the country within a broad set of conventions agreeable to the monarch. They were a 'party', in the loose contemporary sense of the word, bound less by personal devotion to the memory of Pitt than by an acceptance of the principles embodied by Pitt when he first took office as prime minister in 1783. In that central Pittite group Liverpool had been an influential figure ever since 1801. Unlike Grenville, Canning and Sidmouth, who at different times had sailed off on tacks of their own, he had stayed in the mainstream of the Pittite tradition. He had acted as a consistently conciliatory figure; he was liked and trusted; he was without rancour; his enemies were few. He did not intrigue or often quarrel, he did not ostentatiously aim at power. His father had been over-ambitious for him; and it is hardly possible that he had no ambitions of his own. Yet his modesty, good nature and good sense kept his ambition within bounds. He did not push his claims unduly; he hardly pushed them at all. With what for a professional politician was unusual selflessness, he was always ready to subordinate any interest of his own to the larger needs of the administration which he served. One of his disarming qualities was his loyalty to his leader and his colleagues. A constant sense of the collective nature of government, which Wellesley and Canning so conspicuously lacked, in Liverpool was conspicuously present. To this were added qualities of equanimity and good temper which make a greater difference to a politician's relations with his colleagues and subordinates than the public always appreciates. 'He is one of the best tempered men living,' Charles Long said of him in 1812.[1]

All these things of course would not have been enough had he not possessed other professional virtues. His administrative ability was appreciated mainly by those within the government. His debating talents were more generally recognised, though they received less publicity because he was in the House of Lords. From the outset of his parliamentary career he had enjoyed a reputation as a speaker: some thought it was his principal asset. He made no attempt to rival the florid rhetoric of Grenville or Wellesley whose oratory was in the classical literary tradition that still impressed contemporary parliamentarians. He tried instead to explain, demonstrate, and convince. His was the nineteenth- rather than the eighteenth-century mode of public speaking; but both sides in Parliament were ready enough to acknowledge its effectiveness. Tierney said in 1813 that he thought Lord Liverpool 'one of the most prudent ministers and debaters in Parliament he ever knew, and that he is besides a man in the House of Lords who is ready to turn out in all weathers'.[2] By 1812 time and experience had matured both his talents and his temperament. While he never lost his kindness and courage, the early undue sensitivity and tension was now protected by a strength and calmness of manner which impressed most people who had dealings with him. His modest expressions when taking on the premiership resulted not from any inner diffidence but from a realistic appreciation of the difficulties that lay in front of him. Behind the patience and good temper in fact was a more acute intelligence and a firmer will than was usually suspected. The old influences to which he had deferred in the early part of his career – his political mentor Pitt, the old King, his domineering father – had all gone from the scene. At the age of forty-two, with already half his life spent in politics, his nerve had hardened and his judgement ripened. Above all, he had learned the most valuable lesson that politics has to teach: to see men for what they really are and to know how, with all their faults and weaknesses, they can be used for a common purpose. It was a cautious, solid, unheroic, but experienced man who in 1812 was put by his colleagues in the most responsible position that government had to offer. They would hardly have done so had they not trusted his ability to guide them through the critical time ahead.

With the advent of middle age Liverpool had changed physically as well as mentally from the young Jenkinson who had entered Parliament twenty years earlier. The sharp, angular profile still gave an impression of tension and resolve; but the face and neck had thickened and the scrawny appearance seized on by the first caricaturists had largely disappeared; though, after the manner of their tribe, the cartoonists were slow to abandon the pictorial image they had made popular. Those who actually met him found a plain, ungraceful figure with a face which, though occasionally lit up by a pleasant smile, was heavy and thoughtful in repose. The traditional inelegance of the Jenkinsons never left him. He had a clumsy way of standing and his clothes, to a woman's eye at least, generally looked untidy. Unlike his father he did not affect the *haut ton* and the fashions of the *beau monde* (or *biau monde*, as old Lord Liverpool used to pronounce it). His nature was too simple, his life too busy, his position too secure to need such pretences. The death of his father and the succession to the earldom made a difference to his financial rather than to his social position. In all he had inherited an additional income of about £15,000 a year, a figure which included the rental of the two small estates in Gloucestershire, Hawkesbury and Eastwood.

There had been few other claims to reduce the paternal fortune he acquired. His stepmother, the dowager countess, was left a meagre annuity of £700. This, even with the jointure of £1,000 per annum from her first marriage, hardly seemed sufficient in an inflationary age for an earl's relict. Liverpool added another £500 annually to bring her income up to the more respectable figure of £2,200 a year. His half-brother Cecil needed no such additional support even though he had been left an equally modest legacy of only £1,000 per annum. He was not, however, without resources of his own. His varied if slightly dilettante career, which had already included several years as a mere boy in the Royal Navy, undergraduate life at Oxford and a spell as under-secretary at the Home Office under his brother, was only to end with his appointment as Lord Steward to Queen Victoria in the 1840s. In 1804 he had secured a diplomatic appointment with the British legation in Vienna where, undeterred by any notions of diplomatic neutrality, he had fought at Austerlitz as a volunteer with the Austrian army. In 1807, while he was still abroad, he had inherited the Pitchford estate. The last two Ottleys had died in quick succession at the beginning of that year and in Adam Ottley's will Cecil had been finally named as heir to the family property.

Hawkesbury and his wife had already reconciled themselves to the certainty that they would never become the owners of what is still one of the oldest of the black-and-white half-timbered manor houses of Shropshire, and perhaps the loveliest. In 1807, however, they were less in need of either the Hall or the Pitchford rent-roll than when the prospect of acquiring them had first delu-sively opened up. As Louisa, nobly subduing her regrets, explained to her sister in February 1807, about Cecil,

> It is of much more importance to *him* and all circumstances considered is a better arrangement. Lord Hawkesbury feels just the same about it, and we have talk'd it over well. We feel *quite glad* we have not a third country House which we would have felt bound to live at, and which would have made our life something very like a *wandering Arab's*. The estate is rather above £2,000, a very nice provision for Cecil, and what we shall not want; *just now* it would to be sure have set us free from little difficulties – but on the *whole* it will do much more good where it goes. So don't grieve at this apparent disappointment for us, we are really *quite satisfied*. I am particularly pleased at Cecil being call'd home, and to *settle at Home* before his *true English* feelings are spoilt on that *Vile continent*.[3]

As it was, with his official salary and the Wardenship of the Cinque Ports, Hawkesbury's income after his father's death amounted to about £23,000 per annum, which was more than a modest competence even for a peer. The Pitchford estate, if he had received it, would only have been of marginal financial benefit and certainly any prolonged residence in the remoteness of Shropshire would have been out of the question for a busy minister.

More sensibly, one of the first uses to which Liverpool put his new wealth was to improve his house at Coombe. Soane the architect was commissioned to design a library at the dining-room end of the building which considerably lengthened its frontage (and incidentally spoiled its symmetry). Other rooms were still being added in 1817 and a grand new balcony put on the front in 1819. Liverpool also obtained a larger and more permanent home in London. So far he and Louisa had lived in a succession of rented houses in Sackville Street, St James's Square and Charles Street. In 1809, however, he took a long lease of Fife House, a Crown property in Whitehall near Old Scotland Yard, into which he and his wife moved early in 1810.[4] When he became prime minister two years later, he chose not to occupy 10 Downing Street, preferring to use Fife House as his official place of business.

The three houses round which their existence now rotated – Fife House during the session, Coombe in the summer, and Walmer Castle in the autumn – provided more than adequate accommodation for their needs. No children had been born to Louisa. In 1812, at the age of forty-five, she must have given up all hope of becoming a mother, though earlier perhaps, to judge from a crude joke of Lord Holland,[5] there may have been some false pregnancies, or at least false reports of pregnancies. As it was, the Liverpools were always able to place one or other of their houses at the disposal of relatives or friends. When Leveson Gower married the Duke of Devonshire's daughter Harriet at Christmas 1809, Liverpool allowed them the use of Walmer for their honeymoon. Walmer was also lent to his favourite sister-in-law the Duchess Elizabeth when the Duke's death in 1811 obliged her to leave Devonshire House which had been her home for thirty years. Later that year, tired perhaps of a solitary existence overlooking the rough waters of the English Channel, she came to stay with them at Coombe for a while before moving into a house of her own at Richmond.

It was partly, perhaps, because Louisa had no children of her own to absorb her energies and emotions that she was so unusually active in the charitable work to which her evangelical outlook naturally inclined her. Her early training had clearly left its mark. Indeed, as she grew older, her religious utterances increasingly resembled those of her dead mother. Describing to Lady Erne in 1807, for instance, her efforts to relieve the pains of a dying cottager, she added 'but above all, I am most thankful for having been instrumental in bringing her poor ignorant mind to a sense of religious duty and religious comfort'. Criticising the Duchess of Richmond's worldliness in 1803, she concluded piously, 'alas, how far from her is that amiable Christian Humility which we are told is so important to us!' Even more sanctimonious was her comment in 1809 on two aristocratic families of her acquaintance who had both lost a son in the wreck of a troop transport off Cornwall. 'They are just the sort of prosperous people that will suffer peculiarly from such a blow, but it may be wholesome discipline.' This kind of moralising, however, was not uncommon in the age of Wilberforce and Hannah More. In Louisa's case it was redeemed by her genuine sympathy for the poor and unhappy. The following year, when thanking Lady Erne for her assistance in helping an old couple who had fallen on hard times, she burst out with honest feeling: 'But oh, my Dear Sister, what a number there are who I *can not* assist! who are sick and destitute and suffering, whilst I am surrounded with comforts far far beyond my deserts. If I ever had a doubt of a Future State, I think this reflection would convince me.'[6] Among their many charitable acts the Liverpools virtually adopted some of the Boothby children, the progeny of Liverpool's cousin, Fanny Jenkinson, who in 1805 had married William Boothby, the son and heir of an apparently impecunious Derbyshire baronet. In 1815–16 Liverpool was paying the fees for 'Master Boothby' at a boarding school at East Sheen. Later the whole family seem to have taken up residence at Coombe and Fife House, to the astonishment of worldly political acquaintances who encountered them there.

Louisa's childlessness may also account for the maternal note which comes out in the references in her correspondence with her sister to her 'dearest Lord Hawkesbury', her 'poor fagg'd Lord Warden'. They were nearly always together; few of their letters to each other exist because they were hardly ever separated. When duty called him away, she moped and fretted. Left alone at Walmer in September 1807 when her husband was unexpectedly summoned to a cabinet meeting, 'I feel grudging myself every breeze of this balmy air because Lord Warden is not here to share it.' Much as she enjoyed the importance of his position – the dinners, the receptions, the official guests, the atmosphere of confidentiality and excitement, the public speeches and private discussions – her quick emotional nature was easily exhausted by the strain of social functions, crowded rooms and late nights. She was not strong physically and suffered much from colds, headaches, feverishness and 'spasms'. As early as 1801 she was dosing herself with saline draughts and what she called 'poppies' (presumably an extract or tincture of opium) to help her sleep after an unusually active day. That she was something of a hypochondriac is evident; but it is conceivable that her constant talk of ill-health concealed from others how ill in reality she often was.[7]

For Liverpool, a man with few close male friends, her artless affection was a constant solace among the frictions and fatigue of a public career. Many people noted the unusually close relationship between them. In 1816 Lawrence the painter mentioned to his fellow-academician Farington the great fondness they showed to each other. He thought Liverpool communicated much information to her and asked her opinion on many of his letters. His unquestioned devotion to Louisa certainly shielded him from the gossip about marital vagaries which provided so much conversation for modish society and did so much to fortify middle-class distrust of the aristocracy. In the year that saw the collapse of the Portland administration the eminent London surgeon Carlisle opined that Liverpool was the only one of the prominent politicians of the day who had a reputation for respectability; no accusation had ever been brought against him, and there was a general prudence in his conduct. In an age of growing public reaction against corruption and immorality in high places, this was a reputation that stood the Prime Minister in good stead in the wider world which existed outside Carlton House, Parliament, the political clubs, and the fashionable drawing rooms of the West End.[8]

*   *   *   *   *

Liverpool's first full session as Prime Minister, like the proverbial month of March, opened windily and ended in a flat calm. At the start there were awkward debates on the generally deplored outbreak of hostilities with the United States and on the notoriously bad relations between the Princess of Wales and her husband to which with whig encouragement she had chosen to give newspaper publicity. In February 1813 the Privy Council, having examined some of the damaging documents produced in the so-called Delicate Investigation of 1806, upheld the restrictions on the Princess's access to her daughter; but the publicity did more harm to the Prince than to his wife. In the House of Lords an attempt by Wellesley to obtain an enquiry into the conduct of the war in Spain was crushed by Liverpool and Bathurst with contemptuous ease.

Overshadowing all these issues, however, was the long-awaited debate on Catholic disabilities launched by Grattan at the end of February. A majority of the House of Commons supported his preliminary resolutions and in May a bill founded on them was carried in committee. Although, under the new neutrality principle laid down by Liverpool the previous year, the government was not collectively implicated, the Prime Minister was not an indifferent spectator of what was happening in the lower house. The previous October he had told the Speaker that he would resist an enquiry into Catholic claims since an enquiry was in itself tantamount to concession. When Abbot asked what the government would do if an enquiry was forced on it, Liverpool parried by saying that it would be better to allow the supporters of Emancipation to embody their proposals in a bill so that it could be clearly seen what they wanted and what securities they offered. In March 1813, five days after Grattan had won a majority of forty for his motion for a committee, Liverpool sought out the Speaker again. He reiterated his earlier willingness to admit Roman Catholics to all ranks in the army, other than two or three of the very highest posts. He stood firm, however, on his refusal to consent to their admission to Parliament. This, in his view, would either lead to the opening of all high offices of state to Catholics or else create a permanently discontented parliamentary party. The Speaker could have been in no doubt that the head of the administration was as solid as he had ever been in his determination to oppose any further dilution of the principle enshrined in the 1688 settlement of a Protestant king in a Protestant state. The knowledge may not have been without effect. When the crucial vote came on Grattan's amended bill in May, it was lost by four votes in a crowded House after Abbot had delivered a powerful and influential speech against it. For the rest of the session the issue was effectively dead.[9]

The government's own business passed off smoothly. Vansittart's massive budget of £72 million went through with scarcely a dissentient voice; and after Parliament broke up in July, the administration registered another silent success. Canning, who played a leading role in the Catholic debates, had by the summer lost heart and disbanded his little following in the Commons. Liverpool and a few others were willing to take him back into office but the difficulty was to find him a suitable post. Melville was ready to transfer from the Admiralty to accommodate him, but Buckinghamshire refused to give up the Board of Control to Melville. The old followers of Addington had long memories. It was in fact a singularly awkward time to stage a return of the prodigal son; even if all the cabinet (which was clearly not the case) had felt paternally anxious to welcome him. All that Canning secured was the relief of knowing that the Prime Minister was still his friend.

The contented mood at home was a reflection of the startling allied successes on the continent. At the beginning of the year, with the Prussian army about to go over to the Russians as they followed the wreck of the *Grande Armée*, the cabinet decided to assist the war in northern Europe. This they did in a number of ways, by financing Gneisenau's mission to secure Colberg, paying for the German Legion operating with the Russians, and encouraging the intervention of Sweden.[10] Spring saw the entry of Prussia and Sweden into the war. Though Napoleon miraculously organised another army to check his adversaries, Castlereagh's diplomacy, backed by British gold, brought Russia and Austria into a military alliance with Britain, pledged not to make a separate peace. Nevertheless, the armistice signed by Russia and Prussia, and Metternich's diplomatic activities, raised acute and justified British anxieties that the eastern powers were ready to make a settlement with Napoleon that would ignore British interests in Spain and the Netherlands. Wellington's victory at Vitoria on 21 June, which broke the back of French military power in Spain and earned him the rare honour of a field marshal's baton, was therefore of European significance. Copies of the *Gazette* with details of the battle in three languages were sent to northern Europe and special messengers were despatched to the headquarters of the Russian and Prussian armies. If Austria now declared war, Liverpool wrote to Wellington, 'we might really hope to put an end to the tyranny which has been so long oppressing the world, but on this event no reliance can, I fear, be placed'.[11] At home three nights of illumination marked the importance of the victory which no croaking on the part of a few dogmatic whig politicians was able to diminish in the eyes of the British public. In August the eastern powers, joined now by Austria, resumed the offensive and in November the church bells in England rang out to celebrate the great allied victory at Leipzig.

As the end of the war approached, the thoughts of the government increasingly turned to the terms of the peace. Already in November when Parliament met, Liverpool had uttered some thoughts on the diplomatic settlement which, it was hoped, would follow the great military victories to which the speech from the throne had been largely devoted. The war, he said, had changed its character. It had become a war of peoples, Prussia being the most recent example. The policy of the government would be to provide security not only for her friends but for her enemies. He would not consent to any demands on France which went beyond what he himself, in reverse circumstances, would be ready to concede. The present moment was one of noble expectations founded on the cause of European independence.

As a sentiment this perhaps took too little account of the old monarchies of the continent; but at least it put the government on the side of the people against the dynasts. It was an attitude that commended itself to the British public. A general peace would necessarily involve all the great powers and, in the face of Castlereagh's warnings, the cabinet reluctantly refrained from committing itself to that restoration of the Bourbons which had so long been a popular British objective. The desire of the Bourbon princes to join Wellington's army, as it entered southern France, required some thought on the part of the ministers. Wellington seemed in favour of playing the Bourbon card; Bathurst even more so. Liverpool was more cautious and as a result had a couple of difficult interviews with the Comte d'Artois, the French King's brother. In the end, though the Bourbon princes were allowed to go to France (since, as Liverpool pointed out, they could hardly be prevented from doing so), Wellington was instructed not to receive them at his headquarters.[12] The tone of the British press, still more the feeling of the British people, was strongly opposed to leaving Napoleon on the French throne; but the cabinet was ready, for the time being and without much pleasure, to follow Castlereagh's advice. When the Foreign Secretary left for the continent at the end of 1813 the general lines of British policy were clear. France was to be reduced to her old frontiers; Spain and Holland were to be independent. If a satisfactory settlement was made for the rest of Europe, and if the allies were ready to maintain some form of treaty obligation to preserve that settlement, Britain would be ready to return all its colonial conquests except a few of special strategic value. Though Liverpool, to preserve allied unity, was prepared to make peace with Napoleon – if satisfactory terms with such a man could be obtained – he confided to Castlereagh in January 1814 his wish to keep the Bourbon restoration as an alternative and for the moment concealed strategy.[13]

Meanwhile the continued military successes of the allies, the spread of Bourbon feeling in France, and the growing anti-Napoleon fervour in Britain, constituted strong arguments for insisting on a return by France to its ancient territorial limits. 'You can scarcely have an idea,' the Prime Minister wrote to Castlereagh in February, 'how *insane* people in this country are on the subject of any peace with Buonaparte.' The insanity was not confined to the population; it was found in Parliament, at Court, and in the cabinet itself. 'Believe me, it requires every effort of which I am possessed,' he wrote again in March, 'to keep anything like steadiness in our counsels.' His delaying tactics, however, carried Castlereagh safely past the point where the negotiations at Châtillon with the allies might have been endangered. By the time Liverpool finally and apologetically sent instructions not to make peace with Bonaparte, the Châtillon conference had ended and developments in France were pointing to the feasibility of a Bourbon restoration. The issue soon settled itself. In April the guns in Hyde Park boomed out once more to celebrate Napoleon's abdication; and before the end of the month Londoners wearing white cockades turned out in their thousands to greet Louis XVIII on his way from his rural English retreat in Buckinghamshire to the capital of his ancestors.

Liverpool was among the princes, peers, and ambassadors who greeted him in London. Accompanied by Louisa he went down to Dover on 23 April for the embarkation on the Prince Regent's yacht the *Royal Sovereign*. The French

servants arrived late and while her husband talked politics with Pozzo di
Borgo, the Russian minister, Louisa as the only Englishwoman on board had
to act as hostess and chambermaid to the ladies of the French Court. Next day
the yacht sailed for France with Lord and Lady Liverpool at the pier-head
among the cheering crowds to wave them off. So ended what she described as
two 'fatiguing, active' days and an unusual experience which was not only
'most highly Gratifying to my own feelings, but it was pleasing to Lord
Liverpool's and from peculiar circumstances I was *really and truly useful*'.[14] This
was only the start of a summer of rejoicing. In May Liverpool was able to
congratulate Wellington on his dukedom and express a cautious hope that the
exhausted state of Europe, the high reputation British arms had achieved, and
the newly forged friendship between the allies, would together bring about a
lasting peace. In June the Tsar Alexander, the King of Prussia, and (of equal
interest to the English crowds) Marshal Blücher arrived in England to take part
in the festivities. A few days later, at a special ceremony at Carlton House, the
King of Prussia, Liverpool and Castlereagh were invested as Knights of the
Garter: an honour which, in the manner of such things, brought Liverpool a
subsequent bill for £126. 10s. od. in fees and £42. 14s. od. for the insignia. On
a later journey to Oxford the two monarchs were entertained by the Liverpools
at Coombe Wood with a dinner at which the Duchess Elizabeth sat next to the
King and Louisa presumably next to the Tsar.[15]

Before his departure from England the Tsar paid another visit to Coombe
when Elizabeth was again present together with a bevy of nephews and nieces
(children of Lord Bristol) who gazed entranced from the drawing-room window at the Tsar's bearded coachman in his Cossack uniform. During the visit
of the two monarchs general festivities were held all over the country for the
'General Peace'. London was illuminated and vast, orderly crowds paraded
the streets to celebrate the end of the war with which they had lived so long
and made such financial sacrifices to win. In July came a thanksgiving service
at St Paul's, attended by the Regent, Wellington, Blücher, royal dukes, peers
and ministers of state. Later there was a fête at Carlton House where the
short-sighted, neglected Duchess of Wellington walked about with Lord and
Lady Liverpool while her indifferent spouse exhibited himself as guest of
honour in the full glory of his field marshal's uniform, glittering with orders
and decorations.[16]

There were few clouds to mar the brilliance of that victory summer of 1814.
The Princess Caroline did what she could to attract the attention of the visiting
potentates and there was embarrassment when the Tsar manifested a desire to
call on her. The Prince wisely allowed it to be known through Liverpool that
he would place no obstacle in the way of such a visit; but in the end diplomatic
discretion subdued the Tsar's curiosity. Early in August, to the relief of the
Court and the administration, Caroline departed to the continent for what was
generally hoped would be a permanent stay. Her decision was partly in protest
at her exclusion from the thanksgiving celebrations at St Paul's. Nevertheless,

before she left she sent a warning to the Prime Minister through her old friend
Canning that if there was an attempt to use the opportunity of her absence to
procure a divorce, so that the Prince Regent could marry again and provide a
male heir to the throne, thus depriving her daughter Charlotte of the succession, she would instantly return to England to defend her rights. This to
Liverpool seemed a highly fanciful speculation. Writing from Coombe on 5
August he told Canning that he had read her letter 'with no little amusement'.
No assurances of any kind could be given to Caroline; no conditions had been
imposed on her; there was nothing to stop her returning to England at any
time. Her husband could not divorce her without parliamentary authority,
and Parliament would never authorise a divorce except on proof of adultery.
The legal security of her marriage was therefore as safe when she was abroad
as when she was at home – unless, he added drily, the insinuation in her letter
was that 'her conduct is less likely to be correct upon the Continent'. He could
see no reason for Caroline to be alarmed; there was certainly every reason for
the government to feel relieved. It would be good policy, he wrote to Wellington the following month, to make foreign countries agreeable to her so that she
would have no inducement to return.[17]

There were better prospects for amicable relations with the other difficult
individual who also went to the continent in the first autumn of European
peace. Hearing that Canning was to accompany his invalid son to some warmer
climate, Liverpool proposed that he should take up some diplomatic position.
A special embassy to Lisbon to welcome back from Brazil the Prince Regent of
Portugal seemed a suitable appointment. Canning was ready to accept, provided something was done for his parliamentary friends whom he had left
politically stranded. Liverpool generously took over this debt of honour and,
with the Prince in an expansive mood, was able in July to promise a viscountcy
for Leveson Gower and promotion to an earldom for Boringdon. Office was
found for Huskisson as First Commissioner for Woods and Forests (the early
nineteenth-century equivalent of a Ministry of Works), and other posts for
lesser Canningites like Binning and Sturges Bourne. It was with a genuine
sense of gratitude and reassurance that Canning left England with his family
in November. The embassy was clearly a halfway house to high political office.
Privately, in fact, Liverpool had told him that he would be offered the first
cabinet vacancy that came up. It was a magnanimous act; that it was also
politic does not detract from its generosity. Liverpool in 1814 was in almost an
unassailable position compared to 1812. Nothing that had happened, however,
had destroyed his respect for Canning's abilities; and from a wider point of
view the return of the Canningites would mark an important stage in that
reunification of all the Pittites which his father had hoped it would be his
destiny to accomplish.[18]

Liverpool's larger preoccupation in the autumn and winter of 1814 was the
problem of peacemaking on both sides of the Atlantic. The war with America
had run into a stalemate by land and water. It was a war which in Liverpool's

view had never been desired by Britain and which he was anxious to be rid of as soon as reasonable terms could be obtained. Whether what was reasonable would also be popular he did not mind. Negotiations were already under way at Ghent but appeared to be making as little progress as the war which occasioned them. The government's objects were simple: the security of Canada and protection for her Indian allies. By September the Prime Minister was beginning to fear that the limits of British concessions had been reached with still no prospect of a settlement. If the war lasted into 1815, he estimated that it could cost the country between £8 and £10 million. Since Wellington's discouraging opinion was that the American states offered no vulnerable point except New Orleans, which was notoriously the most unhealthy part of the USA, this was a daunting outlook. There was a further disadvantage. A costly war of indefinite duration and uncertain success would be a clog on British diplomacy in Europe at a time when the authority and objectivity which Castlereagh could supply were never more needed.

As the allies turned from the peace treaty with Bourbon France to the reconstruction of Europe, and their negotiating headquarters shifted from Paris and London to Vienna, problems emerged which not only deeply divided the powers but threatened the newly-won peace itself. From being a benevolent spectator, the British government found itself obliged to become an arbiter in the quarrels which split the victorious continental allies after their defeat of Napoleon. It was a task which Castlereagh, going far beyond the original instructions approved by the cabinet, had from the start envisaged for himself. Like his master Pitt, he regarded British and European interests as indivisible and his own role as that of mediator in the Great Power conflicts of which he was already forewarned. In his earlier visit to the continent he had impressed the allied diplomats by his calm courtesy and European outlook. When he travelled to Vienna in September 1814 it was to assume a role in the councils of Europe which could never have been predicted for the unpopular and suspect parliamentary politician of some five years earlier. Castlereagh's achievement at the Congress of Vienna, however, would scarcely have been possible if he had not had in London a prime minister who supported him to the limit of his powers.

When Castlereagh was out of the country the daily superintendence of the Foreign Office was taken over by Lord Bathurst, who had already had some experience of that department. The real direction of foreign affairs, however, was assumed by the Prime Minister who interviewed ambassadors, briefed the Prince Regent on the language he was to employ when talking with foreign diplomats, and maintained a close correspondence with Castlereagh and the other British officials in Vienna. His handling of the Foreign Secretary was similar to his handling of Wellington in the peninsula. He had already discussed with him, immediately before his departure for Vienna, the broad lines of British policy towards the various postwar problems. Once Castlereagh had arrived at the other end of Europe Liverpool took it for granted that he would exercise a wide discretion in adapting his tactics to shifting circumstances and taking decisions when necessary on his own responsibility. He accepted Castlereagh's right to be the initiator of British foreign policy and once action had been taken he steadfastly supported the authority of the absent minister. Nevertheless, the interchange of views between Vienna and London was as close and continuous as the slowness of communications allowed. In a stream of letters Liverpool commented frankly on what Castlereagh was doing, made alternative suggestions, and asked probing questions. He also reported on the reactions of the political world at home and the parliamentary position of the administration as it faced the transition from war to peace. As was his habit, he did not (except on one occasion) issue formal instructions or seek to impose his own views. Instead, by comment, criticism and advice, he made it his task to clarify the issue from the point of view of British interests and to ensure that Castlereagh was always kept in mind of the practical limitations under which British policy had to operate. As against Castlereagh's idealism and European outlook, he exhibited the realism of a prime minister who could never for a moment forget that no foreign policy was possible for a British government which Parliament and public opinion did not sanction or the resources of the country allow.

From Cooke, the under-secretary with Castlereagh in Vienna, he received a dryer, more cynical commentary on what was passing in the Austrian capital: one perhaps nearer to Liverpool's own practical and unflattering assessment of the nature and personalities of the allied powers. Eight years' experience since he himself had been foreign secretary had not elevated his notions of the crowned heads of Europe. He thought the Tsar profligate 'from vanity and self-sufficiency, if not from principle'; the King of Prussia the dupe of Russia; and the Austrian Emperor well-meaning but in the hands of Metternich on whom nobody could rely.[19] He instinctively distrusted therefore any grand European diplomacy based on the assumption of goodwill and honesty among the allies. The defence of the Netherlands, security against a revival of French militarism, the independence of Spain and Portugal – these were the essential British interests he wanted safeguarded and which alone would be understood by the British public.

The crucial issue at the Congress of Vienna was Poland, on the fate of which the secondary problems of Saxony and the Netherlands largely depended. Castlereagh's vigorous, almost aggressive attempt to unite Austria, Prussia and, if possible, the rest of Europe against the Tsar Alexander's plan to incorporate most of Poland in a satellite Russian kingdom, was already in October causing Liverpool some concern. An independent Poland was a traditionally popular cause in Britain; but though Liverpool was anxious that this should be placed on record, he knew that as an actual policy it was completely impracticable. A partitioned Poland would be unpopular, even though it had the merit of reflecting existing Austrian and Prussian interests and past European history. A Russian Poland threatened the balance of power in eastern

Europe. His realistic conclusion was that no possible arrangement existed which was 'either creditable or satisfactory' and he urged Castlereagh to detach himself as far as he could from the issue.[20] To a major anxiety over the crisis in Vienna was added a minor anxiety over the safety of Wellington in Paris. There were reports that the Bourbon princes felt insulted by his presence in France; and warnings of assassination were taken seriously by the cabinet, if not by the Duke. To withdraw him with honour from a post of danger was not easy. Only two courses seemed possible: to appoint him as deputy to Castlereagh at Vienna, or to make him commander in the field in the American war. Liverpool chose the latter as the more convincing reason. It might have the further advantages of galvanising the moribund negotiations at Ghent and it was a post that professionally Wellington could not refuse. Having extracted the unwilling Duke from France, however, the Prime Minister was in no hurry to despatch him to Canada. The fact that peace negotiations, however sluggish, were under way, and the unsuitability of winter for an Atlantic crossing, were legitimate pretexts for delay. February or March, he told the Duke in November 1814, would be early enough. To Castlereagh a few days later he wrote that the cabinet had decided to wind up the American war without insisting on any territorial gains. The disunion at Vienna, the disturbed state of France, the government's own financial difficulties – all argued decisively for an early peace. It is clear that if Wellington had gone to North America, it would have been to preside over a diplomatic settlement and not to conduct a military campaign; but it is not certain that Liverpool ever had any fixed intention of sending him there. While urging to Castlereagh at the start of December the need for his presence when Parliament met in the new year, he added that if necessary Wellington could go as a replacement to Vienna and this would be a perfect excuse for removing him from Paris.

By November 1814 the situation in Vienna seemed to be growing worse rather than better. Castlereagh was bluntly asking what he should do in the event of war between their European allies. Should Britain join in, offer mediation, or remain neutral? If mediation was chosen, should an attempt be made to enlist the support of France? To this alarming communication Liverpool replied on 25 November advising caution and restraint. His colleagues, he wrote, were apprehensive that the course British diplomacy was taking might eventually lead to war, when what the continent needed most was a period of peace in which the new territorial settlement of Europe would have time to consolidate. If hostilities did break out, they might easily turn into another revolutionary war in which all that Britain had gained would be put at risk. If, on the other hand, there was an initial period of peace in Europe, any future war might be no more than the limited contest between states common before 1789. He concluded with a Latin tag to the effect that an unjust peace was preferable to a just war.[21] To emphasise the cabinet's anxieties, a formal instruction in the name of the Prince Regent was sent off two days later (the only important instruction Castlereagh ever received while at

Vienna), enjoining him to prevent the outbreak of war, by all means in his power. To Liverpool, looking at the diplomatic turmoil at Vienna from distant London, it seemed obvious that the only monarch who counted there was Alexander and in him he placed no trust whatsoever. The Tsar, by his ill-bred behaviour over Princess Caroline and his ostentatious cultivation of opposition politicians during his visit to England, had displeased both the Regent and his ministers. His subsequent actions over Poland and Saxony caused Liverpool no surprise. 'He is vain, self-sufficient, and obstinate,' he wrote to Cooke in December, 'with some talent, but with no common-sense nor tact.'[22]

With the receipt of this cabinet instruction Castlereagh's second great initiative seemed to have failed. During December his pessimistic letters from Vienna showed his disillusionment with the conduct of the allies and his despair of realising any grand plan for the pacification of Europe. The cause of Poland was lost; the issue now was whether Austria and Prussia would come to blows over Saxony. While the cabinet was interested in Castlereagh's idea of armed mediation in association with France, they were by no means enthusiastic. Almost any arrangement for Poland, Germany and Italy (Liverpool wrote on 23 December) was preferable to a resumption of hostilities. It would be impossible for a British government to go to war except on a clear point of honour or national interest; and no undertaking could be given, in advance of the circumstances by which such an intervention would have to be judged. British policy must favour therefore the adjustment of allied differences by peaceful means and the consolidation of the peace already signed with France. However, if there was another European war, it would be idle to expect France to remain neutral. In that case the best course would be to associate France with Britain in any diplomatic action.

It was a limited approach; but by Christmas 1814 there was nothing to suggest that there was any other practical policy for Britain to adopt and it still left Castlereagh with some possibility of manoeuvre. In the general wreckage of all he had set out to do at Vienna, the Foreign Secretary now agreed to come back to face the difficulties expected by the ministry in the House of Commons and it was settled that Wellington should replace him at the Congress. At the start of the new year, with the American treaty finally concluded, Liverpool went off to Bath for three weeks. Most of his colleagues were already scattered around the country still enjoying their Christmas vacation. Bathurst alone remained in London to deal with diplomatic correspondence. In the middle of January he received the startling news that Castlereagh had negotiated a secret defensive alliance with Austria and France. The treaty was designed to prevent the total annexation of Saxony by Prussia, supported by Russia, as compensation for the loss of Prussian Polish territory. Though Castlereagh's bold initiative hardly seemed in line with the instructions he had received from London in November, the Prime Minister took the news calmly. He wrote at once to Castlereagh to say that he was thoroughly satisfied with the treaty he had concluded; and though he told Bathurst to arrange a meeting of the cabinet ministers available in London, it was to inform them of what had happened, rather than to request their views. To the grumbling comments of men like Harrowby and Westmorland he paid no attention. It was an episode that revealed much about Liverpool's control of his cabinet. Few British foreign secretaries have enjoyed so much latitude as Castlereagh at Vienna; few have been supported so steadfastly by their prime minister.

It is true that Liverpool was cooler in his attitude to the January treaty than Bathurst. He told the latter that he doubted whether he himself in Castlereagh's position would have proposed such a treaty, though he would have accepted it if proposed by Austria or France. Nevertheless, he could see that Castlereagh by this one stroke had redeemed his previous failures at Vienna and won Britain immense prestige. Loyalty apart, his reasons for supporting the Foreign Secretary's action were intelligible. He did not, in the first place, believe that the disagreements among the allies would lead to war. In the second place, Saxony, unlike Poland, constituted a western European problem in which Britain had a direct interest. He did not want Saxony to be wholly absorbed by Prussia. 'I do not,' he had written to Cooke in December, 'like the annihilation of ancient independent states.' It was important in his view to preserve a portion of Saxony as a buffer between those jealous Germanic rivals Austria and Prussia. It was equally important that some of the territorial compensation for Prussia should be found further west in the Rhineland where it would serve as a bastion against future French aggression. Since the January treaty reaffirmed the settlement of the French frontiers and the integrity of the Netherlands, the vital interests of Britain were also being strengthened. A final advantage was that a formal alliance had been secured with the Bourbon King whom he regarded as the only crowned head in Europe whose interests made him a natural and therefore a dependable ally of Britain. For that reason Louis XVIII was the one monarch whom it was in British interest to maintain on his throne. As he confided to Castlereagh in February, 'The keystone of all my external policy is the preserving the Bourbons on the throne of France. I am satisfied that this alone can prevent a recurrence of the evils which we have suffered for the last twenty years, and that all other dangers may be regarded as contemptible when compared with those which would arise out of another revolution in France.'[23] For one who from 1789 to 1815 had watched the great French drama unfold, it was not an unnatural conclusion; nor, until 1870, was it demonstrably untrue.[24]

While approving Castlereagh's Viennese masterstroke, Liverpool wanted him back for the start of the session at Westminster. Six months after the end of the fighting, the British public was still waiting for the promised blessings of peace. Of what was happening at Vienna they knew little and cared less. What they wanted was a reduction of the war taxation under which they had groaned for nearly twenty years, the return of the army, and a reduction in the navy. The landed interest, alarmed by a heavy importation of foreign grain and a sharp fall in price, was demanding tariff protection. The parliamentary opposition, gratefully emerging from the restraints of wartime patriotism, could see an inviting vista of topics on which they could harry the ministers. Already the short November session of Parliament, held on account of the American war, had revealed to Liverpool a new and ugly tone in politics. Not for many years, he observed more than once, had so much party spirit and rancour been manifested. 'The restoration of general peace,' he wrote to Wellington with restrained understatement in January 1815, 'though it may relieve the country from great difficulties, does not make the government more easy to be conducted in the House of Commons.'[25] While he had been able to parry without undue exertion Grenville's lofty assertion that there was hardly a branch of the public administration that did not require the material consideration of Parliament, things had not gone so well for the leaderless and not particularly distinguished government spokesmen in the lower house. 'Our friends *en première ligne*, in the House of Commons,' the Prime Minister wrote bluntly to Castlereagh on 12 January, 'have proved themselves not equal to the burden.'[26] There were some promising junior ministers, notably Peel, but they necessarily had to confine themselves to their own departmental business. It was the three cabinet ministers – Vansittart, Bragge, and Pole – who constituted the weakness in the lower house.

Liverpool obtained an adjournment of Parliament to 9 February, the latest practicable date, and sent a succession of reminders to Castlereagh to return to his post in the Commons by at latest the middle of February. Apart from the financial measures that would have to be settled, a good start to the session was always of psychological importance. In the undisciplined lower house the appearance of government strength had the effect of creating it; the reverse was unfortunately also true. With no more Wellington victories to sustain their prestige, only the bills for them to be met, the ministry had to relearn the arts of peacetime political management. It was not, as Liverpool realised, going to be easy.

One issue that promised much difficulty for ministers, unless tactfully handled, was corn. The controversy had started as far back as 1813 with the appointment of Parnell's committee. The noisy and confused debates in 1814 had engendered more heat than light, and both houses of Parliament appointed select committees to look more closely into the problem. A temporary measure to facilitate the export of corn had produced an observation from Liverpool that free trade was the one 'sound system of legislation' on such matters. Nevertheless, an abstract devotion to the doctrines of Adam Smith did not imply a readiness to apply them wholesale to the complicated web of British commercial regulations. Over corn the Prime Minister's sympathies lay more with Huskisson and a sliding scale of duties than with his own Chancellor of the Exchequer who favoured a fixed duty. What he was reluctantly obliged to admit was that government could not stand aloof from the national controversy. By mid-February, when the Commons took up the issue once more, they were in possession of more information and had specific recommendations in front of them. It was clear that something would have to be done, and done quickly. The average price of wheat had fallen from 118s. 9d. a quarter in January 1813 to 78s. 6d. in January 1814 and 60s. 8d. in January 1815. The farmers were in a panic and rents were already falling. Behind this immediate pressure were wider issues. Under the stimulus of the war, British agriculture had increased its productivity, its costs and its rewards. The continental blockade had underlined the importance of self-sufficiency; the end of hostilities brought the fear of foreign competition. No government could afford to be indifferent to the fate of agriculture, the largest single economic interest in Britain and the largest employer of its population.

Though the inhabitants of London and the industrial districts as a whole were not unnaturally opposed to anything that might put up the price of bread, an influential body of objective opinion favoured some form of legislative protection for agriculture to ease the painful transition from war to peace. Since a new corn law was inevitable, it seemed to Liverpool only politic for the administration to exercise some control over its provisions and reap some political advantage from its passage. Responsive as he was to the interests of manufacture and commerce, he hoped both to restrain the demands of the more violent protectionists and to lessen the animosity of their opponents. The decision was taken therefore to frame a government bill based on the recommendations of the 1814 committee. Its main finding had been that 80s. a quarter was the minimum remunerative price for the domestic producer and below this the import of foreign wheat should be prohibited. It was a level which seemed high five years later but which only corresponded to the average wartime price. Huskisson and Liverpool would have preferred a sliding tariff scale rather than an absolute prohibition below 80s. Discussions at Fife House, however, between ministers and agricultural members from both sides of the House of Commons, made it clear that there would be strong opposition to any substantial departure from the committee's central recommendation. On the other hand, ministers won concessions over free warehousing and colonial preference which they hoped would help to keep prices steady. Since Robinson, the minister who would have to shepherd the bill through the Commons, favoured this compromise, Liverpool and Huskisson reluctantly gave way.

For the Prime Minister it was essential to avoid a long and perhaps ultimately unsuccessful battle in the Commons. He regarded the 1815 bill as an interim measure. When, as he anticipated, peacetime conditions produced a fall in prices, it would be time to review it. Nevertheless, even as a temporary device, he thought the bill had merit. It would assist agriculture to cope with postwar conditions and enable the country in a few years to feed itself. Since it was unlikely that much corn would be available from Europe, a flourishing farming industry offered the best prospect of providing sufficient food for the mass of the population. When the bill came up to the Lords he made national self-sufficiency his principal argument. In the debate on the second reading on 15 March, in his first important speech as Prime Minister on economic affairs, he vindicated the classical free-trade theory he had imbibed from his early read-ings of Adam Smith but pointed out that until the great countries of the world adopted its principles an individual state should apply them only with a prudent regard to its own interests. The object of the bill, he insisted, was to encourage agriculture: 'not to protect would be to discourage'. If agriculture was strong, the whole nation would benefit, since, he argued optimistically, a flourishing agricultural economy would 'render grain cheaper instead of dearer'. In a rare reference to his own economic education, he informed the peers that 'he himself had been bred in a school where he had been taught highly to value the commercial interest' (the shade of the first earl must have smiled approvingly) but he could not sacrifice the agricultural interest to it. Indeed, he added admonishingly, it was a fallacy to assume 'that these interests were at all distinct from each other. On the contrary . . . they were the same.' It was a balanced, intelligent speech containing a number of economic ideas, not all of which accorded with the candid self-interest which moved most of the bill's supporters. For the moment it was enough that the bill went through with comfortable majorities. Before it became law on 23 March a mass of petitions, rioting in London and other towns, and attacks on ministerial houses, demonstrated that many ordinary members of the public took a simpler view of the 1815 Corn Law than the Prime Minister. Riots and window-breaking were, however, a time-honoured form of popular protest; there could be little doubt that at the time the country on the whole approved the bill.

The important issue for government in 1815 was not corn but finance. In the past five years the ministers had strained the national resources to the limit in their final effort against Napoleon. Wellington's peninsular army and Castlereagh's continental subsidies had together pushed national expenditure to a level sustainable only by vast borrowing; and even though the guns were now silent, it would be some time before the costs of the fighting services and commitments under the postwar settlement sank to tolerable peacetime pro-portions. Whatever happened, there could be no return to prewar standards of revenue and expenditure; inflation, a huge national debt, and an appreciable number of new colonies had made sure of that. The British public, however, looked for immediate relief, above all for the end to the hated income tax which, it was widely and erroneously believed, Parliament was pledged to abolish as soon as peace returned. 'The truth is,' Liverpool wrote to Castlereagh on 20 February, 'the country at this moment is peace mad. Many of our best friends think of nothing but reduction of taxes and low establishments.'[27]

By accepting, however reluctantly, the 80s. limit for corn imports, the Prime Minister undoubtedly hoped to smooth the way for his more controversial finance measures. To meet past debts and current liabilities the government was anxious to continue the income tax for at least a further year. Opposition had been expected but after the November sitting of Parliament it became clear to Liverpool that the most he could hope for was to keep the tax for another twelve months with a pledge to end it after that time. If peace continued, substitutes could then be found, 'though none in my judgement,' he told Canning, 'so equal and just'.[28] That was in December; by February what he felt was an unreasonable, and was undoubtedly a powerful, agitation against the tax forced a further retreat on the government. At best and with difficulty the income tax could only be carried on for one more year, at the end of which the financial situation would be just as bad. To make a virtue in 1815 of what would be a necessity in 1816 might, on the other hand, result in more generous treatment by the House of Commons when it came to consider the fiscal alternatives. On 9 February, therefore, Vansittart announced that unless the American Senate refused to ratify the treaty of Ghent, he would discontinue the income tax and find other forms of taxation more acceptable to the country. Whatever he did, a large gap between revenue and expenditure was now inescapable. Liverpool was left with the gloomy prospect of carrying into peacetime the ruinous system of borrowing familiarised by war. Peace was clearly going to be a costly business.

Dragging himself unwillingly away from the final stages of peacemaking at Vienna, Castlereagh eventually arrived in England on 3 March. A week later came the staggering news that Napoleon had escaped from Elba and landed in France. The response of the British government was immediate. Even before Napoleon reached Paris, the decision was taken to move regiments from Ireland to reinforce the small British force stationed in the Netherlands. As an intermediate step Liverpool sent his half-brother Cecil, now Colonel Jenkinson, to Paris to report on the morale of the French government and army. The Prime Minister was at his best in a crisis; the caution and doubts which often accompanied his ordinary actions seemed to vanish under the spur of events. When Cecil, refused permission by the Bourbon government to visit their suspect troops, wrote back in pessimistic terms, he received a brotherly rebuke.

> In God's name, however, keep up your spirit, or otherwise you can be of no use. I do not mean that you should not see things as they really are, but you should not suffer yourself to despair. I never knew those feelings entertained by anyone, that they did not, however unknown to himself, tinge the language of the person who imbibed them, and thereby produce incalculable mischief. Poor Sir John Moore was a melancholy example of what I am saying.[29]

Meanwhile Castlereagh wrote off to the British delegation at Vienna, authorising the offer of yet another British subsidy to the allies to accelerate their military preparations. Since Wellington was fortunately still in the Netherlands, two cabinet ministers – Harrowby and Pole – were sent across to confer with him. They took with them two memoranda from the Prime Minister. The first was designed to elicit the British commander's professional view on the various military contingencies that might arise in the near future – an allied defeat, a French retreat south of the Loire, or a complete surrender by Napoleon. The second memorandum covered a number of topics – the attitude of the allies, the timing and nature of their operations, the policy towards French loyalists, the possible flight of Napoleon to a neutral country, and future securities against France. Wellington's answers were brisk and reassuring; and by the third week in April there was every hope that the allies would be able to concentrate their armies on the French frontier sometime during May.[30]

Liverpool himself had no doubt of military victory; his concerns were political. Would it be possible to restore the Bourbons to a kingdom from which they had been driven with such ease and ignominy? Would the British public accept more expenditure of blood and gold simply to restore the Bourbons? Meanwhile every effort was made to reinforce Wellington's command. His magnificent army of the peninsular war had been dispersed, a large part to America, other units to colonial stations round the world. By taking 5,000 men from Ireland, all disposable troops in England, and volunteers from the militia, between April and the middle of June the British army in the Netherlands was raised from 4,000 to over 32,000, though inevitably most of them had no experience of fighting. At home there was the delicate problem of sounding public and parliamentary reaction to a renewal of the war. The Prince Regent's message to Parliament of 6 April simply recommended defensive preparations and in his speech next day Liverpool deliberately asked for a postponement of any decision on war or peace on the grounds that it was not just a British but a European question. The peers did not dissent from this; and in the Commons Burdett and Whitbread from the more radical wing of the opposition obtained only 37 votes for their policy of complete non-intervention. Wellesley caused some surprise a few days later with his attack on the ministers over the escape from Elba and the alleged breaches by the allies of their agreement with Napoleon. This was easily answered by the Prime Minister. Elba had been the choice of the continental powers; it had been disapproved by the British government. As to infringements of the treaty, he coolly observed, Napoleon had justified his return simply on the ground of being summoned by the voice of the nation. The House of Commons, by agreeing to an extension of the income tax for a further year by a three to one majority, left no doubt of their support for the government's obvious intention of joining the rest of the allies in a war against Napoleon. By May, when the treaty with Russia, Austria and Prussia of 25 March was laid before Parliament, the argument had become almost academic. In justifying a resumption of hostilities Liverpool put his case on both the violations of the peace treaty and the character of Napoleon. War, he argued, was both just and necessary. Grey's amendment, to the effect that an attempt to remove Napoleon by force would be questionable in principle and hazardous in execution, was beaten by 156 votes to 44; and, even more disastrously, was disowned by his old ally Grenville, who voted with the government.

On 22 June, four days after Waterloo, the Tower and Park guns rattled the windows of London for the last time. Some diehard whigs could still be found to assert that the battle was a sad loss of life which would do nothing to settle the fate of Europe or Napoleon. In less than a week, however, the Emperor had abdicated and by 15 July was a voluntary prisoner on board HMS *Bellero-*

phon. The soldiers had done their work; now it was for the politicians to take up once more the old problems. What to do with France? What to do with the Bourbons? Most urgent of all, what to do with Napoleon? Even before his surrender Liverpool thought the simplest procedure would be to hand him over to the King of France to be tried as a rebel, provided (a cautious proviso) that he would not be allowed to escape again. When it appeared that the restored Bourbon government would prefer not to have this alarming duty, he was ready to accept responsibility on behalf of the British government, with another proviso, that it was given sole discretion. There were, after all, no lack of far-flung British possessions – St Helena and the Cape of Good Hope, for instance – where Napoleon could be held securely. When he actually arrived in British waters, however, the difficulties multiplied. His ingenuous request to be allowed to live in Britain as a private citizen could clearly not be granted. The engrained tendency of the sentimental English public to make a hero of a man they had just beaten was in itself a reason for hurrying him away. 'You know enough of the feelings of people in this country,' Liverpool wrote to Castlereagh on 21 July, 'not to doubt that he would become an object of curiosity immediately, and possibly of compassion in the course of a few months.'[31]

Eldon as Lord Chancellor ruled that Napoleon, as a prisoner of war, could be held until a peace treaty was made with him or including him. What the position would be thereafter and by what right the British government could send him into permanent exile could be and was debated at length by the jurists. In the end Liverpool cut through the web of legal arguments by having a bill of indemnity passed the following year. Meanwhile his distrust of the vagaries of British public opinion was more than borne out. In an attempt to set Napoleon at liberty by a more expeditious process some eccentric and ingenious liberals obtained a subpoena from the Court of the King's Bench for Napoleon to appear in court the following November and were indignant when a boat that put off to serve the writ on the Emperor personally was met with a threat from the captain of the *Northumberland*, to which ship Napoleon had been transferred, that he would sink it if it did not keep its distance. 'We wish,' wrote the Prime Minister with pardonable exasperation at the follies of his countrymen, 'that the King of France would hang or shoot Bonaparte, as the best termination of the business, but if this is impracticable, and the Allies are desirous that we should have the custody of him, it is not unreasonable that we should be allowed to judge of the means by which that custody can be made effectual.' He saw to it that prompt action was taken. Within a week of Napoleon's arrival at Torbay, an order was sent down for his removal to St Helena, the place of confinement recommended by Barrow, the Secretary to the Admiralty, on grounds of its remoteness, salubriousness, adequate residential accommodation, and controllability. On 8 August, when the *Northumberland* set sail, Europe was at last relieved of anxiety about the man; from the consequences of the man it was never to be free during Liverpool's lifetime.[32]

The immediate British diplomatic objective was now a fresh treaty with France; but the continental powers seemed in no particular haste to conclude one. While their armies were in France they were being fed by the French and paid by the British. The crucial issue was whether France should be penalised for supporting Napoleon's Hundred Days adventure. Prussia and Austria looked not merely for a return to the 1790 frontiers but for large territorial gains in Flanders and Alsace-Lorraine from which both could profit. Russia, by contrast, was opposed to a partition from which she herself would be unable to benefit. At times the Tsar showed an alarming tendency to pose as friend and patron of France against his allies. For the British government the dilemma was that a loss of historic French territory, while weakening French ability to stage wars of aggrandisement, would also weaken French support for the restored Bourbon monarch. There was a gloomy conviction in the cabinet that the royalist party in France was quite useless as a means of carrying on the government of that unsettled nation. Liverpool, with personal experience of the Bourbon princes, thought that they were as ignorant of the principles and practices of constitutional government as if they had lived all their lives at the court of Louis xv. On the other hand, it was his constant nightmare that if the Bourbon monarchy was overthrown, its successor would be 'a Jacobin or Revolutionary system'. As early as July, therefore, he pronounced in favour of garrisoning the northern French fortresses for a limited period, rather than dismantling them or annexing them for the allies. Fortified by the opinion of Castlereagh and Wellington, the cabinet agreed in August to a temporary occupation of important centres in northern France but no permanent cession of territory there. This, together with an indemnity, became the basic compromise to which the other European powers eventually consented.

While the allies in the autumn of 1815 haggled over details of compensation, indemnity and security, Liverpool received at the beginning of October a note from Castlereagh enclosing an autograph letter from the three allied monarchs to the Prince Regent, proposing that novel form of engagement, a union of Christian rulers, which later became known as the Holy Alliance. Castlereagh, like Metternich, had tried to prevent this embarrassing development and his letter was apologetic in tone. His motive was clearly to avoid giving offence to the Tsar. Nevertheless, while poking fun, in a well-known phrase, at 'this piece of sublime mysticism and nonsense', Castlereagh did in fact (a circumstance frequently forgotten) propose that the Prince Regent should sign the treaty without the intervention of his ministers as a private autographic record of his concurrence with its objects. Liverpool had a stiff sense of the constitutional proprieties and in his reply came as near as he ever did to a rebuke to Castlereagh for allowing so improper a proposal to get as far as it did. The suggestion that the Prince Regent should be allowed to sign without ministerial authority he flatly rejected. A treaty was an act of state and no British king or regent could be a party to one except through the agency of a minister. Instead he laid the whole correspondence before the Regent and held a cabinet on the matter. 'It is quite impossible,' he wrote '. . . to advise the Prince to sign this act of accession which has been transmitted to him. Such a step would be inconsistent with all the forms and principles of our Government, and would subject those who advised it to a very serious responsibility.' The solution adopted by the cabinet was that the Prince Regent should write an autograph letter explaining that the form of the British constitution precluded him from acceding formally to the treaty, but expressing his concurrence with its sentiments.[33]

For the rest of the autumn there was little left for the Prime Minister to do in the field of diplomacy except watch over Castlereagh's negotiations in Paris for the second peace treaty with France. After the cost in lives and money of the 1815 campaign, it was peculiarly irritating to British opinion to observe the failure in France to punish those who had abandoned Louis XVIII to serve Napoleon again. Even more offensive was the return to office of Fouché, Napoleon's ex-Jacobin police chief: an event which attracted fierce comment in the English press. Liverpool appreciated that his appointment was a precaution, though a desperate one, against the troubles expected from Bonapartist and republican elements in France. Even so, he thought that the authority of the restored Bourbons would never be established unless they took some action against those who had broken their oath of loyalty. 'One can never feel,' he wrote to Canning in August, 'that the King is secure upon his throne till he has dared to spill traitors' blood.'[34] Neither he nor Castlereagh nor Wellington made any move to prevent the execution in December of Ney, the most prominent of the generals who had gone over to Napoleon in 1815. Castlereagh may privately have been disposed to clemency but Wellington, like the Prime Minister, was convinced that an example had to be made.

With the general terms of the second treaty of Paris Liverpool was satisfied, despite the financial provisions which added to the British taxpayers' burden. It accorded with his standing principle that it was an essential British interest not to reduce or dismember France but to assist her to play a responsible and pacific role in a future Europe. For that he was prepared to face much criticism at home. 'The terms are as *severe upon France*,' he commented to Bathurst, 'as would in any way be consistent with maintaining Louis XVIII upon the throne.'[35] Bathurst and the three other cabinet ministers available in London for consultation agreed with that verdict. By November nothing was wanting except the signatures of the principals in Paris. In view of its importance Liverpool came up to London to await the arrival of the treaty, leaving Louisa behind at Walmer. Expected in the middle of the month, the document did not arrive until the 23rd. All that the Prime Minister could do in the interval was to order an instant telegraphic signal of the arrival in port of Planta, Castlereagh's private secretary, who was the bearer of the treaty, and to sit in Fife House writing letters to his deserted wife.

15 Nov. 1815

My dearest Love, I can assure you, I am as much vexed and disappointed as you can be at this delay. Nothing can be more unpleasant than the uncertainty. I must only hope that it will soon be over and if the weather permits, I shall be happy to return again after the 27th.... God bless you my love, I am most affectionately yours, Liverpool.

18 Nov.

My dearest Love, A mail is just arrived but still *further delay*. If Planta should arrive tomorrow, I would still come down on Tuesday and return on Saturday but if he does not come tomorrow I must put off my return till the 28th.... God bless you, dearest, till we are again together.

21 Nov.

My dearest Love ... I have written to Lord Castlereagh by a Messenger tonight to desire he will meet me at Walmer on Monday to dinner. I think if he sets out on Thursday as he intended, he may arrive on Sunday or Monday. I expect Planta to be at Dover early tomorrow, as the Wind is as fair as it can blow.... I fear you will suffer from this Cold which appears likely to last. God bless you, most affectionately yours, Liverpool.

23 Nov.

My dearest Love, I have but a moment. ... Planta has arrived with the Treaties and nothing is likely to occur to prevent me from being as I intended at Walmer on Tuesday.... God bless you, we will soon now meet, Most affectionately yours, Liverpool.

They had been married twenty years and this was possibly the longest period that they had been apart.[36]

So ended the eventful year 1815, with Britain militarily and diplomatically more powerful in Europe than at any time since the reign of Anne. By their skill, their patience, and above all their resolution, Liverpool's ministry had deserved well of the Prince Regent and the country. George himself was more than content with the ministers who had enabled him in 1814 to exercise his undoubted talents for pageantry and ceremonial display and to entertain in his own unravaged capital the victorious monarchs of Europe. How far the prestige of victory would sustain the ministry when it entered the uncharted waters of postwar politics remained to be seen. The British public was not renowned for either gratitude or long memory.

NOTES

1 FD, VII, 90.
2 *The Glenbervie Journals*, ed. W. Sichel (1910), p. 203.
3 LWF, I, 84 (misdated 1803).
4 Details of lease in 38474 fos 50-51, 280.
5 'Lord Holland says it is like Lady Hawkesbury's Children that never come to maturity, and have great doubts of whether they ever existed.' LGC, II, 166.
6 LWF, I, 83, 136, 161, 171.
7 See esp. LWF, I, 73-4, 86-7, 142.
8 FD, V, 170; VIII, 52.

9 Colchester, II, 405-6, 440.

10 Bathurst, pp. 226-7; Webster, pp. 119 ff.

11 WSD, VIII, 49.

12 Yonge, I, 476 ff.; WSD, VIII, 486-90; Webster, pp. 510 ff.

13 Webster, Appendix B, pp. 510 ff. prints a valuable series of letters from Liverpool to Castlereagh, 1813-14.

14 LWF, I, 196-8.

15 38474 fos 37, 39; Stuart, pp. 205, 207.

16 FD, VII, 271.

17 WSD, IX, 259; Yonge, II, 1 ff.

18 LGC, II, 497-8; Hinde, pp. 268-70.

19 WSD, IX, 494; Yonge, II, 89.

20 Yonge, II, 35, 46; WSD, IX, 382.

21 Letters misdated in Yonge, II, 26 and WSD, IX, 285. See Webster, p. 259 n.

22 WSD, IX, 467.

23 Yonge, II, 106.

24 For Liverpool's views during the Vienna diplomacy see generally Yonge, II, 26-9; WSD, IX, 455-538; Webster, pp. 369-75.

25 WSD, IX, 536.

26 Yonge, II, 132 n.

27 Yonge, II, 104-5.

28 Yonge, II, 77.

29 Ibid, 168.

30 Ibid, 169 ff.; WSD, X, 35 ff.

31 Yonge, II, 198-9; WSD, XI, 47.

32 For the problem of Napoleon, see Yonge, II, 185 ff.; Twiss, II, 270-80; Bathurst, p. 375.

33 Yonge, II, 231-2.

34 WSD, XI, 94.

35 Bathurst, p. 388.

36 38474 fos 66, 68, 70, 78.

CHAPTER VII

The Aftermath of War

The parliamentary session in Liverpool's first full year as peacetime prime minister saw a spectacular defeat for the government. It was to some extent a self-inflicted wound since it came over their unexpected proposal to retain the income tax. The reasons for their change of policy were sensible enough, had the British public been disposed to be sensible on the subject. Not only was there additional heavy expenditure and indebtedness arising from the Waterloo campaign and the peace settlement, but strong parliamentary criticism had been levelled at Vansittart's ideas for substitute taxes in the previous session. If, as seemed unhappily the case, all taxes were equally unpopular in the House of Commons, Liverpool thought there was much to be said for fighting that inevitable battle on the issue of the income tax, the best because the most equitable of them all. The basic object of ministers was to restore sound currency and public credit by avoiding as far as possible any further large-scale borrowing. Nevertheless, their change of policy had its risks and to conciliate the Commons the rate of the tax was lowered to 5 per cent, a cut which would immediately relieve the public of £7 million while retaining a useful £6 million for the Chancellor of the Exchequer.

The cabinet calculated on a majority of forty; in the event they lost by almost exactly that margin. The result took even the opposition by surprise. They had expected to run the government close but not to beat them on a major financial measure. What enabled them to celebrate a great if fortuitous victory was the prolonged campaign of petitioning against the tax in February and March, the continual discussions in the House of Commons it occasioned, and an almost uniformly hostile press. Huskisson thought that Liverpool had been frightened off the income tax the previous year; the sequel in 1816 proved that his fears were justified. A large number of the government's usual supporters went away before the division; an equal number voted with the opposition. Defeat on such a scale was demoralising. Having lost the income tax the ministers then voluntarily abandoned the wartime malt tax: a masochistic gesture rationalised by the argument that it would be socially inequitable to retain a tax on an article of popular consumption when a tax on the rich had just been removed. In reality the cabinet was thinking not in financial but political terms. In the general wreck of their budgetary policy, the £2½ million from the malt tax was almost irrelevant. It was obvious now that they would have to live for some time on borrowing; what had to be retrieved was their political authority.

A depressing feature for the Prime Minister was that there was evidently no more gratitude for concessions than there was support for intransigence. The Corn Law of 1815 had failed to attach the agricultural interest; the abolition of the income tax failed to satisfy the economisers. Indeed, it served only to whet the appetite of the House of Commons for further retrenchment. To the opposition it was now clear what the Achilles heel of the administration was going to be in the new world of postwar politics. The proposed level of service establishments was already under attack in both houses, and in the rage for economy attention was being turned to the civil offices of government. While the cabinet's foreign treaties were approved with handsome majorities, every item of domestic expenditure was jealously scrutinised. A couple of days after the income-tax defeat, the government scrambled through a difficult debate on Admiralty salaries only by dint of more surrenders; that kind of undignified retreat could not be allowed to go on indefinitely. On 21 March Liverpool sent Arbuthnot down to Brighton with a letter for the Prince Regent urging him to return to town so that he would be available for consultation. 'The Government certainly hangs by a thread,' he wrote warningly, '. . . the spirit of the House of Commons is as bad now as at any period of the present session, or indeed as at any time within my recollection.' The Prince threw off his gouty affliction to dash off a message in the heroic vein he sometimes affected. 'You have seen me before pretty highly tried and you shall find me now, as at all times, true to the backbone.' Of more practical use perhaps were the letters Liverpool sent off to influential peers and the meeting of office-holders he held at Fife House a few days later.[1]

In the end the navy estimates went through successfully, partly because of the excesses of the opposition, partly because of the residual loyalty of the country gentlemen. Adjusting themselves grimly to the new political climate, the cabinet cut all their original service estimates, ordered similar reductions in the civil departments, and launched enquiries into further possible areas of retrenchment. Even the difficult issues of the civil list and the Prince Regent's debts, which came up in May, were unflinchingly faced. The extravagant expenditure on the Pavilion at Brighton was a favourite subject of popular complaint and one on which the Prince was particularly sensitive. In March, warding off possible royal displeasure with any individual minister by making a collective approach, Liverpool, Castlereagh and Vansittart sent the Prince a formal letter warning him of the damage to which the ministry would be exposed in the House of Commons if his debts continued to mount 'at a time when most of the landed gentlemen of the country are obliged to submit to losses and privations as well as to retrenchment'.[2] The promise they extracted from the Prince that all new expenditure at Brighton and elsewhere would cease, was a material help both in getting the Commons to approve the new civil list and in avoiding a committee of enquiry. By the end of the sesssion the battered government could comfort itself with two reflections. First, the independent gentry in the Commons did not apparently wish to unseat the ministry, only to place a severe curb on its expenditure. Second, the opposition whigs were only effective when exploiting popular feeling; they had little strength of their own and were always liable to be tripped up by their own extravagance.

There were few other comforts for the government. The year 1816 formed a depressing start for the era of peace to which the nation had looked forward with such anticipation. A severe trade recession had set in, with widespread unemployment swollen by the third of a million men discharged from the armed forces. In the early summer there were extensive food riots in East Anglia which needed the use of troops before order was restored. Intermittent Luddite disorders continued in the textile districts of Leicestershire and Nottinghamshire and there was a scattering of minor troubles all over the kingdom from Forfar to Devonshire. For the Prime Minister public discontents were accompanied by private anxieties. In the late summer Louisa was sufficiently ill for the Prince Regent himself to express concern.[3] It was judged inadvisable for her to travel by road to Walmer for their usual autumn visit and plans were made to take her by boat. A harsh and difficult year ended on an alarmist note in December when a meeting at Spa Fields in London to organise petitions about the distress in the country was diverted by the revolutionary radicals of the Spencean Society into rioting and attacks on gunsmiths' shops. Some of the ringleaders were later put on trial for high treason (an unnecessarily portentous indictment) but acquitted by a sceptical or disloyal London jury.

Economic distress and social discontent were the products of forces largely outside the control of government; though not without effect on their policies. What concerned Liverpool more nearly was the fact that the government had been left with a revenue of £12 million to meet an expenditure of £20 million; and that its control over the House of Commons was weaker than at any time since 1812. Some of the early difficulties of the 1816 session were caused by Castlereagh's illness which left poor Vansittart for a time in charge of the House of Commons. Though a better financier than his reputation suggests or contemporary circumstances allowed, he was an eccentric and clumsy speaker whom the House found it hard to listen to with becoming respect. It was a stroke of fortune for the Prime Minister that the accidental death of Lord Buckinghamshire in February made it possible to bring Canning back into the administration. The colleagues he consulted – Castlereagh, Sidmouth and Melville – were not unrestrainedly eager for his return. Sidmouth, while agreeing that it was proper and perhaps obligatory for Liverpool to offer the vacancy to Canning, refused to believe that his services were so valuable as to require any other member of the administration to give up his office. Melville thought that Buckinghamshire's empty post at the India Board was good enough for Canning, and was not prepared to surrender the Admiralty as he had been in 1813. The Prince Regent sanctioned Canning's appointment but added a magisterial warning that he hoped his introduction into the cabinet would not lead to division and want of harmony 'in a Government, with which I am so perfectly contented and with which I and the country have so much reason to be well satisfied'.[4] Luckily for the Prime Minister, Canning, in a chastened mood since 1812, accepted the unfashionable India Board without demur. By the time he had returned to England and secured his re-election the session was virtually over.

The addition of one able orator to the front bench could not, however, transform the situation in the House of Commons. The fundamental weakness of the government in the lower house was that in periods of distress and agitation MPs were influenced more by the press, their constituents, and the general tone of public opinion than by the exhortations of ministers and Treasury whips. By the time the cabinet gathered in London in November 1816 to discuss forthcoming parliamentary business, they knew that they faced as many problems in the next session as they had encountered in the last. Liverpool's momentary optimism over trade figures in September had given way in October to a realisation that the government faced 'a stormy Winter'. Trade remained stagnant and unemployment had grown. The Prime Minister's diagnosis was that the distress had two causes: the bad harvest and the false encouragement given to British manufactures by the coming of peace which had merely resulted in over-production and a glut of British goods on foreign markets. Economic hardship bred political discontent. Even respectable opinion was tempted to ascribe many of the country's difficulties to extravagance in government and to see a remedy in parliamentary reform. The more popular version of the widespread feeling of discontent was riot and disorder, accompanied by vaguer and more subterranean activity by advanced radicals. The cabinet's conclusion in December 1816 was as guardians of the public purse to meet the legitimate demands of the public for further retrenchment but as guardians of law and order to seek stronger powers to deal with sedition and agitation.

Over the last issue Sidmouth, on whose department fell the main responsibility, wanted an early meeting of Parliament and emergency legislation. Liverpool, more cautious, preferred to collect evidence from the country gentlemen before presenting them with legislative proposals. These by their nature could hardly avoid encroaching on historic liberties to which not only the opposition attached constitutional importance. The parliamentary session was opened by the Prince Regent at the end of January. As he returned from the ceremony a bullet from an airgun or similar weapon shattered his carriage windows. This added a sensational item to the government's case for legislation, but most of the evidence to be presented to Parliament had already been put together. On 3 February a special message from the Prince was received by both houses, enjoining them to take into immediate consideration the information laid before them on treasonable and seditious activity in London and other parts of the kingdom. Next day each house appointed a Secret Committee to examine the evidence. It is clear now that the documents they studied over the next fortnight presented an exaggerated picture of the extent, organisation and strength of seditious activities. Some of the information would have come from credulous or dishonest spies; some from timid or alarmist magistrates. The absence of any effective system of either intelligence or police inevitably made the central and local authorities more nervous in time of widespread agitation than was justified; but the information before the committees was not concocted by the government nor was it intended to deceive. On the opening day of Parliament Liverpool told his young colleague Peel that he had been a member of the Secret Committee of 1794 and nothing had come to light then which showed nearly such a disaffected and seditious feeling among the people as now existed.[5]

When Prime Minister and Home Secretary were convinced by the evidence, it was not likely that Parliament would be sceptical. The reports of the Secret Committees, presented before the end of the month, concluded that there was an organised network of clubs and societies, particularly in the larger towns and manufacturing districts, which, under the pretext of agitating for parliamentary reform and other political objects, were attempting to lead the poor and distressed classes into sedition and revolution. The House of Commons, never backward in supporting the executive on matters of law and order, did not quarrel with these findings. In the course of the session therefore a number of additional security measures became law: a temporary suspension of habeas corpus for persons arrested on suspicion of treason; a consolidation of existing Acts against seditious or secret societies; an Act for penalising attempts to tamper with the loyalty of the armed forces; and another for the personal protection of the Prince Regent.

It was not only among politicians and magistrates that there was alarm. In the spring and summer of 1817 Liverpool was favoured with the views of two eminent poets on the state of British society. Southey in March warned the Prime Minister that the spirit of Jacobinism which had possessed ardent young intellectuals like himself a quarter of a century earlier had now descended into the masses. It was essential, he wrote, for the government to retain the loyalty of the troops. 'If the fear of the military were withdrawn, four and twenty hours would not elapse before the tricoloured flag would be planted upon Carlton House.' In July Coleridge sent an obscure philosophic effusion denouncing godless rationalist thought and affirming the need to place the principles of political obligation on a religious basis – 'at least,' ran the Prime Minister's patient endorsement, 'I believe this is Mr Coleridge's meaning, but I cannot well understand him'.[6] What perhaps cheered Liverpool, more than these unsolicited prophets of doom, was the fact that Lord Grenville (himself a member of the secret committee) had given unequivocal support in the House of Lords to the government's legislation, saying he was convinced that the country was in extreme danger.

As the rest of the year demonstrated, the new powers given to the government had no great effectiveness. The Hampden societies, the largest of the parliamentary reform organisations, were disbanded for a time; but press prosecutions during the summer were remarkably unsuccessful. The right of summary arrest and detention, the most formidable weapon given to the executive, was used sparingly – as indeed Liverpool had promised in the House of Lords when asking for the government to be entrusted with that power, 'a most odious one,' he agreed, for a short time in the unusual conditions prevailing in the country. A different set of measures passed on ministerial initiative that year showed that the cabinet was not indifferent to the social distress which made political agitation so dangerous. Legislation put through in the course of the session included a Truck Act to limit the practice of paying wages in kind, an Act to protect and encourage savings banks, a Passenger Transport Act to facilitate emigration, and, most remarkable of all, a Poor Employment Act enabling state loans to be made for public works undertaken by local authorities. None of these measures probably had much effect on their main objective of reducing poverty and unemployment; but at least they demonstrated that the ministry was ready to depart from the orthodox teaching of political economy and intervene directly when abnormal conditions seemed to call for abnormal action. The real obstacle to any social programme of this kind was not so much economic dogma as shortage of money and lack of administrative machinery.

Meanwhile the House of Commons, while giving full support to the cabinet's security legislation, showed no sign of slackening the campaign for retrenchment. At the start of the session, after strenuous efforts to ensure the attendance of their customary supporters, the ministers presented Parliament with a fresh package of economy measures. The peacetime establishments for the army and navy had again been ruthlessly cut back; the Civil List, including the Prince Regent's personal income, was also reduced; and 10 per cent was struck off official salaries. While recognising the honesty of these efforts to reduce expenditure, the Commons ungratefully launched a separate attack on official sinecures which in radical propaganda and the public mind had been given a notoriety out of proportion to their number or purpose. Faced with the threat of further attacks by the opposition on some of the Admiralty administrative posts, the ministers retreated yet another step. In mid-February, after a number of hasty meetings, a gathering of the more discontented country gentlemen at Fife House were told that government sinecures would be abandoned. The saving which resulted was small. Most of the sinecures were used as pensions for retired civil servants and ministers; and a new Pensions Act had to be passed to deal with these genuine cases. The political benefits, however, were immediate. Ministers were now able to protect the working establishment of government departments against further crippling staff reductions and MPs were convinced of the ministry's real desire to eliminate waste and extravagance. One of the sacrifices in the retrenchment drive, indeed, had been the Prime Minister's own salary as Lord Warden of the Cinque Ports. By jettisoning even

the little that was left of its power of 'influencing' the legislature, the government had probably staved off more damaging attacks. For the remainder of
the session the House of Commons gave little trouble.

Liverpool's object throughout had been clear: to pursue retrenchment real-
istically as only so could the ministry's parliamentary support be preserved; but
not to pursue it so insensitively (as some of the opposition were demanding)
that the actual machinery of the state would be damaged. It was a delicate
balance that was achieved in the 1817 session and it seemed to Liverpool that
the limits of concession had virtually been reached. Meanwhile the government's underlying financial difficulties still had to be solved. The economies
that had been achieved were relatively trivial compared with the enormous
gap between revenue and expenditure. The yield from custom and excise was
down; heavy borrowing continued. At most, by continuing the payments to
the Sinking Fund (that doubtful inheritance from Pitt), a façade of stability
and orthodoxy was preserved. The mounting debt arising from regular financial deficits was, however, a problem that grew worse the longer it was left
untouched. Sooner or later it would have to be solved if there was ever to be a
return to normal peacetime practices.

Yet socially as well as politically normality seemed as far off as ever. The
summer of 1817 saw small but alarming radical 'risings' at Nottingham and
Huddersfield, the first of which led to the appointment of a special commission
at Derby and the execution of three of the rioters. The suspension of habeas
corpus was renewed until January 1818; and further reports from the Secret
Committees of Parliament the following February kept alive the general fear
among the propertied classes that an actual armed rising was in contemplation.
There were other more domestic matters to add to the Prime Minister's burdens
as the year 1817 drew to an end. Louisa had never fully recovered from her
illness in 1816 and though as usual she seemed to improve when they made
their customary autumn move to Walmer, she was still far from well. By the
start of 1818 alarming reports of her health found their way into the newspapers
and Prince Leopold sent a friendly message on 18 January to enquire into their
truth. Only a couple of months earlier the attentive, if slightly oily, Coburger
had lost his own newly-married wife, the Princess Charlotte, in childbed. For
her father, the Prince Regent, the loss of his only child was a shattering
bereavement. The news, announced in the *London Gazette* of 6 November,
brought Liverpool hurrying up from Walmer to the side of the afflicted prince.
It was a distressing event for both the Liverpools. Louisa wrote to her sister the
next day that 'the shock was really almost too much for me and I felt afraid I
was going to add to poor Dear Lord Liverpool's painful feelings. He set off for
London last night. I never saw him more overwhelm'd, this blow is indeed a
dreadful one in *every* way.' As usual sudden death evoked her most pious strain
of evangelicalism. 'But He who order'd it can make the chastisement a salutary
one and I trust He *will* do so and that we shall all learn Humility, and see the
full extent of the unsteadiness of all worldly Happiness and greatness.'[7]

It was a chastisement which her husband in his capacity as prime minister would willingly have been spared. The death of Charlotte, the only legitimate grandchild of George III, brought up in an acute form the question of the succession to the throne. Of the seven sons of George III, the Regent, the Duke of York (the heir presumptive), and the Duke of Cumberland, were now unlikely to have children. The third in line, Sussex, had contracted an invalid marriage. It was not surprising that Liverpool pressed behind the scenes for an early decision on the matrimonial alliances being languidly considered by the remaining three middle-aged bachelor dukes, all of whom were well over forty.

It was an unfortunate but inevitable outcome of the crop of royal marriages in contemplation that the ministers would be saddled in due course with the disagreeable duty of going to the House of Commons for increased allowances to support them in their new marital state. A second and even more uncomfortable consequence of Charlotte's death was that it relieved the Prince Regent of his last scruples in seeking a formal divorce from his long-estranged wife. Both matters engaged the attention of the cabinet in January 1818. Over the financial settlement for the royal dukes agreement with the Prince Regent was soon reached. On the matter of the divorce it was less easy to arrive at a coincidence of views. Ever since Caroline had left England, reports had been coming in of her scandalous mode of life which by 1816 satisfied George that he had grounds for a legal divorce. The cabinet was concerned less with juridical probabilities than with political repercussions. When first consulted in 1816 their advice had been discouraging. There were, they pointed out, three courses open to the Prince: an action in the ecclesiastical courts for separation; a divorce bill in Parliament; and proceedings against the Princess for high treason on grounds of adultery. They counselled against the first as unprecedented, and also dangerous, since it would allow Caroline to bring recriminatory charges against her husband; they thought the second unlikely to succeed; and the third inadvisable unless certain of success. Success was doubtful, however, since British courts would always be wary of foreign witnesses. They therefore urged the Prince to be satisfied with his existing position of moral superiority, and deprecated any attempt to secure further evidence against Caroline. Further information in 1817 about the princess's vagaries merely led Liverpool to repeat these eminently sensible but to the Prince highly unsatisfactory sentiments.

Assisted by his Hanoverian officials, George continued to amass incriminating evidence and by November 1817 he was fortified by the opinion of his own personal law officer, vice-chancellor Leach. By the start of 1818 he was once more bringing pressure to bear on the Prime Minister and the cabinet. Though they were again able to temporise, it was evident that the Prince was in a more determined mood than before. For Liverpool the issue was almost entirely one of expediency. Of Caroline's worthless character he needed no convincing. He had read too many depositions from too many unimpeachable witnesses to be left with any doubts. His low opinion of Caroline went back many years.

Talking with his sister-in-law the Duchess Elizabeth in 1813 about the Prince's unfortunate marriage, he told her that the old King had wanted George to send for the pictures of other eligible Protestant princesses but the Prince, impressed by the military reputation of the Duke of Brunswick, had insisted on marrying one of his daughters although anyone could have told him how loose her conduct was even as a girl. In the Duchess's outspoken circle (and no doubt in the more circumspect Liverpool household) Caroline's indelicacy and immorality were common knowledge.[8] What Liverpool wanted to avoid at almost any cost was a royal divorce action in the courts, inevitably giving rise to discussions in Parliament, and taking place in an atmosphere of salacious publicity and political partisanship that would harm both monarch and ministers.[9]

As it was, the royal family continued to be, in Wellington's phrase, 'the damnedest millstone about the necks of any Government'. When the new scale of allowances for the royal dukes was announced to a private meeting of some seventy backbench supporters, mainly country gentry, at Fife House in April, the frosty reception induced the cabinet to make further reductions before they put them before the Commons. Even so the government was beaten twice – on the increased grant recommended for Clarence, the likely ultimate but not yet presumptive heir to the throne, and over a modest allowance proposed for the wife of the Duke of Cumberland. Clarence was unpopular because of his flock of debts and bastards; Cumberland had married a woman who was known to be *persona non grata* at Court. In each case the House of Commons had the happy sense of gratifying personal resentment while displaying financial rectitude. Only the mercifully more obscure dukes of Kent and Cambridge were given the full allowances suggested by the ministers. Even in the more decorous House of Lords the Prime Minister had to ward off some polite heckling on the subject. Much as its parliamentary position had improved, the case of the royal dukes was a reminder to the government that the Commons could be led, but not driven; and that on certain issues it would always make up its own mind. It was an unfortunate episode altogether, since 1818 was also the year of a general election, Parliament having run six of its maximum seven years.

A more congenial employment of public funds as far as the Prime Minister was concerned was the million-pound grant for church building he was able to obtain from the House of Commons before it was dissolved. The money was to be entrusted to a commission and used primarily to meet the needs of the more crowded and understaffed urban parishes. Alarmed by the spread of both political radicalism and religious dissent, a strong movement had been developing in High Church circles for a programme of church extension. In a cabinet which included such evangelically-minded ministers as Liverpool, Sidmouth, Vansittart and Harrowby, there was no lack of sympathy; the task was to find the appropriate moment for putting such a proposal before the legislature. Once the decision was taken, Liverpool was anxious to press ahead while the prospects were favourable. He had satisfied himself that the church leaders approved the government's bill and that no objections would be raised by either of those formidable critics 'the Dissenters or the Economists'. Of his personal interest there could be little doubt. He told the peers in May when moving the bill that it was 'a measure which was the result of his own investigations, and of the deliberations of those whom he thought it his duty to consult'. His calculation was that together with the expected private subscriptions, it would be possible for between 150 and 200 new churches to be built. To Lord Harrowby he expressed a private aesthetic hope that they would be provided with 'that decent decoration which would mark the character of the Established Church'.[10] Aesthetics apart, it was the first occasion since the reign of Anne that the state had taken any responsibility for the spiritual state of the country. In such matters, it seemed, Liverpool was indifferent to the dogmas of *laissez-faire*.

The elections held in June were chiefly remarkable for the return of a large number of new men, about a quarter of the whole House. The government admitted the loss of a few seats; the opposition claimed the capture of many more. Yet all such calculations were unreliable until the new parliament met and a few important divisions took place. What was more disquieting to the government than any loss of seats was the general mood of disillusionment in the country. The prestige gained by the great military victories of 1814 and 1815 had long faded. The ministry, if not unpopular, enjoyed little respect. It seemed to be showing neither initiative nor leadership. Worst of all, the constant radical cry, that the evils from which the country suffered were due to misgovernment, was beginning to colour the attitude of many respectable members of the middle classes who would have indignantly rejected any imputation of radicalism. Huskisson reported to the Prime Minister from Sussex that the farmers and freeholders in the country 'are no longer what they were ten years ago in their attachment to the old Tory interests and principles which are prevalent in the Nobility and Gentry. . . . Be assured that the feeling is strong in the Country, that we have not done enough.' Even for what they had done, the ministers were given little recognition. Inexperienced in the arts of publicity and old-fashioned in handling their relations with the general public, the government never seemed to make the best of their case. Virtually the whole of the national press was in the hands either of critical neutrals or party opponents. The lament of the stout tory Walter Scott in 1817 still lingered on in the following year. 'How we want Billie Pitt now to get up and give the tone to our feelings and opinions.'[11]

Not being a Billy Pitt, the Prime Minister continued patiently with the more prosaic task of reinforcing the parliamentary basis on which ultimately all policy depended. One grain of comfort in 1817 had been the growing separation between the Grenvillites and the opposition whigs. Grenville himself had been as firm as any ministerialist on issues of security and public order. When the House of Lords Secret Committee was renewed the following session Liverpool wrote tactfully to persuade him to continue as a member. Grenville

remained a difficult and prickly figure, but with fading energies he was beginning to feel that his political career was drawing to its close. The heir apparent
to the leadership of the Grenville connection was his nephew Lord Buckingham
whose ambitions were centred on an alliance with the government rather than
a useless and uncomfortable association with the opposition. Since he freely
communicated his views, Liverpool discreetly cultivated good relations with
him and his uncle by small acts of courtesy and friendly unofficial contacts
through junior members of the administration. At the start of the 1818 session
it was announced in the House of Commons on behalf of the small knot of
Grenvillite MPs that they would in future sit as a separate group. Any closer
relationship with the government would clearly have to wait on time and
circumstance. Liverpool was too cautious to make a premature move and in
any case there was nobody among the younger Grenvillites who was of obvious
ministerial material. What promotions took place at this time were confined to
his official men. In January 1818 Rose, who as Vice-President of the Board of
Trade had been running the office under the nominal presidency of Lord
Bathurst, the Colonial Secretary, died at the age of seventy-four after a lifetime
of public service. Liverpool took the opportunity to promote Robinson, whose
abilities he respected as much as he deplored his indolence, to the presidency
of the Board and a seat in the cabinet. The change allowed him to promote his
old friend Wallace, another valued economic expert, to the vice-presidency.

Later in the year he secured an even more illustrious recruit in the person of
the Duke of Wellington. The decision to invite him to join the cabinet was
taken before Castlereagh went off to the Congress of Aix-la-Chapelle in the
summer of 1818. With the French war-indemnity paid off and the allied
occupation forces withdrawn, there was no further need for the Duke's professional services abroad, and none of the purely military appointments available
at home seemed worthy of him. The first idea was to put him in the cabinet
without portfolio; but Mulgrave then offered to give up his office of Master
General of the Ordnance as the one cabinet post that would in a technical sense
justify Wellington's appointment. The Duke, while expressing his personal
attachment to the ministers, was at first reluctant to commit himself publicly
to a political party. It was probably Castlereagh who overcame his professional
soldier's scruples with the argument that if he refused the offer, it would be a
blow to the government's prestige. In accepting Mulgrave's post Wellington
stipulated that if the ministry ever went out of office, he should be free to follow
his own political course: a condition cheerfully accepted by Liverpool.[12] As a
reward for his unselfishness Mulgrave was retained in the cabinet without
office and stayed in the government until May 1820.

Neither the acquisition of the Duke nor the more amiable attitude of the
Grenvillites made much immediate difference to the government's parliamentary position. The work of the 1818 session was scarcely over before the
problems of the next began to loom up. Among Liverpool's concerns, if not
among his direct responsibilities, was the still unresolved matter of the Princess

Caroline. In May the vice-chancellor Leach had submitted his final report in which, while confirming the previous accounts of her private life, he recommended that a more systematic enquiry should be conducted in Italy and other countries where she had been staying. The cabinet considered this unwelcome proposal and in July Liverpool told Leach that while the government declined to set up a public commission to examine the conduct of the Princess, they would meet the expenses of such an enquiry if the Prince Regent thought fit to authorise it. He protected himself with the stipulation that this in no sense constituted a pledge on the ministers' part to take any further action, whatever the result of the investigation. Whether, even without this guarded assent, the Prince could have been deflected from what was rapidly becoming the principal object of his life, is doubtful. Nevertheless, the Milan Commission, as it became known, was one more milestone on a road which the cabinet travelled with increasing discomfort. Any action of the Regent involved his ministers to some degree; and Leach, by consulting the Lord Chancellor over the choice of members of the commission and keeping Liverpool informed of what he was doing, blurred still further the distinction between the private acts of the Prince and the public acts of the government.[13]

More straightforward, though equally difficult, was the remorseless and never-ending campaign for economy. A House of Commons fresh from the embrace of the electorate clearly would not regard the cry of retrenchment as having exhausted all its political possibilities. For the fourth year running, therefore, the cabinet addressed itself to what seemed the unending task of pruning the estimates. The work began in July, earlier than usual in order to accommodate Castlereagh who was due to go off to Aix-la-Chapelle in September. The sole area left in which significant economies could still be made was the unfortunate armed forces. Liverpool and Castlereagh were in agreement that the only effective, if brutal, administrative procedure was to impose an arbitrary limit of expenditure on the army, navy and ordnance, with the subsequent argument revolving round methods rather than principles. Discussions on these points took up much of Liverpool's time during the summer but mercifully all three service heads were sufficiently sensitive to political considerations to cooperate. Only the navy, because of the rapidly deteriorating state of the fleet, proved in practice incapable of keeping within its financial quota. In their case, at least, the bottom of the barrel had been reached.

Nevertheless, Liverpool was insistent that the new establishment cuts should begin to take effect even before Parliament met and before the British army of occupation returned from France. It was not enough to blunt the edge of opposition attacks; their own friends and supporters must from the start be rallied to the side of the government. 'With respect to our reductions,' he wrote to Bathurst at the end of September from Walmer, 'the best argument to appease our royal master is this, that the fate of the Government must depend on the manner in which the first questions are carried in the new Parliament, that economy and reduction are the passions of the day, and that if he wishes to preserve his Government, he must allow them to manage the questions of establishments of all descriptions in such a way as to give no pretext to our friends to vote against us.'[14] The death of the old Queen Charlotte in November allowed the ministers in fact to make a more economical reorganisation of the royal household; though not without a tussle with the Regent and the Duke of York (which the ministry lost) over the proposed use of the Privy Purse for meeting some of the cost of George III's maintenance. Nevertheless, they were able to reduce the Civil List, and gently but firmly insist on economies in the Windsor establishment. The old blind King (as Liverpool was able to see for himself on his periodic official visits of inspection) had now lost all contact with the real world. Looking like a Jewish rabbi with his long, white patriarchal beard, he talked to the living as though they were dead and to the dead as though they were living.[15] In the ministerial view it was morally and politically indefensible to continue to surround him with a household appropriate to an actively ruling monarch.

Retrenchment, however, was at best a negative policy. The larger financial problem haunting the ministers was the intricate relationship of deficits, loans, interest rates and exchange levels. A government which could only make ends meet by heavy borrowing could hardly avoid contributing to inflation and high interest rates; and it was precisely this unpleasing combination which was feeding the whig and radical campaign against stock-jobbers, fundholders, speculators and bankers. By 1818 the country had been off gold for twenty-one years. Legally the Bank of England should have resumed cash payments six months after the signing of the peace, but year after year the government with Bank encouragement obtained a postponement. In theory the cabinet, like Parliament, though not the general public, were in favour of a return to the gold standard. The dispute between ministers was not over ends but methods. The bullionists argued that a deliberate decision to end bank restrictions was the only way to restore normality; the anti-bullionists argued for delay until deflation and favourable exchange rates made the transition relatively painless. The advantage of the bullionist argument was that it proposed a remedy capable of immediate application; the disadvantage of the anti-bullionists was that waiting for favourable conditions might mean waiting for ever. Though in 1810 Liverpool had, with other ministers, opposed the demands of Horner's committee for a return to gold within two years, he was not dogmatic and had been coming round to the view that a resumption of cash payments could not be deferred much longer. The difficulty was that his colleagues were still deeply and publicly divided. Vansittart, the Chancellor of the Exchequer, Castlereagh, the Leader of the House of Commons, and Harrowby in the Lords, were all apprehensive of the effects on government finances of the restricted credit and reduced note circulation which were the expected consequences of a return to gold.

The evidence suggests that by the start of 1818 Liverpool had made up his mind in favour of a restoration of the gold standard. The problem was one of timing; and here it was not only the domestic situation which had to be taken into consideration. International diplomacy had a habit of affecting international finances. In February the Prime Minister told Wellington that he was sufficiently acquainted with the Bank of England's circumstances to know that they could safely resume cash payments were it not for the financial difficulties of the French government. The root of the trouble there was the indemnity due to the allies. The French were naturally anxious to pay off the debt and get rid of the allied occupation; what they lacked was the means to do so. Liverpool was equally anxious that the allies should not evacuate France until a satisfactory financial settlement had been made. By this he meant not necessarily a full payment of the indemnity before the end of the military occupation, but an arrangement which would guarantee payment within a reasonable time after the allies had withdrawn their troops. To prolong the occupation indefinitely solely on the grounds of non-payment of the indemnity was not a course which the Prime Minister, with his usual political sensitivity, thought would be justifiable; but he considered that the allies had a moral right to press the French to come to some arrangement, before the troops left, which would enable them to pay off the debt. Since governments could not be trusted, and bankers could, he gave his encouragement to an agreement for a loan to the French government from a banking consortium headed by the English firm of Baring. The disadvantage of the scheme was that the strain on British banking resources imposed by the massive French loan would delay the resumption of cash payments. This, however, was a disadvantage which had to be accepted for the sake of the larger benefit of ending the occupation. It was not indeed the only loan to a foreign government floated on the London money market between 1815 and 1818. Russia, Austria and Prussia had also drawn on its resources. The French loan, however, was the largest and most conspicuous; and until 1819 no return in the shape of interest payments would be forthcoming. It was not surprising that both the Bank of England and the private bankers were concerned at the strain on British reserves. In May 1818, when all these matters were under discussion in the House of Commons, the Bank's stock of bullion (at about £8 million less than commonly realised) was sinking rapidly.[16]

The decision was, therefore, to continue bank restrictions for at least another year while making preparations for changing back to the gold standard when the time seemed propitious. In January 1819, however, the government's hands were forced by the directors of the Bank of England who now pressed for an enquiry in preference to yet another unsettling and inconclusive delay which was all that the government was offering them. To this the cabinet had no option but to agree; but though this unexpected development drove Liverpool into what Huskisson unsympathetically described as one of his 'grand fidgetts', it proved in the end a blessing in disguise. It enabled the Prime Minister to end without acrimony the deep division in his cabinet; and in the

House of Commons to beat off a hostile motion from Tierney in the neatest possible way by setting up a committee of his own choosing and on his own terms at the start of February. With this enquiry in prospect, a fundamental decision on future financial policy became unavoidable. Indeed, five days after the appointment of the committee on bank restrictions, Castlereagh moved for another committee on the wider issue of national income and expenditure. The cabinet were undoubtedly learning more subtlety in their handling of the Commons and this second committee was the first careful step towards a new financial system. The voice would be that of a House of Commons committee but the words would clearly be supplied by the ministers. Huskisson, who since the corn law discussions of 1815 had been one of the Prime Minister's closest economic advisers, was arguing strongly that a return to gold must be accompanied by a reduction of government debt and an increase in taxation. Liverpool himself was concerned at the mounting level of unfunded debt and a start had already been made in 1818 to repay some of it.

Certainly it needed no great financial acumen to see the illogicality of maintaining the Sinking Fund by borrowing at an even higher rate of interest than the fund itself yielded. It was obvious, as Huskisson and others pointed out, that the only real sinking fund was a surplus of revenue over expenditure. As far as Liverpool was concerned, they were preaching to the converted. Already the previous autumn he had been speaking of a surplus as something 'which ought at this time to be the object of all our efforts'.[17] To impose fresh taxes was to reverse the trend of government policy since the war, but that could not be helped. Indeed, it was no more than taking up again the task of finding substitutes for the income tax abolished against the will of the government in 1816. As Liverpool observed later in the House of Lords, since the peace some £17½ million of taxes had been rescinded and it was questionable whether all this retrenchment had been wise, in view of the heavy burden on the revenue of the National Debt interest payments. Under pressure of circumstances the whole pattern of governmental finance (and not before time) was beginning to change. The cabinet accepted the necessity; the argument once more was over methods. Herries, another of Liverpool's little 'economic cabinet', was bold enough to argue for a resurrection of the income tax. As auditor of the Civil List he was still primarily a civil servant and the professional politicians had too many pungent memories of 1816 to fall in easily with that proposal whatever its technical merits. The cabinet could see the social arguments for a fiscal shift which would enable them to reduce taxes on articles of popular consumption and thereby lower the cost of living for the poor. Whether the House of Commons and the middle-class public could be persuaded to reverse the decision of five years earlier was another matter. In the end the ministers decided to commandeer the Sinking Fund (some £15 million) and ask for another £3 million in new taxes. It was hoped in this way to produce an annual surplus of revenue over expenditure of £5 million during the next three years. It was a modest start; but a start nevertheless.[18]

The final determination to launch what was in effect a new financial policy was taken before the end of April. By that date the government had run into deep difficulties in the House of Commons on other matters. Despite all the work on the estimates the previous autumn, despite the announcement in the Regent's speech of considerable reductions in naval and military expenditure, despite the success on the bank committee issue, the new parliament was showing itself as captious and unreasonable as its predecessor in its passion for retrenchment and indifference to governmental needs. In February the ministerial plans for a reduced Windsor establishment were badly mauled; in March the opposition whig Mackintosh carried a motion for a committee on capital punishment against the government, thereby pre-empting the ministers' own modest scheme for legal and prison reform. Finally, after the Easter recess, Lord Douglas Hamilton won a victory by five votes against government opposition for a committee to consider petitions for a reform of the Scottish burgh electoral system. The defeats on these issues, and a run of dangerously low majorities on others, were only partly due to a new aggressiveness in the official opposition. The real damage was caused by the absence, abstention and often actual opposition of men who were normally government supporters. Defeatism is infectious and morale on the government benches was beginning to give way. Even the official men were becoming culpably slack in their attendance, noticeably so in the second week of March when Castlereagh was unavoidably absent. Twice Arbuthnot wrote to Liverpool to complain; he finally went in person with Huskisson and Long to tell the Prime Minister that unless better discipline was enforced, the government's authority in the lower house would collapse. Liverpool was reluctant to encroach on Castlereagh's sphere of responsibility but eventually called a meeting of office-holders at Fife House to urge better attendance.

Behind the disordered state of the House of Commons which was the despair of the harassed Treasury whips were deeper political currents to which Parliament itself was instinctively responding. Though public opinion did not hold the government responsible for all the economic and social troubles of the country, it did expect the ministers to show some kind of initiative. It was the apparent lack of it which was at the heart of the government's drooping reputation. Since the end of the war the ministry had been at the mercy of events; it had not controlled them. It had deferentially responded to pressure from Parliament and the public, but that deference had brought no honour and little reward either to itself or to the country. Now, belatedly and illogically, having for five years applauded every effort to weaken the government, the country was reproaching it for not showing more strength. By the beginning of May Liverpool had at last made up his mind that the long retreat must be halted. The government must take control of policy or perish in the attempt. Canning had been pressing for some issues on which a stand could be made in the House of Commons. Liverpool's decision was to make that stand on what was arguably the most controversial of all the ministerial proposals, the new financial policy still to be revealed in Vansittart's budget. Dangerous as this appeared, it had a certain logic. There seemed little prospect in any case of putting through their financial proposals unless they were made a question of confidence. If ministers were to put their existence at stake, they might as well make the stakes as high as possible. It was, he told the Regent, possibly their last chance of regaining the weight and influence they needed to carry on the government.[19] It is to be presumed that in this determined attitude he was supported by Castlereagh and Canning, the two leading ministers in the Commons; but not all his colleagues were ready to risk the fate of the administration on what in previous years had been the most vulnerable of all government policies. Eldon in fact warned the Prime Minister that he was inviting the end of the ministry.

Once he had made up his mind, however, Liverpool as usual was firm and uncompromising. He was, he told the Lord Chancellor, sanguine enough to think that they had a reasonable chance of success. If not,

> I am quite satisfied, after long and anxious consideration, that if we cannot carry what has been proposed, it is far, far better for the country that we should cease to be the Government. After the defeats we have already experienced during this Session, our remaining in office is a *positive* evil. It confounds all idea of government in the minds of men. It disgraces us *personally* and renders us less capable every day of being of any real service to the country, either now or hereafter. ... A strong and decisive effort can alone redeem our character and credit, and is as necessary for the country as it is for ourselves.[20]

His resoluteness came from his character; his sober optimism came from a conviction that when an issue concerned the actual existence of the government, the country gentlemen would not deliberately unseat them in order to install the opposition whigs. The very nature of the new taxes, which included a restoration of the malt tax discarded in 1816, would make it an acid test of their loyalty. To the Prince Regent, who was in some trepidation himself at the thought of hazarding the life of the administration on a single measure, and thought the malt tax would be peculiarly unpopular among the very MPs they wished to win over, Liverpool wrote austerely that the only alternative was a restoration of the income tax which would be even more unpopular.[21]

As it happened, the opposition played into the hands of the government. It was not the first time that, flushed with premature success, they overreached themselves. On 18 May, a week after Liverpool's letter to Eldon, the new leader of the opposition, Tierney, moved for the appointment of a committee on the state of the nation. He made it clear that the motion would effectively be one of no confidence by arguing that nothing less than a removal of the existing ministers would satisfy the country. This was meat too strong for the stomachs of most MPs and after four hours of wide-ranging debate the motion was defeated by a two to one majority. It was a reverberating defeat for the opposition – and a gratuitous one. Nevertheless, the fate of the government

Robert Banks Jenkinson aged 26.
From the painting by Sir Thomas
Lawrence *c.* 1796.

d Hawkesbury aged 37. From the
nting by John Hoppner *c.* 1807 in the
ection of the Rt Hon. the Earl of
erpool.

Lord Liverpool aged 50. From the painting by
Sir Thomas Lawrence *c.* 1820.

Lord Liverpool aged 50. From a sketch by
Sir William Hayter, 1820.

Lord Liverpool aged 56. From the painting by Sir Thomas Lawrence *c.* 1826.

Cartoon by James Gillray, 1796.

Lord Liverpool as depicted in the radical press 1820–21.

Lady Louisa Hervey, later Countess of Liverpool, aged 24. From the painting by George Romney *c.* 1791.

Lady Hawkesbury aged 34. A bust by Joseph Nollekens c. 1801.

Coombe House as it appeared *c.* 1930. It was demolished in 1933.

Fife House: a contemporary view from the Thames.

Louisa Theodosia, Countess of Liverpool. A posthumous statue by Sir Francis Chantrey *c.* 1822–4.

Hawkesbury Parish Church. The memorial tablet to the 2nd Earl of Liverpool is on the north wall.

still depended on the outcome of the finance debate. Nothing could be taken for granted and for the fourth time since January whips and ministers sat down to write letters to laggard friends urging attendance on 7 June when Tierney was to propose amendments to the financial resolutions. 'The existence of the present Government depends absolutely on the vote of Monday next,' Robinson wrote to one of his MP acquaintances. 'The difficulty which on more occasions than one we have experienced this year upon questions of no inconsiderable importance has placed the Government under the necessity of undertaking to stand or fall by the result of the debate on finance on that day.'[22] The threat of resignation was effectual. When the time came the Commons accepted, by a majority of nearly two hundred over Tierney's counter-motion, the recommendations of the Committee on Income and Expenditure.

The recommendations included one of which the government was subsequently to make much use. 'It is absolutely necessary that there should be a clear surplus of the income of the country, beyond the expenditure, of not less than £5,000,000.' It was a crucial declaration. Vansittart's belated budget, taking £12 million from the Sinking Fund and imposing £3 million of new taxes, still did not cover all expenditure and he again had to resort to borrowing. Nevertheless, the tide had been turned. The principle of the new financial policy had been accepted by the House of Commons; and the government had at last asserted its mastery in a field which was pre-eminently one of governmental responsibility. That was the great political achievement of the session. Even financially, with the resolution of the committee as a basis for future policy and the acceptance by the Commons of the report of the Bank Committee recommending a gradual return to gold by 1823, normality was returning. The Prime Minister, whose forecast of the result in the House of Commons had been resoundingly vindicated, could feel with justice (as he told Huskisson the following year) that at last they were getting back to a true 'state of peace'. The difficult process of extricating themselves from the abnormal demands, practices and consequences of the long war was nearly over.

It was a satisfactory end to the session; but the year was not over yet. Despite the report of the Secret Committees and the precautionary measures taken by the government in 1817, the radical agitation in the country had only momentarily been checked. By the summer of 1818 political clubs and radical associations were active once more, particularly in the industrial areas. At the start of 1819 the radical reformers embarked on a determined effort to influence public and parliamentary opinion by a display of physical strength, culminating in a series of monster meetings in London, the Midlands, Lancashire and Yorkshire. The popular demonstrations and the reckless language of the radical orators were all the more alarming since they took place against a background of industrial distress and reports of secret drilling by political unions. In August came the Manchester meeting in St Peter's Fields where a dozen people were killed and many hundreds injured in a clash with cavalry and yeomanry and during the general panic that ensued. That the magistrates had acted precipitately and unwisely (indeed, against the earlier cautionary advice of the Home Office) was hardly in doubt. Yet the magistracy was the government's first line of defence against social and political disorder, and in the disturbed industrial areas their unpaid, difficult and sometimes dangerous posts were not easy to fill. The JPs at Manchester had acted in good faith and the law officers of the Crown were agreed that the meeting was of a character which justified dispersal by force. As Liverpool wrote to Canning in September, 'When I say that the proceedings of the magistrates at Manchester on the 16th ult. were justifiable, you will understand me as not by any means deciding that the course which they pursued on that occasion was in all its parts prudent ... but, whatever judgement might be formed in this respect, being satisfied that they were substantially right, there remained no alternative but to support them.'[23] Sidmouth as Home Secretary had in fact promptly conveyed the commendation of the Prince Regent for the quick and efficient measures taken by the Manchester JPs and yeomanry to preserve public tranquillity: an uncompromising expression of official support which redoubled liberal anger. A storm of indignation swept the country and some inspired journalist coined the word 'Peterloo' in satiric reference to the government's other great victory in 1815.

So little had the government been expecting trouble that eight of the cabinet were abroad at the time, leaving only Sidmouth, Wellington, Castlereagh, Vansittart and Eldon available for consultation. They had several meetings with Liverpool during that troubled August but it was decided that no action was called for on their part. Sidmouth fretted at the Prime Minister's caution and continued to press for something to be done. Even before Peterloo he had been advocating further legislation against seditious activities. Now he proposed an early recall of Parliament, changes in the law and an increase in the army. Liverpool was doubtful; he thought this might suggest undue alarm on the part of the ministers. If any appeal was to be made to the independent country gentlemen in the House of Commons, he preferred first to find out how they were likely to respond. At Sidmouth's insistence, however, he summoned the three cabinet ministers still within reach – Sidmouth, Castlereagh and Wellington – to meetings on 15 and 21 September. At the second of these they discussed the Home Secretary's request for an early session of Parliament. The other two agreed with the Prime Minister that there were no adequate grounds for recalling Parliament before Christmas. Except in a few districts of England and Scotland, the country was quiet and the economy prospering. Liverpool did not dispute the need for strengthening the law against mass meetings and seditious publications, but he thought that consideration of these difficult matters could be left until Parliament met in the normal way. He could see no urgency; certainly nothing to change his intention of going off to Walmer on 25 September for six or seven weeks.

Within ten days, however, he had altered his plans. The reason was not the state of the country, about which he had fewer qualms than Sidmouth, but the fact that the opposition had decided to make the Manchester affair a party issue. This unexpected development changed the whole situation. Individual whig politicians had participated in some of the early protest meetings held in various towns; and after some hesitation and internal disagreement the party as a whole began in September to organise a series of formal county meetings. Their intention was twofold: first, to take the protest movement out of the hands of dangerous radicals, and second, to seize on the blunders of the Manchester magistrates as a means of damaging the government. The two objectives were not easily reconcilable and to the ministers seemed contradictory. In Yorkshire the list of signatories requesting a county meeting was headed by two great opposition peers, the Duke of Norfolk and the Earl Fitzwilliam, the Lord Lieutenant. Sidmouth at once renewed his pleas to Liverpool; and the Prime Minister, observing that the proceedings in Yorkshire 'will identify even the respectable part of the Opposition with Hunt and the radical reformers', consented to the holding of yet another cabinet. On 8 October, though still only half-convinced, he bowed to the general feeling in the cabinet that Parliament should be summoned for 23 November.

Vindication for the persistent Home Secretary was not long in coming. At the Yorkshire county meeting on 14 October a series of resolutions were carried which were not only endorsed but in fact drafted by Lord Fitzwilliam. They condemned interference with the right of popular assembly and demanded an enquiry into the proceedings at Manchester. This was an affront which could not be overlooked. The Lord Lieutenant was the direct representative of the Crown in his county and the protest which Fitzwilliam publicly supported was against an action which the Prince Regent had explicitly commended. Liverpool, who had delayed taking any decision until the result of the Yorkshire meeting was known, had now no hesitation in authorising Fitzwilliam's dismissal. 'Our forbearance,' he wrote to Sidmouth from Walmer on 17 October, 'would be ascribed to nothing but timidity, and would discourage our best friends.' However, it was thought right to go through the form of ministerial consultation. A cabinet was held on 20 October and next day Sidmouth despatched a messenger to Fitzwilliam to inform him that he had been removed from the lord lieutenancy.[24] The die was now cast. The opposition, whatever their doubts about associating themselves with Hunt and the radicals, felt obliged to close ranks round Fitzwilliam, one of their oldest, wealthiest and most respected peers. Ministers for their part now had to justify the early meeting of Parliament by bringing forward specific legislative proposals, knowing that they would come under the close scrutiny of their own supporters as well as the more hostile regard of the opposition.

Liverpool did not lack advice on what ought to be done. Lord Kenyon recommended the formation of armed loyalist associations; the Duke of York an increase in the army; a third peer suggested solving the unemployment problem by cultivating waste Crown lands. To this last the Prime Minister replied unsympathetically that had half the capital employed during the war in bringing marginal land under cultivation been used for the better cultivation

of the existing arable, production would have been greater and distress less. To
a proposal that government should give state assistance to industry and commerce, he observed in the pragmatic spirit of a true follower of Adam Smith, 'I
am satisfied that Government or Parliament never meddle with these matters
at all, but they do harm more or less. But sometimes, to avert a present and
very pressing evil, we are obliged to depart from what is sound, both in
principle and practice.'[25] Lord Grenville, in one of his rare direct approaches
to the Prime Minister, sent him a memorandum on the measures needed to
combat the dangers to public order which to his old, sombre mind recalled 'the
beginnings of the French Revolution'. To this unwonted mark of friendliness
Liverpool hastened to return a long, reasoned explanation of his views. Like
Grenville, like many Englishmen of his age and generation, though less excit-
ably, he too was inclined to think that economic distress alone would not have
produced the existing ferment in the country had not the French Revolution
popularised political agitation and weakened traditional deference to constituted authority. Nevertheless, he was not disposed to make much of the isolated
incident of Peterloo. The cabinet had agreed that Hunt, whose forcible arrest
at the meeting had precipitated the bloodshed, should not be prosecuted for
high treason and with his fellow-prisoners should be left to the leisurely process
of the ordinary courts rather than a Special Commission. What concerned the
Prime Minister was the more general problems: the growth of seditious journals, the delays and inefficiency of the legal procedure for dealing with trials
on indictment, and the alarming novelty of huge political open-air assemblies
which seemed to be replacing the traditional constitutional channels of parish
and county meetings.[26]

It was these matters which, together with a prohibition of unauthorised
military training, formed the substance of six bills which the ministers eventually laid before Parliament. The time had been short; the law officers had had
to work hard; and Liverpool had been obliged to come back to Coombe at the
beginning of November to go through the drafts before the text was submitted
to the full cabinet. What was noticeable was the anxiety of both ministers and
law officers not to encroach more than was necessary on the traditional liberties
of the subject; and later in Parliament their readiness to accept amendments
from the opposition. The propertied classes had undoubtedly been alarmed by
the events of the summer and to Liverpool's relief soundings among friendly
MPS showed a general feeling in favour of government action. Even so, the new
legislation was studiously moderate. Indeed, the Grenvillites and many of the
government's own supporters thought it decidedly weak. For this the blame –
or credit – clearly rested with Liverpool. The Home Secretary complained
privately to Ward that he wanted the Prime Minister to consent to 'local
measures of severity and power such as there were in Ireland', a reference
presumably to the right of Irish magistrates by 'proclaiming' a disturbed
district to assume additional security powers. Liverpool, however, had said
that there were too many obstacles to such a policy in England.[27] Apart from

temporary powers for magistrates to search for arms and prohibit mass meetings for specifically political purposes, the Prime Minister could assert with much truth that there was nothing in the bills which conflicted with the principles and traditions of the British constitution.

His main argument in the House of Lords was that it was better to take timely precautions than to allow disturbances to reach a point when forcible repression became necessary. Recalling what he had witnessed on the streets of Paris thirty years earlier, he warned the peers that 'it was the desperate conduct of the few, and the fears of the many, that produced revolution'. Disorder, he argued, engendered panic, and panic bred tyranny. 'The fear of the mob invariably led to arbitrary government and the best friends of liberty were therefore those who put down popular commotion, and secured the inhabitants of the country in the peaceable enjoyment of their rights.' In short, the object of the government's legislation was to strengthen the constitution by defending the peaceable majority against the desperate few. Echoed by Castlereagh in the House of Commons, these arguments probably elicited greater sympathy than the theory put forward by Sidmouth of a general conspiracy to overthrow the constitution. Opposition attempts to postpone the bills until there had been an enquiry into Peterloo and to blame the government for the economic grievances that had produced the disorders, failed to impress the country gentlemen. Few educated people thought that the ministry should be held responsible for the state of the economy, even if it was the state of the economy that produced dangerous demagogues like Hunt and tragic accidents like Peterloo. As Liverpool patiently and somewhat pessimistically observed in the House of Lords when discussing the limitations on governmental action,

> This was a doctrine that could not be too often or too strongly impressed on the people of this country. They ought to be taught that evils inseparable from the state of things should not be charged on any government; and, on enquiry, it would be found that by far the greater part of the miseries of which human nature complained were in all times and in all countries beyond the control of human legislation.[28]

It was a bleak doctrine; but one to which most politicians and economists subscribed even if many of their lowlier countrymen dimly felt that somehow there ought to be a different and better ordering of things.

The six bills went through Parliament with massive majorities, four of them before Christmas, which was as much as the Prime Minister had hoped. It was in a comfortable mood that the cabinet finally adjourned Parliament until 15 February 1820, a later date than usual to compensate for its unwonted pre-Christmas activities. The government's new financial policy had been successfully launched and the opposition, by their half-hearted echoing of the radical cry over Peterloo, had left themselves in an even more discredited position than at the end of the previous session. In politics, however, the only certainty is the arrival of the unforeseen. In the event, 1820 was to prove the most difficult and dangerous year of Liverpool's whole career.

NOTES

1 Yonge, II, 270; Cookson, p. 75.

2 George 4, II, 158.

3 Ibid, 169.

4 Ibid, 148.

5 Parker, I, 237.

6 Yonge, II, 298 ff.

7 38474 fo. 69; LWF, I, 226.

8 Stuart, p. 191.

9 For the Caroline issue see Cookson, pp. 200 ff.; Yonge, III, 12 ff. The cabinet memorandum, misdated in Yonge July 1820, is in fact that of August 1816 (Cookson, p. 206 n.).

10 Yonge, II, 366.

11 J.G. Lockhart, *Memoirs of Sir Walter Scott*, five vols (1900), III, 91; Cookson, pp. 142-3.

12 WSD, XII, 776-7, 812, 822; Oman, p. 257.

13 George 4, II, 410-14.

14 Bathurst, p. 456.

15 Cf. LM, pp. 11-12; *Reminiscences of Captain Gronow*, two vols (1889), II, 309-10.

16 WSD, XII, 267, 364, 375, 539; J.H. Clapham, *Bank of England*, two vols (1944), II, 64-8.

17 Bathurst, p. 457.

18 For the new financial policy see Cookson, pp. 168 ff.; Hilton, pp. 31 ff.

19 George 4, II, 290.

20 Twiss, II, 329.

21 George 4, II, 292.

22 *Letters of the First Earl of Malmesbury*, ed. Earl of Malmesbury, two vols (1870), II, 527.

23 Yonge, II, 407

24 For the Peterloo discussions see Yonge, II, 407 ff.; Twiss, II, 336-48; Pellew, III, 261 ff.; Bathurst, pp. 479-80.

25 Yonge, II, 416.

26 Ibid, 418 ff.

27 Ward, II, 20-27, 30, 32; BCR, II, 359-60.

28 Yonge, II, 442-5. On the Six Acts generally see Cookson, pp. 191-9.

CHAPTER VIII

The Queen and the King

In the spring of 1819 Cooke, the barrister who headed the Milan Commission, returned to England with a dossier of incriminating evidence against Caroline. The Commission's formal report was ready in July and a copy immediately submitted to the cabinet. For the ministers it was an embarrassing and irrelevant business. A shipload of evidence would not have persuaded them that any good could come from a royal action for divorce. All they did therefore was to repeat their warning that the testimony of continental witnesses would always be suspect in a British court and that to start a divorce bill in Parliament would be highly impolitic. If, they suggested, the Prince was not satisfied with their advice, he could consult his own law officers on the various courses open to him. Ministers had reason to be confident of their judgement. In June the Princess's legal adviser, Henry Brougham, had written to Lord Hutchinson, who was acting for the Prince in these matrimonial matters. His message was that he was ready to ask Caroline to agree to a formal separation and the renunciation of any future status as Queen on condition of receiving her existing financial allowance for the rest of her life. George regarded this as a virtual acknowledgement of her guilt and continued to press his own solution. The cabinet pointed out that divorce could not be obtained by consent or collusion, and that the best remedy was an amicable separation as proposed by Brougham. Meanwhile Caroline sent elaborate letters to Liverpool, Castlereagh and Canning, complaining of attacks on her character by false witnesses and threatening to return to England to insist on her rights.

In January 1820 the Prince's law officers delivered their opinion. They advised him that a charge of high treason could not be sustained on the grounds of adultery with a foreigner; that an action in the ecclesiastical courts was not appropriate; and that the only conceivable course was parliamentary legislation. This would, by its nature, involve examination of witnesses and allow the Princess to bring evidence to rebut the allegations made against her. There for the moment the matter rested; the Prince was confident that the Milan Commission had furnished him with irrefutable evidence of his wife's adultery and the cabinet equally confident that the Princess would agree in due course to a compromise settlement. These beliefs were both to be put to the test in the course of the year; for on Saturday 29 January 1820 the old forgotten King died at Windsor. He had been unwell since the beginning of the new year but the end came with great swiftness. Warning of the imminent event only reached Liverpool in time for him to set out for Windsor on the Friday evening. He spent that night at the castle and could have been in no happy frame of mind.

Earlier that day he had received what amounted to an ultimatum from Canning. After four years of decorous behaviour the President of the Board of Control was bored and frustrated; he was also conscious that the best years of his political life were passing. He told Liverpool that he could not go on much longer in his present position and that his talents were being wasted. The Prime Minister enquired whether he would take Sidmouth's place if, as seemed probable, the Home Secretary retired on the death of George III. This was not enough for the dissatisfied Canning. He touched on the possibility of going to India as governor-general (a lucrative appointment which had been in his mind for some time) and made it plain that unless he could have the leadership of the House of Commons as well as the Home Office, he would prefer India. Although in the lower house he was inevitably overshadowed by Castlereagh, he had been an efficient front-bench minister and the loss of his debating power was one the government could ill afford. Nevertheless, a demand of this kind, reviving memories of 1812 and the quarrels of the Portland administration, was one that Liverpool could not satisfy or Canning enforce. The most the Prime Minister could do was to offer him the first refusal of the Home Office when it fell vacant; and for Canning that was useless.[1]

Within twenty-four hours this unwelcome cabinet complication was pushed from Liverpool's mind by the larger and more pressing consequences of the King's death. Among the immediate details attendant on the start of a new reign were the necessary changes in the Prayer Book. George IV was insistent that Caroline's name should not be included in the prayers for the royal family. He was at the time seriously ill with pleurisy and there was a real fear that his reign would be over almost as soon as it had begun. It was not until 9 February that he was able to attend to public business. For over a week therefore the ministers were free to ponder on the fresh set of difficulties that his father's death had created for them. The question of the liturgy was only one of a number of problems connected with Caroline which now had to be confronted. Not unreasonably the cabinet was anxious to deal with them all together: the question of her title, her Civil List allowance, her place of residence, and finally George's long and loudly-expressed desire for a formal separation. It was obvious that his accession to the throne would increase his determination to have a divorce; it made the ministers equally determined that he should not. After a succession of meetings the cabinet by 10 February had arrived at an agreed solution for all these royal matters. There was little hesitation over the omission of Caroline's name from the liturgy though some (notably Canning) wondered whether this decision ought to be taken before the idea of a divorce was finally given up. On that larger issue the cabinet was unanimous. The scandal and mutual accusations that such a step would cause made it impossible to contemplate. If Caroline and her advisers were foolish enough to start parliamentary proceedings on their own account, the question of a divorce could be reconsidered. The moral advantage in that case would be on the side of the King and his government.

A long, carefully argued minute was accordingly drawn up advising the King to forego his right to a divorce and be content with a formal enactment depriving his wife of the title and privileges of queen-consort; any further financial provision should be made dependent on her continued residence abroad. While the document was being drawn up Liverpool saw the King on 9 February to prepare him for its recommendations. No doubt the compromise he and his colleagues proposed seemed to the Prime Minister eminently reasonable. Unfortunately the two people with whom he had to deal were highly unreasonable. Before the cabinet memorandum even reached him, the King sent his law officer Leach (whom the cabinet suspected of currying favour with his master for private reasons) to the Lord Chancellor to convey a warning that the King would insist on a divorce. If his present ministers could not procure him one, he would find others who would; in the last resort he would retire to Hanover and obtain one there. Next day, 11 February, Liverpool had an audience with the King to deliver the cabinet minute. He was told to present himself together with Eldon and Sidmouth for a private interview after the Privy Council on the 12th. At the Council the changes in the liturgy were formally approved. At the private meeting which followed, the King handed the three ministers a cleverly argued memorandum (probably written by Leach) criticising the cabinet's proposals. He told them that he regarded a divorce as a point of honour he could never abandon; he had no wish to change his government but a royal divorce was a *sine qua non*. According to the gossip which went round Whitehall later, it was an uncomfortable and sometimes stormy meeting. At one point the King reportedly asked Liverpool if he knew to whom he was speaking; to which the Prime Minister replied with spirit, 'Sir, I know that I am speaking to my Sovereign, and I believe I am addressing him as it becomes a loyal subject to do.' George apparently realised he had gone too far and later sent for Liverpool who at first refused to go. On a second summons he relented and was told by the King, 'We have both been too hasty.'[2] How far all this was true cannot be confirmed; but the atmosphere at the meeting was certainly unpleasant and the ministers went off anticipating their dismissal. The cabinet that evening sat late and Castlereagh wrote to his brother the following day, 'I consider the Government as virtually dissolved.'[3] Even under the threat of losing office, however, the Prime Minister and his colleagues stood firm. A second memorandum was drawn up on 14 February which reaffirmed, though in more conciliatory language, that they could not consent to initiate a bill of divorce.

It was the calm, courteous Castlereagh who was the first minister to make some impression on the stubborn and angry King. He had an audience with George on 14 February and another on the 16th, when the cabinet went to

Windsor for the funeral of the old King. At the second interview Castlereagh, in what was perhaps an oblique rebuke, apologised for discussing matter more proper to the Prime Minister. At that the King burst out pettishly that it was impossible for him to discuss such things with Lord Liverpool because he was deficient in both manner and temper; but he would always be happy to talk with Eldon or Sidmouth. His resolution was already beginning to crumble, however, as was evident from his suggestion that if an enquiry was brought on at the Queen's instance, it should automatically be followed by divorce proceedings. Even this tentative compromise was firmly rejected by the cabinet. They suspected that the King was only yielding because he had discovered that the opposition also would not support him. If their suspicions were true, any further talk of changing his government was bluff. That in fact was what it turned out to be. On 17 February a message was received from the King expressing his readiness to fall in with the cabinet's wishes. The immediate crisis was over and since ministers had always believed that George was a greater obstacle to a peaceful settlement than Caroline, the way forward now seemed unobstructed.[4]

For the Prime Minister the most unpleasant feature of the crisis had been the way in which he had been singled out as the target for the King's displeasure. Up to that point relations between prince and minister had been good and often cordial. George IV did not pay the same constant and detailed attention to the work of government that his father had done; and on matters of patronage, where his interests were most likely to be aroused, Liverpool's combination of firmness in principle and smoothness in action had avoided any serious friction. It was difficult for the Prime Minister to feel the emotional veneration for the new king that he had for the old; and George IV had too questionable a private life of his own for ministers to have much sympathy for him over his admittedly objectionable and adulterous wife. Eight years at the head of affairs had developed in Liverpool a habit of authority. He had strong constitutional views on the duty of the monarch to accept the advice of his ministers as long as he retained them in his service; and it irked him that, in the face of the formal and informal expressions in previous years of the cabinet's disapproval, the King still clung to the notion of a divorce. After the threat communicated by Leach to Eldon, the Prime Minister must have anticipated a scene with the King on 12 February; and given his temperament, no doubt he was ill at ease when he went in for the audience. This in turn may have made his manner more abrupt. Certainly what the King complained of was not a nervous demeanour but an outspoken tongue. It was a side of Liverpool which perhaps George had never encountered before. If so, it would have come as a disagreeable surprise because of the Prime Minister's normally quiet and even-tempered habits of business.

The King's indignation was natural enough. To free himself from his odious wife had become almost a dominant passion. He would have been less than human had he not expected that his accession to full kingly dignity would bring a corresponding increase in authority and influence. To be confronted at the outset of his reign by the opposition of his own cabinet on a matter so dear to his heart stirred up a deep resentment which understandably vented itself on their leader and spokesman. Once the breach had opened up, the temperamental contrast between the emotional, self-indulgent, weak-willed monarch and the sensitive, morally serious but determined Prime Minister ensured that it could not easily be healed. George IV was not a vindictive man; few of his dislikes and ill-humours lasted very long. Yet over his wife he was implacable; and after February 1820 something of that implacability entered into his attitude towards Liverpool.

The Prime Minister, however, was sustained in his purpose by the conviction that what he was doing was in the best interests of the King himself. The time now seemed propitious for direct discussions with Caroline's advisers. Accordingly he sent for Brougham, that ambitious and not very scrupulous barrister who had become an influential figure among the radical whigs. Liverpool's chief object was to discover whether the proposal of the previous years still held. His chief bargaining weapon was the fact that Caroline's allowance as Princess of Wales had legally expired with the death of George III and no more money could be expected until the government had laid its new Civil List arrangements before Parliament. He was also anxious to prevent her from coming to England before a settlement was reached. Brougham readily fell in with the Prime Minister's proposals and offered to visit Caroline at some convenient spot on the continent to make it clear to her that she should remain abroad while an agreement with the government was worked out. The unpredictable element in the situation, he observed to Liverpool, was Caroline herself who had some right to regard herself as queen already and of whose headstrong temper no man could be sure. At the time it seemed only the kind of remark any shrewd negotiator would make at the start of a hard round of bargaining. Brougham otherwise spoke with confidence about his relationship with Caroline; and since he hinted that his own promotion to KC would obviate any protocol difficulties over his appointment as the Queen's attorney general, it seemed he was not above the kind of worldly considerations which the government had in their power to offer. If that was his price, Liverpool was prepared to pay it; Canning indeed was anxious that he should. It was apparently Eldon the Lord Chancellor who put obstacles in the way of making Brougham a silk, despite a direct entreaty from the Prime Minister. Since Eldon was prepared, however, to recognise Brougham's status as the Queen's attorney general, there seemed no positive necessity for any further professional advancement.[5]

The mistake was to place any reliance on Brougham at all; but this was early in his career. Ten or twenty years later ministers would have been more wary of 'Wickedshifts', as his fellow-whig Creevey nicknamed him. At the time Liverpool thought he would be trustworthy because his own interests required him to be. The quandary for Brougham was that he had far less power than he allowed to appear. Wellington's later assertion that he had betrayed everybody

- the King, the Queen, the cabinet and Lord Hutchinson – was not perhaps literally true. Yet his tactics were so devious, and his control over his client so slight, that the effect was much the same. He had some grounds for believing in 1819 that Caroline would accept a compromise; but he had proposed terms of settlement without obtaining authority from her beforehand or informing her afterwards. He concealed from her the fact that ministers had offered a reasonable arrangement. He tried to frighten the Queen by talking of parliamentary proceedings and the government by encouraging her to come to the French coast. He did virtually nothing he undertook to do and in the end tried to shuffle off the blame for failure on others. It was several months before his complete unreliability was exposed and by then it was too late.

Hard on this first crisis of the reign of George IV came the grisly irrelevance of a plot to murder the entire cabinet. For the public it was a nine days sensation; for the ministers little more than a momentary distraction from their busy official routine. The intentions of the Spencean radicals, Thistlewood and his equally crackbrained conspirators, were serious enough. Their grim preparations showed what might have happened had their security been as great as their fanaticism. There was an informant in their ranks, however, and the Home Office had known for some time of their general purpose. Many of the ministers were incredulous and, in the absence of precise details, no special preparations were made to protect them. Then, on 22 February, it was learnt from more than one source that the attack was to be made the following evening at Lord Harrowby's house in Grosvenor Square where one of the regular cabinet dinners was to be held. To avoid arousing suspicion the arrangements for the dinner were allowed to go forward and there was some discussion on whether to await the attack or arrest the conspirators beforehand at their meeting-place in Cato Street, off the Edgware Road. Wellington, that master of defensive tactics, recommended that the cabinet should lock themselves in Harrowby's dining room and resist the assassins until the troops surrounded the house and caught them redhanded. His more cautious civilian colleagues decided against this spirited course of action. 'We thought it better', Castlereagh wrote lightly to his brother, 'to stay away from the festive board, and not to suffer it to go to single combat between Thistlewood and Marshal Liverpool.' Since the Prime Minister's fencing days were far behind him, this was perhaps as well. Instead it was left to individual ministers to dine elsewhere and assemble afterwards at Fife House.

Harrowby, having sent his wife and daughters to safety, dined with the Liverpools and Lady Erne. The two ladies, not yet in the secret, were naturally curious at this unexpected change of dinner engagements. When told the real reason both had mild hysterics and Louisa, whose health had recently been poor, actually fainted. Later the rest of the cabinet dropped in one by one to await in suspense the first news from Cato Street of the action by police and military. After all the careful preparations to spring the trap on the conspirators, it was a disappointment to learn that, largely because the troops were late in arriving, one police constable was killed in the scuffle and Thistlewood with several of his gang had escaped. Sidmouth, however, assured his colleagues that Thistlewood would be in his hands within twenty-four hours. His confidence in the Home Office network of intelligence was justified. Thistlewood was arrested in his bed the following morning and on Sunday 27 February the cabinet attended the Chapel Royal at St James's to return thanks for their preservation.[6]

The leading conspirators met their inevitable judicial fate on 1 May 1820, the day of the London chimney-sweeps' holiday, when the streets were lively with music, drums and mummers. Long before then Liverpool was immersed in other cares. Although by law Parliament could continue for six months after the death of a sovereign, it had been decided to hold an early election. A House of Commons about to meet the electors was an even more sensitive and capricious body than one recently returned by them. Parliament was dissolved in mid-March and after the elections met again on 21 April. There was little to distinguish the new House of Commons from the old. The polling had been quiet; the government recovered some of the ground it had lost in 1818. There seemed no support among the electorate for riot and sedition; and the Six Acts that were to acquire such exaggerated notoriety in later radical tradition were generally approved. Nevertheless, it was undeniable that an undercurrent of dissatisfaction continued. Liverpool, though maintaining that the government was more popular than the opposition, feared that radicalism was making headway in Scotland and parts of England. What other government supporters lower down in the hierarchy, like Peel and Huskisson, noted was a widespread feeling that not enough had been done and that ministers were out of touch with the restless and critical mood of the country. Perhaps they were less insensitive and remote than their critics imagined. Liverpool needed no persuading that, while more constructive measures were being planned, retrenchment or at least severe economy must continue to be the watchword of the ministry.

One problem that had to be tackled immediately was the Civil List for the new reign. This was something which the House of Commons, who could never overlook George IV's previous architectural extravagances, were certain to submit to an unusually searching examination. The King, not unnaturally, expected that the disappearance of a separate establishment for his father and his own accession would be marked by a more generous provision than he had enjoyed as Regent. Preliminary estimates, from his not entirely disinterested court officials, suggested that an increase of about £65,000 would be appropriate. There was little or no chance that this would be accepted by the Commons and the Prime Minister braced himself for renewed difficulties with his disgruntled monarch. To allow ample time for argument and attendant delays, he obtained estimates from the palace officials in March. On the main issue, however, he probably made up his mind as soon as he was able to talk with Castlereagh after the latter's return from electioneering in Ireland. When

Liverpool and his little financial committee – Vansittart, Huskisson and Long
– looked at the proposals after Easter they were in quick agreement that the
King would have to reconcile himself to a continuation of the establishment
voted for him in 1816. A period of economic depression, with much suffering
among the poorer classes, was no time to go to Parliament with a request for
an increase in the royal allowance. The King, still sore from his bruises over
the divorce question, received this decision with considerable sullenness. It was
not until Sidmouth, one of his more favourite ministers, had been to see him
that Bloomfield was able to inform Liverpool of the King's acquiescence.[7]

As a precaution the draft of the King's Speech, which included an announcement of the unchanged Civil List, was submitted for approval earlier than
usual. The Prime Minister's anticipation of difficulties proved correct. The
King returned the draft with alterations to the paragraph on the Civil List and
a note for Liverpool which to his anxious mind raised once more the possibility
that George intended to dismiss them. 'I have an answer from Windsor of the
most unsatisfactory kind,' he wrote to Bathurst on 23 April, 'and such as *I think*
should lead to the dissolution of the Government.' He summoned a cabinet for
the following day which was attended by all but one of the ministers. To his
colleagues, however, it appeared that the King had not absolutely rejected
their advice and that it would be unwise for Liverpool to regard his reply as
grounds for resignation. A firm memorandum was drawn up, reiterating their
recommendations, with a request that George should give an audience to
Liverpool and Castlereagh as soon as he had been able to study it. Once more
the King surrendered, but with worse grace than usual. When Sidmouth had
an interview on 26 April the King told him that he knew the memorandum
had been drawn up by the Prime Minister and only signed by the rest of the
cabinet as a matter of duty. It was high time, he added sulkily, that they
decided whether they were servants of the King or servants of Lord Liverpool.
To this piece of royal petulance the Home Secretary made the austere reply
that the memorandum had been discussed and approved by the whole cabinet;
that they were all servants of the King; and that they would only continue so
long as they enjoyed his confidence.[8]

When the new parliament met at the end of April the political value of the
King's enforced financial restraint was at once apparent. The new Civil List
proposals (involving a saving of £238,000) secured the hearty support of the
House of Commons which rejected opposition wrecking motions from
Brougham and Lord John Russell by handsome majorities. Yet the jealousy of
the House over any suggestion of waste or jobbery, and the fluctuating nature
of support for the government, were demonstrated only a week later by Hamilton's attack on a Scottish judicial appointment. The matter was relatively
trivial. Relying on Scottish legal opinion, the government had ignored the
recommendations of a recent committee of enquiry and maintained at five the
number of judges in the Scottish Court of the Exchequer. The censure motion
was staved off by only twelve votes and the narrowness of the division was the

equivalent of a moral defeat for the ministers. When another vacancy occurred the following month they prudently refrained from filling it. The incident prompted another bout of discussion in ministerial circles about the weakness of their parliamentary position and possible ways of improving it. Arbuthnot, the Treasury Secretary, spoke with Liverpool about the advisability of recruiting individual members of the opposition. The Prime Minister showed little interest. It would, he observed, merely discourage the younger people on their own side. Mrs Arbuthnot's tart but justified reflection when her husband reported the conversation was that the best way for Liverpool to strengthen his administration was to get 'more hold on the mind and opinion of the nation generally, which is in fact what the present Government wants the most'.[9]

It was a common complaint; yet in his quiet, infinitely cautious way Liverpool was already addressing himself to that task. While ministers, aided by some of the opposition economists like Ricardo and Baring, firmly resisted attempts by the agriculturalists to obtain an even higher level of protection than that afforded by the 1815 Corn Law, Liverpool went out of his way to encourage the spread of liberal economic opinions in manufacturing and mercantile circles. The efforts of Tooke, another economist, to organise a free-trade petition in the City of London were discreetly backed by the government and a deputation which came to Fife House in April was agreeably surprised to discover the Prime Minister's sympathetic views – a revelation which argued no great familiarity with his parliamentary speeches. The following month the eccentric Lord Stanhope tried to win the support of the House of Lords for a poor-relief programme of spade husbandry, wasteland cultivation, and restrictions on the use of machinery. These amateurish economic notions were promptly demolished by the Prime Minister in person. On machinery he was particularly eloquent. Next to the spirit of the people, he told the peers, England was indebted for her commercial power and greatness to her mechanical inventiveness. It had, as he picturesquely expressed it, given legs to the lame and sight to the blind. Not natural advantages of soil or climate but the minds and talents of her engineers had created British economic dominance – men like Watt, Boulton, and Arkwright who were as useful in their generation as any of the legislators of old in theirs. Lord Stanhope, he advised, should go to manufacturing towns and meet the men who from the humblest social conditions were daily rising to wealth, honour and eminence in the state.[10]

Tributes from the minister of the day to the pioneers of the Industrial Revolution were not, perhaps, the common diet of the House of Lords; but it so far agreed with Liverpool as to negative Stanhope's motion without a division. Ten days later, on 26 May 1820, he improved on this lesson by delivering one of the most important free-trade speeches of his career. The occasion was a motion by the whiggish Lord Lansdowne for a committee of enquiry on foreign trade. He opened the debate with a wide-ranging speech and Liverpool, who spoke immediately after him, was similarly expansive. The result was a more illuminating exposition of his economic views than the public

had so far heard. It was a clever, almost artful speech. His purpose seems to
have been threefold: to support the proposal for an enquiry without identifying
himself with Lansdowne's more extreme theoretical opinions; to encourage the
free-trade movement without alarming too many vested interests; and to
camouflage his specific suggestions for reform with generalisations about the
difficulties of rapid change. He emphasised once again the interdependence of
agriculture, manufacture and commerce, and the need for a national policy
covering all three. 'Any attempt to legislate in favour of one of those interests
to the exclusion of the others, would be most destructive to the whole.' On the
other hand, 'what is for the benefit of the one, must be beneficial to the rest'.
Free trade was theoretically the best policy, of that 'I can entertain no doubt'.
Yet in a protectionist world no one country could afford to apply the theory
either completely or immediately. Even so, he did not think Britain was
benefiting particularly from its protectionist system. Some might argue that
the country had risen to greatness because of it. 'Others, of whom I am one,
believe that we have risen *in spite* of that system.' Heavy national indebtedness
and low taxation put it out of the question, however, for Britain to make any
early or drastic changes in its tariff code. Then, turning to topics of current
discussion, he reiterated the government's determination to resist any attempts
to increase corn protection or go back on the recent currency legislation.
Elsewhere, he observed casually, some relaxation could be introduced without
danger. The cotton trade, for example, need not fear competition from anywhere in the world. The same was true of woollens, though not, regrettably, of
those artificially-reared manufactures, silk and linen. An extension of bonded
warehouses would help make Britain an *entrepôt* of world commerce; duties on
foreign timber could be reviewed; restrictions on British trade with India could
be eased. All these matters could be looked at by a committee. He did not
anticipate all the results Lord Lansdowne expected. Difficulties abounded;
hasty and partial legislation was to be deprecated. 'I firmly believe that on all
commercial subjects, the fewer the laws, the better.' Nevertheless, he was most
willing to see what could be done.

His carefully oblique approach pleased advanced free-traders without
alarming practical men. It was a mark both of the importance attached to it as
a statement of policy and of the government's growing awareness of the need
for better publicity that the speech was later published as a pamphlet. After five
painful years ministers were learning something about the arts of peacetime
politics. While admonishing caution, the Prime Minister had in fact provided
a programme. When, early in June, a similar committee was appointed in the
House of Commons, the ground was deftly laid for the first large attack on the
historic protectionist system that had for so long swaddled British commerce.
The government had demonstrated neglected powers of leadership; a tacit
alliance had been made with liberal free-traders on the opposition benches;
and the machinery of tariff reform quietly put in motion. It was a historic
moment. In its review of the economic debates of the session the *Annual Register*

noted with pleasure 'the liberal views of our national interests, adopted and proclaimed by the leading members, both of the Ministry and of the Opposition'.[11] For ministers, however, the sense of progress was shortlived. Before the two committees had presented their reports, the constructive work of the government was brought to a halt by the sudden irruption of the Queen's business. For the rest of the year the royal scandal obsessed the mind of the public and absorbed the energies of the Prime Minister. Scandal at that august level, as Liverpool had realised with sinking heart for many months, inevitably involved the government. The worst sufferer from the divorce affair of 1820 was not the hapless, hated King, nor the vulgar, vanquished Queen but the Prime Minister who saw the parliamentary strength of his administration almost destroyed and his already damaged relationship with the King strained to breaking-point.

After the general election the King expressed a wish that his friend and adviser Lord Hutchinson should be associated with Brougham in any visit he made to the continent to negotiate with Caroline. Liverpool was asked to call them both for a briefing on the government's attitude. After a preliminary meeting the Prime Minister saw them again in the middle of April when he read out a memorandum embodying the cabinet's terms which he then gave to Brougham to retain. Brougham, now officially recognised as the Queen's attorney general, was also told by the Prime Minister that if Caroline came to England, parliamentary proceedings against her would be unavoidable. At the lawyer's request this warning was put into writing and on 20 April delivered into Hutchinson's keeping since Brougham professed a certain delicacy at being the bearer of such a message to his royal client. Some weeks of inaction followed. Brougham showed no sign of hastening across to the continent and in the meantime Caroline started her leisurely journey from Italy. She reached Geneva (where Liverpool had wanted Brougham to meet her) in the second week of May and instructed her attorney general to present himself at St Omer, a town within easy reach of both Calais and Boulogne, on 30 May. On 31 May Liverpool received a letter from her asking for a residence in London and a royal yacht to transport her across the Channel. He at once wrote a note to Brougham urging him to set out at once for the continent and repeating that if the Queen landed in England a message to Parliament would follow immediately. On 3 June Brougham reported to Liverpool from St Omer. His message was worse than unsatisfactory. The Queen was bent on coming to England; Brougham had warned her of the consequences but had not yet mentioned the cabinet's proposals for a settlement; and Hutchinson, though introduced to the Queen, had not had an opportunity to discuss with her the government's attitude.

Further letters from both men made it clear to the angry cabinet that Brougham had grossly exaggerated his influence with the Queen and that such conversations as had taken place with Caroline had been brief and perfunctory. Hutchinson's informal note, setting down from memory what terms the govern-

ment were offering, was only put into her hands five minutes before she set off
for England. Several days later the astounded Liverpool learnt that Brougham,
under the pretext that Hutchinson was responsible for conveying the government's views to Caroline, had never communicated to her at any point
Liverpool's memorandum of 15 April. Deceived and betrayed, the cabinet had
now no option. Both their offer and their threat to Caroline had been designed
for one purpose only: to keep her out of the kingdom. When that failed, their
position would have become ludicrous had they not put the threat into effect.
Whether any further attempt at a negotiated settlement might have succeeded
after Caroline's arrival is doubtful. The fact remained, however, that since 15
April the Prime Minister had virtually lost his freedom of manœuvre. It was
an unenviable and dangerous situation for any politician. On 5 June, when it
was known that the Queen was actually crossing the Channel (she landed at
Dover that evening), the cabinet met at Fife House, broke up at midnight and
resumed at ten the next morning. There could only be one outcome to their
painful discussions. That same afternoon Liverpool went down to the House of
Lords with a message from the King giving notice that in view of the Queen's
arrival at Dover the previous day, certain documents would be laid before
Parliament that called for their earnest and immediate attention.

The government had crossed their political Rubicon; there could now be no
withdrawal. Any compromise proposal, designed to settle the case by consent,
would have to come from Caroline. That bold and brazen woman ('the most
impudent devil that ever lived', according to the Duke of Wellington) was in
no mood for compromise. The cheers of the multitude, the delegations from
corporate bodies, the lavish hospitality of the radical City politician Alderman
Wood, the public sympathy of the middle classes and the private aid promised
from opposition peers, all combined to convince her of ultimate victory. In
reality her strength lay solely in her husband's unpopularity. The radical mobs
adopted her as a symbol of their hostility to the King and his ministers. The
respectable middle classes in town and country, who knew little of her mode of
life on the continent, saw her as an injured and innocent queen. The aristocracy, who knew a great deal about her, thought her no more immoral than
her husband and less to be blamed. The opposition supported her because they
were confident that a divorce bill would never go through Parliament and that
its defeat would bring down the government.

Last-minute negotiations to find an amicable settlement soon broke down.
The Queen demanded recognition of her rank and privileges; Liverpool replied
that both were implicit in the government's proposals of 15 April. She suggested arbitration; the King would only agree to conversations between Wellington and Castlereagh on one side, Brougham and Denman on the other.
These ended in deadlock over Caroline's insistence on either a restoration of
her name to the liturgy or an official introduction as Queen to foreign courts.
In the House of Commons the pious and well-meaning Wilberforce secured a
resolution urging the Queen in complimentary language to make concessions.

Their sympathetic address, presented by a delegation of MPs on 24 June, was politely rejected. The Commons, although it was a Saturday, assembled on that day to hear Caroline's reply. Liverpool also remained in town to learn the outcome. He was given the news personally by Lady Erne's son-in-law, Stuart Wortley, who had been one of the delegates and came round afterwards to Fife House. There was little surprise there at the failure of the delegation's peacemaking mission, though some regret. Louisa was chiefly vexed that she would have to go off alone to Coombe where she and her husband had planned to escape for one night. While sorry for the necessity of proceeding with a public enquiry, Liverpool was quietly confident, as he strolled in his garden that summer afternoon, of the strength of the case against the queen.[12] What seemed beyond all doubt was that she was the kind of woman who would take advice from nobody and that further negotiations were useless.

Nevertheless, not everybody in the cabinet was equally happy over what had been decided. At the start of the Commons proceedings Canning, while defending the action of the ministry, made several flattering (some thought adulatory) remarks about the Queen which revived the old scandal about his relationship with her twenty years earlier. Before the debate he had offered his resignation to the Prime Minister. Liverpool pointed out the embarrassment which this would cause to the government and persuaded him to withdraw it. The King was so enraged by Canning's speech that (if Hobhouse is correct) he put it to the Prime Minister that Canning should be made to resign. Getting no satisfaction, he retaliated on 11 June by refusing to give an audience to Liverpool and Castlereagh until the Prime Minister had furnished him with a satisfactory explanation of Canning's words about the Queen. Liverpool insisted that the speech had been honourable to Canning and useful to the government; and bluntly declined to be a channel of explanation for another minister since that would imply a degree of censure on Canning himself. Within twenty-four hours the King's temper subsided; but at the suggestion of Castlereagh, who had sensitive memories of being kept in the dark by his colleagues during the Walcheren business, the Prime Minister told Canning of the King's displeasure. An audience was then arranged to smooth the matter over. The royal ill-will, in fact, was directed as much against Liverpool for his subsequent defence as against Canning for the original offence. In a private interview with Sidmouth the King spoke angrily of the need to replace the Prime Minister with a more congenial colleague: a notion which the Home Secretary declined to foster. Liverpool for his part in certain moods seemed equally prepared to dispense with the services of the King. Talking in private towards the end of June about George's intense unpopularity – even the soldiers of the Household Brigade in London, he said, drank the Queen's health – he observed with unusual acerbity that if the King did not show himself more to the public, it might be better for him to withdraw to Hanover until the storm had subsided. With the Duke of York as regent there would be more tranquillity.[13]

Meanwhile, in an atmosphere of sustained and concentrated public excitement such as nobody could remember, the parliamentary proceedings against the Queen got under way. Because of the action already taken in the Lords, the Commons had postponed their own committee of enquiry. The Secret Committee in the upper house (which included Liverpool, Eldon and Sidmouth) made its report, recommending legislative proceedings, on 4 July. The Prime Minister, who like Castlereagh and the Lord Chancellor had previously been against a formal divorce, was now persuaded that this was the least complicated course of action. Next day he introduced a bill of pains and penalties to deprive Caroline of her rights as Queen Consort and to dissolve the marriage with the King. The second reading was fixed for six weeks later. In the interval, while radical mobs with banners and cockades roamed the West End cheering for the Queen and groaning outside the houses of ministers, and the air was thick with rumours of mutiny among the household troops, the two sides prepared for what was in effect, if not in form, a judicial trial.

On 17 August, in a House of Lords ringed by horse, foot and artillery, with gunboats patrolling the Thames, the submissions of counsel and the examination of witnesses began. All that month a procession of couriers, cooks, chambermaids, porters, grooms, and equerries poured out the unsavoury details of Caroline's private life to a half-shocked, half-fascinated audience of peers and commoners, and within the space of a few hours, through the medium of the press, to the British public at large. When the prosecution case was concluded early in September, Brougham was granted a further delay of a month to prepare his defence. In this, as in other ways not generally known, Liverpool acted with scrupulous fairness towards Caroline and her legal representatives. The government put up the money to provide her with a residence in London; they paid the legal costs of the defence; they permitted on her behalf the introduction of evidence not usually allowable; they left officers of the King's household, normally expected to vote in Parliament with the government of the day, free to act as they pleased. Though the opposition treated the issue as a party matter, and only two of their number (Lauderdale and Donoughmore) in the event voted for the bill, no corresponding ministerial pressure was brought to bear on peers friendly to the government.

All this was unknown to the public and ignored, even if known, by the generally hostile national press. In the winter of 1819–20 the radical cartoonists and pamphleteers had already been exploiting the extravagances of the Prince Regent, the 'massacre' of Peterloo and the Six Acts. The divorce issue enabled them to turn with redoubled zest to the congenial task of presenting Caroline as a high-minded, courageous and innocent queen persecuted by a loathsome and licentious husband. Though their attacks inevitably concentrated on the vulnerable and portly figure of George iv, ministers did not escape the odium being heaped on nearly all the institutions of the state. In previous years Liverpool had been handled lightly by the popular press. Their particular detestation was for Sidmouth as Home Secretary, Eldon as Lord Chancellor, and Castlereagh as Leader of the Commons against whom old, malicious charges of brutalities in Ireland during his period as Chief Secretary were kept continually alive. Since the Cato Street conspiracy he habitually carried a brace of pocket pistols even in his own house and for a time during the Queen's trial he slept at the Foreign Office for greater safety. There is no evidence that the Prime Minister took any special precautions, but even he had to endure his share of radical abuse. In the immensely popular pamphlet by Hone and Cruikshank, *The Queen's Matrimonial Ladder*, for example, which ran into over twenty editions, he and Castlereagh were depicted as the fawning lackeys of a fat, royal voluptuary. It was as well that ministers were less sensitive than their master to this kind of press scurrility.

During the trial the cabinet met regularly after the House of Lords' sittings in order to discuss the progress made and the reactions in Parliament. It soon became evident that some bishops and many peers, on grounds of conscience or expediency, had scruples about a divorce, irrespective of any proof of adultery. Liverpool himself, in a short debate in the Lords early in August, had indicated that he did not regard the divorce clause as an integral part of the bill. Though the majority of the cabinet still wanted it retained, the Prime Minister (to the annoyance of some of his colleagues) subsequently took the view that he was pledged by what he had said to support any formal motion for its omission. On 1 September he wrote a letter to the King which was remarkable as being an expression of his personal views and at no point invoking cabinet authority. In it he said that from his extensive communications with peers and bishops he was convinced that there was little chance that the divorce clause would pass. He requested permission, therefore, to offer to abandon it before the defence proceedings began. The King hesitated and suggested a personal interview with the Prime Minister and some of his colleagues. After Liverpool, Castlereagh, Wellington and Sidmouth had been to see him, he granted the Prime Minister's request and it was announced in the Lords the following day. Even so, it was still far from clear what the fate of the bill would be despite this prospective lightening of its load. Though a majority was confidently expected on the second reading, there were doubts whether it would be large enough to constitute a moral victory for the government: that is to say, a majority of the independent peers, not counting ministers and household officers.[14]

The case for the defence took up the whole of October. It was not until 3 November, on the second reading, that Liverpool made his one important contribution to the debate. He intervened on the second day of the discussion, immediately after Lord Grey, the leader of the opposition. Apart from Eldon, who made a brief and ineffective speech, and Harrowby, who uttered a few words, he was the only cabinet minister to speak. As manager for the bill on behalf of the government he had already won general admiration for his dignity, calmness and impartiality. Louisa's niece Caroline, who usually had sharp words for her aunt, and is therefore in this instance an all the more credible witness, wrote to her mother on 10 September that 'her vanity and her better feelings must at this moment be highly gratified about Lord Liverpool, who is constantly gaining himself more and more credit and respect'.[15] In his speech of 3 November he excelled himself. It was a model of that species of advocacy, the more deadly for being dispassionate, which consists in making every reasonable concession to the opposing side, voluntarily discarding all doubtful or uncorroborated evidence, and concentrating instead on proved and relevant facts to produce a cumulative and irresistible effect. For mastery of debate and forensic skill, it could not have been bettered by any professional advocate.

At the start he seemed nervous and embarrassed, and made Arbuthnot, as he listened to his chief, feel nervous too. The future Earl of Albemarle, standing near the throne in the crowded chamber, made even more congested by the temporary galleries put up to accommodate the press reporters, thought from the odour wafted towards him that the Prime Minister was taking doses of ether to quieten his nerves. The simpler explanation possibly is that Liverpool, who had a cold and was very hoarse, was using some vapour to clear his nose and throat. He finished his speech the next day with growing power and assurance. All who reported on it were unstinting in their praise. 'He was admirable,' wrote Arbuthnot, 'and made her guilt as glaring as we know it is. Castlereagh was close to me and was as much pleased with it as myself.' Wellington, though he was out of humour with the Prime Minister because of the way in which he had kept the management of the trial in the hands of the Attorney General and himself, told Mrs Arbuthnot that he spoke 'most remarkably well'.[16]

On 6 November the second reading of the bill was carried by 123 votes to 95, a smaller majority than the government had hoped and expected. Many peers who had no doubt of the Queen's guilt were unconvinced of the bill's utility. Nevertheless Liverpool felt some relief that a clear majority of peers had been found to condemn her. After his earlier misgivings and hesitations, now that a firm course had been chalked out he was characteristically resolute. By contrast most of his colleagues were becoming increasingly lukewarm about the whole business. Castlereagh for one wanted the bill quietly put out of the way in the Lords without ever coming to the Commons. Yet with admirable loyalty even those with the greatest doubts felt it their duty to stand by the Prime Minister despite his growing isolation. The King, somewhat illogically, had hoped for a good majority for the bill in the House of Lords so that he would obtain greater popularity by withdrawing it before it went down to the Commons. This, however, the Prime Minister refused to sanction. Having pledged himself to the King to introduce the bill, he was determined to go on with it until he succeeded or success was clearly seen to be unattainable. His distaste for the Queen's private life had probably not been lessened by the frequent sight of her in the House of Lords as she listened to the proceedings: the corpulent figure and protuberant breasts, the coarse defiant face, and the bizarre contrast between her naturally blonde complexion and the thick black painted eyebrows and wig of black curls that appeared beneath a variety of startling hats. To his sense of moral repugnance was added the more practical conviction that discussions in the Commons could not be staved off indefinitely and that it might be as well to let the topic exhaust itself sooner rather than later.

On 8 November, however, the government was beaten by 62 votes to 129 on the divorce clause. Ministers had supported a motion for its removal but the whole force of the opposition now switched their tactics and voted for its retention as a way of making the bill more objectionable. It was a cynical but not ineffective manœuvre. In the cabinet next evening Liverpool at last admitted doubts about the wisdom of proceeding any further. It was an ill-humoured discussion. Most of the ministers were worn out by the interminable meetings of the Lords; and tempers had been strained by the repeated arguments in the cabinet. The Prime Minister himself was weary and on edge. To Eldon, who stubbornly opposed the abandonment of the bill, he at one point spoke sharply and with untypical discourtesy. It was not the first time that he had betrayed his nervous tension by sudden gusts of emotion within the privacy of the cabinet. Few realised in fact what inroads the strain of the divorce was making on his physical and mental resources. 'In the whole course of my life,' he confessed to Canning on 12 September, 'I do not recollect to have undergone such continued fatigue as during the three weeks of proceedings in the House of Lords.' The whole time too he had the added burden of his wife's ill-health. Throughout the summer and autumn of 1820 Louisa was seriously unwell. While her husband carried out his distasteful duties in the Lords, escaping from London only at the weekends, Louisa was being nursed by her sister Mary in the tranquillity of Coombe Wood. Not until October, when she seemed a little better, was Lady Erne able to return to her own home for a short time. In the end it was agreed in cabinet that if the majority on the third reading of the bill dropped to something like ten or twelve, Liverpool should be at liberty to withdraw it, since there would then be no rational prospect of getting it through the House of Commons. As usual, the final decision was left to the Prime Minister. In the debate the next day on the third reading, Eldon, at Liverpool's personal request, spoke on certain technical aspects of the bill. When he sat down Liverpool passed him a note. 'Most admirably; I am much obliged to you for it; and sorry if what I said last night gave you pain. L.'[17]

In the division which followed the government majority sank to nine: for the bill 108, against 99. Liverpool immediately rose to say that in view of the narrow division, the government proposed to withdraw the measure, though (he added defiantly) had the figures been as favourable as on the second reading, he would have thought it his duty to send the bill to the House of Commons. For the cabinet as a whole, and perhaps for the Prime Minister as well, it was a happy deliverance. Ministers had justified both their original decision to bring in the bill and their final decision not to press it further. They felt that they had proved the case against the Queen, and already fancied they could detect a reaction against her in the country. Nevertheless, though they might find comfort in the rectitude of their behaviour, the political situation in which they found themselves after the withdrawal of the bill in the House of Lords was hazardous in the extreme. The King wanted Parliament to make an immediate financial provision for the Queen so that she would have no excuse for remaining in the kingdom. The cabinet, rather more knowledgeable about parliamentary management, wanted time for the popular excitement to subside and for soundings to be taken among MPs on what would be an acceptable provision for Caroline. After an unpleasant tussle with the King they carried their point, and Parliament was prorogued until the end of January. George's unwilling surrender concealed an even greater hostility to his ministers than they realised. In secret he was trying to screw himself up to dismiss them. By a typical piece of self-deception he had persuaded himself that his unpopularity was due to the mistakes of his government and that his credit would be restored by a change of ministers. During November he had been rehearsing argument and counter-argument with his confidant Knighton and sounding prominent opposition whigs on their views. Finally on 25 November he had a private interview with Lord Grenville in which he made him a virtual offer of the premiership. Liverpool had been notified beforehand of the Grenville audience but not its true purpose. It put him, according to Arbuthnot, 'in a fever' since little imagination was needed to guess George's intentions. Secret talks between the monarch and elder statesmen out of office could scarcely be reassuring to any administration.

By mid-November the government to all appearances was in a precarious state. Caroline was demanding a royal palace and a suitable establishment to go with it; the opposition were joyfully anticipating the collapse of the administration in the new year; faithful government supporters were divided and dismayed. Liverpool's own reserves of mental and physical strength were running dangerously low. 'I feel', he wrote tiredly to Arbuthnot from Coombe on the 13th, 'I have few, very few, publick friends in the world. I wish only to be thoroughly and honourably released. I will not abandon others but I am by no means sure that they will not abandon me and leave me to be the *sole* victim of the present clamour.'[18] Many members of the public shared this gloomy view of his personal future and looked forward with relish to his impending departure from the political scene. A cartoon by Cruikshank published the following January showed the bowed, dejected figure of the Prime Minister, the notorious Green Bag containing the documents for the Secret Committee slung round his neck, riding a melancholy ass towards a waiting gallows. Beneath was a slightly garbled text from 2 Samuel: 'And when Ahithophel saw that his Counsel was not followed, he saddled his Ass and arose and went and hanged himself.'

Nevertheless, though the bill had been abandoned, Liverpool refused to give way on what he believed to be the issue of principle. As he had explained to Wilberforce at the end of November, he was ready to make a generous and unconditional financial provision for the Queen (an income of £50,000 was what he had in mind) but the government would pay her no honours beyond what was strictly her legal right, would not provide her with one of the royal palaces, and above all would not reinsert her name in the liturgy.

No consideration will induce me to be a party to any such measure. If Parliament should determine upon it, the country must dispense with my humble services. I would rather live in retirement the remainder of my life than give any sanction to a measure which will, I am satisfied, give a deadly blow to the moral character of the nation.[19]

By giving express permission to Wilberforce to show this letter in confidence to his friends, the Prime Minister was clearly preparing for the crucial test in the House of Commons at the start of 1821. What was now at stake was the fate of the government itself. It was a mark of the desperate position in which ministers saw themselves that once more they invoked this final sanction.

The Prime Minister's depression in November was not lifted by Canning's return to the cabinet after an absence abroad of several months. He at once made it known that he disagreed with Liverpool's intentions with regard to Caroline and in mid-December he finally resigned his office. To Liverpool's tired mind Canning's desertion, at a time when the administration faced a hostile inquest on its conduct as soon as Parliament reassembled, was of a piece with the rest of his past political career. He told Arbuthnot angrily that Canning had no moral principles in public affairs, looked only to his private advantage, and never considered himself bound in honour to act fairly by his colleagues. Nevertheless, mastering his feelings, he did what he could to coax Canning from his determination, inviting him down to Walmer for 'a long and thorough talk', and allowing himself to be half-persuaded that Canning could not, for purely personal reasons, be an active member of the government until all repercussions of the Queen's affair were over. When resignation could no longer be postponed, he helped to draft Canning's farewell letters to the King and the other members of the cabinet so as to cause as little offence as possible.[20]
The vacancy created in the cabinet was offered to Peel, who, since the conclusion of his highly successful Irish Secretaryship in 1818, had been an obvious candidate for higher office. Peel, however, like Canning, had disagreed with the ministry over their tactics in dealing with Caroline and felt reluctant to join at that moment. Liverpool had some sympathy with this attitude and, realising that other possible candidates might feel similar scruples, decided to postpone decision on the permanent appointment. As an interim arrangement Bragge Bathurst was asked to assume responsibility for the India Board.

Liverpool's own future, if not actually threatened, still had much uncertainty about it. When the King received Canning's letter of resignation he sent, not for the Prime Minister, but for Sidmouth. It was a snub which was felt. Next morning Liverpool went off for a weekend with Wellington at Stratfieldsaye, leaving Lady Erne to look after Louisa at Coombe. He had sufficiently re-

covered his spirits on his return to entertain his two ladies with an account of
the charades in which he had taken part. His youthful distrust of his acting
abilities had apparently died down; Arbuthnot, who was also a guest at the
house-party, thought he had shown himself very expert in that species of
entertainment. In view of his bad leg, however, the Prime Minister had wisely
declined to join the younger members of the company in a game of blind-
man's-buff.[21] After these mild diversions he had an interview with the King on
18 December which passed off tolerably well.

Time had also allowed tempers to cool elsewhere. The government, by
printing in pamphlet form the speeches of Liverpool and Lauderdale, and
recommending favourable articles extracted from the London newspapers
(notably the *New Times* and *Courier*) to friendly provincial journals, had ex-
ploited what publicity they could to strengthen the growing reaction against
Caroline. Stout, if somewhat scurrilous work was also being done on their
behalf by a new and independent conservative newspaper, *John Bull*.[22] By the
time Parliament came together at the end of January there were signs that
opinion in the provinces was rallying to the ministry. Soundings among friendly
MPs by the Treasury indicated that most of the government's usual supporters
approved the cabinet's policy of making suitable financial provision for the
Queen but refusing her both a royal residence and reinstatement in the Prayer
Book. When the inevitable post-mortem debates took place in January and
February, the ministerial confidence was more than justified. Particular motions on the liturgy and general motions on the government's handling of the
divorce issue, resulted alike in even more comfortable majorities for the government than their whips had forecast. Ministers pointed to the majority obtained
in the Lords as a moral justification of their action against the Queen but at
the same time made it clear that they neither wished nor intended to proceed
any further against her. The opposition whigs, on the other hand, tried to whip
up popular feeling less with any hope of achieving something for Caroline than
as a last desperate attempt to overturn the government. Satisfied that the long
sorry affair was over and that no vindictive action would be taken against the
Queen, the majority of MPs could see little point in sacrificing the ministry and
letting in the whigs simply for the sake of Caroline's fly-blown reputation.

As public support receded, the Queen's ability to embarrass the government
disappeared. Though at first she declined to accept any financial allowance
until her name was restored to the Prayer Book, she accepted it in the end.
When she asked whether she could attend a Drawing Room at Court to present
a personal petition to the King, George refused to admit her. The cabinet took
precautions in case she presented herself at the palace but in the event she
merely sent her petition to the Prime Minister who returned an official rejection. In April she notified Liverpool that she wished to come to the coronation.
He advised that her letter should be ignored but George, fearing that silence
might be interpreted as consent, instructed him to send a formal intimation
that the King declined to give permission for her to attend. Some argumenta-

tive correspondence followed and the Privy Council finally had to give a ruling that the Queen's presence had never been an invariable, still less an obligatory, feature of royal coronations. The tragi-comedy of desperate entreaties and official rebuffs ended on coronation day when Caroline was turned away from the doors of Westminster Abbey and drove off to the jeers and catcalls of the onlookers. The sudden collapse of popular support for the Queen seemed at the time as inexplicable as the sudden frenzy of enthusiasm on her behalf the previous year. In retrospect it is obvious that the violence of the 'Queen's affair' was little more than a symptom of the gap between the machinery of royal government and the sentiments of the mass of the population which had opened up so alarmingly since the end of the war. If so, the end of the extraordinary divorce crisis did not mean that this fundamental weakness in the position of the administration had been cured. That could only be achieved by the ministers themselves and there was still much to be done. At most it could be said that Liverpool had successfully steered his cabinet through an unprecedented and dangerous episode with little help from either King or Parliament. Though at the start the cabinet had allowed themselves to be boxed into a dangerous corner they had been extricated from it by a combination of firmness in principle and flexibility in tactics which once again demonstrated Liverpool's indispensability to the administration. The Prime Minister, remarkably enough, had emerged from the crisis with his personal reputation enhanced; the same could hardly be said of the government over which he presided.

NOTES

1 Dixon, p. 198; Hinde, p. 296.
2 Greville, 20 Feb. 1820.
3 CMC, XII, 210-13.
4 For this early crisis see Yonge, III, 12ff.; Hobhouse, pp. 4-10; Cookson, pp. 210-13.
5 Yonge, III, 54 (Liverpool's memorandum); Cookson, pp. 229-31; Chester W. New, *Life of Henry Brougham* (1961), pp. 228 ff.
6 Pellew, III, 311-25; Foster, p. 344 (wrongly dated 1810); A. Alison, *Lives of Lord Castlereagh and Sir Charles Stewart*, three vols (1861), III, 112 n. See also J. Stanhope, *The Cato Street Conspiracy* (1962).
7 Hobhouse, pp. 18-19.
8 Ibid, pp. 19-20; Bathurst, p. 483; George 4, II, 324-6.
9 ARJ, I, 19.
10 16 May 1820.
11 AR, 1820, p. 93.
12 LWF, I, 269.
13 Hobhouse, p. 27; ARJ, I, 26; George 4, II, 344-5.
14 George 4, II, 361-3; Hobhouse, p. 36.
15 LWF, I, 277-8.
16 ARJ, I, 50, ARC, p. 19; Earl of Albemarle, *Fifty Years of My Life* (1877), p. 233.
17 Twiss, II, 398-9; Hobhouse, pp. 39-40; ARJ, I, 51-2; Yonge, III, 106 ff.

18 ARC, p. 21; Bathurst, p. 490.

19 Yonge, III, 111 ff.

20 ARC, pp. 21-2; ARJ, I, 55; Cookson, pp. 286-90.

21 Hobhouse, pp. 44-5; LWF, I, 290; ARJ, I, 59-60.

22 Bathurst, p. 489; LM, p. 102; A. Aspinall, *Politics and the Press* (1949), p. 151.

CHAPTER IX
The Turn of the Tide

With the nightmarish experience of the Queen's trial behind them and politics beginning to flow back to their normal channels, ministers could at last take up once more the economic measures foreshadowed in 1819. Their policy was very much of their own devising. It owed little either to promptings from the floor of the House of Commons or to pressure from the business world outside or to the stimulus of returning national prosperity. It was a policy sired by hope out of necessity. Members of the trading and manufacturing world, while tepidly subscribing to free trade as a general principle, tended to oppose its application in any specific instance where their own livelihood was involved. There were, in the Prime Minister's words, too many 'connected and complicated' vested interests in the commercial system to make liberal legislation an easy matter. The House of Commons, with few pretensions to erudite economic wisdom, preferred to tread the well-worn path of retrenchment and economical reform, varied by periodic inquests on the depressed state of agriculture. It was in any case too divided to be able to produce any coherent programme. The radicals under Hume concentrated on reducing government expenditure; another group led by Lord John Russell had taken up the cause of parliamentary reform; whig legal experts like Mackintosh were pressing for widespread changes in the criminal law; and the Webb Hall agricultural protection movement in the English counties had secured a voice in Parliament through such MPs as Gooch and Western. Ministers, painfully conscious of endemic unrest among the poorer classes and impatient at the slowness of economic recovery, increasingly realised that they would have to take action themselves to guide the country back to order and prosperity. With sharp memories of Peterloo and the Queen's trial, and a House of Commons that seemed as unmanageable as ever, they faced the task with some caution. The tactics of the indirect approach exemplified in Liverpool's 1820 speech led to a preference for working through parliamentary committees rather than making direct ministerial proposals. It was not heroic but it was sensible and it worked.

The first fruits of the new policy were the reports of the two committees on foreign trade set up in 1820. That of the Commons committee, drawn up by Liverpool's protégé Wallace, the Vice-President of the Board of Trade, was particularly forceful. The greatest advantage that could be bestowed on British commerce, it argued, was as much freedom from interference as possible. All restrictions not justified by special considerations should be abolished; the Navigation Acts should be modified; and the system of bonded warehouses should be extended in order to encourage international trade. All this had been foreshadowed by Liverpool's speech two months earlier. Reappointed in February 1821, the committee issued a further series of reports which paved the way for specific legislation. One bill, lowering the duty on timber from northern Europe, was passed the same session and five more under Wallace's guidance followed in 1822. A committee of a different nature was that on agricultural distress, set up by the government to mollify the discontented agriculturalists rather than to lead to any action. Its report consisted of an historical explanation of the troubles afflicting British agriculture and a philosophic argument that legislation could do little or nothing to remove them. Huskisson, who was largely responsible for the report, had only with difficulty been persuaded to serve on the committee and the rough handling he received from the disappointed country squires strengthened his general sense of grievance at the inferior position he occupied in the ministry. Nevertheless, the consistency of ministerial economic policy had been preserved and the way left open for a reduction rather than the increase in agricultural protection for which the agriculturalists had been asking. Liverpool had never regarded the 1815 Corn Act as more than a temporary expedient and it was becoming clear to the cabinet by 1821 that the case for admitting foreign supplies at a reasonable price would soon have to be looked at more closely.

By 1821 in fact the government's policy was beginning to take on a more unified and active appearance than at any time since the start of the peace. While the Board of Trade was busy with plans to liberalise and stimulate the economy, Vansittart was able to promise a large reduction in the estimates and in the end was better than his word. Even the Home Office under Sidmouth was making progress with a general measure of prison reform. While the departmental heads were busy, however, Liverpool was still oppressed by a sense of the political weakness of his administration. With both the King and the House of Commons its roots seemed planted in shallow soil. In the lower house not only did ministers have to contend with continual and unreasonable demands for even more retrenchment and tax-reduction, but opinion, even among the more responsible members, seemed to be moving in directions which to his mind, growing more conservative with age, seemed inherently dangerous. A small but typical example was Grampound, a Cornish borough which had been condemned for gross corruption a few years earlier. In March 1821 Lord John Russell's bill to give the two seats to the unrepresented town of Leeds was carried in the House of Commons. Liverpool was horrified; he not only objected in principle to this disturbing precedent but was alarmed that some of the solid country gentlemen (including his unreliable nephew Stuart Wortley who moved the third reading of the bill) apparently were ready to make fundamental constitutional concessions in the hope of silencing radical demands for a general measure of parliamentary reform.

Unlike some of his colleagues, notably Eldon and Bathurst, who opposed any change, Liverpool was not against the actual disfranchisement of Grampound. In the House of Lords he supported the principle of transferring the two seats but obtained an amendment giving them to the county of Yorkshire. As he made clear to the House, he favoured reform in particular cases where abuses had been proved; but he did not like any general schemes of remodelling the electoral system. 'He supported the present bill, not because he was a parliamentary reformer, but because he was an enemy to all plans of general reform.' It was a traditional conservative policy of conceding a little immediately in order to avoid conceding a great deal later. As a concession, however, it was hardly calculated to satisfy the growing movement for enfranchising some of the larger, unrepresented towns. There was, in fact, a respectable case for giving Leeds or Manchester their own MPs since they were not only important industrial centres but had actually been parliamentary boroughs in an earlier period.

On that narrower issue Liverpool had already expounded his views in a memorandum he had circulated to the cabinet in an endeavour to get an agreed government policy on the issue of parliamentary reform. His argument was that to give separate representation to such places was the worst remedy of all. It would create a source of constant political turbulence in what were already, particularly Manchester, notorious centres of political agitation and would swell the list of large, corrupt boroughs of which there were already too many.

> I do not wish to see more boroughs such as Westminster, Southwark, Nottingham etc. I believe them to be more corrupt than any other places when seriously contested; and I believe the description of persons who find their way into Parliament through these places are generally men who from the peculiarity of their character or their station, are least likely to be steadily attached to the good order of society.

He had no prejudice against boroughs or in favour of the counties as such. If any satisfactory scheme of borough reform could be devised, he would prefer to keep the existing balance of town and country representation. Failing that ideal vision of the future, however, the best practicable course was to give the two disposable seats to a county.

> County elections are the least corrupt of any in the kingdom. The representatives of them, if not generally the ablest members in the House, are certainly those who have the greatest stake in the country and may be trusted for the most part in periods of difficulty and danger.[1]

It was a carefully qualified tribute to what most conventional political wisdom regarded as 'the soundest part of the House'. Liverpool had experienced too much trouble of his own from the country squires to heap superlatives on them.

Nevertheless, his recipe was admirably adapted to win over a cabinet which contained some notable reactionaries like the Lord Chancellor. It had the disadvantage, however, of concentrating too much on preserving the character of the House of Commons and too little on making more acceptable to the general public a system that was increasingly being regarded as anachronistic.

The Commons accepted the revised bill, even though they had previously rejected a similar one in their own House. The fact that the government had actually assumed responsibility for the disfranchisement of Grampound was an interesting item in the annals of parliamentary reform; but it was of minor significance compared with the refusal to sanction the enfranchisement of Leeds. How long it would be possible for the House of Lords, even backed by the authority of the Prime Minister, to overrule the lower house on such an issue was questionable. The same doubt applied to an even greater constitutional principle which came up during this session. In April, for the first time, the Commons passed by nineteen votes a bill for the enfranchisement of Roman Catholics. Under Liverpool's neutrality rule, this could not strictly be regarded as a challenge to the government. In any case the defeat of the bill in the Lords, if not entirely assured, was made predictable by a hostile speech from the Duke of York, the heir presumptive to the throne. The Prime Minister, Eldon, and Sidmouth all spoke against it, Liverpool as uncompromisingly as his two colleagues. There was not, he said flatly, three lines in the bill with which he could agree. Civil and religious liberty was something all should enjoy; but political privilege and power should be bestowed by the state in the light of its own security. The bill was rejected, but only by thirty-nine votes, a frail enough screen against the formal decision of the Commons. Even before the debates in the lower house were over, the Prime Minister was sufficiently pessimistic to send a warning to the King not to commit himself publicly against the bill in case, sooner or later, Emancipation had to be conceded.[2] Times were changing, but in 1821 he was too old or too tired or too depressed to change with them.

The difficulties of the government in the Commons were made even greater by the poverty of speaking talent on the front bench. Almost the whole burden fell on Castlereagh (now Lord Londonderry since the death of his father in April), who was never regarded even by his friends as a dexterous speaker. Vansittart only spoke on departmental business and not effectively even then. Bragge Bathurst commanded little respect; Wellesley Pole was unable to control his temper; Huskisson was shy and unpopular (free-trade intellectuals were not greatly beloved by the country gentlemen). The indolent Robinson largely confined himself to answering questions about trade. Since what the administration needed was a more authoritative presence in the lower house, it was not surprising that the Prime Minister constantly turned his thoughts towards Canning and Peel, the best orator and the best debater respectively in the House of Commons. With Sidmouth ready to lay down the burden of the Home Office the time seemed propitious for a general overhaul of the ministry.

In March there were cabinet discussions of a plan to move Melville to the Home Office and Vansittart to the Board of Control, making room for Canning to come in as First Lord of the Admiralty and Peel as Chancellor of the Exchequer.

Objections to these proposals came unexpectedly from Londonderry who, although constantly complaining of overwork, seemed unnaturally disturbed by the talk of a cabinet reshuffle. He opposed Peel's appointment with the curious argument that it would diminish his own influence as Leader of the House. The matter was left open for a time but when renewed discussion in May failed to overcome Londonderry's resistance, Liverpool abandoned the idea of shifting Vansittart and decided instead to offer Peel the Board of Control. Even with this truncated scheme he made no headway. He spoke to Peel at the end of May about coming into the cabinet, but disconcerted the younger man by his hesitant manner and failure to name any specific office. When a few days later he mentioned the India Board, Peel showed no interest. Asked by Liverpool whether his disinclination extended to other posts, he replied somewhat stiffly that the time to consider that would be when an actual offer was made. It was an unhappy interview. The Prime Minister was tired and under personal strain. Louisa's protracted illness had recently taken an ominous turn and though Liverpool had for long refused to give up hope of a recovery, he was now having to steel himself for the inevitable end. There were other complications of which Peel was unaware. No other post could be made the subject of an offer until the Prime Minister knew what Canning wanted; and no firm proposition could be put to Canning until the King's permission had been secured.

To obtain this permission was in itself a political problem. Not only had George's grievances against Canning not disappeared but his discontent with Liverpool was still simmering. In an audience with the King in February Wellesley Pole had been obliged to listen to a tirade against his leader which (on Wellington's maladroit advice) he had repeated to Liverpool. All it elicited was a testy remark from the Prime Minister that he was tired of serving such a master and would willingly resign his office when the circumstances allowed. In April there was a sharp clash over George's wish to appoint a young if blameless curate, tutor to the Conyngham children, to a canonry at Windsor. Liverpool, who prided himself on the quality of his ecclesiastical appointments, refused to sanction the promotion and enlisted the support of Sidmouth and Castlereagh. In the end the King gave way but took paltry revenge by encouraging Lady Conyngham to flirt with the whigs and inviting Lord Lansdowne and other leading opposition members to dine at the Pavilion.[3] When at the end of May Liverpool first raised with him the project for bringing Canning back into office, he found the King in a highly obstructive mood. The Prime Minister's proposal was for Melville to take Sidmouth's place at the Home Office and Canning to go to the Admiralty. The King put an instant veto on this and in the next few days did his best to make bad blood between Liverpool and Sidmouth over the question of the latter's retirement pension. The Home Secretary had sense enough not to be taken in by fulsome royal support and not only rejected a hint from George that he might become Prime Minister himself but disinterestedly urged him to accept Canning.

The King, however, remained adamant. He was ready, he told Liverpool on 9 June, to gratify Canning by an appointment as governor general in India but he would not permit him to enter the cabinet. Next day by agreement the Prime Minister submitted a paper with a full list of the changes he wished to make, including not only the Melville–Canning arrangement but an offer of the India Board to C.W. Wynn, a Grenvillite, and (a sop to George) the retention of Sidmouth in the cabinet without portfolio. The following evening a box with the King's reply arrived at Fife House where Liverpool, Lady Erne and Cecil Jenkinson were gathered at the dying Louisa's bedside. The letter was short and discouraging. Sidmouth's retention was approved; for the rest, 'the King can see no necessity, and consequently has no wish, or intention, of changing the present frame of his Government'. On reading this Liverpool's overstrained nerves gave way. He threw the box on the floor, tore up the letter, and declared passionately that he would resign office.[4] A few hours later, at half-past five on the morning of Tuesday 12 June, Louisa died.

For the next few days Liverpool was completely prostrated and unable to see anyone. At Castlereagh's instance Arbuthnot sent him a note to inform him of a softening of the King's attitude (he now merely asked for a postponement of any decision over Canning) and of the feeling in the cabinet that no ministerial changes at all should be made until the following session. Liverpool replied in a tired emotional letter in which only his willpower seemed to survive. 'I feel', he wrote, 'I have neither strength nor health to engage in a protracted discussion.' Nevertheless, to allow Canning to remain excluded from the cabinet when a vacancy existed for him would be the equivalent of a proscription. 'Upon such a principle, so applied, I cannot agree to remain at the head of the Government.' He referred morbidly to a scheme which he thought was on foot 'not to destroy the Government at present, but to have the means of destroying it whenever the opportunity may be more convenient', and added wearily that 'it is not affectation in me to say that I am ill in body, as well as in mind'. Until he returned from Louisa's funeral in Gloucestershire, he wished to be spared further discussion, but if the King then still adhered to his previous decision, 'he must look out for another minister'.[5]

At his request this letter was shown by Arbuthnot and Castlereagh to Wellington, Bathurst, Sidmouth and Melville on 16 June. This inner group of colleagues concurred in thinking that nothing should be done until the Prime Minister was able to discuss the situation once more with the King. The only shade of difference between themselves and Liverpool was, as they honestly stated in another sympathetic letter sent by Arbuthnot to Liverpool's secretary Willimott, a doubt whether the entry of Canning (in itself clearly desirable) should be forced on the King immediately. Otherwise they stood loyally by their leader and Wellington undertook to tell George that he should admit Canning and adopt any other measure Liverpool advised to strengthen the administration. The touchstone of the King's intentions towards the ministry, they argued, would be his reaction to the proposal to bring in the Grenvillites. If that was refused, it would be obvious that he wished to keep the government weak, so that it could more easily be dismissed on some future pretext. If accepted, it would be a sign that there was no such covert intention since the Grenvillites would be an indispensable element in any alternative administration. On 18 June Sidmouth was at last able to see the Prime Minister. Though distressed and agitated, Liverpool probably derived some comfort from their conversation. As often happens when men are still suffering from shock, he talked more freely and personally about Louisa than he had ever done before with Sidmouth. In turn the Home Secretary did his best to persuade him that there was no sinister purpose behind the King's behaviour and that it would be best for the moment not to force the issue of Canning's appointment.[6]

Immediately afterwards Liverpool went off on his depressing journey to Gloucestershire. The funeral of Louisa was a harrowing time for him. It was reported (and in view of the morbid streak in her nature it would not be uncharacteristic) that she had left directions that no one was to touch her body but her husband; and that he nearly fainted when he had to lift her slight, emaciated corpse into its coffin.[7] On 19 June the funeral procession left Fife House for its long, slow progress to the west country with all the conventional pomp of the period. Six horsemen riding two and two preceded the hearse which was drawn by six horses with plumes of black feathers and covered by a pall with Louisa's armorial bearings. Behind came three mourning coaches each with six horses. For the first part of the journey out of London the cortège was lengthened by a great train of over seventy carriages belonging to sympathetic peers and gentry, among them those of the royal dukes of York and Clarence, her kinsmen the Duke of Devonshire and Lord Verulam, the Duke of Wellington, and Lords Hertford, Bridgewater, Harcourt, and Spencer. The interment took place in the family vault of the Jenkinsons in the little parish church of Hawkesbury on 22 June. All through the service Liverpool sat blinded by tears and almost oblivious of those around him. Even when it was over he insisted on going down into the vault for one last look at her coffin.[8] He returned to Coombe Wood early the following week, quieter but exhausted, and did not appear in town until Tuesday 26 June when he had long talks with Londonderry and Sidmouth.

Canning had already written twice to release him, in view of the King's opposition, from any obligation over office; though he could not resist the temptation to put in a strong plea for Huskisson's promotion.[9] The Prime Minister's two colleagues probably stressed once more the unwillingness of the cabinet to see the administration break up over Canning, especially now that the King had relaxed his uncompromising attitude and Sidmouth was ready to serve a while longer at the Home Office. To this the Prime Minister was prepared to assent, though only up to a point. To Bathurst, who had written to him in similar language, he replied on 27 June that while there might occasionally be good reasons why a monarch should object to a particular cabinet appointment, the utmost caution should be observed in exercising this right, especially when no specific reason was given. The practical usefulness of admitting Canning was in a sense unimportant compared with the constitutional principle. 'It is not *Mr Canning out of office*, but Mr Canning *out of office by the personal exclusion of the King, agreed to by his Government*, which is the question.' In a letter to the King a few days later he acquiesced guardedly in the postponement of any changes in the ministry. He pointed out, however, that the choice of ministers should be made on public, not personal grounds; and, referring to the King's assurance that he did not intend the permanent exclusion of Canning, he added firmly that he must be at liberty to renew his proposal the following session.[10]

This was putting a more liberal construction on George's deliberately vague words than the King intended; and though the immediate crisis was surmounted, distrust and ill-will continued to sour relations between king and minister throughout the summer and autumn of 1821. Liverpool excused himself from the coronation ceremony in July but the occasion was marred by disagreements with the King over the award of honours, particularly the proposed promotion of Lord Conyngham as Master of Horse. The King's infatuation with Lady Conyngham was too notorious for this to pass as a reputable appointment and the cabinet stood solidly behind Liverpool in his opposition.[11] There were more angry feelings the following month over the Prime Minister's handling of the Queen's funeral. Caroline died on 7 August while the King was at Holyhead about to start on his state visit to Ireland. In sending him the news Liverpool suggested a burial in Westminster Abbey and a brief period of Court mourning. Next day he learnt from the Queen's solicitors of her testamentary wish to be buried in Brunswick, and he at once assumed responsibility on behalf of the government for carrying this out. On 10 August George sent instructions that her body was to be taken by water from Brandenburgh House and transferred to a warship for the rest of the journey. This had been the Prime Minister's own original intention, principally to avoid popular demonstrations if the cortège passed through London. To that plan the Admiralty raised professional objections and the decision was then taken to send the coffin by land to Harwich. A route from Hammersmith through the northern outskirts of London was chosen, avoiding the City, and full instructions were issued by the Home Office and the Horse Guards to ensure security against interruption. In the absence of all three secretaries of state (Londonderry and Sidmouth were with the King, Bathurst at his home in Gloucestershire) the Prime Minister took general charge of the arrangements. By the time the King's instructions arrived, preparations were already well advanced and Liverpool felt justified in not acceding to a plan which had already been considered and rejected by his naval experts.

On the day of the funeral the procession found the official route blocked at various points by barricades and large crowds demanding that it should go through the City. There were clashes between the demonstrators and the cavalry escort; injuries to soldiers and horses from brickbats and stones; and two civilians killed when some exasperated troopers fired their carbines. Eventually Sir Robert Baker, the senior Bow Street magistrate in charge, agreed to divert the cortège through the City despite repeated messages from Liverpool and pleas from the officers in charge of the escort. It was an unseemly but characteristic end to Caroline's unseemly career; and as usual everyone's reputation suffered. The cabinet was angry at the cheap radical victory and even before the King returned from Ireland had decided to recommend the dismissal of Baker and Sir Robert Wilson, an army officer of radical views who had been prominent in the disturbances. Liverpool thought that his own sin in the King's eyes was his failure to carry out George's directions. He instructed Admiral Cockburn to draw up a memorandum explaining the technical reasons which had persuaded the cabinet to change the route: the difficulties of getting a frigate to the mouth of the Thames in the teeth of the prevailing westerly gale, the narrow arches of London Bridge which made a passage only passable for half an hour at high tide and low tide, the impossibility of ensuring a strict timetable along a river crowded by boatloads of spectators and demonstrators, and the danger of an actual accident on the water to the coffin itself.[12]

The affair was one more addition to the growing list of royal grievances against the Prime Minister. From the reports that came in to him of the King's uninhibited private talk, Liverpool was now inclined to think that George wanted not so much to replace the ministry as to displace his chief minister. When on 16 September the King returned to London he displayed ostentatious resentment, keeping the Prime Minister waiting twenty-four hours for an interview and insisting on an apology for not having been told at an earlier stage of the Queen's illness. Since, however, he had been warned by Sidmouth that any affront to Liverpool would be met with the resistance and if necessary the resignation of the whole cabinet, that was as far as he went. A week later he set out for Hanover, taking Londonderry with him, and remained abroad until November. As Warden of the Cinque Ports Liverpool presided over his embarkation at Ramsgate and did what he could to ensure proper marks of respect from the public. 'His manner to me was not OVER cordial,' he reported wryly to Arbuthnot, 'but not sufficiently otherwise to attract observation, and upon the whole I have no right to complain.'

The consolation for the ministers left at home was that, if the King really intended to change the government, he would have done so before he went off to Germany. As the autumn wore on Liverpool's exaggerated anxieties and suspicions of the summer began to die down. He had at least the reassurance that on any issue of principle the cabinet would stand behind him; there was no danger of intrigues within the government. Both Sidmouth and Londonderry, his two possible successors, had rejected suggestions from George that one of them might take over as prime minister. On the other hand, senior colleagues like Bathurst and Wellington and junior men like Arbuthnot and Croker had made it abundantly clear to him that there was a general unwillingness to allow the administration to break up simply because of Canning. While in Hanover the King told Londonderry that, despite his resentment at what he called the 'monstrous' behaviour of the Prime Minister, he had no wish to change his government and would even consent to Canning's return to the cabinet provided it was understood that he should not be put in an office which would bring him into contact with the King and would go to India as soon as the opportunity arose. Primed with this welcome news, the Foreign Secretary returned to England a day ahead of the King in order to have a preparatory discussion with the Prime Minister.

The main reason for George's change of mood was that he had already learnt that the Prime Minister would raise no objection to Lord Conyngham's appointment to a lesser household office such as Groom of the Stole and was ready to notify the directors of the East India Company of the government's approval for Canning's nomination as the next governor-general. Though on the return journey George declined Liverpool's offer of hospitality at Walmer on the grounds of his displeasure with the people of Dover for their welcome to the Queen the previous year, this was sufficiently credible to rob the refusal of any offence. When Liverpool finally had an audience with the King on 13 November, he was given a more cordial reception than he had known for over a year. The question of Canning's immediate future still had to be settled, but the diplomatic Londonderry did not think that George would now raise any insuperable difficulties. 'Such a changed man as the King you never saw,' he wrote to his brother eleven days later. 'He is in the highest spirits, and says that he, L., is again entitled to all his confidence.' The different atmosphere at Court affected the Prime Minister also. For the first time since Louisa's death he was noticeably cheerful and confident. Londonderry, pleased with the success of his mediation, even thought that the incident had cleared the air and that affairs would go better in future. 'It will be good as experience,' he told Princess Lieven at the end of the month, 'for the King will learn that it is not so easy to dismiss a Minister, and the Prime Minister will learn that it must be remembered, above all things, that the King is master.'[13]

The way was now clear for the long-delayed ministerial changes. Sidmouth was ready to vacate the Home Office for Peel, though he first wished to settle matters in Ireland where Talbot, the Lord Lieutenant, and his Chief Secretary Grant had never pulled together. The cabinet's choice of a successor to Talbot was the 'grand Mogul' Wellesley himself with the sober 'Protestant' Goulburn to keep him in order as Chief Secretary. This fitted nicely with a resumption of the old plan of an alliance with the Grenvillites which had hung fire like much else since the early summer. On 21 November Wellington summoned W.H. Fremantle, a junior Grenvillite, for a preliminary discussion with the Prime Minister. At the interview Liverpool outlined the main inducements he was prepared to offer: a dukedom for Lord Buckingham, the presidency of the Board of Control for Charles Wynn with a seat in the cabinet, the Irish attorney generalship for Plunket, and the possibility of a few minor appointments for other members of the party. This was less than the Grenvillites had hoped for but as much as Liverpool was prepared to give. As a collective bribe, however, it was calculated to overcome both the distrust of Lord Grenville (too old and indifferent to want office himself) and the 'Catholic' principles of Charles Wynn. The later news of Goulburn's Irish secretaryship and the retention of Sidmouth in the cabinet (at the wish of the King) caused some heart-burning. Nevertheless, as anticipated, Wellesley's lord lieutenancy and Buckingham's dukedom together formed an irresistible lure. Though he had fed the Grenvillites occasional crumbs of patronage Liverpool had never shown excessive eagerness for their alliance; but Londonderry urged it strongly for tactical reasons. As he wrote to the Prime Minister on 9 December,

> In this way you will be sure of taking this connection out of that central position in the House of Commons which invites intrigue, and might facilitate an intermediate arrangement. I regard this as constituting the preponderating motive for forming this connection which, having once incorporated with your management, I think your Government will be equal to any emergency.[14]

The chief, in fact almost the only substantial reason for the alliance from Liverpool's point of view was that it denied the King the sole possible alternative ministry other than a pure whig ministry under Grey and Lansdowne.

The future of Canning proved more complicated and more acrimonious. Until Lord Hastings actually retired from his governor-generalship in India little more could be done about Canning's succession. In the meantime an interim appointment to the cabinet was an obvious expedient. In the second half of November, however, the Prime Minister learned that Hastings's resignation was imminent. When Canning still hesitated, Melville withdrew his earlier offer to vacate the Admiralty since there was now nothing to prevent Canning's immediate Indian appointment. Since Canning would not go back to the India Board and could not (in view of the King's earlier stipulation) go to the Home Office, the cabinet door seemed still effectively closed against him. Liverpool, who had hoped to the last to retain Canning in England, now bowed to the inevitable. Taking Londonderry with him he went down to Brighton on 26 November with his final plan for the new ministerial arrangements. With royal approval the various interlocking moves were soon put into operation. Peel accepted the Home Office on 28 November. The negotiations with the stiff-necked Grenvillite connection took a little longer. In an interview with Buckingham on 30 November, however, Liverpool made enough progress to go off to Bath for most of December, leaving Londonderry in charge of the rest of the negotiations. Though this to the touchy mind of Lord Grenville argued a singular failure to appreciate the importance of the Grenville alliance, by the middle of the month everything had been satisfactorily concluded with an exchange of letters between Liverpool and the duke-to-be Lord Buckingham.[15]

The Prime Minister clearly deserved a few weeks of relaxation before the parliamentary grind resumed. It had been a hard year for Liverpool and he had still not solved the problem of Canning. Having sought India when it was not vacant, that incalculable politician now seemed beset by doubts when it was his for the asking. Fortunately the business of Hastings's resignation dragged on and Canning was able to enjoy the luxury of keeping the offer of the governor-generalship in his pocket without the necessity of returning an immediate reply. This suited Liverpool equally well for other reasons; at least it ensured that Canning would keep reasonably quiet. As he wrote from Bath to his frequent confidant Bathurst a few days before Christmas, 'I must say that I hold the keeping the situation of Governor General open for Canning as a question of VITAL *importance*. We shall find the greatest inconvenience in his being here for any time out of office, and yet his return to office now is rendered nearly impracticable, even if the King's objections could be overruled.'[16] As a mild gesture to the Canningites the Prime Minister sounded Palmerston about vacating the secretaryship at war for Huskisson in exchange for Woods and Forests and a British peerage. Palmerston declined, however, and Liverpool was reluctant to press him. So Huskisson, who wanted the India Board and had refused the Irish secretaryship, remained promotionless and aggrieved.

For the rest the Prime Minister could feel with some justice that his administration had taken out a new lease of possession. To outsiders in fact it looked as though there had been a grand plan for the reconstruction of the government. This was an illusion. A number of separate problems had been solved in different ways and with different objects. It was the reconciliation with the King that had made it possible to carry them out simultaneously. Talking with Fremantle, the Grenvillite, in November Liverpool was reported as saying that 'the great and material point to which the Government looked was strength in the House of Commons' and any changes in the cabinet would be prompted by that consideration. In neither votes nor debating power, however, did the changes bring much additional reinforcement. The Grenvillite connection mustered only a dozen or so members in the Commons, and while Peel added solidity to Castlereagh's thin front bench, Wynn – 'Squeaker Wynn' – was only a lightweight figure in the House. For the historically-minded the union with Grenville healed a breach which had existed since 1801. In a letter to Huskisson in January on his return to London Liverpool himself referred to the 'public importance which has been attached to the reuniting with the Government the Grenville part of Mr Pitt's original connection'. If so, it was the practical contemporary aspect rather than the sentimental one that was important to the ministry. Now, short of surrender to the old Foxite opposition, which was almost inconceivable, George IV had been deprived of any real choice. That knowledge in itself was likely to restore political stability after the uncertainties of the previous eighteen months. The Grenvillites, or some of them, believed that the alliance would strengthen the 'Catholic' element in the government; and there was much nice but futile calculation of the new religious balance of power within the administration following the promotion of Wellesley and Wynn on the one side, and of Peel and Goulburn on the other. This was not a guessing-game which Liverpool wished to encourage. As he observed to Wynn in another letter from Bath, the government was based on a principle of neutrality and 'fewer public evils are likely to arise from the adoption or rejection of the Catholic claims under a Government of a mixed character, than might occur under one which for brevity I designate as exclusively Protestant or exclusively Catholic'.[17]

The problems of the 1822 session were in any case likely to be economic rather than religious. As far as the estimates were concerned, much preliminary work had already been done. In July a list of proposed reductions in the armed forces had been laid before the King, and although the reluctance of the royal assent had been underlined by a tart remark that the King 'expects from his cabinet that he shall not again be called upon to sanction any further measures of this discription', a more understanding royal attitude could now be expected. With the agricultural depression beginning to affect rents as well as prices, the Commons would certainly require some economies; and (as the cabinet pointed out to the King) it was better that these should be proposed to Parliament by government than forced on government by Parliament. The Prime Minister himself felt that they could not cut the service establishments back much further; but since he was determined to defend the revenue, the only way of satisfying the economical instincts of the Commons was to reduce expenditure. A rough parliamentary session was clearly in prospect. Three good grain harvests in succession had glutted the market, kept prices for farmers permanently low, and slashed the landowners' rents. The winter of 1821-2 was marked by meetings and petitions in the agricultural districts, complaining of distress and demanding a remedy. In their panic many farmers and a few misguided gentry were looking with approval on such radical expedients as parliamentary reform, the abolition of tithes, and an arbitrary reduction of interest on government stock. Vansittart was sufficiently impressed to suggest to Liverpool before Christmas that it might be necessary to bring in a new corn bill, offering moderate protection for agriculture generally, and to combine this with an attack on monopolies and protective tariffs enjoyed by manufacture and commerce. Such a two-pronged policy, he thought, would at least soothe the feelings of the landed gentry and at best give a stimulus to the economy from which everyone would benefit.[18]

The cabinet was prepared to make minor tax concessions to the agricultural interest on malt and salt; to renew the committee on agricultural distress; to prune the estimates still more; to borrow money to make loans available for public works; even to reduce official salaries. Within limits, Liverpool's policy was always flexible. The difficulty was to discover what the administration could do that would be helpful. At the beginning of February he and the

Chancellor of the Exchequer called the Governor and Deputy Governor of the Bank of England, together with other leading bankers, to a meeting at Fife House. He addressed them on the subject of agricultural distress and asked whether a loan of £5 million in exchequer bills would enable the country bankers to assist the farmers. The prompt and unanimous reply was that it would be useless. It was not lack of money in the country banks but the poor security offered by the farmers that constituted the problem.[19] On the other hand the Prime Minister was still anxious to keep a surplus available for the Sinking Fund as a symbol of the government's determination to maintain public credit. On agricultural distress, which was the real cause of the back-benchers' revolt, he delivered his considered views in a speech of 26 February 1822 which ranks with that of May 1820 on foreign trade as an exposition of his basic economic thinking.

The starting-point of his argument was a flat rejection of the popular view that the current distress was caused by excessive taxation – 'one of the grossest delusions,' he said crisply, 'that was ever attempted to be instilled into the minds of the people'. Since the war a quarter of the whole taxation of the country had been given up and it was now £17 million less than in 1815. The growing wealth and population of the country, the vast increase in trade, made the current level of taxation easily sustainable. Tax reduction in itself would do nothing for agricultural distress, much of which was attributable to the sudden fall in demand when the war stopped. 'What the agriculturalist really wants is a market ... But it is not in the power of Parliament immediately to give the farmer a market adequate to his needs.' To abandon the £5 million surplus earmarked for the Sinking Fund would damage public credit, while affording no perceptible assistance to agriculture. The duty of government and Parliament, he said boldly, was 'to hold the balance between all the great interests of the country as even as possible ... the agriculturalist is not the *only* interest in Great Britain. It is not even the *most numerous interest.*' It was no bad thing, he pointed out to the peers, that the rest of the population could buy meat at 4d. a lb, instead of 8d., and other foods equally cheaply. Agriculture, he concluded, must be left to right itself. Low prices would increase consumption; low profits would decrease production. Market forces would thus in time produce a balance. After going through in detail all the economic measures proposed by the government, the only hope he held out on the corn laws was some modification to smooth the transition from complete prohibition to unchecked imports at the 80s. a quarter level.

The speech, buttressed by numerous appendices with statistics of revenue and expenditure, was later published as a pamphlet. Whether it made converts among the agricultural protectionists is impossible to tell. In March Liverpool and Castlereagh went down to Brighton, where Princess Lieven gave the Prime Minister advice on how to behave in the exotic surroundings of the Pavilion (once compared by Wellington to a high-class brothel) and where he found himself with some embarrassment the table companion of Lady Conyngham.

The object of the visit, however, was secured with unexpected ease. When it was suggested that the 10 per cent cut in official salaries might be matched by an equivalent reduction in the Civil List, the King said at once that 'as a gentleman he could not do less himself than he had imposed upon his servants'.[20] In the House of Commons, however, wrangling over estimates and occasional reverses for the government continued after Easter until in May, over the Civil List, the government were driven yet again to their last resource of threatening to resign if they were again defeated. This brought the discontented country gentry to their senses and the remainder of the session passed off with only moderate discomfort. Nevertheless, Liverpool was left with a heavy heart when he took stock of the government's position in August. Despite all their preparations ministers seemed to have yielded rather than gained ground; they had lost the initiative once more and had been continually forced back on the defensive. 'To concede every thing and propose nothing,' he wrote to Huskisson, 'was a course of Administration neither creditable for the Government, nor safe for the Country.'[21] At the start of the 1822 session a pamphlet, *The State of the Nation* (anonymous but with no attempt to hide its official inspiration), had been put out by the ministry to explain government policy and improve relations with the public. It listed the achievements of the ministry, especially in reducing taxation and cutting the costs of government; and for good measure described their future intentions. The gist of the argument was that the ministry wished to stand well with the public and be seen to be actually promoting the welfare of the country. If this could be generally recognised, it would promote social harmony and render unnecessary the repressive legislation required in more disorderly times.

. Aimed principally at the independent country gentry and the more educated members of the public, the pamphlet was not without effect. It attracted publicity, running into at least seven editions in the first twelve months.[22] One pamphlet, however, though a novel form of propaganda, could not work a miracle. As a statement of aims it was admirable; the drawback was that they were still aims rather than accomplishments. Even worse, the classes whose support the ministry hoped to win for its policy of social conservatism were perversely being attracted towards various forms of political liberalism. In April a motion by Lord John Russell in favour of parliamentary reform secured 164 votes, more than any similar motion had drawn for over thirty years. In May Canning's bill to admit Roman Catholic peers to the upper house passed the Commons by a majority of twelve. In the House of Lords it was opposed comprehensively and bitterly by the Lord Chancellor, narrowly and more temperately by the Prime Minister as invidious, illogical and inconsistent so long as Roman Catholics remained excluded from the House of Commons. The bill was duly defeated but as a parting shot from the governor-general-designate it could only have strengthened Liverpool's conviction of the danger of having Canning running wild in the House of Commons. Other members of the government held even stronger views. 'I know not', Lord Lowther wrote cynically in September, 'whether he is most to be dreaded as *friend* or *foe*.'[23] In those ambiguous circumstances a gilded exile in India seemed by far the best solution.

In the late summer, however, this soothing prospect was shattered in a peculiarly brutal manner. On 7 August a cabinet was held to consider the instructions for the Foreign Secretary at the forthcoming congress of Verona which Londonderry had himself drawn up. Nothing unusual happened on this occasion but Wellington and the King who saw the Foreign Secretary on the 9th were deeply disturbed by his manner. Early on Saturday 10 August Liverpool to his surprise received an urgent and secret summons from the King who was at Woolwich about to embark for his state visit to Scotland. When he arrived at Woolwich the King expressed his fears about Londonderry's sanity and possible suicidal tendencies, and told Liverpool to ensure that he was not left alone for an instant. Inured to George's habit of exaggeration, Liverpool found it hard to believe that Londonderry's state was quite so alarming, even though the Foreign Secretary had already confided to him that he was being blackmailed on charges of homosexuality. He went, however, to St James's Square only to find that Londonderry and his wife had gone off to Cray, their home in Kent. His personal physician Bankhead had already bled him the previous day and was going to stay with him at Cray for the weekend. Liverpool contented himself therefore with sending a note to Londonderry asking him to come up to London the following week; the receipt of this was said to have had a calming effect. He received a reply from Lady Londonderry the same day, saying simply that her husband had been very unwell and was being nursed under Bankhead's supervision. She asked him instead to come down himself to Cray on the Monday or Tuesday. Liverpool agreed and told her to keep her husband quiet in preparation for his imminent departure for the continent. He then went back to Coombe. There, on Monday morning Dr Bankhead arrived in a hurry with the shocking news that Londonderry had cut his throat only a few hours previously.[24]

For the Prime Minister the event was a staggering blow. Writing at once to Peel to ask him to break the news to the King, he ended his letter with obvious anguish, 'what a conclusion to such a life! May God have mercy on his soul!' Even when talking to the Russian ambassador a couple of days later, he seemed 'quite overwhelmed'. Afterwards some blamed him for not having taken more stringent precautions to prevent the tragedy against which the King had specifically warned him. Yet it is difficult to see what more he could have done. Lady Londonderry clearly suspected that there was a risk of suicide; Bankhead had been told by Wellington that his patient was suffering from delusions. For his own part Liverpool expressed himself bitterly about Lady Londonderry in a conversation with Princess Lieven some ten days later. According to the Princess's possibly heightened account, Liverpool declared that Lady Londonderry knew of her husband's real condition but 'her pride was stronger than her anxiety' and she had not wanted anything to stand in the way of their continental trip.[25]

More important than any subsequent recrimination, however, was the task of filling the immense gap left in the cabinet and the Commons. Liverpool had long looked upon Londonderry as his natural successor as head of the government, and his death (as he expressed it to Lord Melville) 'strikes off from us the right arm of the Administration'. There was, in fact, only one man who in his view could take Londonderry's place. Peel, though comparatively young, would probably be an effective Leader of the House of Commons; but he had no apparent interest in foreign affairs and his unrivalled knowledge of Ireland made him doubly valuable in his existing post at the Home Office. Wellington had wide European and diplomatic experience, and great prestige with the courts of Europe, and he was some ministers' first choice for the Foreign Office. Liverpool, however, had a wise instinct against the employment of a professional soldier, despite all his military prestige – or perhaps because of his military prestige – as a civilian minister or in any situation which would expose him to party attacks. 'I do not think that anything would be more inexpedient,' he observed to Melville, 'for the sake of the Duke of Wellington and of his public utility, than to put him permanently into any political office.' This was not an argument coined for the occasion. He had expressed the same opinion to Londonderry a year earlier.[26] The only solution then was Canning; the only obstacle the King.

On hearing the news in Scotland George at once wrote south desiring Liverpool in peremptory tones not to make any change in the arrangements respecting India, 'as it is *my decision*, that they should remain *final and conclusive*'. While somewhat evasively assuring the King that he would do nothing before the King's return that would preclude unfettered consideration of the question, Liverpool made his own preparations for a clash of wills. His old friend and adviser Bathurst came to stay at Coombe; Wellington several times went down there for dinner and no doubt much conversation after dinner; and through Croker and Arbuthnot the Prime Minister got in touch with Canning's friend Huskisson. After his failure the previous year, he was perhaps more determined than ever to secure Canning's return to the ministry. In the last resort he seemed even ready to contemplate resignation on the issue. 'I cannot wholly put out of my head,' he wrote to Arbuthnot on 27 August, 'now my *own age and personal situation*. If an efficient Government can be formed I will not desert my post, but *this* is a *crisis*, and I must see my way before I take a new lease.'[27] By the end of the month he knew that the majority of the cabinet were ready to acquiesce in Canning's return to office; that the Grenvillites were threatening to resign if he were not appointed; and that Canning would only accept the Foreign Office and the lead in the Commons, Londonderry's 'whole inheritance'. The crucial figure was Peel, now the senior minister in the Commons and *de facto* leader of the 'Protestant' party in the lower house. In a two-hour conversation on 2 September, the day after he arrived back from Scotland, the

Home Secretary made it satisfyingly clear that his only wish was to assist the government. He would cheerfully accept Canning as successor to Londonderry; equally he would be ready to serve as Leader of the House, if that was required.

When he saw the King later that day the Prime Minister was in a nervous but determined mood. Indeed, to the alarm of Arbuthnot he spoke at one point of giving the King only twenty-four hours in which to decide. He agreed, however, that the proper course was to keep calm and postpone full discussion until the following day. The expected clash came on 3 September. Told by the Prime Minister that he wished to appoint Canning to the Foreign Office and was supported in this by Wellington, Bathurst and Westmorland (none of whom were particularly partial to Canning), George asked pointedly whether his continuance in office as Prime Minister depended on the issue. To this Liverpool wisely declined to answer. The King then summoned Peel, Wellington, Sidmouth and Eldon, the leading 'Protestants' in the government, and wrote a sharp note to Liverpool regretting that no alternative proposal had been put before him. 'If there be no alternative the King takes it for granted that Lord Liverpool and the other members of the Cabinet are prepared to break up the Government.' In the event the anti-Canning influence of Eldon and Sidmouth was more than outweighed by Peel's loyalty and the trenchant advice of Wellington. The Duke, who had been writing firm letters to Knighton from a sickbed, eventually saw the King privately on 7 September. 'I must wait', wrote the neglected Prime Minister to Arbuthnot on that day, 'with philosophical patience for the King's letter.' His only fear was that the King might take up some intransigent position from which it would be difficult for him to recede. George, however, as several people at Court had long suspected would happen, yielded to the Duke's brisk assault and on 8 September came the royal permission for Liverpool to propose Canning's readmission into the Government – the 'greatest sacrifice of my opinions and feelings that I have ever made in my life'.[28] Liverpool at once wrote off to Canning with the news. While taking offence at certain expressions in the King's letter (which the Prime Minister had been required to pass on to him), Canning after two days finally accepted. The crisis was over and somewhat fortuitously Liverpool had finally won his two-year battle with the King.

It was not, however, the last of the ministerial changes. Other moves had already been under discussion, though Liverpool did not want to start fresh difficulties by linking them with Canning's appointment. Once in office Canning gave fresh impetus to some of the older plans. In the course of the autumn therefore another round of retirements and promotions took place which reflected the altered balance of power within the administration. Canning's idea was to send Manners Sutton, the Speaker, to India; Wynn to the empty Speaker's chair; and Huskisson to Wynn's place on the Board of Control. This proved impossible because neither Sutton nor Wynn was prepared to move, even though as a sop to the Grenvillites Liverpool was persuaded by Canning to raise with the King the question of admitting the Duke of Buckingham to the cabinet. In November the Prime Minister put through an alternative scheme which involved the retirement of Bragge Bathurst and Vansittart, leaving the way open for Robinson to go to the Exchequer and Huskisson to the Board of Trade. These were reasonable and not unexpected changes. Bragge, elderly and in poor health, was anxious to quit; Vansittart not disinclined to follow his example. A sound if conservative economist, he had been unlucky in having to deal with the intractable problems of the postwar finance and his administrative usefulness was impaired by his notorious clumsiness as a parliamentary speaker. He had long been the target of bitter criticism from both the Canningite and Grenvillite parties. In making both changes Liverpool's concern was to gratify Canning's wish for Huskisson's promotion without showing harshness or ingratitude to the two ministers who were to be replaced. Sidmouth's aid was enlisted to get his brother-in-law Bragge to accept a retirement which was sweetened by a pension for his wife and daughters. Vansittart he tackled himself in a warm, persuasive letter on 14 December. Though reluctant to promote to the House of Lords a man of notoriously limited income, the Prime Minister agreed in the end not only to reward Vansittart's long services with the sinecure but cabinet post of Chancellor of the Duchy of Lancaster but to grant his wish for a peerage.[29] The two transactions were carried through in a friendly fashion but they meant unmistakably the eclipse of the old Sidmouth connection. Long before his formal resignation at the end of 1824, Sidmouth himself had become a largely passive figure in the cabinet. It was the Canningites who were now in the ascendant. Robinson had the approval of Vansittart and the reputation of having been Londonderry's favourite for the post. Yet he, like Huskisson, was also Canning's man and the two appointments to the key posts of trade and finance were taken as proof of Liverpool's weakness and Canning's dominance.

The Prime Minister, on whom the burden of the negotiations had mainly fallen, was perceptibly torn between conflicting impulses: constant urging from the ebullient Canning; a conviction that a stronger front bench in the Commons was necessary; and a dislike of causing offence to old colleagues. After the long strain of 1820 and 1821, the renewed complications of the ministerial reconstruction in the latter part of 1822 drained his energies once more. Canning told the sulky and obstinate Huskisson that 'Liverpool's agitation has, in some stages of this business, amounted almost to illness'. Huskisson, whose insistence on a seat in the cabinet had almost dislocated the whole operation, was a peculiar irritant to the Prime Minister. 'I am more provoked with Huskisson than I can tell you,' he wrote to Arbuthnot at the end of the year. 'I cannot conceive anything in worse taste than a man endeavouring to *force* himself into a Cabinet against the wishes of the King and his own friends.'[30] Indeed, it was the Prime Minister rather than the King who kept Huskisson out of the cabinet until November 1823. These were not the only embarrassments which the victory of the Canningites brought in their train. Arbuthnot, for example, a great friend and admirer of the dead Castlereagh, was particularly anxious not to remain as patronage secretary under his rival Canning. After thirteen years in the Treasury he had strong claims for promotion and Liverpool offered him the post at Woods and Forests vacated by Huskisson.

Another unhappy man was Wallace, the Vice-President and acting head of the Board of Trade, who had won much prestige by his commercial legislation of the previous session. He was so mortified by Huskisson's promotion over his head to the presidency of the Board that he promptly resigned. Liverpool was considerably distressed at this reaction from a personal friend who had served him and the government well. Having nothing else to offer, he unwisely thought (or had it suggested to him by Canning) of asking Arbuthnot to forego his promised promotion to Woods and Forests in favour of Wallace and for the time being to serve as Vice-President of the Board of Trade himself. It is possible that he meant no more than that the possibility of this should be discussed with Arbuthnot; but even more unwisely he authorised Canning to make the initial overture. Though deeply hurt by both the matter and the manner of the proposal, Arbuthnot loyally agreed to do what was asked of him. In the event Liverpool's better judgement and the vigorous intervention of the Duke of Wellington led to the abandonment of this particular scheme; but a certain soreness of feeling remained. It was an age when prime ministers, in redistributing offices, acted more as brokers than butchers; and Liverpool's kindness made him a clumsy operator in matters where personal sensitivities were so easily aroused. The exchange of letters between himself and Arbuthnot which ended the episode did credit to their long friendship. Nevertheless, conciliatory by nature and apt to think that everything could be solved by temperate discussion, Liverpool had given the impression over this incident of being at best timid and evasive, at worst a shamefaced tool of Canning. The Prime Minister for his part was heard to lament the disastrous effect on politicians of their wives' pretensions and rivalries.[31]

Petticoat influence apart, it was clear that the return of Canning put a greater strain on the internal unity of the cabinet than anything which had happened since 1812. 'Ours is not, nor never has been, a *controversial* Cabinet,' Wellington had written with emphatic negatives in December 1821. Castlereagh only three days later made the same point when he spoke of the government being 'not one of controversy, but of union within itself'.[32] All that was now changed. With his remarkable gift for either attracting or repelling people, Canning from the start created divisions in the cabinet which had not existed before. There were thus two paradoxes about the state of the ministry after the summer of 1822. One was that the outward strengthening of government in the House of Commons and in the eyes of the public had been accompanied by a weakening of its one great previous source of strength, the unity within the cabinet. The other was that the Prime Minister, now physically and emotionally less robust after ten harassing years in his responsible office, was now even more necessary to his colleagues than before precisely because of the new divisions among them.

NOTES

1 Yonge, III, 137 ff.
2 George 4, II, 424.
3 George 4, II, 425-34; Hobhouse, pp. 52-3.
4 ARJ, I, 100; Hobhouse, p. 64; George 4, II, 437.
5 Yonge, III, 146-7; Hobhouse, p. 64.
6 Hobhouse, p. 65; ARC, pp. 23-4.
7 M. Villiers, *The Grand Whiggery* (1939), p. 346.
8 ARJ, I, 103; GM, 1821, Pt I, 565.
9 GCOC, I, 24-7.
10 Bathurst, pp. 499-501; Yonge, III, 147.
11 Bathurst, pp. 502-3, 507; George 4, II, 447-9.
12 For the history of the Queen's funeral see George 4, II, 452-64; Hobhouse, pp. 71-4; Bathurst, pp. 508-9; Croker, I, 203-9; Creevey, pp. 164-8; Yonge, III, 132-3; AR, 1821, pp. 125-8. It may be observed that the statements in R. Fulford, *George IV* (1935), p. 237, about the behaviour of Liverpool and the cabinet are contradicted by the facts.
13 George 4, II, 465-8, 671-2; LM, p. 143.
14 Yonge, III, 163; BCG, I, 231-5.
15 BCG, I, 235-6; George 4, II, 475-6.
16 Bathurst, p. 527.
17 BCG, I. 232, 252; Hobhouse, p. 132.
18 Yonge, III, 165; George 4, II, 451.
19 AR, 1822 (Chronicle), p. 24; cf. Cookson, p. 350 n.
20 ARC, pp. 29-30; LM, p. 160.
21 Quoted in Cookson, p. 365.
22 It was published by J. Hatchard & Sons, Piccadilly, who also published Liverpool's speeches of 26 May 1820 and 26 Feb. 1822 in pamphlet form. See also *The Diary of Philipp von Neumann*, ed. E.D. Chancellor, two vols (1928), I, 91.
23 George 4, II, 537.
24 A. Montgomery Hyde, *Strange Death of Lord Castlereagh* (1959), pp. 43 ff., supplemented by Hobhouse, p. 89 & n.
25 LM, pp. 192, 201.
26 ARJ, I, 83; Yonge, III, 197.
27 ARC, p. 30; Yonge, III, 194-5; Cookson, p. 369.
28 Yonge, III, 199; George 4, II, 535 & n.; ARC, p. 32.
29 For the ministerial changes see Yonge, III, 204-10; WND, II, 9; Cookson, pp. 375-90.
30 ARC, p. 37; Huskisson, p. 152.
31 ARC, pp. 37-44; ARJ, I, 201-8.
32 Yonge, III, 161; BCG, I, 237.

CHAPTER X

Public and Private Life

In June 1823 Liverpool reached his fifty-third birthday. He had been Prime Minister for eleven years, longer than any of his predecessors except Walpole, North and Pitt. Honours had accumulated round him and were to continue to do so for the rest of his life: Knight of the Garter, Commandant of the Cinque Ports Regiment of Militia, Master of Trinity House, High Steward of the Borough of Kingston on Thames, Trustee of the National Gallery, Trustee of the British Museum, Hon. LL.D. Cambridge, Freeman of the City of Bristol. After Louisa's death there was gossip that he might give up politics altogether. It was a singular misjudgement. Despite his occasional talk of retirement, the emptiness of his private life made work more necessary to him than ever. In politics since 1792, in office first in 1793 and continuously since 1807, Prime Minister since 1812, he would not have known what to do with himself had he abandoned his career in 1821. Not only were politics and administration the only form of life he understood, but he had the sober satisfaction which came from a sense of his own professional competence. For that the best testimony was the value set on him by his fellow-ministers. Wellesley Pole, Wellington's brother who sat in the cabinet as Master of the Mint, agreed with Plumer Ward in May 1820 that 'Ld. Liverpool could not exist out of office, and never would resign; but even if he were willing, and were to state to his colleagues that he thought the King would be more inclined to them without him, they would not permit it, and would all think it right to follow him.'[1]

The remark was the more noteworthy since Pole was critical of other aspects of Liverpool's leadership – his unsociability, for example, and lack of attention to the minor arts of party management. Pole thought that he spent too much time shut up with clerks and had no facility in mixing with other people. Certainly he had not of recent years been a very clubbable man. As a young politician he had joined White's, the rival establishment to the Foxite Brooks's and one (according to that knowledgeable man about town Captain Gronow) to which it was much more difficult to get elected. In the spring of 1806, the youthful Lord Aberdeen noted in his journal dining at White's with some twenty-five Pittites, including Hawkesbury (as he then was), Castlereagh and Canning. But with middle age and high office White's saw him less and less. More than once he even forgot to pay his membership dues. In his private papers is preserved a polite request from the club in March 1815 for the annual subscription of twelve guineas. Next year apparently it slipped his memory again, since another reminder arrived in the autumn of 1816. Finally, in April 1823, he asked the club to remove his name from the list of members. Cards and political gossip perhaps had little appeal for him, even if he had been able to spare the time. Doubtless a more congenial occasion was that in July 1820 when London was buzzing with anecdotes of Caroline and rumours of disaffection among the troops. On the 25th Liverpool was present at a pleasant and evidently non-party dinner at The Club (Dr Johnson's literary club), in the company of Canning, the two Sir Williams – Grant and Scott – and that sociable inheritor of the Foxite tradition, the whig Lord Holland.[2]

It was not, however, necessary to frequent the clubs to pick up political news. In another conversation six months later Pole (who had no great liking for Liverpool) confessed himself impressed by the way the Prime Minister kept himself informed of all that was going on in the parliamentary world. 'There is hardly a thing said or done, hardly a conversation, or even a joke, that is not carried to him.' While this perhaps exaggerated the degree to which whips and Treasury officials like Arbuthnot acted as his eyes and ears, at least it suggested that Liverpool was not without sources of intelligence to offset his social inadequacies. Ward (outside the cabinet) had criticisms of a different kind. He admitted that 'no man can lead the House or the Cabinet so well; on all subjects every one looks up to him in debate'; but he considered that Liverpool relied too much on this narrow parliamentary basis and had not sufficiently attended to the management of public opinion.[3] This second discussion took place in November 1820, only a few days before the defeat of the government in the House of Lords over the divorce clause; and a few weeks before the first serious attempt was started by the ministry to obtain better newspaper publicity. At that point the gap between the government and public opinion was perhaps at its widest. Ward's comment not only seemed justified but probably reflected what many other government supporters were saying.

The fact remained, however, that few of Liverpool's colleagues thought that the ministry could survive his departure. 'You deceive yourself,' the shrewd and sympathetic Bathurst wrote to his chief a year later, 'if you think that your resignation will not be followed by a complete change.' Whatever the government's standing with the public, there was no doubt about Liverpool's standing in his own cabinet. Their reasons are not without interest. Analysing his qualities as Prime Minister, Sidmouth, his colleague for a quarter of a century, singled out three attributes: his integrity (the word recurred time and again when people spoke of Liverpool), his prudence and foresight in cabinet discussions, and his skill and fairness in debate. Once the feverish excitement of the divorce was over, even the public at large was able to perceive something of these virtues, despite the isolation of his office and the narrowness of the parliamentary world. 'He has', wrote the Grenvillite Fremantle emphatically in June 1821, 'more footing and support in the country than any one of the

Ministers.' An identical, though more flowery tribute was paid by the *Annual Register* six years later. It was seldom, observed that publication in its review of 1827, that a minister not distinguished by brilliant genius or popular oratory had 'gained so much weight, and conciliated such universal favour, by the mere force of his personal character. ... Above all, the country trusted in his pure and unquestioned integrity.' His opinions, it added, carried more weight than those of his more brilliant colleagues and the public felt assured that as long as he guided the cabinet, its policy would display 'prudence, consistency, and integrity'.[4]

What the wider public did not know was the other, more emotional side of his nature, the nervous agitation which he showed in time of crisis, the irritability which broke out increasingly after 1820 and manifested itself, if Arbuthnot's subsequent gossip is to be believed, in some unusual and uncharacteristic behaviour. When particularly incensed he would catch up a chair and dash it on the floor, sometimes breaking it in pieces. On one occasion, when informed at a meeting at Castlereagh's house that Lord George Cavendish was not going to vote for them on some question, he burst out 'Damn the Cavendishes! Damn the Cavendishes!' and continued with his ejaculations as he went through the hall to his waiting carriage, much to the astonishment of the servants. These exhibitions probably happened when he was under nervous strain or suffering actual pain from his bad leg.[5] The other things of which he was accused – the lack of social gifts, the outward coldness – are more understandable. Many prime ministers have incurred similar reproaches. Busy men in responsible office are apt to appear brusque and unsociable to lesser individuals who intrude on their time unnecessarily. An underlying anxiousness, however, was part of Liverpool's character. Beneath the phlegmatic physical appearance of middle age was the same highly-strung temperament he had possessed in his youth. His close colleagues, if not the public, were well aware of this. 'A most nervous mind', wrote Arbuthnot in 1819; and he of all men was in a position to judge. The Duke of Wellington told Lady Salisbury long afterwards that Liverpool, though 'a very superior man, was like a sensitive plant'. Yet, though he was easily hurt, he had remarkably little rancour or jealousy in his composition. He astonished Princess Lieven at a dinner at Fife House in May 1822 by pointing across the room to Peel and telling her that 'there is a man who will be Prime Minister before ten years are out'. He appeared to be as pleased with the thought, remarked the Russian woman (whose life in European diplomatic society made this a rare experience), 'as if it were not his own post he would have to give up. His pleasure is typically British and does him credit.'[6]

The calmness and good temper that were his outstanding qualities between 1809 and 1820 were in a sense acquired characteristics: the product of experience, maturity, and self-control even though they accorded with his natural kindliness and goodwill. From the time of the Queen's trial, however, as age, ill-health and recurrent political crises scraped away this protective covering, the older temperamental weaknesses, even the tendency to cry in moments of emotional strain, showed themselves once more. To junior members of the administration these feminine traits were a subject for ridicule. Huskisson spoke disparagingly of his 'grand fidgetts'; Palmerston of 'spoonies like Liverpool' and of the Prime Minister labouring under an attack of 'the weaks'. In the list of code-names Canning drew up in 1819 for use in letters to his wife, Liverpool appeared as Magdalen, a transparent pun. Yet over-anxiousness, an agitated manner, even occasional tearfulness, are not complete indications of a man's character.

Those who knew Liverpool better attached less importance to these idiosyncrasies than those who knew him less. When that relative newcomer to the cabinet Charles Wynn noted in January 1823 that Liverpool was in 'a state of worry and dejection which exceeds anything I have yet seen', he was cheerfully assured by Lord Melville, who had been in the cabinet since 1812, that 'this is not for him extraordinary when hard worked'.[7] What his older colleagues knew, and his younger colleagues soon learned, was that underneath the worried manner and pessimistic remarks was a capacity for resolution amounting at times to obstinacy. Even though he preferred to coax rather than command, Liverpool could become uncommonly peremptory when his patience wore out, as Palmerston himself discovered on at least one occasion. It was only a minor incident though interesting as a side-light on Liverpool's administrative methods. In 1822 the running feud between the Secretary at War and the Horse Guards came to one of its periodic crises with appeals to the Prime Minister from both Palmerston and the Duke of York. Liverpool's first move was to send Charles Long to talk sympathetically with Palmerston and ask him for the sake of peace to make a conciliatory gesture. Palmerston high-handedly refused to budge, telling Long that Liverpool 'must make what he can of the matter'. To this piece of impertinence the Prime Minister responded sharply two days later with a minute to both disputants, impartially condemning the conduct of each.[8]

Few prime ministers are geniuses; and it is as well for the comfort of their colleagues that they are not. Not many prime ministers are in a position to be autocrats; and Liverpool was not autocratic by nature. All successful prime ministers, however, must be men of business; and Liverpool's influence was visible in all branches of the administration. It would be fatuous to regard him as a mere chairman of the cabinet. An assembly of some fourteen ministers (rising to fifteen in 1822, too large in the opinion of George IV), it contained men like Eldon, Harrowby, Westmorland and Wynn who, outside any departmental responsibilities they might have, carried little weight with the Prime Minister. For matters of general policy and when a quick decision was needed, he tended to rely on an inner group consisting principally of Bathurst, Wellington and Castlereagh and later Canning and Peel. For financial affairs he had his little 'economic cabinet' of Vansittart, Robinson, Huskisson and Long. In that field, of course, he and not the Chancellor of the Exchequer was the acknowledged master. Arbuthnot in 1819 spoke of Vansittart's bearing responsibility for measures not his but of 'the sort of commission which has had to decide upon the duties of his own office'. Wynn in 1823, when commenting on Robinson's appointment, opined that he would be an improvement on his predecessor in manners and popularity, 'but as to measures, Liverpool must of course give the orders, and he obey'. The Prime Minister's technical office as First Lord of the Treasury was in no sense a nominal appointment. Indeed, Liverpool told Peel in 1813 that if he were asked to define the respective duties of first lord and chancellor, he could not do so. Herries, the veteran wartime financial administrator who was promoted Financial Secretary of the Treasury in 1823, noted the contrast between the indolence of Robinson and the care with which the Prime Minister attended not only to general financial arrangements but to the departmental business of the Treasury. Liverpool's correspondence with Herries, wrote the latter's biographer, revealed a man 'who did his work conscientiously and thoroughly ... always clear and to the point, showing perfect acquaintanceship with the subjects'.[9]

With so much transacted, especially during the parliamentary session, by verbal and largely unrecorded discussions, it is impossible to gauge with any exactitude the degree of control exercised by the Prime Minister over his colleagues. It is evident, however, that Liverpool never allowed his ministry to become a mere collection of departments. The authority of the office of Prime Minister, which he defended so powerfully against the King, did not suddenly become a fiction when he turned to dealing with his colleagues. Indeed, he wrote on one occasion that 'the first minister is necessarily at the head of every department when *important business* is concerned'.[10] Even with Bathurst, Secretary for War and Colonies, for all that he was one of his most senior and trusted colleagues, his correspondence descended to such minute details as colonial governorships, the value of artillery for use against insurgent Negroes in Demerara, the pay of army generals going overseas, and the provision of a man-of-war to transport a new bishop of Barbados to his distant diocese. With the younger but energetic and capable Peel at the Home Office, he was equally ready to give specific instructions, such as the inclusion of a measure on Irish tithes in the programme of domestic legislation for 1823. There can be little doubt that Peel's reforming activities, including Scottish legal reform, English criminal law, and the policing of London, owed much to the Prime Minister's appreciation of the need to take note of the work of Mackintosh's parliamentary committee and (as far as the police of the metropolis were concerned) of the unfortunate experiences at the time of the Queen's trial and her subsequent funeral. Peel discussed much of what he proposed to do directly with Liverpool before going into any detail in the cabinet.

On Ireland, though Liverpool observed once with a certain English pessimism that it was 'a political phenomenon not influenced by the same feelings as appear to affect mankind in other countries',[11] he was not without knowledge and experience of his own. He had after all been given responsibility for that country as Home Secretary between 1804 and 1809. When Peel was Chief

Secretary Liverpool frequently corresponded directly with him and on occasions provided him with more practical assistance than Peel's nominal departmental head Lord Sidmouth. From whatever source he gained his information,
Liverpool's speeches on Ireland indicated more than a superficial knowledge
of the troubles of that unhappy country. In the great parliamentary debates
on the state of Ireland in the spring of 1816, Liverpool assumed the leading
role for the government with a wide-ranging speech which at the time attracted
some attention. In another Irish debate of 1822 he argued (twenty-one years
before the appointment of the Devon Commission) that 'nine-tenths of the evils
which afflicted Ireland were not to be ascribed to the measures directed by
Government, but to the state of society in that country and the relation of those
who laboured to those who possessed property'.

The most independent of the great departments of state was, to outward
appearance, the Foreign Office under those two distinguished but contrasting
statesmen Castlereagh and Canning. Yet this independence was to some extent
illusory. With all his respect for Castlereagh and his unique position in the
administration, Liverpool had decided views on the objects of British diplomacy which did not always accord with those of his Foreign Secretary. In
particular the Prime Minister's influence was consistently thrown on the side
of diminishing rather than increasing British commitments in Europe. It was
a difference of emphasis rather than of principle; but Liverpool was always
more cautious and more insular than his colleague. At the time of the Aix-la-
Chapelle congress in 1818, for example, Liverpool was doubtful of the propriety
of admitting France to full membership of the Quadruple Alliance. He preferred the compromise which was eventually adopted by the allies, and was
certainly more congenial to Parliament and the British public, of simply
allowing France to participate in the discussions at the conference. On this
issue, whatever Castlereagh's private feelings, there was little real divergence
of views among the allies. On other matters – the invitation to France to join
a 'diplomatic concert of the Courts' and British participation in a regular series
of congresses with her European partners – there was a more serious difference
of opinion. In Liverpool's view, as he once wrote to Canning, such congresses
'without a clear necessity and definite object, would always breed mischief'.[12]
It was not the practical issues at Aix-la-Chapelle – the evacuation of the armies
of occupation from France and the payment of the French indemnity – which
caused him concern, but 'what is intended further to be done on other points'.
When Castlereagh's despatches on these matters reached London he called a
special cabinet to consider them. As a result Bathurst was deputed to convey
the collective doubts of his colleagues on the question of a public announcement
by the great powers of their intention to hold periodic meetings at fixed
intervals.

Though Canning objected in principle to the whole congress system, the
other ministers consulted by Liverpool – Bathurst, Melville and Vansittart –
were not so intransigent. Liverpool gave his own views in a separate letter to

Castlereagh. He thought that where machinery for regular consultation between the allies was already present, there was no point in adding unnecessary public commitments. 'It is often as unwise to look too far into futurity,' he observed with typical caution, 'as to put narrow and contracted limits to our views.' The nature of British politics, he added for good measure, made such extensive vistas impracticable. Three days later, on 23 October, he wrote once more to express his anxiety about any new treaty to which France would be a party. 'The Russians must be made to feel that we have a Parliament and a public, to which we are responsible, and that we cannot permit ourselves to be drawn into views of policy which are wholly incompatible with the spirit of our Government.' Though Castlereagh lightly pointed out 'how little embarrassment and how much solid good grow out of these reunions, which sound so terrible at a distance', this constant pressure from home ensured that nothing came out of Aix-la-Chapelle to complicate life for Liverpool's administration in Britain.[13]

When between 1818 and 1820 the European powers seemed to be moving towards a new, authoritarian form of interventionism, the British attitude was conveyed in the famous state paper of May 1820 which declared in emphatic language that the Quadruple Alliance was 'an union for the Reconquest and liberation of a great proportion of the Continent of Europe from the Military Dominion of France. . . . It never was intended as an Union for the Government of the World or for the Superintendence of the Internal Affairs of other States.' Drafted by Castlereagh but carefully reviewed and emended by the cabinet, this classic document represented not so much the individual views of Castlereagh or Canning as the collective policy of the cabinet under the Prime Minister. After Castlereagh's death, one of the unacknowledged objections to Wellington as a possible successor was precisely (as Liverpool put it to Arbuthnot in December 1822) that 'he is rather *more continental* than we either are or ought to be *permanently*. I say *permanently*, because from circumstances we were brought into a course which was quite right at the time, but to which (with our different prejudices and forms of Government) we never could expect to adhere indefinitely.'[14]

If, after 1822, the Prime Minister's influence over foreign affairs was less obvious, it was because of the close similarity of outlook between himself and Canning. This was the result, however, not of any change of mind on Liverpool's part, but of an attitude towards Europe which he had consistently held from the time of the Congress of Vienna. General agreement with Canning did not imply lack of personal interest or participation in the conduct of British foreign policy. The published correspondence of both men makes it clear that Liverpool maintained a close supervision of the Foreign Office even on such matters as the disposal of diplomatic patronage. There was close consultation on details; Canning regularly submitted drafts of his more important despatches, and not infrequently accepted the Prime Minister's suggestions. Between the two men there was in fact a close working relationship. In November

1824, for example, Canning was writing that it might be better for him to abandon his proposed visit to Walmer 'and look to Coombe for our conference, for which, however, we must allow ample time'.[15]

Certainly there was no question of allowing foreign policy to become the preserve of one man, or even of the Prime Minister and Foreign Secretary acting in concert; Liverpool saw to it that all major issues were discussed in cabinet. That same month, for instance, he was discussing in a letter to Canning the relations between Portugal and its former colony Brazil. Liverpool was anxious that no encouragement should be given to the Portuguese government to attempt the repossession of Brazil by force. On the other hand, he realised that Britain could not prevent such an action and in itself it would not justify the abandonment of British protection to Portugal, since that would merely drive it into the arms of France and her allies. The whole question, he concluded, was of 'so much importance that I do not see how you can take your line until we have held Cabinet meetings upon it; and before this can occur, I shall be glad to have an opportunity of fully discussing with you the whole question'.[16] In some respects, indeed, Canning enjoyed less freedom of action than Castlereagh because he was not absent for long periods abroad attending conferences; his very insularity made him more controllable. The publicity and flamboyance he brought to the conduct of foreign affairs gave the impression of a highly personal policy; but this image did not square with the realities of what went on behind the scenes. It was true, nevertheless, that the combination of the two men, leaders of their respective houses of Parliament and armed with the cumulative authority of Prime Minister and Foreign Secretary, was a formidable one in all ministerial discussions.

There can be no doubt, however, that Liverpool had his own ideas about foreign policy and did not take his opinions ready-made from anyone. On the Greek problem, for instance, he was writing in firm tones to Canning in November 1824 that the Russian policy of nominal Turkish sovereignty was unlikely to succeed. In that case, he added, he was not prepared to join with any other powers and his decided opinion was that all the allies should remain neutral. On occasion he was quite capable of using his authority to make the Foreign Secretary do what he otherwise would not have done. Thus in June 1826 he told Canning in front of the whole cabinet that a particular set of printed papers on the Oregon dispute gave a very imperfect view of the question and asked for more information from the Foreign Office. Despite Canning's unmistakable pique, Liverpool's insistence seems to have been justified. The documents produced in response to his questionnaire included some which Canning confessed he had forgotten.[17]

Liverpool's general authority in the cabinet was strengthened by the fact that he was by far the ablest government speaker in the House of Lords. In contrast to the unhappy Addington between 1801 and 1804, his prestige as Prime Minister never suffered from personal deficiencies in the skills of parliamentary debate. Lady Erne's son-in-law, the by no means uncritical Stuart

Wortley, went so far as to say in December 1819 that 'I am not sure whether I don't think him now the best speaker in either House of Parliament'. For clarity, command of detail, and objectivity, he had no superior and few equals. Sidmouth said of him that he was the best, fairest and most perspicuous debater on any knotty and important question in Parliament that he had almost ever known. One quality in particular which impressed supporters and opponents alike was the scrupulous justice with which he handled the arguments of those who differed from him. A whig peer, unnamed but identifiable as Lord Dacre, speaking to Plumer Ward about the time of the Queen's trial, paid him a particularly striking compliment. Liverpool, he observed, was 'the honestest man that could be dealt with. You may always trust him ... though he may be going to answer you after a speech, you may go out and leave your words in his hands and he will never misrepresent you.' Some people criticised his appearance and gestures, among them the witty and malicious Princess Lieven. In May 1823 she paid a visit to the House of Lords to hear Lord Grey speak for two hours on the Spanish question and stayed on for another hour to listen to Liverpool's reply. 'Heavens, what attitudes he gets into!' she related to Metternich. 'All the same, he speaks well. He is not careful in the choice of his words, but he makes his points soundly. He speaks with force and clarity and one remembers what he has said.' The Prime Minister, who was less embarrassed by the elegant Russian woman's rare presence in the peers' chamber than his rival, would probably have appreciated this measured compliment more than Grey her summary of his own performance – beautiful diction, noble posture, pure style but arguments which were sometimes false and conclusions sometimes exaggerated.[18]

What has been less often the subject of comment is the strain of modernity and liberalism which was as much a part of Liverpool's mental outlook as his constitutional conservatism. In common with the more sensible British politicians and administrators in the first decade of the nineteenth century, he realised that without its industry and commerce Britain could scarcely have won the war against Napoleon. It was a debt he never forgot. Compared with his critical or at best neutral attitude towards the landed interest, he was always ready to emphasise the importance of Britain's Industrial Revolution. In 1824 when asking the King's sanction for a grant of £500 from the Treasury for a statue of James Watt, he described him as 'the inventor of the steam engine, the greatest and most useful invention of modern Times'.[19] He had previously made a personal trial of its usefulness, in fact, by travelling to Walmer by steamboat the previous year. An equally modern touch was his attendance at the Ricardo memorial lecture on political economy given by J. R. McCulloch in 1824. While he took care to mix the wine of economic theory with the water of political caution, he was never out of touch with the teachings of contemporary political economists. 'It is not requisite to inform his Majesty's ministers', the government pamphlet The State of the Nation observed drily in 1822, 'that the first and best principles of commerce would be a perfect freedom of trade, and that in almost all cases legislators would act wisely in leaving it to find its own way. The same text books are open for them as for their political adversaries.' It was only justice to remind the country that for all the practical restraints on government action, 'under no former administration has so much been conceded to the commercial interest of the empire'.

It was not only in matters of economic policy that Liverpool's liberalism manifested itself. At the time of the church building grant in 1818, he drew the attention of the House of Lords to the rapid growth of manufacturing towns and the need for more schools. 'For himself, he had always been of the opinion that the benefit of instruction ought to be extended to all classes of his Majesty's subjects.' If in this particular instance he saw social reform as part of the defences against radicalism and disorder, there could have been no political motive behind his support for a reform of the game laws or for the elder Peel's Act to regulate the employment of children in cotton factories. When that bill came before the peers, he told them bluntly that no eloquence or personal testimony would make him believe that children of seven could labour for twelve hours a day without injury; and he dismissed as puerile the idea that a child of that age could be regarded as a free agent. For Liverpool such issues were essentially moral rather than political or economic; and between morality and religion he saw no clear dividing line. Despite his long opposition to Catholic Emancipation, all his instincts led him towards charity and toleration. The sympathy he had shown for Methodists and dissenters at the time of his 1812 legislation was not dictated solely by expediency; at heart he was himself a liberal evangelical. This was seen in small ways, such as his dislike of travelling on Sunday 'without necessity', as he once confessed to Arbuthnot; but also on larger issues. Together with the Archbishop of Canterbury and the Bishop of Exeter, for example, though opposed by Lord Eldon and many occupants of the episcopal bench, he unsuccessfully supported the relief bill of 1824 designed to legalise Unitarian marriages. In his private life he set a quiet example of regular religious observance. When Collins the painter spent a weekend at Coombe in 1820 he recorded not only that his host went to Kingston Church on Sunday morning but that in the afternoon 'the whole family, including the servants, assembled in the great room and Lord Liverpool read the evening prayers at $\frac{1}{2}$ past 5 o'clock from the book of Common Prayer after which the Company dined'.[20]

On the great and increasingly urgent question of Catholic Emancipation his conflicting religious and political instincts resulted in a complex attitude not always understood by his contemporaries. In 1823, for example, he supported, together with the rest of the cabinet peers, except Eldon and Wellington, a bill for admitting Roman Catholics in England to the parliamentary franchise already enjoyed by their co-religionists in Ireland. The following session he both spoke and voted for Lansdowne's two bills to admit English Roman Catholics to the franchise and the magistracy, though they were in the event rejected by his fellow peers. On these two occasions he argued that concession on minor grievances would strengthen the ability of Protestants to defend their monopoly of the legislature. In 1821 there is some evidence that the Prime Minister may momentarily have faltered in his lifelong defence of even this constitutional principle. When Plunket's Emancipation bill passed the Commons, Liverpool (according to Hobhouse, the under-secretary at the Home Office who was in a position to know) asked Sidmouth whether it might not be wiser to improve the bill where possible and then allow it to pass. In the end he made a strong speech against it; but he had evidently said enough in private for a rumour to go round that the Prime Minister was not unfriendly to the bill. It is of course possible that on this occasion Liverpool was sounding opinion rather than asserting a conviction; it is possible also that he was in a state of genuine indecision. Mrs Arbuthnot, a shrewd observer where her own predilections were not involved, implied on a similar occasion in 1825 that Liverpool had a divided approach to the Emancipation problem. Politically he saw that it was inevitable; religiously he wished to have nothing to do with it. If so, he was only anticipating in his own mind the conflicting arguments of conscience and expediency which Peel had to resolve three years later.[21]

Over patronage, that inevitable accompaniment of power which took up so much of every prime minister's time, Liverpool was usually at his best - urbane, adroit and purposeful, particularly in his earlier dealings with the King. He had firm views on the undesirability of lavish additions to the peerage, for instance, or on the general unsuitability of royal dukes for responsible office. He accepted, however, the realities of political life: the need to reward friends, conciliate the influential, and allow the monarch the illusion of power by consulting his preferences whenever possible. Over episcopal appointments he was a shade more exacting. During his premiership he had twenty-one vacancies to fill, though since some were the result of a translation, only seventeen bishops were actually involved. Like Pitt he had a certain partiality for men of good family, but he was more insistent than his illustrious predecessor on high standards of scholarship, impeccable moral respectability, and a conscientious performance of pastoral duties. Not all his cabinet colleagues were troubled by such scruples. Arbuthnot had a story about a clerical protégé for whom Lord Westmorland made repeated applications for preferment. In the end Liverpool sent Arbuthnot as patronage secretary to tell him that the clergyman in question had not sufficient merit for a bishopric. 'Merit, indeed,' said Westmorland in surprise. 'We are come to a pretty pass if they talk of merit for a bishopric.'[22] Liverpool, however, persisted with his peculiar notion that certain standards were demanded of the episcopacy.

Many of his younger bishops formed the vanguard of those enlightened diocesan administrators who paved the way for wider reforms in the Church of England after 1832. To find suitable men in an age of social unrest and in the face of the King's express wish for bishops of political and theological orthodoxy, preferably connected with the aristocracy, was not a light task. When with difficulty Liverpool obtained the transfer of Ryder, the solitary evangelical on the bench, from Gloucester to Lichfield in 1824, the King stipulated that it should be his last preferment, since his opinions, if they became general among the episcopacy, might be 'attended with great inconvenience to the State'. The election of the reactionary Huntingford for Hereford in 1815 probably owed much to the influence of his patron Lord Sidmouth; that of the self-seeking Pelham for Lincoln in 1820 to royal favour. Pelham, son of an earl, cousin of a duke, friend of George IV, continued to press the Prime Minister for further favours until Liverpool finally told him that he need not look for any more promotion. The only nomination of his own which savours of nepotism was that of his cousin J. B. Jenkinson to St Davids in 1825. Though his elevation was criticised by Peel's tutor, Lloyd of Oxford, because of his lack of theological distinction, this donnish opinion was not perhaps entirely disinterested. Lloyd was busy himself at this time trying to impress on Peel his own claims to the bishopric of Oxford based entirely on scholarly grounds. Though doubtless Jenkinson arrived on the bench only through his family connection, it was not a disreputable appointment; and in the field of education for the poor, at any rate, Bishop Jenkinson, whatever his theological shortcomings, ranked with the more progressive members of the episcopate. For the rest the Prime Minister had nothing to be ashamed of in a list of bishops which included the active pious Law, the reforming administrator Kaye, the evangelical Ryder, the able and scholarly Bethel, the learned energetic Marsh, the gentle, liberal-minded Howley, the serious devout Burgess, and the respected van Mildert. 'The world will at least give me credit,' Liverpool wrote with a touch of complacency to Hobhouse in 1825, 'for my ecclesiastical promotions, whatever they may say or think of me in other respects.'[23]

It is the nature of patronage, however, that many hope and most are disappointed; what begins with impartiality often descends into acrimony and ends in resentment. One particularly painful episode concerned Knighton, the intelligent but intriguing physician who had succeeded Bloomfield in the duties if not the title of private secretary to the King. In July 1823 the Prime Minister received what was virtually a royal command to create Knighton a privy councillor. Liverpool, with strong support from Peel and the more qualified approval of Wellington, Bathurst and Canning, declined to fall in with the King's wishes. He thought the appointment wrong in principle and the precedents for such an action dubious. The refusal made a dangerous enemy of Knighton and added another item to the King's lengthening tally of grievances against him. Yet despite the politic arguments for concession urged by Arbuthnot and Wellington later in the year, the Prime Minister would not give way.[24]

An even more painful, and politically hardly less critical, dispute took place in 1826 with a colleague he respected more than he did the King and in a branch of patronage where he was even more fastidious. Gerald Wellesley, the younger clerical brother of Lord Wellesley and the Duke of Wellington, had once before been refused promotion by Liverpool. He was separated from his wife because of her adultery but had not instituted divorce proceedings, thus leaving himself open to the imputation that he feared recriminatory action. Lord Wellesley, in his capacity as Lord Lieutenant of Ireland, nevertheless recommended him for an Irish bishopric which had become vacant. Liverpool replied that he had not altered his views on Gerald Wellesley's ineligibility and observed pointedly that the vulnerable position of the Church of Ireland and the Lord Lieutenant's own official position were additional reasons against the appointment. Lord Wellesley concurred with apparent good grace but privately wrote to his other brother Arthur urging him to take the matter up with the Prime Minister. Wellington accordingly wrote a strong and injudicious letter at the end of August, pressing Gerald's claims largely on family grounds, citing his own services to Liverpool and implying with extraordinary tactlessness that the earlier refusal to promote Gerald to a canonry resulted from prejudice and bad temper. Liverpool, deeply pained, replied with a firm restatement of his reasons, adding that 'I can only say that I am discharging a duty which I feel to be of the most sacred nature' which no political or private motive could be allowed to influence. Wellington returned to the charge with a long, argumentative letter; Liverpool in turn enlisted the support of the Home Secretary, the Irish Chief Secretary, and the Archbishop of Canterbury. The anxious Arbuthnot, a close friend of both men, then intervened on Wellington's behalf with a letter to the Prime Minister which Liverpool told him later had made him so ill that he had not slept all night.[25]

It was an unhappy episode. The Duke, already dissatisfied with Canning's foreign policy, seemed peevishly ready to quit the cabinet. The Prime Minister, resolute but profoundly upset, longed to get away to Walmer 'for there only have I any rest'. Tiredness and worry sometimes made him unnecessarily stiff in his language; more so than he probably realised. He could sometimes be thoughtlessly brusque even to old and loyal friends like Arbuthnot, Wellington, and Peel. Yet all this was superficial. Sooner or later a characteristic expression of warmth and approval would disarm those whom he had unwittingly offended. He was not a man with whom it was easy to be out of humour for very long; his fundamental kindness and modesty soon won people back. If he annoyed others on occasion by his apparent prudishness, he for his part showed patience towards men with whose tastes and habits he had little in common. He put up with the presence in the cabinet for fifteen years of the coarse and ill-mannered Lord Westmorland. He could even find something to say for the vain, loose-living and dilatory Lord Wellesley who as Lord Lieutenant of Ireland continually exasperated Peel the Home Secretary and Goulburn his own Chief Secretary. 'The truth is, he is a great *compound*,' Liverpool wrote once to Arbuthnot, 'and if one is to have the use of him it must be by making as little as possible of some of his absurdities. We have known him for thirty years. The acquaintance of Peel and Goulburn has been but recent and they cannot therefore see as well as us, that a man may be wise in some things and most foolish in others.'[26]

*   *   *   *   *

The outward appearance of the Prime Minister in the last years of his life was caught by two well-known painters. Hayter dashed off an impressionistic sketch of him in profile – still the same sharp, eager profile of his youth – at the time of the Queen's trial. The more familiar appearance known to contemporaries – middle height inclining to stoutness, the serious reflective countenance: this was recorded for posterity in two portraits by Sir Thomas Lawrence. The first, commissioned by George IV for his Waterloo room at Windsor Castle (where it may still be seen) was a three-quarter-length painting showing Liverpool in a black coat adorned with his Garter star, his hands (surprisingly graceful hands) lightly clasped in front of him. The intent, almost anxious look of the early Hoppner and Lawrence portraits has gone. The face is firmer and above the strong chin and long nose the eyes look out with a steady regard. Peel commissioned the second portrait some years later for his private collection of political contemporaries. It was finished in 1827 and exhibited at the National Gallery, where it now hangs, in May of that year. It is a full-length study of Liverpool sombrely dressed in a long dark coat, standing at a table by an open despatch box. Of the two, it was the first, put on public show in London in 1821, which attracted most attention. Some praised the painter at the expense of his subject. Henry Fox, who went to see a display of Lawrence's pictures in December 1821, wrote: 'I was very much struck indeed with one of Ld. Liverpool, which is a triumph of art to throw any noble expression into such an *ignoble* face: it is very fine indeed.' Allowance must always be made for a measure of flattery in the work of a fashionable court painter; even so, perhaps an Oxford undergraduate of whiggish persuasion was not likely to be the most sympathetic of critics. Mrs Arbuthnot, who had seen the portrait in September, was more generous. 'It is impossible to conceive anything more exquisitely like or where the character and the *manière d'être* of the individual is more perfectly caught. It has exactly his *untidy* look and slouching way of standing; it has, too, all the profound and penetrating expression of countenance which marks this distinguished statesman.'[27] As though to prove her impartiality she went on to complain of his cold manner and irritable temper: criticisms which doubtless reflected in an exaggerated form her husband's experiences. A few years earlier perhaps her comments would not have been so tart. As far as command of nerves and temperament was concerned, Liverpool was probably at his most impressive between 1808 and 1820. It was in the latter year that not only political anxiety but an actual physical worsening began to affect him. The irritability and gusts of passion so foreign, as Hobhouse noted, to his usual calm and cold manner, only started to show themselves about a year before Mrs Arbuthnot wrote her comments.

It could scarcely have been a coincidence that this was the exact period when his health began slowly but steadily to deteriorate. Although, like many other politicians and men of fashion, he often in earlier years used Bath as a place of rest and recuperation, there is no evidence that he was ever seriously unwell until his wife's death. He had been suffering for some years, however, from a form of thrombo-phlebitis in his left leg. Fremantle mentioned 'a serious attack of inflammation in the sinews of his thigh' in July 1822 and added that it was 'his old complaint'. It was probably a similar attack from which he was recovering in the spring of 1816 when he stayed away from the wedding of Princess Charlotte and Leopold of Saxe-Coburg because his doctor feared that the heat and standing might bring on a relapse. Whatever the cause of the trouble (and there are many possibilities, including hereditary weakness) his sedentary occupation would undoubtedly have made it worse. The diagnosis advanced by Sir Henry Halford some years after the Prime Minister's death, that he suffered from *phlegmasis dolens* or Whiteleg, a disease of the legs associated with women after childbirth, is not one that would commend itself to many modern physicians. His further suggestion that this condition ultimately caused his death is even less credible. Halford was a vain, pompous careerist and it is difficult to resist the impression that his unusual diagnosis, put forward in a public lecture delivered to the Royal College of Physicians, owed much to the illustrious position of his patient and a desire to embellish his own professional reputation.[28]

Whatever the cause, it was a painful complaint and as time went on, it became a persistent condition. A similar weakness may well have affected in later years the blood vessels of the heart and also his pulse rate; this would suggest a general vascular inadequacy. Two years later the state of his legs had become observably worse. Lord Colchester noted in June 1824 that whereas the Prime Minister had for some time been in the habit of resting one of his legs along his bench in the House of Lords, he was now putting both up. In May of that year his doctors had been afraid that the disorder was spreading from the left to the right leg; and Knighton reported to the King in June that Liverpool was in constant pain whenever he sat with his legs down. Though the condition was not stable and showed improvement from time to time, he had bouts of acute discomfort for the rest of his life. He bore the physical marks of his suffering in the swollen state of his left leg and thigh, and the varicose appearance of the veins. After his death it was ascertained that there was complete obliteration of the external iliac veins on both sides with widespread ossification of the walls of the blood vessels. The liver, however, was quite sound which suggests that alcoholism played no part in his disorders.[29]

Despite this disability the Prime Minister seemed perfectly able to carry on with his duties after 1821. He even found time and inclination to marry again. That he would do so sooner or later was not unexpected in his own small circle. He liked the company of women and after Louisa's death was obviously pining for sympathetic companionship. Lady Erne came to stay with him for a while and later in the year the dowager Duchess of Devonshire, now over sixty, good-heartedly made the long journey from Italy to be with him. She arrived soon after the coronation in July and stayed at Fife House until November. The following year Lady Erne, from her nearby home at Hampton Court, continued to keep a sisterly eye on him. In May 1822, on one of her regular visits to Coombe, she found her brother-in-law still in low spirits but had the comforting feeling that 'our quiet *tête à tête* dinner and evening just suited him'. Louisa's brother, the Earl of Bristol, had just returned to England and Liverpool was dreading the prospect of their meeting, the first since Louisa's death, which was bound to renew his sense of loss. When Lady Erne spoke to him about it, the tears poured uncontrollably down his cheeks. From time to time, however, he found other feminine solace. That same spring there was a party at Coombe consisting of his half-brother Cecil Jenkinson, the lively Georgiana Bathurst, daughter of his cabinet colleague, and what Lady Erne described as 'his two *Cronies*, the Duchess of Wellington and Lady Bathurst, and they will be such excellent aids I cannot be wanted'. She was still disquieted about his health. He looked ill and had been troubled by a return of his leg complaint, for which he had been applying leeches to reduce the inflammation.[30]

For a man who found such pleasure in women's society, remarriage was almost a personal as well as a domestic necessity. As early as September 1821 Georgiana Bathurst, who was then about thirty, was being teased over her prospects of becoming the second countess of Liverpool. It was not on her, however, but on the older and quieter Mary Chester, his wife's long-standing friend and companion, that his choice more sensibly fell. Socially it was an irreproachable if not exciting match. She was the daughter of the Rev. Charles Chester, a niece of Lord Bagot, and a grand-daughter of the Earl of Dartmouth. The only circumstance which caused surprise was the fact that she, like Louisa, did not enjoy good health. Louisa, however, had been fond of her and the gentle Lady Erne said of her that 'she is a Person of more than ordinary merit'. The Duchess Elizabeth, who had a strong affection for both Louisa and Lord Liverpool, felt a twinge of jealousy at his prompt remarriage, but she took the news better than her sister expected. 'I am sure that we feel alike about it,' she wrote from Rome to Lady Erne, 'and most sincerely do I wish him happy.' The quiet wedding planned for August 1822 had to be postponed because of Londonderry's suicide; it took place a month later on 24 September. To Liverpool it brought the comfort and companionship he needed, as was clear from the letters he wrote to the Duchess of Devonshire. 'I am delighted to hear from you that you are so well and that Walmer has agreed with Lady Liverpool,' she replied at the end of the year. 'Every letter I receive is full of her praise and I do assure you that if I may look to another excursion to England I should have a sincere pleasure in cultivating my acquaintance with her as I feel I should love a person who constitutes your happiness.' That meeting never took place. In April 1824 Liverpool was writing to the King to announce the death in Rome of 'his poor sister the Duchess of Devonshire' and to deplore in stately language the loss of 'so near and dear a connection, from whom he never experienced during the course of more than thirty years, any feelings but those of the greatest kindness'.[31]

It was probably Mary Chester's close relationship with his dead wife, and his own long acquaintanceship with her, that explained Liverpool's choice.

Nevertheless, though Mary could bring him a measure of content, she could never replace her predecessor in his affections. After her death he commissioned the famous sculptor Francis Chantrey to carve a statue of Louisa. The seated life-size marble figure, though bearing the date 1825, was sufficiently advanced by the end of 1822 for the Duke of Devonshire to tell his stepmother how beautiful it was. It was a likeness of Louisa not as she was in 1821 but as Liverpool must have liked to remember her: as a young woman, little more than a girl in appearance, looking upwards with a wistful expression on her small, regular face, dressed in a long gown that recalled the more natural fashion of twenty years earlier. The similarity between it and the portrait of Louisa done by Romney about 1792 is considerable. It is not beyond conjecture that Chantrey may have used that painting when executing his posthumous commission. On the pedestal was carved a simple inscription so unlike the conventional florid tributes of the period as to suggest that Liverpool himself composed it. The last four lines are an adaptation from the definition of pure religion in the General Epistle of James I, 27.

Louisa Theodosia
Countess of Liverpool
Born February 1767
Died June 1821
She visited the fatherless
and widows in their affliction
and kept herself
unspotted from the world.

The statue was probably intended from the start as a funerary monument, but perhaps because Liverpool could not bear to let it out of his sight, it was still in Coombe House at the time of his death. It stands today in the parish church of All Saints in Kingston on Thames where she and her husband in their lifetime were regularly among the congregation.

Even without the presence at Coombe of Louisa's pensive statue, life with her elderly husband was quiet enough for the second countess. When Arbuthnot went to stay at Walmer for a couple of days in October 1823, he was bored to death, or so his wife said – 'they breakfast before 9 and go to bed soon after 10'. Charles Wynn was equally bored and equally uncomplimentary when he stayed at Coombe the following year. 'This is unquestionably', he pronounced, 'the dullest house in which I ever passed a day.' Most of Liverpool's entertaining had been at Fife House; but when Louisa became an invalid even that rambling old Whitehall mansion offered few social attractions for the political and diplomatic world. Much depended on the company; as host Liverpool was too reserved and serious to give a lead. He needed the stimulus of more extrovert characters to reveal the lighter side of his nature. While the Duchess Elizabeth was at Fife House in November 1821, he gave a dinner-party at which the company included the Duke of Wellington, Sir Thomas Lawrence,

George Lamb and his wife, who was the eldest of the Duchess's illegitimate children by the fifth Duke of Devonshire. Wellington was in a talkative vein and over port, when the ladies had retired, 'he had been delightful,' Liverpool told Elizabeth afterwards; 'they had made him relate his battles'. The Duchess, who had been reduced to discussing clothes with Mrs Boothby in the drawing room, was understandably displeased at the barbarous English convention which had excluded her from those conversational delights. Liverpool himself could be sociable, almost frivolous, when in the mood; though this was not often. In December 1823 when he was at last graciously permitted to pay a courtesy visit to old Lord Grenville at Dropmore, he obviously laid himself out to please. His diplomatic journey to this shrine of the Grenvillites went off surprisingly well and Wynn, a fellow-guest, described him as 'chatty, full of anecdotes and evidently anxious to please'.[32]

With women he did not find it difficult to unbend. The Princess Lieven, in her time the confidante of many British politicians, was a frequent visitor at Fife House. In June 1820 she described in her own witty style a 'long and solemn dinner', enlivened in the drawing room afterwards when her host took the odd fancy 'of jumping over the back of a big sofa on which I was seated, and establishing himself on a little footstool in front of me. The great Liverpool hovered and then settled on the ground, looking very comic. It is a common joke in this circle of society that he takes a very great interest in me; I quite like Prime Ministers.' That a sedentary man suffering from incipient thrombo-phlebitis would amuse himself by jumping over furniture in his own drawing room is not altogether easy to believe; perhaps the Princess's notion of a 'big' sofa referred to length rather than height. The Duchess Elizabeth, who during her life had charmed more men than Princess Lieven, certainly knew and approved of Liverpool's partiality to her own sex. When Sir Thomas Lawrence visited Rome in 1819 he found Canova at work on a statue which had been commissioned by her famous brother-in-law. The Italian sculptor, thinking perhaps that the grave office of British Prime Minister required an equally grave subject for his chisel, chose to carve the figure of a recumbent Magdalen. Canning would have been highly amused at the appropriateness of this but the Duchess was in strong disagreement. 'Canova must not', she wrote to Lawrence, 'do too holy a figure for Lord Liverpool, who is a great admirer of female beauty and would like a Nymph or a Venus better than a Magdalen.' Canova, however, was not to be swayed, even by a duchess and patroness of the arts. The statue, one of the last he completed, was still in his Roman studio at the time of his death in 1822; though by the following spring Liverpool was making arrangements for its shipment to England and the payment of the purchase price (£1,200) to Canova's executors.[33]

This interest in the arts was not new. In 1815 he had pressed at an early stage, against the views of Castlereagh and Wellington but with ultimate success, for the return of the art treasures looted by the French from other European countries. He subscribed to monuments for Canova at Venice and

Rome; and besides the statue of Louisa, he commissioned Chantrey in 1822 to do a bust of Wellington. His interest in painting was even greater than in sculpture; and he seems to have been particularly anxious to encourage native British artists. In 1818 he was competing, unsuccessfully, with the Prince Regent for a picture of fishing boys by William Owen; and he engaged William Collins to paint the portraits of the two Boothby children whom he had virtually adopted. Some of his own collection appeared in an exhibition in the British Gallery in 1823. His greatest contribution to the arts in Britain, however, was the foundation of the National Gallery in 1824.

For some years the art-connoisseur Sir George Beaumont had been urging such a scheme on the government and had promised to bequeath his own collection of pictures to the nation if a suitable building could be found. An opportunity came in 1823 when the wealthy London merchant and art-patron J. J. Angerstein died and his choice collection of paintings came on the market. In September Liverpool was writing to the Duchess Elizabeth about the government's intentions 'to lay the foundation of a National Gallery in this country'. His particular wish, he confided to her, was to have a building where outstanding canvasses could be displayed to the public.

> The great object is large Pictures of eminence. Small pictures are as well displayed in private collections but there are scarcely any houses in London capable of containing large pictures and the consequence is, that they are either not bought or sent to great Houses in the Country where few can see them.

In March 1824 he notified the Treasury Board that on behalf of the government he had concluded an agreement with Angerstein's executors for the purchase of his whole collection of thirty-eight pictures (among them works by Claude, Titian, Rubens, Van Dyck, Carracci, Poussin, Velasquez, Raphael, Correggio, Rembrandt, Cuyp, Hogarth, Reynolds, and Wilkie) for the sum of £57,000, together with a lease of the house at 100 Pall Mall where they were hung. Provision was made for the appointment of a Keeper of the Gallery at a salary of £200 a year and in May 1824 the National Gallery opened its doors to the public.

Two years later the government purchased Titian's *Bacchus and Ariadne*, Poussin's *Bacchalian Dance*, and Carracci's *Christ appearing to St Peter*, for a further £9,000. At the time of his death, according to Seguier, the first Keeper of the Gallery, Liverpool was intending to do something further to stimulate British painting. It was in acknowledgement of the Prime Minister's services to the arts that Lawrence depicted him, in the portrait he painted for Peel, with his hand resting on a bundle of papers on the table beside him marked 'National Gallery'. At the first dinner of the Royal Academy after Liverpool's stroke in 1827, when the President gave a toast for his speedy recovery, this painting by an apt coincidence was on display in the same room.[34]

Liverpool's only other discernible interest outside his work was in literature. His library, a miscellaneous collection of history, English antiquities, law, divinity, general science, languages and travel, together with some French and Italian books and the usual Greek and Latin classics, was sufficiently large to be sold at Christie's after his death. Good prices were obtained, though many of the volumes with marginal notes by the Prime Minister were bought back by the family. Even in literature, however, what attracted him most was politics and political history. His correspondence with Croker in 1824, on the late eighteenth-century political world into which he was born, displayed an informed and critical mind as well as some interesting personal judgements. He ascribed the agitation of the first few years of George III's reign, for example, to the succession of shortlived ministries which destroyed public confidence. Lord North, he thought, though a man of considerable talent, was not suitable as Prime Minister despite maintaining a strong government until after the outbreak of the American war. He deplored the failure of Glenbervie, who had married Lord North's daughter, to write a complete *Life* of his father-in-law. 'The American War having been a losing cause,' he added drily, 'it is not likely to find now even an apologist: all that will be written, will be written with a strong bias the other way.'

In this exchange of views his monarchist family tradition and his approval of rulers who retained long-serving ministers, were humanly evident. It was a curious historical fact, he ruminated, that Queen Elizabeth, reputedly capricious, was 'the most steady Sovereign in her politics' that ever reigned. 'She knew when she was well served, and kept the same Minister for more than forty years.' The unspoken comparison with that unsteady sovereign George IV is almost audible. Burke's writings, he thought, 'contain the whole strength and secret of the Whig cause during the last reign'. Though differing from him on many points, 'I look to him as one of the great oracles of my country. I wish the Tory cause had found as good an expositor. Dr Johnson is admirable as far as he goes.' Prior's *Life* of Burke he thought excellent; his only criticism was that it made Burke too much the leader of a party. This he never was.

> He was undoubtedly the oracle of the Marquis of Rockingham, and of all the *pure Rockingham party*, but the House of Commons never did, nor ever would, have submitted to him as leader of any party. . . . Why, it may be asked, being gifted with acquirements beyond all other men perhaps, living or dead, and surpassing all his contemporaries in the *highest flight* of eloquence, was he not the leader of his party? First, because he wanted taste, and secondly, because he was the most impracticable of men. He never knew when not to speak, he never knew when to speak short.

This whole passage, redolent of Liverpool's practical outlook on politics, may be set beside a brief comment he once made to Peel about Fitzgerald: 'he is unfortunately deficient in two qualities more important in the concerns of life than any talents, *judgement* and *temper*'.

His literary verdicts were as severe as his political. Of Bishop Tomline's deplorable scissors-and-paste *Life* of the younger Pitt, he wrote scathingly that any drayman, given Pitt's letters and the volumes of parliamentary debates, could have done as well; and though he said he would assist Croker with his edition of Horace Walpole's correspondence, he confessed to an ineradicable prejudice against that writer – 'as bad a man as ever lived . . . the most sensuous and selfish of mortals'. Any letters of his were not likely to be of much service to history and 'will rather mislead than instruct the rising generation'.[35]

Outside politics, in fact, Liverpool allowed himself few diversions and seemed to have fewer interests. Even when the coming of peace in 1815 made continental travel fashionable again, he showed little desire to retread the paths of his youthful tours of Europe. His only trip abroad in later life seems to have been in 1825 when he took his second wife to France, the Hague, and Amsterdam on a kind of sedate and much-delayed honeymoon. 'Lady Liverpool was much pleased with an opportunity of seeing Holland,' he reported to Arbuthnot, 'and it answered thoroughly to me, who had been in that country before, though at a distance of thirty-five years.' The appeal of foreign countries, however, was clearly limited and in other years they confined themselves to the small, familiar triangle of Fife House, Coombe Wood and Walmer Castle. In the absence of a suitable dwelling-house at Hawkesbury, his Gloucestershire estates rarely saw their owner. Though his father had left money in trust for the acquirement of more land, the son's ventures into the property market were only fitful. He bought an estate in Wiltshire in 1821, probably the 577 acres in that county which the *Return of Owners of Land of 1873* recorded as owned by Sir George S. Jenkinson. Earlier, in 1818, his estate steward Biedermann suggested the purchase of the Upton house and estate near Hawkesbury. Liverpool took no action, apparently because he did not want to burden himself with yet another residence – 'I have already more Houses than I want.' Nevertheless, in 1820 he did apparently begin the building of a house (Eastwood Park) on his other estate at Falfield, though it seems not to have been finished until Sir George Jenkinson took it over in the 1860s. Possibly the death of Louisa the following year destroyed any incentive he might have had to secure a house in Gloucestershire.[36]

He remained, therefore, something of an absentee landlord, leaving the details of management in Biedermann's hands. Even at one remove, however, he was able to experience some of the problems and pleasures of a country landowner. In January 1818 he was noting the smallness of the rent-remittances from Gloucestershire and hoping that better prices for cheese and cattle would enable his tenants to pay off their arrears in the spring. This optimistic expectation, which no doubt he shared with many MPs, was only partially realised. While the Hawkesbury tenants paid up, the Eastwood tenants remained in default; though they promised to work off their arrears before Christmas. His west-country estates at least enabled him to impart an agreeably bucolic aspect to his property at Coombe Wood. Biedermann obtained milch cows and live poultry for him in Gloucestershire and sent them up to Surrey to provide fresh milk and eggs for the Coombe household. In 1818 Liverpool was asking for no less than five cows, adding that he was in great need of them. A herd of five dairy cows for one household seems a generous provision, but contemporary notions of the domestic staff needed by an upper-class family were equally generous. In 1819 Liverpool was paying taxes on fifteen full-time male servants, eight occasional helpers, three carriages, ten driving or riding horses, three farm horses, and four dogs. Nine of his servants wore livery and powdered wigs, which attracted a further tax. This was not, however, by the standards of the time, an extravagant domestic establishment for a man in his position.[37]

The permanent presence of the Boothby family at Coombe and Fife House probably made only a small difference to the costs of Liverpool's household. While poor relations do not add conspicuously to the social attractions of a noble household, at least they provided Liverpool with something of the family atmosphere which Louisa's childlessness had denied him. The Boothbys were still there in 1824 though at some time later in the 1820s Liverpool procured an appointment for Fanny's husband as commissioner in HM Customs which probably resulted in their departure at long last to an establishment of their own. To two of Mrs Boothby's children the Prime Minister was particularly attached – Cecil and Fanny. To each of 'these dear children' he left £10,000 in his will as well as £2,000 to each of their four brothers and sisters. This, though the most munificent, was not the only example of his generosity to relations and other protégés who had either thrown themselves on his charity or been bequeathed to him by Louisa. A noble benefactor, reputedly wealthy and as Prime Minister credited with unlimited patronage, was a natural target for the needy and importunate. Even William Boothby, now Sir William, whose family had lived so long on Liverpool's bounty, was still asking in 1826 for some sinecure that would bring him in two or three hundred a year to augment his salary in the Customs. To this brazen request the Prime Minister returned a long, helpful and considerate letter discussing Boothby's financial and professional situation but pointing out that salaried offices with no work attached to them no longer existed in government and that there was nothing compatible with his duties at the Board of Customs which Liverpool could creditably give or Boothby creditably receive.[38]

Other connections were even more grasping. Charles Jenkinson, Fanny's elder brother, wrote in 1825 from Paris (that haunt of impecunious Britons) describing himself as a penniless debtor and imploring Liverpool to find him employment. To this the Prime Minister circumspectly replied by offering £100 towards his debts and an annual allowance of £50 for his two elder daughters, the youngest being already assisted by her uncles. Much correspondence also took place about another protégé, Captain Ricketts, probably the son of Sophia Watts on his mother's side of the family. In 1818 Ricketts had contrived to get himself expelled from the Royal Military College, Sandhurst, for 'extreme insubordination'. There seemed an hereditary proneness to such accidents among the male Ricketts. Having put several opportunities in the way of Captain Ricketts, Liverpool was confronted in 1824 with a plea from Mrs Ricketts on behalf of her son, who had just been thrown out of the East India Company's College. Despite this discouraging record, Liverpool was trying the following year to obtain a consulate in Colombia for the younger Ricketts.

Perhaps his most wearisome correspondent was a certain Captain Edmund Burke, apparently a former protégé of Louisa, whom Liverpool had helped to educate and get a commission in the army. For years Edmund and his mother Anne Burke, to both of whom Liverpool was making small allowances, stuck to their benefactor with the tenacity and appetite of leeches. Querulous, extravagant, idle, incorrigible, given to writing long screeds which fluctuated ludicrously between grovelling self-pity and petulant haughtiness, Edmund Burke was a character who might have been created by Thackeray at his most satirical. Eventually the long-suffering Liverpool hardened his heart. When Edmund went off to the Cape of Good Hope in 1818 he refused to see him before his departure or answer his voluminous letters, though he continued to pay the bills which perpetually fluttered in Edmund Burke's wake. This forbearance merely encouraged more appeals. In August 1821, in the middle of the crisis with the King, Liverpool was driven to writing a long letter declining to see him, reviewing his past conduct, and ending 'harassed as I am, publicly and privately, I cannot feel myself called upon to continue Discussions which must be very irksome to me and can lead to no practical result'. Even then his sorely-tried patience did not run out. Two years later at Burke's request he agreed to postpone repayment of a loan of £50 he had made to him, though he accompanied this with a warning that it was more than Burke had a right to expect and he must look for no further assistance. 'I have more just claims on my Bounty than I am able to meet and I do not feel that I should be warranted in refusing relief to others in order that I might feed your extravagance.'[39]

These were not the only recipients, deserved or undeserved, of his generosity. In his last will, drawn up in December 1821, he left small annuities to a number of people, mainly women, but including one of £100 to the ineffable Captain Burke, and another of the same amount to his wife. Besides this miscellaneous flock of protégés, there was a constant flow of begging requests from the public at large. A reputation for benevolence was a mixed blessing in an age in which private charity, because socially approved and expected, was peculiarly open to abuse and the art of the begging-letter-writer a remunerative branch of the Grub Street profession. Though Liverpool and his second wife faithfully carried on Louisa's tradition of charitable activities, he was sensible enough to take some precautions against cheats and impostors. Since most of these unsolicited letters were addressed to Lady Liverpool, a certain Miss Robertson was engaged to read them and make personal enquiries where necessary into alleged cases of distress. This lady seems to have performed her task with exemplary thoroughness and scepticism. The familiar docket going forward to Lady Liverpool – 'Miss Robertson's report – unfavourable' was frequently backed by brief but trenchant comments – 'The Man is frequently drunk', or 'they live rent-free and seem to be in no want of blankets'.[40]

At nearby Kingston, of which he had become High Steward in 1816, Liverpool's philanthropy took a more permanent form. Besides dispensing much private charity, he contributed to the upkeep of the Almshouse, was the principal founder and patron of Kingston School, and was chief subscriber for the building of the new bridge over the Thames of which he laid the foundation stone in 1825. In his will he left a small annuity of £25 to be distributed each Christmas among the five most industrious and deserving heads of families in the parish, methodically defined as poor persons, male or female, who had at least two children.

Whatever the begging-letter-authors imagined, Liverpool does not appear to have been regarded by his contemporaries as a particularly wealthy man. If his income was comfortable, his expenses were heavy. In those aristocratic days no provision was made for official entertainment, secretarial staff, and travelling on duty. These incidental expenses (which could be heavy) were expected to be met from official salaries and often, in the case of a man in Liverpool's position, consumed them almost entirely. Liverpool's personal estate on his death was returned by his executors as under £120,000. Of that amount, nearly two-fifths were either given away in bequests or charged with life-annuities, leaving only £46,500 to the residuary legatee, his half-brother Cecil Jenkinson.[41] This figure did not of course include the main settled estates in Gloucestershire held in trust which in 1873 amounted to 3,000 acres with a rent-roll of £4,300. This was probably a much larger sum than Liverpool ever received in the era of agricultural depression after Waterloo. His biographer C. D. Yonge says that Liverpool left office poorer than when he entered it; this may well be true. Unlike his father, nobody ever accused him of being in politics for what he could make from it.

NOTES

1 Ward, II, 53.
2 *Journal of H. E. Fox*, ed. Earl of Ilchester (1923), pp. 35–6; 38474 fos 48, 123; 38475 fo. 53; Muriel Chamberlain, *Lord Aberdeen* (1983), p. 94.
3 Ward, II, 71.
4 AR, 1827, p. 91; BCG, I, 165; Bathurst, p. 501.
5 Arbuthnot's anecdote is in Oman, p. 212.
6 LM, p. 170; ARC, p. 17; Oman, p. 210.
7 BCG, I, 419.
8 The story is told in Kenneth Bourne, *Palmerston, The Early Years* (1982), pp. 170–73.
9 Herries, I, 120 & n.; ARC, p. 17; BCG, I, 411; Parker, I, 109.
10 Bathurst, p. 581 (4 May 1825).
11 Parker, I, 207 (1816).
12 Yonge, III, 192.
13 CMC, XII, 54–63; Bathurst, pp. 457–8; Yonge, II, 344–5.
14 ARC, p. 36.
15 GCOC, I, 200, 203.
16 WND, II, 336.

17 Yonge, III, 307 ff.; GCOC, II, 58, 62, 71-2.
18 LM, pp. 262-3; LWF, I, 261; Pellew, III, 418; Ward, II, 57.
19 Yonge, III, 288.
20 FD, VIII, 241.
21 Hobhouse, pp. 54-5; ARJ, I, 392.
22 Oman, p. 188.
23 Hobhouse, p. 32 n.; see generally R. A. Soloway, *Prelates and People 1783-1852* (1969), esp. pp. 11, 45 n., 84 n.
24 See A. Aspinall, 'George IV and Sir William Knighton', *English Historical Review*, LV, 37-82.
25 Yonge, III, 382-95; Bathurst, p. 614; ARC, p. 83.
26 ARC, p. 45.
27 ARJ, I, 121; *Journal of H. E. Fox*, ed. Earl of Ilchester (1923), p. 91.
28 Sir Henry Halford, *Essays and Orations* (2nd edn., 1833), pp. 111-17; BCG, I, 343; Foster, p. 415.
29 Colchester, III, 330; ARJ, I, 315, 321; *Gloucester Journal*, 2 Dec. 1828.
30 LWF, I, 305-7.
31 George 4, III, 70; 38474 fos 396 ff.; LWF, I, 305-7, 310; II, 134.
32 BCG, II, 19, 33; ARJ, I, 271; LWF, I, 299-300.
33 38475 fos 55, 79; Stuart, pp. 231-2; LM, p. 37.
34 For Liverpool and the National Gallery see 38475 fos 73, 79; AR, 1824, pp. 272-3; FD, VIII, 175, 241; *Diary of B. R. Haydon*, ed. W. B. Pope, five vols (1960-63), III, 324-5; Colchester, III, 494.
35 Croker, I, 270-75. For Liverpool's library see GM, 1829, II, 453.
36 38474 fos 199, 206, 364; ARC, p. 78.
37 38474 fos 168, 236, 305.
38 Liverpool's will is in the Public Record Office (Prob. 11/1751 fo. 92). For Boothby see 38475 fos 327, 329.
39 38474 fo. 360; 38475 fo. 65.
40 38474 fos 391 ff.
41 The valuation of Liverpool's estate sworn by his executors is in the Public Record Office (IR/26/1200-33).

CHAPTER XI

The Years of Prosperity

The years from 1823 to 1825 were the halcyon period of Liverpool's administration: a time of prosperity and liberal reform, when the opposition was silent and discouraged, and even the farmers and country gentry ceased their complaints as wheat prices rose once more. The emergence into political sunlight after the gloom and depression of 1822 came with surprising suddenness. In January 1823 Liverpool was instructing Vansittart that any surplus left after the Sinking Fund had claimed its £5 million should be applied to a reduction in taxation. His object was clearly to ease the distress in the country, particularly that affecting the landed interest. He suggested to the Chancellor of the Exchequer that he should surrender £1 million on malt and reduce by half all assessed taxes (that is to say direct taxes on horses, carriages, servants and windows).

By the time the financial proposals were laid before the House of Commons in February, Vansittart was no longer Chancellor. It was his successor Robinson who had the good fortune to introduce the first popular budget since the end of the war. Though in the event the malt tax was left untouched, various small taxes on employment were abolished entirely, along with all the assessed taxes in Ireland. The remaining assessed taxes in England and Scotland were reduced by 50 per cent. In all well over £2 million of taxes were removed at one stroke. Not surprisingly Robinson's statement was 'received with loud applause by both sides of the House'. It was true that the ostensible revenue surplus of over £7 million, which made this bounty possible, was (as Ricardo pointed out) in a measure fictitious since it hinged on Vansittart's scheme for converting the 'deadweight' of service pensions into a fixed annuity charge, thereby relieving current taxpayers at the expense of the next generation. Against this it could have been argued that the £5 million set aside for the Sinking Fund was in effect merely an unacknowledged addition to the government's financial reserves. While maintaining it as a symbol of public credit and financial orthodoxy, Liverpool was sceptical of its importance to the national economy. 'I have never considered the Sinking Fund as increasing the wealth of the nation,' he confided to Lord Grenville when giving him a sketch of the cabinet's policy in July, 'nor do I consider the National Debt as in any way impoverishing the nation at large.'[1] Such heretic views, however, were not for public consumption.

It would have been equally inadvisable to admit the other demonstrable truth; that the Deadweight scheme was simply a disguised method of adding to the National Debt. Since it was essentially a funding operation involving immediate borrowing at the cost of paying a fixed charge for many years to come, it ran counter to the principle of meeting expenses as they arose. To try to pay off the National Debt through the Sinking Fund and simultaneously add to the Debt in order to reduce the current charge for the Deadweight was to propose two contradictory policies in the same budget. Even if the House of Commons had understood, however, the technical arguments of the economists (which was doubtful), they were not disposed to pick holes in a budget which was obviously going to relieve their own pockets of immediate expense. For Robinson, a happier debut as Chancellor of the Exchequer could scarcely have been imagined; that it was largely undeserved passed without comment. For the Prime Minister it constituted the first, if precarious, sign to the world that recovery was on the way.

By the summer of 1823 the mood of the country had changed miraculously. Towards the end of August Liverpool was cheerfully telling Canning that 'Great Britain was never in such a state of internal welfare and content as at present'. The following day (24 August) Princess Lieven was unconsciously echoing his words in a letter to Vienna. 'Never was the country so happy and peaceful as England at the moment,' she wrote to Metternich. 'I have lived in this country for eleven years and for the first time I hear no grumbling.'[2] For a nation of born grumblers this was a rare state, nor was it a transitory phenomenon. In 1824 and again in 1825 the tranquillity and wellbeing of the nation was the keynote of the King's speeches at the opening of the parliamentary sessions; and the refrain was naturally taken up by government spokesmen in both houses. In the debate on the address in 1825 the Prime Minister used unaccustomed adjectives to describe the 'unprecedented, unparalleled prosperity of every part of the country'. From this, for the benefit of their lordships, he drew two morals: one looking back on the past, one looking forward to the future. What they were now enjoying, he pointed out, was a reward for the discipline and resolution the country had shown in meeting its postwar difficulties. At the same time the opportunity was presented to them to remove restrictions on trade and industry which might have been unsafe to touch in less fortunate times. Though he admitted that he had on occasion argued for the retention of particular types of protection, 'he had nevertheless always laid down the general principle of free trade as the great foundation of national prosperity'. The moment had arrived, was his clear implication, to translate that economic truth into action.

The budgets of 1824 and 1825 gave practical effect to these general aspirations. That of 1824 was important more for the principle it embodied than for the size of the achievement. It was in effect the first free-trade budget of the nineteenth century. With an estimated surplus of £1 million, over and above the £5 million for the Sinking Fund, Robinson was able to reduce the duties on rum, coal, wool and silk as a first significant step towards a liberalisation of the economy. It was a clear shift of tactics from 1823. The aim now was not to cut still further the amount of direct taxation but to make a frontal attack on the vast structure of prohibitive and protective duties which encased the British economy. The 1824 budget was only a start; but a start in the right direction. In October Canning, who had little interest in economic policy compared with Liverpool and Huskisson, suggested yet another round of reductions in direct taxation similar to that of 1823. It was a proven formula for parliamentary popularity and as Leader of the House this was an argument which probably weighed more strongly with him than anything. Liverpool, however, saw no reason for purchasing superfluous support at the cost of bad economics. He acknowledged that all the reports on the state of the revenue which had been collected in preparation for the cabinet meetings in December were satisfactory; but, he said firmly, there was no margin for any further tax cuts. The 1823 concessions had been legitimate in view of the general distress in the country but no justification existed for reducing still further a national revenue that was already scarcely adequate for the country's needs. Direct taxation in Britain, he pointed out, amounted to less than £4 million, a smaller proportion of the total national revenue than was paid by the population of any other country in Europe. He continued in words which shed some light on his own economic thinking.

> If we *could* do what we *ought* to do (do not be alarmed, I am not going to propose it) we should make an augmentation in our direct taxes of at least two millions; and, as a compensation, take off indirect taxes to the amount of four or five millions. By such an arrangement we should not materially reduce our revenue, and we should considerably increase the wealth and resources of the country, by the relief which might be afforded to commerce.[3]

For the Prime Minister the cry of 'cheap government' had clearly lost any constructive value; what he was looking for was the creation of new wealth.

As yet, however, neither the House of Commons nor the public at large were ready for a fiscal approach which combined both severity and imagination. The budget of 1825 adopted a more gradual method of tackling the problem of commercial policy. Despite the tariff cuts of the previous year the revenue had recovered with remarkable buoyancy and Robinson had a surplus of nearly £1½ million instead of the mere half-million that had been anticipated. In contrast to the budget of 1824, which had chiefly aimed at reducing the cost of raw materials for industry, that of 1825 was designed to encourage home consumption and (a not unimportant accompaniment) reduce smuggling by making it less profitable. Large reductions were made in the duties on spirits, wine, rum, cider, coffee and hemp. All that was done by way of direct relief to the taxpayer was the abolition of a number of small taxes amounting to little more than £¼ million out of a total loss to the revenue by the budget changes of over £1½ million. Since these small taxes were administratively expensive to raise, the revenue department probably gained as much as the taxpayer by their removal.

There was some grumbling at the niggardly amount of direct relief but in general the appearance of a third budget surplus, with all the excess money returned in one form or another to the public, was greeted with satisfaction. After years of deficit finance and constant borrowing, a solvent government came as a pleasant novelty. These were the years when 'Prosperity' Robinson earned both his nickname and a credit for his finance which more justly belonged to the administration as a whole, including those forgotten men Vansittart and Wallace. Looking ahead in the sanguine mood created by the financial achievements of the past three years, the Chancellor of the Exchequer could even entertain his House of Commons audience with talk of a budget surplus of over £800,000 in 1826 and one of £1¼ million in 1827. For the moment, at any rate, it seemed as if all promised well in a better world than any one could have prophesied two or three years earlier.

Free trade in the literal sense remained an objective rather than an accomplishment; but what Liverpool's government now clearly possessed was an integrated policy designed to remove prohibitive or extremely high duties, to encourage both the export trade and home consumption, and to assist the domestic manufacturer. More perhaps could have been done, on the lines of the 1825 budget, in removing small duties which made little or no contribution to the exchequer. The principles inspiring the government were, however, self-evident; and in view of Robinson's optimistic forecasts in 1825 there was no reason to think that the programme of economic reform had reached more than a halfway stage. The limitations were practical rather than intellectual; the pace of government policy would have to be adjusted to financial and political circumstances. Though accepting Adam Smith's views on the nature of an ideal economy, neither Liverpool nor his chief economic advisers were doctrinaires. Indeed, Huskisson's interest in reciprocity treaties, a number of which were concluded in these years, and his policy of imperial preference, cut across any absolute free-trade philosophy.

From a narrow point of view it could even be argued that the work of Liverpool's ministry between 1822 and 1825, in effect if not in intention, was simply to make the tariff system more efficient. Monopolies and prohibitions were swept away; what was left was a more rational revenue-producing structure of moderate protectionism. As Liverpool realised, the point had nearly been reached when little further headway could be made in liberalising the economy until new forms of direct taxation could be devised to replace the tariff revenue that would have to be sacrificed by any wider free-trade policy. With his practical sense and political patience, however, he could at least feel that they were moving in the right direction at a rate that was politically and economically sustainable. Free trade could not be achieved in a day, or even a decade. Nevertheless, by producing a coherent long-term programme, his administration had done what no previous government had attempted; equally significantly, visible signposts had been set up for the future. It could scarcely be a coincidence that when the next important stage in the free-trade movement came sixteen years later, it owed everything to men who had been members of Liverpool's ministry - Peel, Robinson, Goulburn, and Herries - in the pioneer years of the 1820s.

The optimistic outlook of these financially carefree years was reflected in the cheerful mood of the House of Commons. 'I hear that we are vastly popular, and all the country gentlemen disposed to support us,' wrote Wynn to his patron the Duke of Buckingham in January 1824. Six months later Canning was able to report with complacence that Parliament had dispersed after a short session 'in the course of which there has not been an angry discussion'.[4] As Leader of the House, in fact, he never had to face the kind of difficulties that had harassed Castlereagh year after year from 1815 to 1822. Not only were the Commons more amenable to government direction than under his predecessor; but he was supported by a much abler front bench in the persons of Peel, an invigorated Robinson, and the intellectual, if unpopular, Huskisson. So far from trying to demonstrate his superiority to his dead rival in the leadership of the House, Canning seemed content to rely on his younger colleagues and take pride in their achievements. He told Knighton in 1825, in the course of the long interview which paved the way for a reconciliation with the King, that the tranquillity of the government was to be ascribed not only to Liverpool and himself in their respective offices but to the 'extraordinary efficiency with which those other great departments of the State are filled by Peel, Robinson and Huskisson; those offices were never so filled all together before'. He even incurred the criticism (a rare one in his controversial career) of leaving too much to his colleagues. At the end of his first session as Leader of the House, Fremantle told Buckingham that Canning had done nothing, had allowed Peel to take command, and the government would have done as well without him as a leader as with him.[5] An exaggeration, no doubt; yet the fact that Canning was never called upon to show his skill as Leader of the House was at least a proof that Liverpool was spared the endless anxiety about the position of the government in the Commons which had been a feature of the stormy period from 1815 to 1822. Out of the ministerial changes of the early twenties had come a demonstrably abler, and to outward appearance a more integrated, administration than Liverpool had ever possessed before. Of this the public at large were in no doubt.

Yet the paradox remained that while the ministry basked in the sun of popular favour and the Commons seemed now more the ally than the watchdog of government, relations inside the cabinet had become brittle and uncomfortable. At the centre of the tension, though perhaps only partly conscious of the fact, was Canning. He had still not lived down his past; some of his colleagues distrusted his foreign policy; even more disliked the ascendancy he seemed to have over the Prime Minister. More important than any specific grievance, however, was his actual character and temperament. With all his talents, no politician of his generation created so much hostility and so much suspicion among his contemporaries. Wellington, who had done all he could to assist Canning's return to the government, soon became his bitterest enemy and was not over-discreet in allowing it to be known in his own social circle. At Court there was an active anti-Canning faction, the so-called Cottage coterie, working to keep alive the King's animosity to the Foreign Secretary. It included not only the two royal favourites, Knighton and Lady Conyngham, but the not unskilful diplomats who represented Russia, Austria and France. If the ultimate object of this cabal was to secure the removal of Canning, it was an intrigue which had little chance of success. Behind Canning was Liverpool; and he was too strongly entrenched politically to be evicted by anything short of a complete reconstruction of the government. While the tension lasted, however, not only did Canning have to struggle against backstairs influence, but the Prime Minister himself shared in the unpleasantness because of the constant accusations that he was under the domination of his brilliant and dangerous colleague.

Much of the antagonism towards Canning was caused by the restless energy he showed in the cabinet and the administration generally as contrasted with the easy-going methods of Castlereagh when he was Leader of the Commons. Part was also due, as far as Wellington was concerned, to the new aggressiveness he brought to the conduct of British foreign policy. At the start of his foreign secretaryship Canning had tried to divert the attention of his colleagues away from the affairs of the continent which had been Castlereagh's main preoccupation towards what Canning asserted was the more vital interest of protecting British commerce, and regularising British relations, with the South American colonies which had broken away from Spain. This issue, however, was soon overshadowed by the threatened French military intervention in Spain sanctioned by Britain's allies at the Congress of Verona. The ostensible object was to defend the Spanish monarchy against the liberal, constitutional party; but the method used implied inevitably a restoration of the traditional French influence in the peninsula which had been a feature of both Bourbon and Bonapartist policy. The British government pointedly refused to be associated with the action of its allies and proclaimed a strict neutrality in Spanish internal affairs as the proper policy for all states. Something more than virtuous inactivity seemed necessary, however, if the British example was to have any effect.

In the debate on the address on 4 February 1823 Liverpool, while reaffirming British neutrality, spoke in praise of the Spanish liberal constitution and the party which had been responsible for its introduction: a revolution, he affirmed, less tainted by bloodshed, crime or violence than almost any similar event in recent history. In case neutrality should be interpreted as weakness he went on to deny that Britain lacked the means to fight on behalf of its vital interests if these were ever challenged. Ten days later, in an interview with the Russian ambassador, he warned him that Britain would never allow France to recover its previous influence in Spain and would oppose it in any struggle that ensued, even if it meant supporting the revolutionary party on the continent. This strong diplomatic language reflected, however, a position of undeniable weakness. In private he admitted that little could be done to prevent French intervention. A memorandum apparently drawn up early in 1823 by Canning but almost certainly approved in advance by Liverpool, pointed out that Britain had neither the military nor the financial resources to engage in another peninsular conflict. A decade of government retrenchment and savage cuts in the service establishments had put it out of Britain's power to fight a continental war. In any case the circumstances were very different to those of 1808. The great powers of Europe were on the side of France; a large part of the Spanish people was opposed to the liberal constitution. The only source of comfort was the hope, born of historical experience, that the French might find themselves enmeshed in greater complications than they anticipated once they were established in Spain. Neutrality, therefore, remained the only prudent policy. Only two eventualities might in the end justify British action: an attempt by France to recover the liberated Spanish colonies, and a threat to the independence of Portugal.[6]

All this became the substance of the speeches delivered in the middle of April by the Prime Minister in the Lords and Canning in the Commons. The only noticeable difference between the two was that Liverpool issued a more forceful warning that the government's neutrality should not be taken as implying an unwillingness or inability to fight if British interests were directly menaced. 'A great country like this', he said proudly, 'will always find the means of protecting itself when its safety, its interests or its honour are really endangered.' Popular as this language was with the British public, it was received with almost as much distaste at Windsor as at Vienna or St Petersburg. 'Royaliste par métier', as Wynn sardonically observed a year later, George IV was angrily sensitive to the charge that his ministers were not only abandoning the union of monarchies which had defeated Napoleon but even invoking the Jacobin spirit of the French Revolution against which they had fought for many years. At a private dinner at Brighton in March he told Princess Lieven, the wife of the Russian ambassador, in the presence of Lord Bathurst, a cabinet minister, that he was royalist to the core and he warmly agreed with her deft rejoinder that Liverpool's speech of 4 February seemed a direct encouragement to the revolutionaries on the continent.[7] For Liverpool and Canning, however, the one point of importance was the failure of both their public threats and private offer of mediation to prevent the French military occupation of Spain, peacefully accomplished in the spring and summer of 1823. It was followed by a collapse of the liberal regime and the institution once more of absolute monarchical rule. For Canning it was particularly galling to have to stand by impotently while French influence was restored at Madrid within a bare six months of his taking office. Even more galling was the silent contrast with his political rival Wellington who had made his reputation ten years earlier by driving the French out of the peninsula to which they had now returned.

The question of recognising the rebellious Spanish colonies as a counterstroke to French intervention in the mother country was therefore taken up by Canning with redoubled energy. It was not, however, a new policy; merely a continuation and enlargement of one started by Castlereagh. For Liverpool it was a step that was necessary in the interests of British maritime and commercial strength and made inevitable by the developments in Spain. As early as 1821 he had told Bathurst that 'I have long been of opinion that the independence of South America (which is now decided) must make an alteration in our whole policy.'[8] His motives were purely practical. He wanted to secure for Britain as large a share as possible of the trade with the new Spanish republics. To abandon that lucrative traffic, in which British merchants had already established themselves, would simply hand it over to the eager Yankee traders. This in turn would mean not only a loss of potentially great commercial profits but a shift in the balance of sea-power in the south Atlantic to Britain's detriment. For a minister who remembered the inconclusive and damaging war of 1812 this was a powerful consideration. Trading with South America, however, which in 1821 had involved little more than a loosening of the Navigation Acts, in 1823 meant defying the Spanish monarchy and offending the legitimate rulers of Europe generally, including his own royal master.

The issue was debated with some acrimony in the cabinet in the early months of 1824. At one point Wellington's opposition to Canning's policy looked as if it might end in his resignation. The Duke, like George IV but with perhaps a shade more justification, could never forget that he had fought beside three of the crowned heads of Europe to restore two others. He was instinctively and understandably antagonistic to any deliberate disruption of the great wartime alliance. Ultra-conservative in his political views, his anti-Canning prejudice made it even harder for him to free his mind from his old diplomatic attitudes. The resultant combination of these personal and political disagreements made Canning's first full year of office a time of great strain for the Prime Minister. Liverpool had to defend himself against not only the reactionary wrath of the King but the more subtle reproaches of some of his closest colleagues.

The most remarkable of these came in a letter sent to the Prime Minister by Arbuthnot in October 1823. As Liverpool himself may have gathered from the opening paragraph, the initiative for such an approach originated with the King who had summoned Arbuthnot to Windsor for the purpose. What Liverpool did not know was that despite Arbuthnot's request that the contents of the letter should not be communicated to any other person, Wellington had read and extensively revised the document. As trusted adviser of the King in the past, an old friend and associate of Liverpool, and a recent but warm adherent of the Duke, Arbuthnot was probably the best choice for a commission which in anybody else would have been a piece of gross impertinence and would have been regarded as such by anyone less kindhearted than Liverpool.

The gist of Arbuthnot's long letter was that the King was deeply dissatisfied with the Prime Minister. For this two reasons were alleged. One was Knighton's bitter resentment at Liverpool's refusal to give him a privy councillorship; the other the undue influence Canning was deemed to have over him. Though the King disliked Canning and did not want to part with Liverpool, he would rather have Canning in the open exercise of the premiership than Liverpool as a mere mouthpiece of the Foreign Secretary. The remedy Arbuthnot suggested was for Liverpool to give Knighton what he wanted and at the same time demonstrate to his colleagues, particularly those devoted to him personally but sharing the King's feelings, that he was determined to follow his own judgement and not be led by Canning. Though deeply hurt, Liverpool replied at once in terms which were kind to Arbuthnot personally, but indignant towards those who had inspired this more than candid communication. He denied point-blank that Canning had 'an unbounded influence over my mind and opinions'. For government to function properly, he pointed out, there had to be complete understanding and confidence between the prime minister and the leader in the other house such as had existed between himself and Castlereagh and before that between himself and Perceval. In no single instance, as far as he was aware, had Canning ever assumed an authority or influence that did not belong to him.

> The whole (if it has any foundation) must be grounded upon the notion that Canning and I happen to have agreed more nearly than some of our other colleagues, not upon what was to be *done*, but upon our views of the possible result of the successful French invasion of Spain.

He continued with mounting feeling.

> The K. will find himself very much mistaken if he supposes that if he dismissed me because it was *his royal will and pleasure*, or if he created an obvious pretence for this purpose, that Canning, Peel, or anyone of my colleagues would remain behind. . . . The K. is mistaken if he supposes that I have any anxious desire to remain in his service. He cannot be too strongly apprized of this truth. If I see I cannot go on with honour and with credit, it will be for me to consider *when* I can most easily retire, but let the K. take care that he does not make the close of a reign which has been hitherto most glorious, and upon the whole most prosperous, stormy and miserable.[9]

The matter of Knighton he dismissed contemptuously in one brief paragraph. Though he admitted the force of the counter-arguments, the issue of the privy councillorship could not be reopened and what Arbuthnot had said about Knighton personally, he added crushingly, merely confirmed the man's utter unfitness for such an office.

Direct pressure on the Prime Minister was clearly self-defeating. Nevertheless, ill-feeling persisted and Canning continued, wittingly or unwittingly, to involve Liverpool in further difficulties with the Court. The Waithman affair was a case in point. Waithman, the Lord Mayor of London in 1824, was a radical City alderman who as Sheriff of Middlesex had behaved so provocatively on the occasion of the Queen's funeral that ministers had considered taking legal action against him. The cabinet had boycotted his inaugural Lord Mayor's banquet the previous November; but Canning argued, and Liverpool agreed, that a permanent proscription would merely present opposition politicians with a gratuitous advantage. Invitations to another City banquet came in April 1824, during the Easter recess. Liverpool was then, on medical advice, at Bath taking the waters, but most of the other cabinet ministers went out of town to avoid the event. Canning and Wynn attended, however, and the King was furious. When Liverpool returned to London he found a strong royal remonstrance waiting for him. He replied almost as strongly. Though Wellington secured the insertion of a softening paragraph, the bulk of the Prime Minister's letter consisted of a vindication of Canning's conduct and a firm statement that had the Prime Minister been well enough, he would have gone to the banquet himself. He took the precaution, however, of writing privately to Canning who responded with a long defensive letter. This Liverpool forwarded to the King with a covering note emphasising that what Canning had done was from a sense of duty to the King's service and that he was sincerely sorry if he had incurred the King's displeasure. On this tactful note the incident closed.[10]

The illness which prevented Liverpool's appearance at the Lord Mayor's Easter Monday banquet was genuine enough. Its most disquieting and puzzling symptom was a dangerously low pulse rate. From a normal 75 it had sunk to 50 and though his doctors had called in the royal physician, Sir Henry Halford, nothing their combined medical wisdom suggested had any effect on the patient. He was listless and depressed, and talked to Arbuthnot of the possibility that his ill-health might force him to retire. The egregious Halford, even more alarmist, informed the King that he did not think the Prime Minister would be fit for office much longer: intelligence which George promptly sent Knighton to impart to Wellington. Since the King had been confiding to a number of people at court that the Duke was his chief supporter in the cabinet, this additional mark of royal intimacy made it uncomfortably clear to Wellington that he was being regarded as Liverpool's successor. Meanwhile, on 12 April the Prime Minister went off to Bath. Whether the medicinal virtues of the water were responsible, or merely the quietness and relief from official duties, a visit to that fashionable resort always seemed to do him good. It did on this occasion. Eleven days later he was able to send an optimistic report to his doctor in London, Sir Astley Cooper. Within the last few days his pulse had risen to a regular 52 and was maintaining that more favourable rate. A long, fast ride on horseback in drenching rain which soaked him to the skin had brought no ill effects and he was therefore contemplating an earlier departure from Bath than had been planned so that he could make a short tour to Bristol, Gloucester, Cheltenham and Oxford. He proposed to be back in town on 1 May in comfortable time for the meeting of the House of Lords two days later.[11]

The unpredictable invalid duly reappeared in London, looking and professing to feel much better, with his pulse (now the subject of eager political enquiry) back to a respectable 60. Speculation continued, nevertheless, throughout the summer months as signs appeared that the beneficent effects of Bath were beginning to wear off. Though in June Liverpool was discussing in cabinet, with the casual air of a man who had no doubt of his continuance in power, measures that might have to be postponed to the following session, an expectation that he would soon retire was gaining ground. Those who stood to profit by such an event were naturally the most assiduous in predicting it. Knighton in June, probably not without a certain relish, reported to the King that the Prime Minister's heart was defective, his blood vessels obstructed, and his head affected in a manner reminiscent of the deaths of his father and grandfather. The King raised the subject once more with the embarrassed Wellington and effusively assured him that he was the person who possessed his entire confidence. This was a possession which the Duke could well have done without. Whatever George might say, most politicians in the government were acutely conscious of the difficulty of finding any acceptable replacement for the Prime Minister. 'If anything was to induce Lord Liverpool to retire,' Croker wrote warningly to Bloomfield on 10 May, 'we should have what is vulgarly called a blow-up.'[12] The divisions within the cabinet made it almost certain that if Liverpool resigned, the administration would be unable to continue without extensive changes. The man with the most obvious claims to succeed Liverpool was Canning; but his only supporters among the ministers were the indecisive Robinson, the unpopular Huskisson, and the uninfluential Wynn. The rest, particularly Wellington, Eldon, Sidmouth, Bathurst, West-morland and Peel, would (it was thought) be unwilling to serve under him. Wellington in June was being urged by the Duke of York to hold himself in readiness for a summons if Liverpool retired; and though he properly refused to do or say anything until that retirement actually took place, he made it plain to his intimates that he would resign office if Canning succeeded. Canning, on the other hand, could hardly be expected to serve under the Duke; and though the King affected to view with equanimity the prospect of losing Canning's services, men with a greater sense of parliamentary realities were more cautious.

The only way out of the difficulty in fact was for Liverpool to recover his health; and this, in the autumn of 1824, he seemed to be doing. At times during the summer he was certainly irritable and depressed; at one point he talked to his subordinates at the Treasury of wishing to settle various measures which, if postponed, he might not be in office to deal with when the time came. As soon as was decent he escaped to Walmer and there, away from London and political harassment, his health once more markedly improved. Visiting Wal-mer at the start of September Peel found him looking 'uncommonly well' and apparently fully restored. Huskisson, who spent a couple of days there a fortnight later, reported that the Prime Minister was looking as well as he had seen him for several years. Rest and sea-air clearly agreed with him. What seemed certain, to most of those who knew him well, was that only sheer necessity would make him retire. As Wynn put it bluntly in June, 'he has no habits of any but official employment, and I cannot imagine him being happy in retirement'.[13]

At the start of the new year he went off for a short stay at Bath from which he seemed to get benefit and where he had Canning to keep him company as well as his private secretary Willimott and his relative Sir William Boothby. There, in the first week of January the two eminent politicians had an unexpected visit from the sheriffs of Bristol bearing an invitation to attend a civic banquet and receive the freedom of the city. It was, as Canning admitted with becoming modesty, the Prime Minister whom the Bristolians chiefly wanted to see. About himself he acknowledged there were reservations, both as the parliamentary representative of a great rival port and as a champion of Catholic claims. The ceremonies and feastings took place on 12 January. The guests were met by the sheriffs at the outskirts of the town and escorted in state to the Mansion House for a reception by the Mayor and corporation. Despite the relatively brief time for preparation, invitations had been sent out to local MPS, gentry and professional people in the surrounding counties as well as to the merchants and tradespeople of Bristol. At the dinner (held at the Mansion House, as the Merchants Hall was deemed too uncomfortable and cold for the Prime Minister in his existing state of health), Liverpool and Canning sat on one side of the Mayor, the Duke of Beaufort and the Bishop of Bath and Wells on the other.

It was a notable civic event in a town where the tory corporation of late years had been more economical in their entertainments than in their unregenerate and lavish past. In addition to the freedom of the city, the two visitors received the freedom of the incorporated Society of Merchant Venturers and an address from the Bristol Chamber of Commerce. For Liverpool it was in a sense a renewal of an old family connection, as he reminded his hearers in a reference to his forebear Anthony Jenkinson, the Bristol merchant who had been the founder of the family's fortunes. He preferred, however, he continued tactfully, to receive his honour in the way it had come since every public man must feel that 'the approbation of his fellow subjects was a just reward of public service'.

For Liverpool it was a rare, possibly unique occasion. It was unusual for senior members of government in those days to make speeches outside Parliament or public appearances outside London or their own locality. For the merchants of Bristol it was also an opportunity to express their sentiments on the national policy of the government since the end of the war. In a succession of speeches and addresses there was a gratifying emphasis on the success of the ministers in overcoming the disorders of the postwar years, on the attention paid by the government to commerce, trade and navigation, on their liberal policy and enlightened principles, on the opening up of new fields for commercial enterprise, on the reduction in taxation, economies in the public service, and the blessing of peace – all leading to the recent unprecedented degree of prosperity enjoyed by the nation. Even allowing for the complimentary nature of the day's proceedings, it was a heartening public tribute to the work of the government since 1815.

Much of what Liverpool himself said in the four short speeches he delivered that day was a repetition with reciprocal compliments of the approving sentiments of the Bristol business community. There were, however, two passages which had a particular interest as revelations, one of his public, the other of his private feelings. When replying to the Merchant Venturers, he declared significantly: 'to Commerce this Country owed much of its prosperity and greatness, and the Landed Interest its present revival and improvement - that indeed no interest stood alone - all were links in the great social chain, all connected with and dependent on each other for that mutual welfare he was pleased to witness, and believed to be increasing'. The other interesting passage came during the dinner in the evening. When proposing the Prime Minister's health, the Mayor had made a flattering reference to his talents, principles and virtues which had raised the country to an unexampled height of glory, wealth and happiness. Liverpool's reply was modest. If there were any merit on his part in his administration of public affairs, he said deprecatingly, it came only from good intentions and best endeavours. Yet good intentions and best endeavours alone would not have been successful 'if they had not received the valuable support, and been aided by the talents, of my excellent and able Colleagues' and if they had not been backed by the great commercial as well as the other great interests of the nation.[14]

He must have been pleased, if also a little exhausted, at the end of this long day of speechifying and entertainment. Public appreciation of his administration's achievements had not been an invariable accompaniment of his lot as Prime Minister. He returned the same evening to Bath, leaving Canning to spend the night in Bristol. They came together again a few days later at Oxford, where Canning stayed in Canon Pett's house in Christ Church and Liverpool enjoyed the doubtless greater luxury of Bishop Legge's hospitality for a couple of nights in All Souls. From Oxford he went home to Coombe where there were to be ministerial meetings to settle the text of the King's speech at the forthcoming meeting of Parliament.

NOTES

1 Yonge, III, 253.
2 Ibid, p. 259; LM, pp. 283-4.
3 Yonge, III, 311; GCOC, I, 179.
4 BCG, II, 41; Bagot, II, 246.
5 BCG, I, 469-70, 475, 481; GCHT, p. 443.
6 LM, p. 237. For memorandum of Feb. 1823 see Yonge, III, 231 ff. (where, probably wrongly, attributed to Liverpool) and GCOC, I, 85 ff.
7 LM, pp. 245-8.
8 Bathurst, p. 526.

9 ARC, pp. 46–58; cf. Greville, 31 July 1831.

10 Yonge, III, 279 ff.; George 4, III, 72–5; GCOC, I, 147–9; WND, II, 250–52; BCG, II, 65–6; Croker, I, 266; cf. Bathurst, p. 513.

11 38475 fo. 118; ARJ, I, 299–300, 314–15.

12 Croker, I, 265; ARJ, I, 321–2; LM, p. 318.

13 BCG, II, 85, 110; Bathurst, p. 573; Huskisson, p. 177.

14 For the Bristol festivities and speeches see *Bristol Gazette*, 13 Jan. 1825; *Farley's Bristol Journal*, 15 Jan. 1825; GCOC, I, 324.

CHAPTER XII

Commerce, Catholics and Corn

In the latter half of 1824 considerable progress was made in arriving at a decision on the South American question. In July the cabinet had accepted a memorandum from Canning in favour of negotiating a commercial treaty with Buenos Aires, the most stable of the Spanish settlements, with which close trading relations already existed. The argument in the cabinet was not over ends but over methods and consequences, particularly the reactions of other states. With increasing pressure from the merchants of London and Liverpool, and the failure of direct diplomatic negotiations with the French and Spanish governments, the Prime Minister by October was inclining to the view that Britain should now ignore other powers, except where bound by previous engagements, and follow a policy based solely on national interest.

When, after a protracted interval of three months, cabinet meetings were resumed in December 1824, South America bulked large in their deliberations. In November Canning had long private discussions with Liverpool on the subject and for the first cabinet on 1 December prepared a memorandum proposing the recognition through commercial treaties of Colombia and Mexico. By 7 December ministers had agreed on the principles to be followed in their South American policy. First, decisions should be made without further reference to the views either of Britain's continental allies or of Spain. Secondly, the question of giving recognition to South American states should be decided on the merits of each individual case. The only important opposition came from Wellington who wrote to the Prime Minister pointing out the difficulties which would be encountered with the King and expressing a readiness to resign from a ministry in which, as he put it, his isolated dissent must be irksome to his colleagues. It was a friendly letter and Liverpool replied in equally friendly terms. 'Nothing', he assured the Duke, 'could give me more sincere pain, privately and publicly, than your separation, from any cause, from the Government.' The King's views he treated less respectfully. 'The opinions which he sometimes avows on the subject of legitimacy would carry him the full length of the principles of the Emperor of Russia and Prince Metternich.'[1]

Even though his views were despised, however, the King still had enough power to make life difficult for his brisk, progressive ministers. Two more memoranda, one composed by Liverpool on the need to protect British interests in South America now that the Spanish government was controlled by France, and the other by Canning discussing the attitudes of other countries, in particular France and the USA, were presented to the King in the middle of the month. Liverpool, who on 16 December made one of his infrequent visits to Windsor to discuss them, thought he would be disinclined to put up any strong resistance. While the King, in characteristic fashion, hesitated and consulted others, the Prime Minister tried to soothe the irritated Canning. He had learned from his own experience, he told his impatient colleague, that it was unwise to press the King too forcibly towards an unwelcome decision. Left to himself, he would always stop short of provoking a crisis. His prediction came true, though not without a difficult passage at the end of January when the King sent a letter to Liverpool denouncing the 'Liberalism of late adopted by the king's government', and demanding to be informed in distinct terms whether the cabinet had abandoned the great principles which governed the allies at the close of the war. An ill-tempered cabinet followed during which Canning got into a passion about the King's unconstitutional behaviour in giving private audiences to the Russian and Austrian ambassadors. In the end a placatory, non-committal reply was concocted to George's rhetorical questions and by February the excitement had subsided.[2]

Even though the outcome of the dispute with the King had never been seriously in doubt, the Prime Minister showed all his old skill and patience in handling the crisis. The proposals laid before the cabinet had been carefully prepared; Liverpool and Canning had given a firm lead in the discussions; and the rest of the cabinet with two exceptions had either supported or at least concurred with their views. Of the two dissidents, Wellington was eventually mollified and reconciled. Indeed, the counter-argument which weighed most strongly with him was Liverpool's point about the need to safeguard British maritime strength. National defence took precedence in the Duke's soldierly mind even over allied solidarity. Westmorland, the other opponent, confined himself to sniping criticisms which, though they enraged Canning, made no real impact. Despite his victory, however, Canning continued to be a disturbing influence in the administration. It was true that once Knighton had effected a reconciliation between the King and Canning in the spring of 1825, foreign policy ceased to be a source of major dissension either with the King or inside the cabinet. Its place was taken, however, by an issue on which Prime Minister and Foreign Secretary were in fundamental disagreement. Catholic Emancipation, on which the government had no collective policy, was still an issue on which ministers individually held entrenched positions and Parliament regularly provided opportunities for revealing them.

The pre-sessional deliberations of the cabinet in December 1824 had been overshadowed by the reports from Ireland of the startling growth of Daniel O'Connell's Catholic Association. The King himself, through the Home Secretary, sent one of his impulsive but impotent warnings to the Prime Minister that if O'Connell's activities were allowed to continue, he would no longer allow Emancipation to be treated as an open question by his government. He was given some reassurance by the bill brought forward by the Irish Chief Secretary Goulburn early in the new session which demonstrated the determination of the government not to acquiesce tamely in the spread of Irish agitation. The desirability of suppressing the Catholic Association was something on which most English politicians could agree. What they found singularly elusive was a practical means of doing so. The real divisions, both in Parliament and in the cabinet, came over the entirely separate issue of Catholic Emancipation for which Burdett subsequently brought forward a carefully prepared bill. To disarm Protestant opposition it was flanked by two auxiliary measures, the so-called wings, providing for the payment of Irish Roman clergy and the disfranchisement of the 40s. freeholder in the Irish county constituencies. As a reform programme it was the greatest threat posed so far to the flagging Protestant party in the legislature.

Already in March rumours had been going round, encouraged if not actually started by the Burdett party, that the Prime Minister was about to give way on the bill. Lord Colchester, the former Speaker, was sufficiently disturbed by them to remark to Liverpool in the House of Lords that he hoped there was no truth in the report that he had changed his mind on the Catholic question. 'Certainly not,' replied the Prime Minister stoutly, 'and those rumours have been contradicted.'[3] The fact that he had taken steps to have the reports denied was in itself a mark of his concern; but what he was contemplating was not retreat but retirement. On 1 April he wrote a pessimistic letter to Wellington about his personal situation. The gist of it was that the voting in the lower house on Burdett's bill would demonstrate that there was a settled majority in the Commons in favour of Emancipation; that for the House of Lords to defeat the bill could only be in the nature of an expiring effort; and that the more he reflected on his own position, the more he felt it impossible to assent to any change of policy, let alone assist in passing it into law. Resignation was therefore the only honourable way out of a hopeless position. He would be ready, he added, to be guided by his colleagues on the timing of that event, except that if Peel also resigned, as was not unlikely, he might have to go out with him.

His fears about the Home Secretary were well founded. On 21 April Burdett's bill gained a majority of 27 on its second reading in the Commons and the two 'wings' were approved in principle before the end of the month. Following the acceptance on 29 April of a motion for the payment of Irish Roman Catholic priests, Peel tendered his resignation. Liverpool immediately summoned Wellington and Bathurst for a private conference at Fife House. At that meeting the Prime Minister and the Home Secretary informed their two colleagues of their definite intention to resign: Liverpool for the reasons he had indicated to Wellington a month earlier; Peel because he felt his isolated position in the Commons, as the only 'Protestant' on the government front bench, was no longer tolerable. It was, by the surviving accounts, a curious and disjointed discussion, in the course of which Wellington put forward a plan for endowing and legalising the Roman Church in Ireland by means of a concordat with the Pope. This remarkable proposition, which Peel briefly dismissed as impracticable, Liverpool seems virtually to have ignored. He did, however, agree to take no step over resignation until the fate of the bill had been decided in the House of Lords.

During most of May Bathurst and Wellington tried to dissuade their two colleagues from giving up office, the Duke concentrating on Peel, Bathurst mainly on Liverpool. To assist their efforts Arbuthnot and the King were brought in as reinforcements. Bathurst's arguments were that the Prime Minister's retirement would break up the government and would not be understood by the public since it was well known that the administration had always been based on the principle of neutrality over Catholic Emancipation. Liverpool, on the other hand, took the line that the state of the Catholic question was now materially different from when his ministry had been formed in 1812. The crisis, he thought, could only be postponed, not averted; and when it recurred, a Catholic victory was inevitable. If Peel left, he would not have a single cabinet colleague remaining in the lower house to represent his views. He would be seen by the public as clinging to office when his principles had been rejected in the Commons and were unlikely to be upheld much longer in the Lords. 'You could not wish me, I am sure,' he wrote tiredly on 4 May, 'to close a long political life with disgrace.'[4]

Liverpool's fixed intention to retire was the more ironic since the public at large, following the defeat of the bill in the House of Lords on 17 May by 48 votes, assumed that the crisis was over and the Prime Minister's position actually strengthened. In the debate Liverpool had made a speech which was forceful not only in matter but (unusually for him) in the manner in which it was delivered. He cast doubts on the loyalty of Catholics – Protestants, he declared, gave an undivided allegiance to the sovereign, Catholics a divided one; he attacked the baneful influence of Catholic clergy in private relationships; he criticised the House of Commons for unfairly tacking on to the main bill measures designed merely to catch votes for it; and he prophesied finally that if the proposed changes in the constitution were sanctioned, they would reduce the Protestant succession laid down in 1688 to a cypher. Though he probably did not realise it, it was the most vehement anti-Catholic speech he had ever made. It was also perhaps the speech of a man under great stress. To the King, who sent him a warm note of congratulation on his 'most powerful' contribution to the debate, he replied pessimistically that the majority in the upper house, though satisfactory, was in some respects a hollow one and could not be trusted for the future.

For Canning the speech came as a deep disappointment. As early as January he had been hinting that the Catholic question could no longer be kept in abeyance; and Liverpool's unexpectedly hostile language in the debate possibly helped to decide his next action. The day afterwards he asked for a special cabinet on the Catholic question and made it clear to the Prime Minister that the government would have to settle the issue one way or the other. Liverpool was convinced that the end of his administration was now clearly in sight. He thought Canning would resign if he did not get his way and that the government would break up if he did. Unless some miraculous recipe could be discovered to reconcile irreconcilable views, he felt it would be his duty to resign and tell the King at the same time that the only possible administration to succeed him was one which would concede Catholic claims. Bathurst, who was prepared to face the consequences of allowing Canning to go out of office, remonstrated against this needless capitulation. He wrote on 23 May:

> At the height of your power, at the head of the most popular administration which this country has for some time had, you resign; and by your resignation the King will appear to have been deserted, and those who are in the midst of their triumph will be delivered over to their adversaries. It will require a very strong proof of your resignation having been necessary, before you can stand excused.[5]

The difference between the two men was a fundamental one. Liverpool was convinced that the Catholic issue had virtually been decided and that Canning was abstractly right in his view that government ought now to take the matter in hand. Bathurst believed that the Protestant cause could still be upheld and that the ministry could survive the loss of Canning without undue damage. For Liverpool it was the strategic, for Bathurst the tactical argument that counted.

When the cabinet met to discuss Canning's disruptive proposition, the Prime Minister simply pointed out that if it was accepted, it would change the whole basis on which the government had been formed. The implication was obvious and one too daunting to face. After a few days of deliberation it was clear that none of the 'Catholic' ministers, not even Canning himself, was ready to take responsibility for destroying the ministry. On 26 May Canning told his colleagues that he was content to have vindicated his right to raise the matter. In their turn Liverpool and Peel adopted the formula that had the majority in the Lords been less emphatic, they would have thought it their duty to resign. Honour was thus satisfied; but the essential fact was that both sides had receded from the extreme positions that had originally been taken up. It had been a curious, compound crisis. Canning's intervention had in effect created a second issue which destroyed the substance of the first. Had he succeeded in having his way, he would have provided Liverpool with a real and intelligible reason for resignation. When he accepted defeat, he removed any justification that Liverpool and Peel might otherwise have had for leaving the government. His misjudgement on the timing of his otherwise logical proposal merely presented the Protestant party in the cabinet with an opportune reprieve.[6]

With public and Parliament unaware of the severity of the crisis within the administration, it was generally accepted that the Catholic issue was buried for the brief remainder of the 1820 Parliament's life. The only question now for ministers was whether to hold the general election in September 1825 or June 1826; these being the two traditional months on either side of the harvest when the still largely agricultural British society could conveniently spare the time for such distractions. The 'Protestants' in the government, headed by Wellington, wanted an early election to take advantage of the current anti-Catholic mood of the public created by the Burdett debates. The 'Catholics' for the same reason wanted to wait until 1826. Other arguments were more finely balanced. Continuing commercial prosperity and the prospect of a good harvest made September 1825 an attractive time to go to the country; and, as most prime ministers discover sooner or later, such opportunities having once beckoned tend not to return. On the other hand, the more dignified and statesmanlike attitude was to let Parliament run its normal course. Whatever the new House of Commons ultimately decided on the Catholic question, it would then at least represent the considered view of the electorate.

Though the Prime Minister's first impulse was to dissolve in 1825, neither he nor Canning held immutable views on the subject. For Liverpool perhaps there was a subconscious relief at the prospect of one more parliamentary session before the Catholic issue raised its Medusa head again. That it would come, and that it would destroy his government, he had less doubt than ever. Indeed, Canning's utterances both public and private made it clear that he now thought he had gained the right at any convenient (or inconvenient) time to renew the initiative in the cabinet which he had been content to drop in May. In September it was finally decided to hold the general election the following summer on the understanding that in the interval ministers would do their best to keep the Catholic question in abeyance and that the new corn bill already under consideration would be held over until 1827. Wellington's rearguard resistance was finally overcome when Liverpool was able to produce letters from Protestant peers deprecating any immediate dissolution as harmful to their electoral interests: a practical if not a very principled consideration.[7]

The recess, however, provided no respite for harassed ministers. Prosperity brought problems of its own and despite Liverpool's warning in the House of Lords in March 1825 that speculation in stocks and shares, particularly overseas investment, was getting out of control, gold continued to pour out of the country. By September the Bank of England was growing nervous. Having fed the boom with lavish credit it now tried to contract the home market instead of restricting payments abroad as Liverpool and Huskisson would have preferred. In December 1825 came a financial panic. The Bank wanted the authority of the government to stop cash payments. Liverpool refused; he thought the only sound cure for excessive credit was an increase in the rate of interest. To suspend cash payments within half a dozen years of returning to the gold standard would undermine the government's whole monetary policy. There were angry meetings with the Bank governors and friction inside the ministry where Herries and Arbuthnot, aided by Vansittart (now Lord Bexley) argued strongly for concession. Finally, after a cabinet meeting on 16 December which lasted until the small hours, the decision was taken. To the Prime Minister's relief, Wellington (so often in the minority) came down on the side of Liverpool, Huskisson, Canning, Robinson and Peel; and the Bank of England was told to ride out the storm. In the event money soon began to flow in to replenish its reserves and ministers were able to depart to their country homes for Christmas with the assurance that yet another crisis was safely surmounted.[8]

Nevertheless, the shock to the money market had been severe. By the end of the year over sixty principal banks had failed and more were to follow. To the Prime Minister it seemed an opportune time to introduce some reforms in the country's banking system. When the government introduced its remedial legislation the following session, however, it was evident that feeling in the cabinet as in the City was still divided. Liverpool held severe monetarist views and while approving the Bank of England's emergency measures to restrict credit and discounts, he felt that they should have taken action much earlier. Bexley, in a memorandum of 11 January, attributed greater importance to the export of capital in the form of loans to foreign governments and investment in commercial enterprises abroad. Still, there was general agreement that the indiscriminate issue of bank notes by the small country banks should be brought under some sort of control. Liverpool would have liked to abolish £1 notes entirely and force the Bank of England to give up its monopoly of joint-stock banking. The question of a territorial limit (a fifty-mile radius round London was the one preferred by the government) for that monopoly had been raised before in 1822. Liverpool distrusted the growth that had taken place in his lifetime of hundreds of small, weak, private banks, confined by law to no more than six partners. He was attracted by the example of Scotland where a few strong central joint-stock banks operated through local branches. The Bank of England directors for obvious reasons were less happy with the Prime Minister's policy but in the unfavourable circumstances bowed to the inevitable. The currency and banking legislation put through in the course of the next session represented much of what had been in Liverpool's mind for many years.[9]

Once the initial resistance of the Bank of England had been overcome, the Banking Act (conceding to the Bank the larger radius of sixty-five miles) passed without undue difficulty, though not until May. The bill to restrict small note circulation, though provoking noisy opposition from merchants, country gentry and provincial bankers, also passed easily enough when it came to a vote. In the Lords Liverpool announced a small concession for Bank of England notes to assist its progress, to the annoyance of Canning who had been neither consulted nor warned. More difficult to contend with was the pressure on the government to issue exchequer bills to ease the credit shortage. Liverpool, who felt himself pledged publicly and privately against such a step, took a stronger line than some of his colleagues either understood or approved. 'But, as a question of department,' Canning admitted the following month, 'it was for him to decide it; and it is but fair to add, that Huskisson entirely concurred with him.'[10] The Prime Minister in fact told Canning just before the critical debate in the Commons on 23 February that if the opposition was as powerful as was made out, it might be better if he and Huskisson resigned. As a result Canning on his own initiative bluntly told the House that, if they insisted on an issue of exchequer bills, they would have to find another administration to undertake it.

This brandishing of the executive's ultimate weapon took not only their supporters by surprise but the King and cabinet as well. It seemed an unnecessary menace, especially as the government subsequently assisted the Bank of England to find other means of advancing money. For House of Commons purposes Canning had put a sharper interpretation on Liverpool's worried words than was perhaps justified. He was himself concerned as Leader of the House to maintain the government's authority and in a letter to the Prime Minister written on 23 February before the debate he had observed that if, after all their declarations, the issue of exchequer bills were adopted, 'it must be adopted, I think, by another Ministry'.[11] On the other hand, Liverpool's talk of resignation was unreasonable (as Peel told him reprovingly), since it was absurd to think that his retirement could be treated as a personal matter not involving the fate of the ministry as a whole. Liverpool's language, whatever form it had taken, was probably caused as much as anything by tiredness and ill-health. He said to Arbuthnot just before Christmas that the financial crisis had affected his health so much that he was convinced he had not enough strength to cope with the difficulties and could not go on much longer. There was no doubt that his health was in a poor state once more.

It was fretted nerves probably which accounted for the scene at the first cabinet dinner on 25 January when Liverpool finally and conspicuously lost his temper with Westmorland. When the latter uttered one of his typically disparaging remarks, the Prime Minister rounded on him angrily, told him that having stayed idle in the country he had no right to find fault with colleagues who had been taking the decisions in London; and then for good measure threw in a remark about Westmorland's habit of going round all the clubs gossiping. The outburst was out of proportion to the offence; but it resulted from an accumulation of grievances in the Prime Minister's mind. Fortunately Westmorland, as proof against abuse as he was careless of offence, remained calm.[12] Nevertheless the continued friction within the cabinet during the early months of the session depressed Liverpool's spirits still further. His bad leg had been giving him pain again; and his doctors were themselves beginning to doubt whether he was fit for the strain of office. On the tactical issue of the exchequer bills, however, he had the satisfaction of being proved right by events. Not only was the government spared an awkward precedent of intervention but the Bank itself discovered in the end that there was less demand for new credit facilities than it had expected. Without any visible interference by the government, the money market righted itself.

Before the Parliament elected in 1820 ended its life, there was one more flurry of excitement. The run of exceptionally good harvests came to an end in 1825 when the average price of wheat rose to its highest point since 1819. In the spring of 1826 the United Kingdom faced the dangerous combination of a general food shortage and a depression in the manufacturing industries in the wake of the financial crash of the previous winter. In both houses of Parliament the clerks' tables were piled high with petitions from an angry public. Some came from agriculturalists demanding the retention of the existing Corn Laws, the larger number from manufacturers and artisans praying for their instant abolition. Widespread rioting and machine-breaking in Lancashire during April underlined the intensity of popular feeling and the urgency of the problem for the government. No ministers, least of all the Prime Minister and the Home Secretary, wanted a recurrence of the troubles of 1816 and 1817. In a debate at the start of May on the distress in the industrial districts, Liverpool warned the peers that a revision of the Corn Laws was absolutely necessary. Next day he outlined in cabinet his proposals for meeting the immediate food crisis. Since the cumbrous machinery of the 1815 and 1822 Corn Laws prevented any opening of the ports to foreign grain until mid-November, by which time sea-borne traffic with the Baltic would be impossible because of the ice, emergency measures would have to be taken. In the last few weeks of the session, therefore, the government obtained authority for the immediate release of bonded wheat for the home market and for the admission of further quantities of grain during the recess should they be required. Though vehement opposition was put up by the more intransigent agriculturalists, the resolution passed both houses of Parliament with large majorities, opposition votes more than compensating for the defection of many of the government's customary supporters. In the Lords the Prime Minister reminded the peers that since the end of the eighteenth century almost a third of British harvests had been deficient. When bad harvests coincided with manufacturing depression, he observed warningly, there could be little justification for a protective duty on corn; a starving population could not be asked to pay more than the natural price for food.

At the general election, contested somewhat tepidly at the end of June, corn rivalled Catholic Emancipation as the principal topic of public interest. A demand for a change in the Corn Laws, even their abolition, was clearly a popular sentiment, though the parliamentary candidates who found it expedient or unavoidable to refer to the subject generally tended to shy away from any specific proposal on what should be done. Over the Emancipation question there was more clarity and therefore greater conflict. In England there was still a strong undercurrent of anti-Catholic feeling from the events of the previous year and such electoral changes as could be directly ascribed to the religious issue favoured the Protestant party. In Ireland, on the other hand, the widespread intervention of the Roman priesthood in the elections on the side of the Catholic League brought about an ominous number of defeats of 'Protestant' candidates in the large county constituencies. As far as the government was concerned, however, Liverpool steadfastly upheld the official principle of neutrality and made no attempt to throw what marginal influence the executive still possessed to one side or the other. 'He was scrupulously impartial, I can bear witness for him, in Parliamentary arrangements,' Canning wrote the following year, 'so far as the distribution of seats in the power of the Government could go – for of ten seats placed at his disposal half were given to Protestants and half to Catholics, friends of the administration.'[13]

Once the passing bustle and excitement of the elections was over, however, public concern soon shifted to the excessive heat and abnormal drought which prevailed throughout July and August and threatened to damage all food crops other than wheat. Over the harvest the government had little control. For the Prime Minister there was a more practical issue claiming his attention that hot summer – the worsening situation in Portugal. The death of John vi early in 1826 had brought that country to a state of virtual civil war. Against the legal government under the regent Isabella, which instituted a new liberal constitution, was arrayed a powerful absolutist party demanding the throne for the infant queen's uncle Don Miguel and backed by the resources and influence of Spain. The absolutist party, reinforced by deserters from the regular Portuguese army, organised their forces along the frontier, retiring into Spain when threatened by loyal government troops. By the autumn the regency government was sufficiently alarmed to ask for the services of General Beresford who had been in charge of the Portuguese forces during the peninsular war and had been given rank in the Portuguese nobility.

In September there was a triangular discussion between Liverpool, Wellington and Canning on the advisability of acceding to this request. Canning, who distrusted Beresford as a Wellingtonian officer with little sympathy for the liberal party in Portugal, was reluctant to let him go except in a purely military capacity, and as a Portuguese subject whose actions would not involve the British government. Liverpool, while accepting the latter point, felt with Wellington that Beresford should be allowed to decide for himself on arrival in Portugal whether a political appointment would assist his mission. Neither the Prime Minister nor the Duke wanted to plunge the country into another peninsular war, but Liverpool at least was disposed to reap what advantage might ensue from the loan to Portugal of a high-ranking British officer.

In October, when it looked as if open war between Portugal and Spain was imminent, Liverpool proposed an alternative strategy to direct British military involvement in the peninsula should hostilities actually commence. He suggested to Canning that in the first instance Spanish ships should be seized in any part of the world where they were encountered; and secondly that an appeal should be made to the great powers of Europe, who had all recognised the regency government in Portugal, to dissuade the Spanish government from aggression. If these measures failed, then as a last resort Britain should give direct encouragement to the liberal party in Spain as a means both of bringing pressure to bear on the Spanish government and of protecting the liberal regime in Portugal. His one misgiving was that the Portuguese themselves might not be ready to take up arms in defence of their own constitution. The basis of his attitude was understandable. In spite of his bold words in public about Britain's ability to fight, he knew too much about the country's unpreparedness not to exhaust every possibility before committing its slender resources to a conflict which might be long and would certainly be costly. A war of ideas was cheaper than a war of armies; and a mobilisation of liberal opinion in the peninsula preferable to a mobilisation of an expeditionary force at Portsmouth or Plymouth. It was in effect a policy of deterrence: a threat calculated to have an effect not so much on the headstrong Spanish government as on the other monarchies of Europe still nervously obsessed with the fear of a general European revolution. This readiness to exploit liberal movements abroad fitted in admirably with Canning's own attitude and was undoubtedly popular with the British public. In some respects it presaged the Palmerstonian liberal foreign policy of the middle of the century. Whether it would have had the desired effect in 1826 is an open question, since in the event it was never put to the test.[14]

Before the Portuguese issue came to a head, however, the government was faced with another crisis at home. By the autumn of 1826 the unprecedented drought had driven the price of oats and pulse crops to record levels and at the end of August the cabinet decided to take action. On the first day of September the ports were opened for the import at a nominal duty of oats, rye, beans and peas. Since these were articles not covered by the emergency powers granted earlier in the year, Parliament was summoned at the unusual date of mid-November to provide the necessary legal indemnity. Though few MPs were disposed to question the rightness of the government's action, it inevitably fanned speculation over the future of the Corn Laws themselves. To allay the excitement Liverpool and Canning announced in their respective houses that the ministers would propose a general revision of those laws after the Christmas recess.

Work on the new Corn Law had in fact been going on since midsummer and not entirely in secrecy. At his election in Liverpool Huskisson was reported as having uttered some startling words about free trade in corn which enraged the already suspicious agriculturalists and provoked a written remonstrance to the Prime Minister from the Duke of Wellington. In his reply Liverpool argued reasonably that he was himself personally pledged to a reconsideration of the Corn Laws in the 1827 session and that deflation since 1818 made the 80s. prohibition level for wheat no longer defensible. On details, however, he maintained that he was completely uncommitted. During the rest of the year these details were worked out between himself and Huskisson. To emphasise the importance which the government attached to the measure – and to separate it from the hostility with which the landed interest, and indeed some of his own colleagues, viewed the President of the Board of Trade – Liverpool decided that Canning and himself would be responsible for bringing forward the new proposals both in cabinet and in Parliament. 'God knows,' he wrote to

Canning in August, 'this is not a pleasant undertaking for either of us.' What was essential therefore was for the government to reach agreement internally on its measure by the time Parliament met.

In October Huskisson produced a memorandum on the Corn Laws which, by Liverpool's cautious direction, was circulated only to Canning, Peel and later Robinson. As he had indicated in his May speech in the House of Lords, the Prime Minister's concern was to balance safeguards to the consumer when corn prices were high with protection to the farmers when prices fell. The logic of this was a sliding scale of duties; and there was no difference of opinion between himself and Huskisson on the need for such a regulating device. The scale of duties suggested by Huskisson, however, seemed to Liverpool unacceptably low. At Walmer that autumn he had been talking to local agriculturalists on the subject at public meetings and dinners. He found that there was, inevitably, an unpractical minority who wanted even greater protection; and he noted the pathological suspicion of Huskisson which seemed almost universal in farming and landowning circles. His enquiries satisfied him, however, that the more sensible gentry would be content with a price of 60s. a quarter for wheat.

His own proposal, drawn up in a final memorandum for the cabinet after he had discussed it with Canning, was to take 60s. as the 'remunerative price' and build a scale round it that would provide effective protection below that point and above it would decrease sharply until at 70s. the duty on foreign imports would become only nominal. He read out his paper at a cabinet dinner at Fife House on 8 November, the first meeting of ministers for six weeks; and after several more meetings the cabinet finally accepted his proposals on the 22nd. Huskisson reported that the discussions had been carried on in 'perfect good humour'. That was not the impression of the Duke of Wellington, who told Mrs Arbuthnot that there had been 'a great deal of ill-humour', and was himself dissatisfied at what he conceived to be the inadequate protection provided by the bill.[15]

Of the two the Duke was possibly in this instance the more objective observer. Liverpool certainly had been much more apprehensive of the difficulties of the issue than Huskisson who was curiously oblivious of his own unpopularity. It was significant that the Prime Minister's success in winning the support of his cabinet was followed by a nervous reaction which took a characteristically physical form. In the first week of December he was suffering from a violent cold with disquieting symptoms of dizziness in the head. The doctors blistered and leeched him; and for some days he was forced to remain in bed extremely unwell. He was still there when the long-expected appeal for assistance came from the Portuguese government. It therefore fell to Bathurst to announce the news and outline the government's policy in the House of Lords.

In reality the Prime Minister's incapacity at this juncture was of little consequence. The crisis had long been foreseen and the necessary military preparations made. All that the ministers had been waiting for was a clear proof that the situation in Portugal had deteriorated to the point where British intervention was unavoidable under the terms of its treaty obligations. That proof came early in December when two invasions of Portugal by rebel troops aided by Spanish irregulars brought a direct appeal from the regency government for British military aid. On 9 December the cabinet, meeting without their chief, approved Canning's draft of a royal message to Parliament and on the 12th the two houses debated and approved the decision to send a British force to Lisbon. The speed of the British reaction was evidence of the government's preparedness. There was no disagreement among ministers on the course to be followed and the expeditionary force was organised with admirable celerity. On Christmas Day 1826 the advance troops arrived at Lisbon and the whole force was in position by the start of the new year.

During all these excitements, while a startled country rallied enthusiastically round the government and Canning thrilled the House of Commons with his rhetoric of calling the New World into existence to redress the balance of the Old, the Prime Minister remained in the obscurity of a sick-room. Though after a few days the external symptoms seemed to be disappearing, he spoke despondently to his colleagues about the desirability of his early retirement. What perhaps weighed with him was his increasing vulnerability in every period of political strain. To Robinson, who expressed an inopportune desire to move to the shelter of the House of Lords, he wrote on 16 December: 'I must begin by telling you that I have been *very ill*. I am recovering, but this last illness I cannot but consider as a hint that I am better fitted now for repose than for the labours, and still more the anxieties, of the situation which I have held for so many years.' In an even greater burst of frankness he told Arbuthnot that his illness had given him 'a great shake' and that he would need great care, and above all repose, if he was to prolong his life for many more years. He had said much the same on other occasions but what possibly induced the Arbuthnots to take his remarks more seriously on this occasion was the outspokenness of his remarks about Canning. Though he insisted that they were the best of friends and had no disagreements, he complained that being in office with Canning was very different from when Castlereagh had led the Commons. He spoke with feeling of Canning's habit of sending him constant notes. Any trifling circumstance was enough for him to fire them off, sometimes a dozen in a day. 'I live in continual dread every time the door opens that it is to bring a note from Mr Canning, till I am driven half distracted.'[16]

Liverpool was only one of a crop of distinguished invalids that winter, the most notable casualty being the Duke of York who died on 5 January 1827. Liverpool travelled to Windsor to arrange with the King that Wellington would succeed him as commander-in-chief of the army (firmly putting aside George's wistful desire to resume in his own person that old Hanoverian prerogative) and then went off to Bath where he had been ordered to stay for at least a month. Canning, whom he invited to keep him company for a few days, arrived on the 21st. After all Liverpool's talk of resignation he excusably read more into the invitation than mere sociability and assumed that he had been summoned to Bath to be given private warning of the Prime Minister's decision to lay down his office. On the way there he chatted with his secretary Stapleton about the consequences of Liverpool's withdrawal from politics; though he clearly took it for granted that he would succeed him as Prime Minister. When they arrived, however, they found the inconstant invalid apparently fully recovered and in the best of spirits. The waters of Bath had once more demonstrated their surprisingly recuperative effects on the Prime Minister's fragile constitution. The three men went riding each day, and in the evening, on the plea of entertaining their younger companion, Liverpool and Canning amused themselves with playful reminiscences of their early days. From the Prime Minister, however, as Canning ruefully confessed on the way back, came not a word about retirement.[17]

It was the last time the two old friends saw each other. When Canning arrived at his home in Brighton he took to bed himself with a severe cold and rheumatic fever, thought to have been brought on by exposure at the Duke of York's funeral and his subsequent journey to Bath. He was for many days unable even to write and Stapleton sent daily bulletins of his health to the concerned and sympathetic Prime Minister. When Parliament reassembled on 8 February Peel took over as acting Leader of the House of Commons. The situation was all the more awkward for the government since one of the first trials of strength to be faced in the lower house besides the corn bill was a renewed motion by Burdett to take Catholic claims into consideration. The Prime Minister was left to hope, as he expressed it with a certain optimism to Canning, that each of these acrimonious issues would draw the sting of the other. He was not best pleased, however, to discover that Canning had been using Huskisson as a channel of communication with Burdett on the timing of the two measures and reminded him that in his absence Peel was in charge of government business in the lower house. To underline this rebuke he called a meeting of Peel and Robinson the next day (11 February) when it was agreed to postpone the corn question until the 26th in order to give Canning plenty of time to regain his strength. Meanwhile Robinson was authorised to arrange with Huskisson and Burdett for the Catholic motion to be brought forward on the 1st or 2nd of March.[18]

On the Catholic question the Prime Minister had been urged by Lord Colchester to anticipate the outcome of the Burdett debate with a firm announcement that he would make no concessions. This, for various reasons, seemed to Liverpool unacceptable and he had already made up his mind to await the verdict in the lower house before deciding his own line. One of the last acts of the Duke of York had been to send him a formal protest against any alteration in the laws affecting Roman Catholics. Since he had also sent a copy of his paper to Windsor, Liverpool felt obliged to write to the King reminding him of the government's principle of neutrality and pointing out once more the impossibility of forming a purely 'Protestant' administration. In his own heart he probably felt that Burdett would be successful and the end of his administration was now imminent. If Canning is to be believed, he even welcomed the prospect of a trial of strength early in the session so that the interminable conflict could at last be brought to an end.[19]

On the other hand, there was still his new corn bill, which he wished to put on the statute book as probably the last legislative achievement of his long career. On his return to town early in February, he had been struck by the ill-feeling and opposition that was building up against any change in the existing level of protection for corn and he anticipated a difficult passage for the bill at every stage. His only comfort was that this might make the emancipation debate flat by comparison, since whatever MPs might be saying about Catholics, they would be thinking about corn. It seemed more important than ever to keep the unpopular Huskisson in the background and introduce the bill as 'a measure of general government and not a Departmental question'. If Canning did not recover in time, he wanted Peel to take charge of the bill in the Commons, however much Huskisson might resent this arrangement. He told the King (or so George later alleged) that he would resign if he could not carry his corn bill; and left him with the impression that he would not in any case want to remain in office after the end of the session. George IV had too much love of the histrionic to be an invariably honest witness; but in this case what he said was confirmed many years later by Arbuthnot who stated that Liverpool had told him also that he would resign after the 1827 session. It would have been an eminently sensible decision; though whether Liverpool would have had the resolution to act on it when the time came is another matter.[20]

On the more pressing matter of Portugal, to which he was now able to give more attention, his views (in marked contrast to Canning's public rhetoric) were eminently cautious and limited. The immediate effect of the British expeditionary force having been achieved, his main aim was to bring the military intervention to a close as soon as was consistent with its diplomatic aim. Already in January, in a letter to Wellington which recalled their peninsular correspondence of fifteen years earlier, he expressed himself strongly against any deployment of the British force as an army of observation along the Spanish frontier: such a situation, he pointed out, might easily provoke incidents with the Spaniards and even possibly lead to war. Both tactically and politically, he held that the best position for the British troops was in the vicinity of Lisbon. On 6 February he wrote to Canning to endorse a conciliatory policy of timing the British evacuation of Portugal to fit in with a French withdrawal from Spain if this could be done without embarrassment. He agreed on the need for British forces to stay in Portugal until Spain had fulfilled its promises and taken its army away from the Portuguese frontier; but he was inclined to think that British policy should be limited to this objective. It would make the role of the British force clear and intelligible, and its withdrawal straightforward and expeditious. To remain in Portugal longer than was strictly necessary would run the risk of involvement in Portuguese politics; and that, he concluded, was the last thing the British public would want. For the Prime Minister, it was clear, the Portuguese episode was a limited operation, under specific treaty obligations, with a specific object. For romanticism in foreign policy, as for rhetoric, he had little taste.[21]

Meanwhile Parliament had reassembled and formal business began. On 12 February the Prime Minister moved an address of condolence to the King on the death of his brother. A few days later, on 16 February, he secured the unanimous adoption of a loyal (and favourable) reply to the King's request for an increased allowance for the Duke of Clarence, now heir presumptive to the throne. He seemed in excellent spirits. Planta, the Treasury Secretary, who saw him in the morning and Eldon, the Lord Chancellor, who was with him in the House of Lords in the afternoon, both remarked that they had never seen him looking so well and cheerful. The Prime Minister's precise state of health baffled his colleagues to the last.[22]

Yet, despite the relief afforded by his long stay at Bath, he must have realised that his physical and emotional strength was steadily declining. It is not impossible that he had already, without knowing it, suffered a slight stroke. His sight had been affected and he had been complaining significantly that when reading he missed a word or two in every line. To Peel, who told him that he was looking better than for some time, he made the sombre response that no man knew what it was like to have been prime minister for fifteen years and never in all that period to have opened his morning letters without a feeling of apprehension. That was the language of a weak and tired man.[23]

NOTES

1 Yonge, III, 305.

2 For the whole episode see WND, II, 364-404; GCHT, pp. 416-26; Yonge, III, 305-7; ARJ, I, 366, 372-4. The paper printed in Yonge, III, 297 ff. is Canning's first memorandum to the cabinet and not, as stated by Yonge, by Liverpool.

3 Colchester, III, 373-4.

4 Bathurst, pp. 579-85; WND, II, 435, 451; ARJ, I, 386-98.

5 Bathurst, p. 584.

6 ARC, pp. 74-8; ARJ, I, 398-401; Hobhouse, pp. 115-16; Hinde, pp. 396-8.

7 WND, II, 463-5, 499, 562; GCOC, I, 289-95; Huskisson, pp. 188-94; Hobhouse, pp. 118-19; Oman, p. 135.

8 Yonge, III, 365 ff.; cf. Hilton, Ch. VII.

9 See J.H. Clapham, *The Bank of England*, two vols (1944), II, 89-107.

10 GCHT, pp. 231-7.

11 Canning's version of the incident (in GCHT, pp. 235-8) is to be preferred to that in Croker (I, 314-15).

12 ARJ, II, 6; cf. Ibid, I, 352; Oman, p. 210.

13 Wellesley, II, 161.

14 Yonge, III, 397 ff.; GCOC, II, 128-9, 141-55; GCHT, pp. 519-29.

15 For the corn law discussions see Yonge, III, 429 ff., 450 ff.; WND, III, 343; Huskisson, pp. 204-

16 ARJ, II, 65; Yonge, III, 438.
17 GCHT, pp. 479-80.
18 GCOC, II, 252-65.
19 Wellesley, II, 160; Colchester, III, 459; Yonge, III, 432.
20 Yonge, III, 450 ff.; WND, II, 588, 632-5; Parker, III, 358.
21 WND, III, 510, 583.
22 Twiss, II, 583; GCFM, p. 20.
23 *Speeches of Sir Robert Peel* (1853), III, 456; Sir Henry Halford, *Essays and Orations* (1833), p. 116.

Postscript

On Saturday 17 February Liverpool opened his morning post at Fife House as usual with the assistance of Willimott, his private secretary, and Brooksbank, his chief clerk and personal secretary in the Treasury. Some of the letters he carried away to read over breakfast which he took alone soon after ten o'clock. The servant who brought in the meal noticed that his master was sitting oddly and that he made no attempt at conversation but he did not suspect there was anything amiss. When he returned some twenty minutes later he found the Prime Minister lying inert and unconscious on the floor. By chance his usual physician Dr Drever happened to be in the house and so medical aid was instantly forthcoming. Within a few minutes he was bled and a messenger despatched to Sir Henry Halford. He arrived within the half-hour, to find his patient incapable of speech and paralysed on one side. Cupping was again resorted to but with no discernible effect. During the next few days there was a slight improvement. Liverpool regained consciousness though his right side remained paralysed and he was still unable to talk. On 22 February he was cupped yet again and the doctors were now guardedly hopeful of a partial, though not of a complete recovery. As soon as he was fit to travel, he was taken from Fife House to the quieter surroundings of Coombe Wood.

It was clear that the Prime Minister had suffered a severe cerebral haemorrhage – in the language of the time a paralytic stroke or apoplectic fit. Gossip in anti-Canning circles subsequently alleged that it was opening a letter from Canning that had brought on the attack. This was both ill-natured and ill-founded, though it is not difficult to see how the story arose. Canning's last letter to him had been written on 12 February and Liverpool had replied to it on the following day. Stapleton, however, continued to send him brief reports on Canning's state of health and one of these notes had been found in Liverpool's hand. His valet told Stapleton afterwards that his name was the first word the Prime Minister uttered when his power of speech began to return.[1] It was not, however, until the second week in March that Liverpool recovered sufficient use of his right side to be able to walk; and his speech was still only semi-articulate. With the impetuous kindness that was one of his more endearing characteristics, the King wrote to Lady Liverpool telling her that on no account was her husband to be upset by any talk of resignation and that he would take no step to replace him until it became absolutely necessary.

On 23 March Liverpool for the first time showed signs of regaining his mental awareness. He enquired from his wife the result of the Catholic Emancipation debate (ironically Burdett's motion had been lost by four votes on 6 March) and then asked faintly 'who succeeds?' Lady Liverpool told him of the King's message and expressed the hope that he would soon be well enough to resume work. To this he muttered, 'No, no, not I - too weak, too weak,' and slid back into unconsciousness once more. For some days lucid intervals alternated with utter physical and mental prostration and it was obvious that any chance of recovery depended on complete rest and freedom from anxiety. He still suffered from a sense of painful pressure in the head. Sometimes he would put his hand to his forehead and in a confused state of physical suffering and loss of memory say 'I am but a child,' while the tears ran down his cheeks. Towards the end of March the King at last sent Knighton to tell Lady Liverpool that the pressure of public business no longer permitted any delay in finding a successor to her husband. She broke the news to Liverpool who seemed to understand and acquiesce. By the beginning of April he was perceptibly better; he was sleeping well and seeing a great deal of his half-brother Cecil. He was fidgety, however, and seemed worried about political developments. As a precaution the doctors were still applying leeches in order to reduce his blood pressure.

All that summer he remained in seclusion at Coombe. Other than the members of his own household he saw only his doctors and one or two close relatives. His physical condition continued to fluctuate and early in July he had another stroke, not so severe as that of February but attended by alarming convulsions. After copious bleedings he slowly recovered but to the practised eyes of his physicians it was evident that the end was only a matter of time. On 20 August he was sufficiently lucid to sign a codicil to his will, leaving a sum of £1,600 to be divided between the School for the Indigent Blind in St George's Fields and the Middlesex Refuge for the Destitute, together with a hundred pounds each to his steward James Child and his valet and personal servant John White. There was one further bequest on that date - 'I also leave to my dear wife Mary my Jewels.' Arbuthnot was later in a fret because he believed that the Prime Minister had neglected to make any arrangements for a financial provision for Lady Liverpool after his death. This seems to have been a groundless fear. Already in 1825 her husband had added a codicil to his will leaving her a house with garden and stabling at Walmer; it seems improbable he would have failed to ensure that she would have an adequate income if he predeceased her. The customary procedure would have been to set up a separate trust. The bequest of the jewels, valued at only £1,457, was clearly for sentimental rather than practical reasons. Another worry of Arbuthnot was that the Prime Minister's cousin Robert Jenkinson, behind whom he darkly suspected the intriguing hand of Canning, was trying to get access to

Liverpool's papers. Warned by Willimott, however, Cecil Jenkinson intervened in July to take them into safe custody.[2]

After the brief rally of August 1827 Liverpool lingered on for another fifteen months, a mental and physical shadow forgotten by the world. The end came on Thursday 4 December 1828. Soon after breakfast on that day he was attacked with spasms and convulsions, and before the local doctor Mr Sandford could get to the house he died in the presence of Lady Liverpool, Cecil Jenkinson, and his house steward Child.[3] On 15 December his body was taken out of Coombe House to begin the long journey to Hawkesbury. The six-horse coach with coronet and armorial bearings was followed by three mourning coaches carrying domestic staff. Then came his own carriage and those sent as a traditional mark of respect by Cecil Jenkinson, the new Earl; his brother-in-law, the Earl of Bristol; that warm-hearted if eccentric Royal Duke Clarence, the future William IV; his old colleague Viscount Sidmouth; and his neighbour C.N. Pallmer, MP for Surrey. It was a smaller escort than that which had accompanied Louisa's coffin on the first stage of a similar journey in 1821. He had been Prime Minister then and a figure of consequence. In December 1828 the political world was absorbed with speculation that Wellington and Peel were about to concede Catholic Emancipation; it had no thought to spare for political figures from the past. Only in his own neighbourhood was the dead statesman remembered. At Kingston the cortège was met by a long line of heads of families who had received Liverpool's bounty over the years; by the corporation of the borough in full mourning; and, drawn up on the new bridge over the Thames where he had laid the first stone three years earlier, by the children of the local school he had helped to found and endow.

After that last formal mark of respect from the town to which he had been a benefactor for a quarter of a century, the funeral hearse and coaches (relieved of their more ornamental escort) quickened their pace for the hundred miles which still separated them from Hawkesbury. They reached Cirencester a couple of days later, travel-worn and dirty, the outside of the vehicles caked with white mud. On hearing of their arrival Lord Bathurst, from his nearby seat at Oakley Park, offered his own carriage to attend them for the first mile out of town; but the undertaker in charge, with a nice sense of the propriety to be observed towards a living, if not to a dead earl, declared that since they were 'in an undress state' he must decline the honour. As soon as the horses had been baited, hearse and coaches trotted briskly away followed by the yells of scores of boys who had gathered to watch the unusual spectacle.[4] On 18 December Liverpool's body was laid to rest in the vault of Hawkesbury church beside the coffins of his father and mother, and that of his beloved Louisa. Not until another thirty years had passed was a tablet placed on the wall of the church by the eleventh baronet, Sir George Samuel Jenkinson, to remind the casual tourist that this was the burial place of the man who had been prime minister at the time of Waterloo.

*   *   *   *   *

Dead politicians, even dead prime ministers, are soon forgotten by their contemporaries. Yet there was something unusual about the oblivion which descended on Lord Liverpool after 1827. He had, it is true, never sought popularity. A serious and self-conscious man, he had no circle of young followers
devoted to his memory. He was, pronounced Hobhouse, the Home Office
under-secretary, with a certain harsh truth, a man 'who had fewer personal
friends and less quality for conciliating men's affections than perhaps any
Minister that ever lived'.[5] There were other less personal, more political reasons
why he was soon forgotten. The last of the true eighteenth-century type of
prime minister, he had no organised political party to sustain him in office or
perpetuate his policy after his departure. He was a great conservative statesman; but it was before the rise of the Conservative Party and there is no niche
for him in the party pantheon. After fifteen years at the head of affairs he had
acquired something of the permanence of an institution, and for that reason
alone it was difficult for anyone to inherit his position. His departure marked
the end of a political era; when he retired he seemed to belong at once to the
past. Canning succeeded as prime minister, and, as had been foreseen, the
ministry immediately broke up. Of Liverpool's twelve cabinet colleagues,
exactly half refused to serve with his successor. Canning died in August 1827,
ironically while Liverpool was still alive, having settled neither corn nor
Catholics. Robinson, raised to the Lords as Viscount Goderich, found his new
dignity insufficient to sustain the burden of continuing the uneasy
Canningite-whig coalition. Wellington, whom Liverpool had once said he
never wished to see in a political office, became prime minister only to demonstrate how hard it is for a general to become a politician. The conscious effort
he and Peel made in 1828 to reassemble the Liverpool 'party' ended in failure
with the resignation of the Huskissonites after only four months.

In the next four years the two great measures which Liverpool had opposed
passed into law – Catholic Emancipation in 1829 and the Reform Act in 1832.
A decade of whig reform legislation began and between it and the Liverpool
regime there seemed the gap of a generation rather than of a few years. Whigs,
liberals and radicals, looking back on the past by the light of their own partisan
prejudices, depicted the years from 1793 to 1827 as an unbroken period of tory
misrule, characterised by costly wars in support of European despotisms,
profligate expenditure, excessive taxation, a swollen National Debt, jobbery
and corruption in government, popular repression, press prosecutions, and
Peterloo. When eventually the creative work of government in the 1820s was
tardily recognised, Liverpool himself received little credit. His more obvious
qualities were acknowledged – his integrity, conciliatoriness, moderation and
tact – but there was as little awareness of his toughness, persistence and skill as
there was of his highly-strung temperament. Because he had the virtues of a
good chairman, it was too easily assumed that this was his only significant role.
Because he sat in the Lords, greater attention was given to his colleagues in the
lower house. The responsibility for the liberal policies of his government after

1821 was ascribed to the men who were promoted about that time and the credit apportioned on a departmental rather than a collective basis. The praise for foreign policy went to Canning; for police and legal reform to Peel; for budgetary policy to Robinson; for commercial reform to Huskisson. For the more partisan it was even possible to claim these ministers as honorary liberals. Canning could be regarded (and indeed was regarded by Lord Holland) as a renegade whig; Huskisson as a Canningite who would have joined, Robinson as one who actually did join, Lord Grey's ministry in 1830. Even Peel, a more difficult case to get round, could be later described as having chosen the wrong party. For Liverpool, however, no such posthumous rehabilitation was possible or thought necessary.

Even his personal qualities were effaced. A statesman who was prime minister at the time of the peninsular war, the Six Acts, the Queen's trial, and the free-trade budgets of 1824 and 1825, seemed to lack all symmetry and consistency. Liverpool the man was lost in the generalised concept of the 'Liverpool administration'. That great phrase-maker Disraeli's description of him as 'the Arch Mediocrity who presided rather than ruled over this Cabinet of Mediocrities' (slapdash and inaccurate like most of his political judgements) was allowed to pass muster for almost a century. That to hold the office of prime minister for fifteen years argued a degree of political skill and fortitude; that he brought to that office an unprecedented departmental experience; that the reluctance of his colleagues to see him retire said something about the value they attached to his leadership – these considerations, though not unnoticed, were rarely given the weight they deserved.

What overshadowed much historical judgement was the fact that the Liverpool system broke down permanently within a few years of his death. Yet even this is only a half-truth. Admittedly the long Liverpool administration was in a sense the mild British version of the *ancien régime*. It was the final phase of the old constitution before the revolution of 1828–32. Like many such regimes in their decline, it was a reforming administration; and as often happens in such circumstances, its reforms seemed afterwards to have been too limited in scope and too late in execution. Liverpool sought by parsimonious government and enlightened economic policy to demonstrate the continuing value of the traditional institutions of the state. In the event all he was able to do was to postpone for a few years those organic constitutional changes which the altered circumstances of British society rendered inevitable. Liverpool had fought against Catholic Emancipation and parliamentary reform because he feared their effects on the historic British state. Yet even before he left office he knew that resistance to the first was no longer practical. That parliamentary reform would also come was equally certain, though nobody could have foreseen in 1827 how soon.

Yet to classify Liverpool merely as one of the great European conservatives of his age – less cynical than Talleyrand, more imaginative than Metternich, more creative than Guizot – is not enough. When the history of nineteenth-century Britain is looked at as a whole, the last half-dozen years of Liverpool's administration take on a significance beyond their immediate time. It is easy to forget that having won the war, Liverpool also won the peace. The work of the 1820s laid the foundations of that great liberal free-trade revolution in financial and commercial policy which was carried on by Peel in the 1840s and consolidated by Gladstone in the 1850s and 1860s. From this point of view the whig decade of constitutional reform from 1831 to 1841 becomes a mere interlude in the continuity of economic policy between Liverpool and Peel. The parallels between the legislation of 1819–26 and that of 1841–6 are in fact remarkable. The replacement of the prohibitive Corn Law of 1815 by one providing for a sliding scale of duties built around a lower 'remunerative price' level was one of Liverpool's chief legislative ambitions in his last couple of years. Though he was not able to see his own bill through in the 1827 session, the principle was eventually put into force by the modified version of his bill passed under Wellington in 1828. Peel continued the process of lowering the corn tariff with his Act of 1842 and abolished the Corn Laws altogether in 1846. Liverpool in 1824 had seen that the key to further free-trade advance lay in having another £2 million of direct taxes. He was never in a strong enough political position either to obtain that or to restore the income tax, the abolition of which in 1816 he had never ceased to deplore. Fourteen years after Liverpool's death Peel brought back the income tax, imposed not £2 million but £4 million of new taxation, and used that additional revenue to recommence the work of extending free trade which had been at a standstill since 1826. Peel's Bank Charter Act of 1844 complemented Liverpool's 1819 currency reforms and provided a remedy for the weakness of the public credit system exhibited in the financial panic of 1825 against which Liverpool had tentatively legislated in 1826. The fiscal and financial policies of the latter years of the Liverpool administration were in effect prototypes of those put into force by Peel twenty years later. As with most prototypes, their significance was as much in the concepts themselves as in the degree of immediate effectiveness. Peel's measures were in every case bolder and more integrated than those of his pioneer predecessor; that is in the nature of things. The philosophy and the objectives, however, were identical.

There were other continuities of a wider political, even moral nature. The emphasis on trade and industry, on the relation between population and food supply, on the interdependence of agriculture, manufacture and commerce, on the need to safeguard the standard of living of the poor, and on the importance of pursuing national, not class or sectional interests – all these issues which bulked so large in Peel's arguments after 1841 are to be found, though more quietly expressed, in Liverpool's parliamentary speeches between 1820 and 1826. If the purpose of Peel's policies was as much social as economic, so too was Liverpool's; and for the same reasons. Liverpool clearly ranks as one of the great though unacknowledged architects of the liberal, free-trade Victorian state, second only to Peel in importance. For a man who had already led the country through the closing, victorious stages of the Napoleonic Wars and the equally strenuous postwar years of disorder and discontent, this was no small achievement.

It would be an injustice to Liverpool's qualities as a politician, however, to let the final emphasis rest solely on his contribution to the classic financial and free-trade policies of Victorian Britain. A verdict appropriate for an economic specialist like Huskisson is inadequate for one whose ministerial life was incomparably longer, more varied and more responsible. The great legal writer F. W. Maitland has been called an 'historian's historian' because of the classic qualities he brought to the study of erudite topics which do not in themselves attract much public interest. Lord Liverpool could be described as a politicians' politician because of the professional qualities he displayed in the course of a career which neither in his own day nor subsequently ever caught the popular imagination. He lacks any qualification for the heroic; his appeal (if he has an appeal) is to a discerning few. It is a taste which has to be acquired and can scarcely be appreciated without a sympathetic understanding of the political environment in which he lived. Liverpool had none of that elusive quality which men call brilliance; he did not have the formidable intellectual powers of Pitt and Peel; he did not possess the dominant personality of Chatham or Churchill; he could never have become a great demagogue or a great autocrat; he was not even supremely gifted in one particular branch of politics or administration. What he did have was a number of more than average talents which in their aggregate constituted a kind of composite talent of its own. He was that comparatively uncommon and always valuable thing in politics, a man of genuine all-round ability.

In any analysis of his premiership three features are outstanding: his competence in every important branch of public business; his successful handling of an extraordinary variety of problems; and his gift for getting the best out of his colleagues. There seemed a fusion of his own qualities and those he elicited from his cabinet which makes it in fact almost impossible to distinguish between them. In that sense it is right to talk of the 'Liverpool administration' as an entity. His rule was not a one-man affair as Pitt's so often seemed to be; it was one of collective strength and unity. His individuality was sunk in that of his cabinet because this was his style of leadership. Few prime ministers have had a stronger sense of cabinet identity; few have defended cabinet authority so strongly. Few indeed have been, as he was, the direct choice of his colleagues.

It can be said of Lord Liverpool, as of Dr Johnson, that he possessed ordinary virtues to a very extraordinary degree. Just as transcendent commonsense is a form of wisdom, so sustained and comprehensive political achievement is a form of statesmanship. With Sir Robert Walpole and the younger Pitt he was one of the most professional British prime ministers ever to have served the country.

NOTES

1 GCHT, pp. 580-81; GCOC, II, 252-70; Oman, p. 210.
2 Bathurst, pp. 639, 657.
3 For Liverpool's last illness see ARJ II, 81, 85; Bagot, II, 373, 376; Bathurst, p. 639; Colchester, III, 463-5, 477, 521-3; Creevey, p. 450; Croker, I, 362, 366; GCFM, p. 35; George 4, III, 209; Hobhouse, p. 127; LWF, II, 11; WND, III, 596.
4 For Liverpool's death and funeral see GM, 1829, Pt I, 81 ff.; ARC, pp. 112-13.
5 Hobhouse, p. 136.

Notes on Sources

I have used the seven volumes of private correspondence in the Liverpool Papers (British Library Add. MSS. 38469-38475) together with a few transcripts or extracts from the Peel, Canning, Huskisson, Soane and Pitchford Papers and the Christ Church, Oxford, muniments. I have also looked at Liverpool's will and the trustees' valuation of his estate in the Public Record Office.

For the rest this book is based on the rich store of printed sources available for this period. The starting point is C.D. Yonge's *The Life and Administration of the Second Earl of Liverpool* founded primarily on the Liverpool Papers. Much Liverpool correspondence is also located in the printed collections of papers of other central political figures of the time. First in importance are the many volumes of letters of George III and George IV, edited with valuable introductions and commentaries by the late Professor A. Aspinall to whom all historians of early nineteenth-century Britain are deeply indebted for having made available a larger range of primary political sources for the period than any other scholar before or since. Other indispensable published collections of political papers are those of Wellington, Castlereagh, Canning, Bathurst, Huskisson, Peel, Arbuthnot, Wellesley and the Grenville family. Much firsthand material is also to be found in the older lives of Pitt, Perceval, Sidmouth and Eldon. There is no diary of a cabinet minister during Liverpool's administration in print but the gap is partially filled by the Colchester and Hobhouse diaries, Mrs Arbuthnot's journal, Ward's memoirs, and at one remove (and with suitable precautions) the Croker papers and Princess Lieven's correspondence.

The contemporary *Memoirs of the Public Life and Administration of the Rt. Hon. the Earl of Liverpool* (anon., 1827) is a mere compilation mainly drawn from parliamentary debates and of little value. Of its 650 pages, 500 are occupied by the period up to 1815. I have, however, made some use of contemporary pamphlets and newspapers. There is no good modern life of Lord Liverpool though recent scholarly biographies of such politicians as Canning, Castlereagh and Sidmouth throw further light on his career. In addition there are two outstanding books published since 1975 on his administration. The first, by J.H. Cookson, is a general study of the crucial years 1815-22. The other, by Boyd Hilton, is on government economic policies from 1815 to 1830. My debt to these, especially the former, will be evident from the notes. The only specialised study in print for the period before Liverpool became prime minister is G.D. Knight's pioneer monograph on his work at the War Office. For the years after 1822 W.R. Brock's *Lord Liverpool and Liberal Toryism 1820-27*, though over forty years old, is still of enduring value not only as an administrative but as a personal study. An even older book, A. Brady's *William Huskisson and Liberal Reform*, is also still useful for commercial policy.

On the personal side J.F. Newton's *Early Days of Canning*, supplemented by the Leveson Gower correspondence, throws some light on Liverpool's undergraduate days; and Dorothy Marshall's *The Rise of George Canning* is indispensable for Liverpool's early relationships. The first Lady Liverpool and her family are exceptionally well documented in *Lady Wharncliffe and Her Family* and in the various books devoted to the colourful careers of her father the fourth Earl of Bristol (the Earl-Bishop) and her sister Lady Elizabeth Foster. The Rev. H.L.L. Denny's monograph on *The Manor of Hawkesbury and its Owners* and the Victorian antiquary W.P.W. Phillimore's contributions to *Gloucestershire Notes and Queries* are important for the Jenkinson connection with Hawkesbury. Further genealogical information can be gleaned from the privately printed *House of Cornewall* (Hereford, 1908) by the fourth Earl of Liverpool and Compton Reade. Some additional information is to be found in the obituary notices in the *Annual Register* and *The Gentleman's Magazine*, and in those indispensable works of reference Burke's *Peerage* and *Landed Gentry*.

Index